Freedom of Expression in England and under the ECHR: in Search of a Common Ground

A Foundation for the Application of the Human Rights Act 1998 in English Law

SCHOOL OF HUMAN RIGHTS RESEARCH SERIES, Volume 6

The titles published in this series are listed at the end of this volume.

Freedom of Expression in England and under the ECHR: in Search of a Common Ground

A Foundation for the Application of the Human Rights Act 1998 in English Law

Heleen Bosma

INTERSENTIA – HART

Antwerpen – Groningen – Oxford

This volume is an adapted version of a dissertation defended at Utrecht University on 27 September 2000.

Heleen Bosma
Freedom of Expression in England and under the ECHR: in Search of a Common Ground.
A Foundation for the Application of the Human Rights Act 1998 in English Law

ISBN 90-5095-136-8
D/2000/7849/29
NUGI 698

© 2000 INTERSENTIA Antwerpen – Groningen – Oxford

ACKNOWLEDGEMENTS

First of all, I would like to thank my supervisors Henk Kummeling and Deirdre Curtin for their continuous support and their suggestions and comments. I am particularly grateful to my daily supervisor Leonard Besselink, whose unfailing interest and willingness to discuss any part of my thesis, from the general outline to the most insignificant details, greatly stimulated me to look further than the surface of the problems I encountered in this study. Thanks are due also to Tom Zwart, whose enthusiasm and encouragements often gave me a renewed interest in my research. The comments and suggested improvements of these four people were invaluable.

Many others have contributed to my thesis. The people I owe thanks to are too numerous to detail in full. Some I wish to mention in particular. These are, first of all, my colleagues at the Institute of Constitutional and Administrative Law, who provided a friendly working atmosphere and who were always available for lengthy discussions on the hard life of those who write a dissertation. I would also like to thank my colleagues at the Netherlands Institute of Human Rights: the enthusiasm of these 'happy researchers' rubbed off on me and the spirit of co-operation in this institute supported me greatly in the final phase of my thesis.

I would like to thank prof. dr C. Flinterman, prof. dr A.W. Heringa, prof. dr T. Koopmans and prof. dr R. de Lange for taking part in the reading-committee. I would like to thank the librarians of the Squire Law Library of the University of Cambridge, who assisted me in finding my way in their wonderful library and freely let me gather any material I needed.

Further thanks goes to Alison McDonnell, who patiently corrected the English spelling and grammar of the manuscript, and to Wieneke Matthijsse, who edited and did the lay-out of the manuscript and whose considerable experience and expertise helped me stay calm when the schedule to get the manuscript to the publisher was rather tight.

Special thanks are due to my parents, my two brothers and my friends who encouraged and supported me throughout the years in which I have been engaged on this study, and who undoubtedly are as relieved as I am to see it finished.

Ton, I thank you most.

Alkmaar, 26 June 2000

TABLE OF CONTENTS

Chapter III
Freedom of Expression in English Law

Chapter IV
Methods of Protection Applied by the Court

PART II – COMMON GROUND

Chapter V
The Notion of the Right to Freedom of Expression

Chapter VI
Margin of Appreciation

Chapter VII
Proportionality

LIST OF ABBREVIATIONS

AC	Law Reports: Appeal Cases
A-G	Attorney General
All ER	All England Law Reports
CA	Court of Appeal
Ch.	Law Reports: Chancery Division 1991-
Ch.D.	Law Reports: Chancery Division 1875-90
CML Review	Common Market Law Review
Cr App R	Criminal Appeal Report
Crim LR	Criminal Law Review
DPP	Director of Public Prosecutions
ECHR	European Convention for the protection of Human Rights and Fundamental Freedoms
EHRLR	European Human Rights Law Reports
EPL	European Public Law
HL	House of Lords
HRLJ	Human Rights Law Journal
HRQ	Human Rights Quarterly
ICCPR	International Convention on Civil and Political Rights
J.	Justice
LJ.	Lord Justice
L.Q.R.	Law Quarterly Review
MLJ	Maastricht Law Journal
MLR	The Modern Law Review
NILR	Netherlands International Law Review
NLJ	New Law Journal
OJLS	Oxford Journal of Legal Studies
PL	Public Law
QB	Law Reports: Queen's Bench Division
Reports	Reports of judgments and decisions. Publication of the case law of the Court as from 1996
TLR	Times Law Reports
UKNCCL	United Kingdom National Committee of Comparative Law
WLR	Weekly Law Reports
YEL	Yearbook of European Law

PART I
TWO DIFFERENT SYSTEMS OF PROTECTION

CHAPTER I
INTRODUCTION

On 2 October 2000 the European Convention for the protection of Human Rights and Fundamental Freedoms (ECHR) becomes part of English domestic law as a result of the coming into force of the Human Rights Act 1998. By means of this Act two different systems of protection of fundamental rights are integrated. The two systems of protection are the continental and the common law systems of protection. The continental system of protection is applied in most European Countries that are party to the European Convention of Human Rights. In the United Kingdom an common law system of protection is applied. The continental system of protection is the system that is used by the ECHR. The integration of the ECHR in the national system of protection requires a change of approach in English law. Just how great a change is required, is determined primarily by the protection currently provided under English law and by the manner in which the ECHR is incorporated in English law. So what then is an English judge required to do exactly when called upon to protect the rights of individuals after the Act obtains force of law and how is this different from what he used to do when confronted with such issues before the Act became law? In this book I attempt to provide an answer to this question by analysing the protection of freedom of expression in the ECHR, its protection by English law and English courts before the coming into force of the Human Rights Act and finally by examining the changes required of the English protection to realise the incorporation of the Human Rights Act.

The Human Rights Act and the manner in which incorporation is established by it is discussed in chapter two of this book.

First however, I wish to define the central problem I examine in this study. In order to do so, it is necessary to give a brief introduction to the two systems of protection discussed in this book: the English system of protection and the system of protection of the ECHR. The discussion of these systems in section 1 of this chapter provides an overview of the differences between the protection of fundamental rights under English law and under the ECHR and as such provides a framework for this study. In this overview I emphasise the difference between a national system of protection and a supranational system of protection. Also I address the influence of the latter system on the former, since the United Kingdom is already party to the ECHR.

After the introduction of the two systems of protection in sections 1.1 and 1.2, I summarise the differences between the two systems of protection that may cause tension between them. In section 2 I indicate that the scope of this study is limited to freedom of expression and to English law,[1] before going on in section 3 to elaborate on the central question and the relevant sub-questions and preliminary questions addressed. In section 4 I deal with the terminology used in this study. And finally in section 5 I set out the structure of this book.

1 TWO DIFFERENT SYSTEMS OF PROTECTION OF FUNDAMENTAL RIGHTS

1.1 The System of Protection in English Law[2]

There are four aspects of English law which are relevant to the protection of fundamental rights. First, in English law there is a general right to freedom. Secondly, there are three distinct sources of law, each of which governs areas of law which can, and do, restrict freedom in some way. These sources are: statutory legislation coming from parliament; common law; and equity, the latter two developed by the courts. Thirdly, in English law parliament is sovereign, which to a large extent determines the location of the responsibility for the protection of fundamental rights. Finally, there is the fact that the United Kingdom has signed and ratified a number of human rights treaties, including the ECHR. I elaborate on these four aspects in the following four sections.

1.1.1 Freedom

Under English law the protection of fundamental rights is not regulated by any law which lists those rights exhaustively. Although the Magna Carta of 1215 and the 1689 Bill of Rights provide for the protection of a number of rights and as we shall see below also common law recognises some rights, the principal approach to the protection of 'civil liberties' is not rights based but freedom based.[3] In this approach, 'civil liberties' are not divided into specific rights that are subsequently defined in laws that protect those rights. Instead, there is freedom where freedom has not been restricted. In other words: in principle anything is allowed as long as it is not prohibited. It is from this traditional approach of 'residual liberty' that the current manner of protection of fundamental rights developed.

The current scope of particular fundamental rights has to be derived mainly from the scope of freedom. In other words it has to be derived from the restrictions that

---

[1]   As explained in section two this means that this study is limited to English law, and does not examine the situation in Northern Ireland and Scotland.

[2]   See for an extensive discussion of the protection of fundamental rights under English law: Feldman, Civil Liberties and Human Rights in England and Wales, 1993.

[3]   Feldman, Civil Liberties and Human Rights in England and Wales, 1993, p. 61.

exist on that particular right or freedom. Freedom is not absolute, but any restriction of freedom has to be authorised. This means that a restriction has to have its foundations in law. The sources of law indicate the authorities on whom the responsibilities for the adoption of restrictive law rest. The sources of law are a second particularity of the English legal system and are the topic of the next section.

1.1.2 Sources of Law

English law has three distinct sources. These are statutory law, common law and equity. Fundamental rights may be restricted by parliament, which is responsible for statutory law.[4] Common law and equity may also restrict freedom, however both common law and equity are law that does not result from legislation. Common law has been created by the custom of the people, and has been justified and developed by the decisions and rulings of the courts.[5] Equity is the law originating from the rulings of the Court of Chancery on petitions presented to the King. The distinction that is usually made between equity and law, means no more than that equity is not a part of common law.[6] Statute law, common law and equity together constitute the law of England. Beside the existence of a number of restrictions it has also been held by the English courts that common law recognises the existence of a number of rights. As will become apparent in the third chapter, freedom of expression is one of the rights acknowledged to exist under common law.

Before I turn to the third relevant aspect of the protection of fundamental rights under English law, I wish to emphasise the role of English courts in this context. They are not only interpreters of statutory legislation, they also develop common law and equity.[7] In their role as developers of common law and equity the courts are bound by custom and previous case law in which the existence of a custom has been recognised. The difference between the role of the courts as regards the development of common law and equity on the one hand, and the interpretation of statutory law on the other, may have an influence on whether, or the extent to which, the courts consider civil liberties in their judgments. I come back to this issue in the conclusions to this study.

The courts' role as interpreters of legislation is determined by the relation of the judiciary to the legislature. This relation is mainly determined by the 'doctrine of

---

4   The presumption in favour of freedom together with the doctrine of parliamentary sovereignty, left parliament with the power to restrict (or protect) rights and freedoms. See also Feldman, Civil Liberties and Human Rights in England and Wales, 1993, p. 62.

5   Williams, Learning the Law, 1973, p. 25. Card, Cross & Jones, Criminal Law, 1995, p. 9.

6   From: Williams, Learning the Law, 1973, p. 24-29.

7   See for an extensive discussion of the relation between statutory legislation and common law, and the position of rights under common law, respectively chapter 4 and 6 of Allen, Law, Liberty and Justice, 1993. See also: Allen, Constitutional Rights and Common Law, 1991, p. 453-480.

Parliamentary Sovereignty'. This doctrine also determines the scope of parliament's legislative powers.

1.1.3 Doctrine of Parliamentary Sovereignty[8]

Smith and Bailey described the doctrine of Parliamentary Sovereignty as follows: 'A measure which has received the assent being given separately and in the two Houses of Parliament by simple majorities, is accepted to have the force of law as an Act of Parliament. Its validity cannot be questioned in the courts and any earlier inconsistent legislation or the manner and form of its enactment cannot succeed. Acts of Parliament, thus defined, are the supreme form of law; the rule of judicial obedience to them is the ultimate political fact on which the whole system of legislation hangs'.[9] The legislative powers of Parliament are thus unrestricted. They are not restricted by laws from previous parliaments, nor by common law or equity. Common law and equity are overruled by Acts of Parliament that cover the same topic. The legislative powers of parliament are not restricted in content, neither are they restricted by powers of review of the courts. As a consequence, the possibilities to restrict fundamental rights by way of statutory legislation is unrestricted.[10] This means, therefore, that the primary responsibility to protect freedom lies with parliament.[11] The text of an Act may give an indication of considerations regarding the protection of fundamental rights. Considerations regarding the restrictive effect may appear from the definition of the behaviour restricted, and from any exceptions and justifications which are formulated. The definition of Obscene Publications in the Obscene Publications Act 1959, for example, is rather broad. The legislature, however, apparently did take account of the impact on freedom of expression, since an offence under the Act can be justified if the publication is 'in the interest of science, literature, art or learning or of other objects of general concern'.[12] The exact impact on freedom of expression, however, will only become clear when the legislation is applied by the courts. The extent to which parliament in fact has taken account of freedom in the legislative process of a restrictive statute, can be derived mainly from the relevant parliamentary debates. The possibilities of the English courts to refer to the parliamentary debates when they interpret Acts of Parliament are limited however.[13]

---

8   See for an extensive discussion of the doctrine of Parliamentary Sovereignty: Loveland, Constitutional Law, a critical introduction, 1996, p. 27-62.
9   Smith and Gunn (eds.), Smith and Bailey on the Modern English Legal System, 1991, p. 242.
10   Feldman, Civil Liberties and Human Rights in England and Wales, 1993, p. 62.
11   Feldman, Civil Liberties and Human Rights in England and Wales, 1993, p. 69.
12   Obscene Publications Act 1959, s.4.
13   See Pepper v. Hart [1993] 1 All ER 42, HL.

The doctrine of Parliamentary Sovereignty does not only determine the legislative powers of Parliament, but it also regulates the relationship between Parliament and the judiciary: the courts do not have the power to assess the validity of a statute.[14] The courts can only influence the restrictive effect of statutory legislation by way of interpretation,[15] and their role as interpreters of legislation is influenced by the dominant position of parliament in the English constitution.[16] This is apparent from the fact that they will follow the wording of the statute unless the meaning is unclear or ambiguous.[17] Such ambiguity provides the courts a possibility to give some protection to fundamental rights. There is, in fact, one aspect of the doctrine of Parliamentary Sovereignty that enables the courts expressly to take account of fundamental rights when interpreting legislation. This aspect is precisely the dominant position of parliament within the organisation of the state. This implies, as I said above, that primary responsibility to protect freedom lies with parliament; consequently the courts have adopted the 'presumption' that Parliament does not intend to restrict freedom.[18] By way of 'presumptions' the courts can provide a certain measure of protection to fundamental rights when they interpret statutory law. The presumption that parliament does not intend to restrict freedom implies that when the wording of a statute is ambiguous, the courts are allowed to interpret the Act in such a way that its impact on fundamental rights is kept to a minimum.[19] The fundamental rights referred to are those specifically recognised by common law, but also those adopted in the Convention.[20] This is where the fourth aspect of English law that is relevant to the protection of fundamental rights comes into play. This fourth aspect is the fact that the United Kingdom is a party to the ECHR and that by way of presumptions the fundamental rights protected in the Convention have an impact on English law even though the Convention is not (yet) a part of English national law.

Before going into this I wish to remark that the sovereignty of parliament also influences the relation between the judiciary and the executive. This is apparent, for example, from the approach of the courts to judicial review of administrative

---

14   See also Wade and Bradley, Constitutional and Administrative Law, 1993, p. 69.
15   Feldman, Civil Liberties and Human Rights in England and Wales, 1993, p. 54 and 70.
16   See for a brief discussion of the present rules of interpretation: Marshall, Two kinds of compatibility: more about s.3 of the Human Rights Act 1998, 1999, p. 377-383.
17   Marshall, Two kinds of compatibility: more about s. 3 of the Human Rights Act 1998, 1999, p. 377.
18   Feldman, Civil Liberties and Human Rights in England and Wales, 1993, p. 63.
19   See Allan, Law, Liberty, and Justice, The Legal Foundations of British Constitutionalism, 1993, p. 136-138.
20   Feldman, Civil Liberties and Human Rights in England and Wales, 1993, p. 70.

action.[21] The executive powers, the exercise of which can be the subject of review by the courts, were granted to the administrative authorities by parliament.[22] The review of the use of those powers is limited for that reason. I elaborate on judicial review in chapter VII of this book.

1.1.4 Impact of the ECHR

The Convention is about to be incorporated into domestic law by way of the Human Rights Act 1998. Until that Act enters into force, however, the English courts are not able to review a restriction of a fundamental right on its compatibility with the UK's obligations under the Convention. The ECHR has already had some influence on English law by way of the application of presumptions however. The presumption that parliament does not intend to restrict fundamental rights is complemented by the presumption that parliament does not intend to act contrary to its international obligations.[23] Where it is obvious that the legislation is ambiguous, this can be resolved by way of reference to these obligations. The ECHR constitutes such an obligation. And although the UK is for instance also a member to the UN Declaration of Human Rights and the ICCPR, it is the ECHR that is most frequently referred to when the courts interpret ambiguous statutory legislation that restricts one of the rights adopted in the Convention. The reason for the frequent occurrence of the Convention in the considerations of the courts can be explained by the fact that the UK had already recognised the individual right of complaint as of 1966.[24] This means that the European Court of Human Rights reviews individual claims by UK citizens of violation of a right protected under the Convention. Such claims are regularly brought before the Strasbourg Court. That Court regularly finds the UK to have acted in breach of the Convention. This will require the UK in most cases to pay damages to the person whose right was violated, and to prevent the rights of other citizens being violated in similar circumstances. This influence of the ECHR on English law increases the necessity for the courts to interpret statutory law (and also develop common law) in accordance with the obligations under the ECHR. If the wording of the legislation is not ambiguous, and leaves the courts no other possibility than to decide contrary to the UK's obligations under the ECHR, then parliament

---

21 See for an extensive overview of the grounds of challenge and the reserved approach of the courts towards judicial review: Jones and Thompson, Garner's Administrative Law, 1996, p. 178-281.
22 Jowell, Of Vires and Vacuums: Constitutional Context of Judicial Review, 1999, p. 449.
23 Feldman, Civil Liberties and Human Rights in England and Wales, 1993, p. 66.
24 On the 14 January 1966 the UK made a declaration under Article 25 recognising the right of individual complaint in respect of events occurring after that date, as opposed to the ICCPR, with regard to which the UK has not recognised the individual right of complaint.

must amend the legislation concerned in order for the courts to be able to decide cases in accordance with the UK's obligations under the Convention.

1.2 The System of Protection under the ECHR[25]

The Convention provides for the protection of certain human rights, which are to be protected by law in each Member State. The rights protected are confined to certain basic rights and liberties, which the framers of the Convention considered would be generally accepted in the liberal democracies of Western-Europe.[26] Four aspects of the manner in which this protection is realised need to be discussed in order to complete the frame of reference that is required to be able to formulate the central problem of this study. These aspects are: first, the procedures by which alleged violations of adopted rights are brought before the European Court of Human Rights; second, the manner in which fundamental rights are protected in the text of the Convention; third, the location of the responsibility for the protection of fundamental rights; and fourth the manner in which the European Court of Human Rights approaches the protection of fundamental rights. I elaborate on these four aspects and on why they are relevant to the protection of fundamental rights. In this section I refer to the European Court of Human Rights, as 'the Court'.[27]

1.2.1 Procedural Aspects

The procedural aspects of the system of protection of the ECHR are of importance to the protection of fundamental rights, because they establish the Court's powers to decide on whether or not a State violated the Convention.

Three procedures have been adopted in the Convention to ensure that the States party to the Convention observe their obligation to protect the rights set out therein. A Contracting State has the obligation to report to the Council of Europe at the request of the Secretary General (Art. 57) on the manner in which it ensures the rights protected. A state-complaint procedure has been provided for (Art. 24), and there is an individual right of complaint (Art. 25).[28] Mostly under the last provision a great many cases have been brought before the Commission and the Court, consequently giving these organs the possibility to develop case law on the different

---

25 See for a more extensive discussion of the system of protection under the ECHR: Van Dijk and Van Hoof, Theory and Practice of the European Convention on Human Rights, 1998, p. 1-69.

26 Wade and Bradley, Constitutional and Administrative Law, 1993, p. 416.

27 In the following chapters of this book, where necessary I use the term 'European Court of Human Rights'. In those instances in which it is clear that I am referring to this court I use the term 'the Court'.

28 From 1 November 1998 on the individual right of complaint is no longer optional.

provisions of the Convention. Most cases discussed in this book will stem from the background of decisions of the Commission and judgments of the Court. From 1 November 1998 onwards all individual complaints come before a permanent Court which replaces the previous Court and Commission.[29] Depending on whether the decision concerns the admissibility of a case, a decision on the merits or a rehearing of the case, it is considered by a Court of three, seven or seventeen judges. Once a case comes before it, the Court reviews whether the State concerned acted in conformity with the Convention. The protection of the rights concerned depends on what the Convention says should be protected, what the Court says the Convention says should be protected and the locus of responsibility to protect the rights adopted in the Convention and its Protocols. First I discuss the manner in which the text of the Convention provides protection for fundamental rights.

1.2.2 The Manner of Protection of Fundamental Rights

Under the system of protection of the ECHR a number of rights are defined in the Convention and its Protocols in order to protect them from violation by the States party to the Convention. These rights are usually not absolute, in the sense that no restriction on them is allowed at all. The impact the Convention has on the protection of fundamental rights in the States party to it is influenced by the character of the rights protected. The whole catalogue of rights of the Convention would therefore be relevant to a discussion concerning the system of protection of the ECHR. Since I limit the scope of this study to one fundamental right, namely freedom of expression, such elaborations are beyond the scope of this book. I address the reasons for selecting that freedom of expression and other restrictions to the scope of this study in section 3 of this chapter.

In Articles 7 to 11 of the Convention, of which Article 10 protects freedom of expression, the Article first defines the right concerned in its first paragraph, whereas in the second paragraph the circumstances under which the right in question may be restricted by the national authorities are formulated. The restriction has to be 'prescribed by law'. Furthermore a limited number of 'legitimate aims' are enumerated the pursuit of which may entail justification of the restriction of a right. And finally the restriction has to be 'necessary in a democratic society'. The restriction imposed may consist of 'formalities, conditions, restrictions or penalties'. This is so generally formulated that virtually any measure preventing an individual from freely exercising his right or freedom, is accepted as such.[30] The requirement

---

29 11 Protocol, Art. 28-Art. 44.
30 In relation to this, the Court does review whether the measure taken is proportionate to the legitimate aim pursued. This, however, is an issue under a different question, namely whether the measure is necessary in a democratic society.

that the restriction be 'prescribed by law' is rarely a matter of dispute in the case law of the Court also.[31] The European Court of Human Rights also tends to accept a State's claim that one of the legitimate aims is served by a restriction.[32] In determining whether a State violated the Convention, the European Court of Human Rights focuses on the question whether a restriction was 'necessary in a democratic society'.[33]

1.2.3 Location of the Responsibility for Protection

The European Court of Human Rights and the Commission have had to determine their own role with regard to the protection of the rights of the Convention. They had to decide who was competent to interpret the provisions of the ECHR and who was competent to decide whether a right had been violated.[34] In settling these issues they took into account two aspects characteristic to the ECHR. The first aspect is the purpose of the Convention to establish within Europe 'the respect by States of rights and fundamental freedoms, as well as the general principles of democracy by a system of collective guarantees'.[35] The second aspect, however, is that the ECHR, which is to accomplish this with respect to the protection of fundamental rights, is a treaty between sovereign states.[36] The state's own perception of the behaviour covered by a right and the restrictions that should be allowed, could not be put aside. In other words, on the one hand the interpretation of the Convention could not be left entirely to the States party to the Convention,[37] on the other hand the Commission and the Court could not impose their own views on the meaning of the provisions in the Convention, completely disregarding the assessment of the national authorities on

---

31 See Van Dijk and Van Hoof, Theory and Practice of the European Convention on Human Rights, 1998, p. 763-771. A rare exception with regard to Article 10 was Harshman and Harrup v. United Kingdom, ECourtHR 25 November 1999.

32 See Van Dijk and Van Hoof, Theory and Practice of the European Convention on Human Rights, 1998, p. 771-773.

33 See Van Dijk and Van Hoof, Theory and Practice of the European Convention on Human Rights, 1998, p. 771. They refer to the Dudgeon case, A. 45, p. 18-25 as an example of the approach of the Court.

34 See Van Dijk and Van Hoof, Theory and Practice of the European Convention on Human Rights, 1998, p. 81-84.

35 Council of Europe, Collected Edition of the 'Travaux Préparatoires' of the European Convention on Human Rights, 1975, p. 264.

36 Article 1 ECHR provides that the Contracting Parties 'secure to everyone within their jurisdiction the rights and freedoms defined in Section I of this Convention'.

37 Article 19 provides that the Court ensures 'the observance of the engagements undertaken by the High Contracting Parties'.

a matter.[38] This, together with the fact that the national authorities are the authorities with which a citizen is confronted when he feels his rights have been violated, led to the conclusion that the responsibility to protect the rights of the Convention is shared between the European Court of Human Rights and the States party to the Convention.

1.2.4 Manner of Protection of the Court

The manner in which the Court has approached the cases brought before it, demonstrates how it translated its approach to the location of the responsibility to the protect rights. It translated the shared responsibility by introducing the 'margin of appreciation', which implies a variable scope of review.[39] The 'margin of appreciation' is a method for determining the discretion of the state in deciding the restrictions on a right that are permissible. In the course of time, the Court has developed the way in which it applies the margin of appreciation. The 'margin of appreciation' varies according to the facts and circumstances of a case. The Court has also formulated substantive criteria of assessment. The substantive criteria of assessment do not concern the scope of the review of the Court, but concern the content of the requirement formulated by the Court in order to determine whether a restriction is 'necessary in a democratic society'. 'Necessary' according to the Court means that there has to be a pressing social need, the measure has to be proportionate to the legitimate aim pursued, and the reasons to justify the measure have to be relevant and sufficient.[40]

The application of the margin of appreciation together with the methods of substantive review constitute the methods of protection that can be derived from the case law of the Court. I extensively discuss the methods of substantive review in the Court's case law and what they entail in chapter IV of this book. There I also elaborate on the 'margin of appreciation' as a method of protection. The manner in which these methods of protection are applied I discuss in detail in chapter VI, VII and VIII of the second part of this study, and therefore, do not elaborate on them here.

---

38 Also see: Wiarda, Extensieve en restrictieve verdragstoepassingen door het Europese Hof voor de rechten van de mens; een middenkoers?, 1981, p. 371-374.
39 See Van Dijk and Van Hoof, Theory and Practice of the European Convention on Human Rights, 1998, p. 82-95.
40 Handyside v. the United Kingdom (1976) A.24, par. 48-50, Sunday Times v. United Kingdom (1979) A.30, par. 62; See also Harris, O'Boyle and Warbrick, Law of the European Convention on Human Rights, 1995, p. 396.

1.3 Essence of the Tension between Protection of Fundamental Rights in English Law and under the ECHR

From the description of the basic features of the two systems of protection, a number of aspects can be identified that will raise difficulties for attempts to integrate the protection of the Convention into the system of protection of English law. The English system of protection is freedom based, in the sense that fundamental rights are not defined, but exist insofar as they are not restricted by law. The ECHR system of protection defines rights which are the starting point of the considerations of the Court. The English courts do not have the possibility to review Acts of Parliament on their consistency with fundamental rights; the primary responsibility to protect liberty lies with the democratically elected Parliament. The possibilities of the English courts to review the exercise of powers granted to the executive by the legislature is also limited. With regard to common law and equity, however, the English courts do not only interpret but also develop law. The Court reviews acts of the national authorities on their consistency with Convention rights. Such acts may consist of national legislation or acts of public authorities, including decisions of the national courts. The scope of the review, however, differs with each case depending on its facts and circumstances.

The two systems of protection are different, but already linked. The ECHR influences the protection of fundamental rights under English law. The United Kingdom is a party to the Convention and, as observed, has already recognised the individual right of complaint in the past. Consequently the European Court of Human Rights reviews whether acts of the United Kingdom are consistent with its obligations under the ECHR. Moreover, the European Court of Justice has held the Convention to be a fundamental principle with which Community acts should comply. Consequently, with the increased Community legislation the influence of the ECHR through 'the back door' has increased.[41] Still the possibilities of English judges to take account of the UK's obligations under the Convention up until now have been restricted.

The new Human Rights Act incorporates the one system into the other. The Act suggests that a change in the protection of fundamental rights is required. The central issue addressed in this book concerns the extent to which the protection of human rights currently provided in England – specifically in the field of freedom of expression – already meets the requirements of the ECHR. I realise that the Human Rights Act does not necessarily require the rights incorporated to be protected to the degree provided by the Court. I discuss the exact requirements of the Human Rights Act and the manner in which they are to be met in chapter two of this book. We

---

41 Besselink, Fundamentele Rechten in het Gemeenschapsrecht, 1998, p. 9.

already know however that the Act incorporates Convention rights and in this book I aim to find a foundation in the system of protection in English law on which the protection of Convention rights in national law can be based. In order to locate such a foundation, it is necessary to know the extent to which the two approaches are comparable.

2 SCOPE OF THIS STUDY

In order to make this study workable, I restricted my research to one fundamental right. I selected the right to freedom of expression as focus. This right touches upon a broad range of legal concepts, which give a good impression of the sort of issues that arise under English law and under the ECHR regarding the protection of fundamental rights. Freedom of expression is one of the rights considered to need protection in the democratic states that have signed and ratified the Convention. It protects that right in Article 10, in the following terms:

> Article 10 ECHR:
> 1. Everyone has the right to freedom of expression. this right shall include freedom to hold opinions and to receive and impart information and ideas without interference by public authorities and regardless of frontiers. This article shall not prevent States from requiring the licensing of broadcasting, television or cinema enterprises.
> 2. The exercise of these freedoms, since it carries with it duties and responsibilities, may be subject to such formalities, conditions, restrictions or penalties as are prescribed by law and are necessary in a democratic society, in the interest of national security, territorial integrity or public safety, for the prevention of disorder or crime, for the protection of health or morals, for the protection of the reputation or rights of others, for preventing the disclosure of information received in confidence, or for maintaining the authority ad impartiality of the judiciary.

Under English law the freedom that remains after all restrictions resulting from legislation, common law and equity are deducted, constitutes the protected freedom of expression. The areas of English law that pose a restriction to freedom of expression include criminal law, civil law and administrative law, the latter involving judicial review. The laws that restrict freedom of expression are governed by statutory law, but also common law and equity. Common law is a significant part of English law and includes a number of areas of law that restrict freedom of expression. Common law governs, for instance, decency offences, blasphemy law and part of defamation law. Equity may also impinge on freedom of expression. Under equity the courts have recognised the existence of an obligation of confidentiality. As for statutory law, there are a number of examples of Acts of Parliament that have a significant impact on freedom of expression. The Contempt of Court Act 1981, the Public Order Act 1986 and the Official Secrecy Act 1989 are notorious examples. Under English law, as well as under the ECHR, a broad range of case law on freedom of expression exists, which makes it a well developed area of law. This adds to the usefulness of freedom of expression as a field of research.

In the parts of this study concerning English law, attention is also paid to the protection that is provided to freedom of expression by Acts of Parliament and by common law and equity, and on the protection that is subsequently provided by the courts in applying this law. The role of the executive in the protection of freedom of expression is a subject of discussion to the extent that restrictions imposed by the executive are subject to judicial review. Finally, this book concerns only an examination of the ECHR and its case law coming from the European Court of Human Rights, and English law. Wales, Scotland and Northern-Ireland are not included in this research. And although the decisions of the Commission are relevant to the degree of protection realised under the ECHR, it is the judgments of the European Court of Human Rights which establish the interpretation of the Convention that is binding upon the State whose act has been challenged in Strasbourg, and which informs the other States party to the Convention of the degree of protection they are required to provide. After these limitations, I can deal more fully with the specific questions examined in this book.

3 THE QUESTIONS

3.1 The Central Question

In order to find a basis for the protection in English law of the rights of the ECHR that are incorporated by the Human Rights Act 1998, I ask the following question in this book: What is the extent of common ground between the protection of freedom of expression in English law and under the ECHR? A number of sub-questions need to be answered to be able to formulate an answer to the central question.

3.2 The Sub-Questions

The central question I have just posed, raises the general issue of what is required of national systems of protection to meet the requirements of the system of protection under the ECHR. To answer the central question it is necessary to identify the aspects that determine the protection of a fundamental right. When all the aspects that determine the protection of a right or freedom are taken together, this reveals the degree of protection that is provided. The aspects that determine the protection of a fundamental right can be distinguished at three levels.

A first level is the approach to the notion of a right. I already indicated above that the topic of this study is freedom of expression. The types of expression that are covered by this freedom, the relations in which it functions – between citizens and the government or between citizens –, and the possibility of prior restraint indicate the approach to the notion of freedom of expression.

From the discussion of the relevant aspects of the systems of protection under English law and under the ECHR in section 1, it was apparent that there are differences in the locus of responsibilities regarding the protection of fundamental rights. This has an effect on the way in which freedom of expression is protected by the courts. This constitutes the second level of protection of a right. The fact that the English courts are faced with a sovereign legislature limits their possibilities for protecting rights or freedoms. This fact influences the scope of the review of administrative action and it influences the possibilities for the courts to provide protection to rights or freedoms in their role as interpreters of legislation and as developers of common law. On the other hand, the European Court of Human Rights reviews not only the decisions of the English courts, but also the restrictions imposed by the English legislature. The second level of protection of a fundamental right is therefore the manner in which this protection is established. The manner of protection of freedom of expression consists of the methods of protection applied. As indicated above, the first element in this is the role the judiciary accepts when it reviews administrative action. This concerns the constitutional relationship between the judiciary and the executive. The methods of protection of freedom of expression under English law furthermore is found in statutory legislation, common law and equity. With regard to law, the methods of protection is first of all determined by the wording of restrictive law as established by the legislature and the judiciary. Second, the interpretation and application of this law by the courts, determines the manner of protection of a right or freedom. The role of the judiciary in providing protection when it interprets and applies law, influences the manner in which a fundamental right or freedom is taken account of. The manner of protection in the system of the ECHR is found in the text of the Convention and in the application of the rights and freedoms by the Court.

Finally, the third level of protection of a right or freedom is determined by the value attached to the right or freedom and to the opposing interests in a particular case. This comes down to the 'consideration and appreciation of facts and circumstances' of the English judiciary and the European Court of Human Rights. If for instance the seriousness of a restriction is not considered in a national system of protection, but is a circumstance that is considered by the European Court of Human Rights, this may lead to a difference in protection of freedom of expression. Similarly appreciation: if, for example, commercial speech is held to be of great value in a national system of protection but is held to be of little value by the European Court of Human Rights, this also will influence the degree of protection provided under the systems of protection.

The sub-questions I consequently examine in this study are: What is the extent of common ground between the notions of freedom of expression in English law and under the ECHR? What is the extent of common ground between the methods of protection applied under English law and by the European Court of Human Rights? What is the extent of common ground between the consideration and appreciation of facts and circumstances by the English courts and the European Court of Human Rights? These questions are examined in the second part of this book.

3.3 Preliminary Questions

In order to be able to conduct this examination, some preliminary questions have to be answered. To determine the approach of English law to the notion of freedom of expression, the methods of protection applied under English law and, also, the consideration and appreciation of facts and circumstances by the English courts, an examination of English statutory law, common law and equity is required first. An examination of the manner in which this law has been formulated by the responsible organs, and the manner in which the English courts interpret and apply this law will make it possible to comment on the approach to the notion of freedom of expression under English law. It will also make it possible to elaborate on the methods of protection applied under English law and on the consideration and appreciation of facts and circumstances by the English courts, in particular on the value freedom of expression is held to have under English law.

With regard to the ECHR such an extensive discussion of the approach to freedom of expression is not necessary, since it provides for a positive protection of this freedom under Article 10. The protection of freedom of expression is located in those cases that deal with restrictions of Article 10. For a separate overview of the ECHR case law on Article 10 a number of excellent publications are available.[42] However, in order to determine a common ground between the methods of protection applied under English law and under the system of protection of the ECHR, it is necessary to determine the methods of protection applied by the European Court of Human Rights. This is the second preliminary question that needs to be dealt with.

I take the methods of protection applied by the European Court of Human Rights as point of departure, since it is the ECHR that is incorporated into English law and not the English protection of freedom of expression that is incorporated into the system of protection of the ECHR. Logically, the system of protection under English law will be required to adjust to the system of protection under the ECHR.

---

[42] E.g. Van Dijk and Van Hoof, Theory and Practice of the European Convention on Human Rights, 1998, p. 557-585; Bailey, Harris, Jones, Civil Liberties, cases and materials, 1995, p. 823-844; Clapham, Human Rights in the Private Sphere, 1993, p. 222-231; Fawcett, The Application of the European Convention on Human Rights, 1987, p. 250-273.

17

4 ANALYTICAL TOOLS

The use I make of a number of terms in this study requires further explanation. Firstly, the term 'common ground', which is my ultimate analytical tool, is discussed in section 4.1. The other terms which require explaining are 'methods of protection' and 'manner of protection' and 'freedom of expression'. I consider the meaning of these terms to be clear, but I will discuss the manner in which I use them for the purpose of this study.

4.1 Common Ground

As the specification of the sub-questions indicated, the term 'common ground' in this study is used in connection with the approach to the notion of a right, the sharing of the responsibility between the judiciary and the legislature in providing protection for a right, the substantive methods of protection that are used when restrictive law is applied and when administrative action is reviewed, and the consideration and appreciation of facts and circumstances of cases in which a right is restricted. Finally the degree of protection resulting from the combination of these aspects, is also part of the term 'common ground'.

Common ground in the sense I use it in this study is formal or institutional to the extent that it refers to the manner in which the standard of protection comes about. The material use of the term 'common ground' with regard to the resultant degree of protection concerns the consideration and appreciation of facts and circumstances which indicates the value a right is held to have. Consequently, the term 'common ground' in this study concerns the notion of freedom of expression, the methods of protection applied by the ECHR, the Court, the English legislature and the English courts and finally the consideration and appreciation of facts and circumstances by the Court and the English courts. These aspects consequently are topic of my search for a common ground.

It is important to note that my use of the term 'common ground' includes a formal or institutional approach. This approach should be distinguished from the purely material approach to this term in the judgments of the European Court of Human Rights. In its judgments, the European Court of Human rights regularly refers to the practices common to the States party to the Convention with regard to the protection of a right.[43] The existence or lack of existence of a common ground in such instances is used to justify the scope of review and the degree of independent evaluation of the facts and circumstances of a case (see chapters VI and IX). Thus material use of the term common ground by the Court does not refer to the position

---

[43] See Heringa, The 'Consensus Principle', the role of 'common law' in the ECHR case law, 1996, p. 108-145.

of the legislature or the judiciary with regard to the protection of a right, nor does it refer to the methods of protection by which the degree of protection is achieved by the national authorities. Instead it refers to the resultant degree of protection of the right at issue. In that context the Court has referred to the fact that many States party to the Convention protect a negative freedom of association,[44] it has referred to a common ground regarding equal treatment of legitimate and illegitimate children,[45] and it has referred to for example a lack of consensus regarding the legal status of transsexuals.[46] The sources of these common standards may be an international treaty to which a number of the States party to the Convention are a signatory or a legal tradition common to the national legal systems of a majority of Contracting States. The Court refers to the source and content of the common standard, but the manner in which the standard came about in the treaty or national legal systems is not specified, let alone examined, as to the existence of a common ground.

4.2 Methods of Protection and Manner of Protection

In section 3.2 above, in which I specified the sub-questions addressed in this study, I indicated that the methods of protection constitute one of the aspects that determine the protection of freedom of expression. As I said, the methods applied by the European Court of Human Rights are discussed in chapter IV. Here suffice it to say that the methods of protection concern the manner in which freedom of expression is considered by the English legislature, the English courts and by the European Court of Human Rights. I want to emphasise that this includes both the scope of the review of courts and the requirements that restrictions have to fulfil in order to be justified. The methods distinguished in chapter IV are 'margin of appreciation', review of proportionality and balancing of interests. These three methods of protection together constitute the manner of protection, that is the manner in which freedom of expression is taken account of.

4.3 Freedom of Expression

Because I restrict this study to freedom of expression, I consider it is beyond the scope of this book to discuss in detail the meaning of the term 'fundamental right'. I merely assume that fundamental rights or civil liberties are those rights and freedoms regarded as such by the authorities responsible for their protection. The

---

44 Meaning that there is a freedom not to join an association. Sigurdur A. Sigurjónsson v. Iceland (1993) A.264.
45 Marckx v. Belgium, (1979) A.31.
46 B v. France, (1992) A.232-C.

fundamental nature of freedom of expression is undisputed. In this study the terms fundamental rights, civil liberties and human rights are used interchangeably.

In this study I do not use a particular definition of freedom of expression. The meaning of this term is determined by the use of it in the English system of protection and in the system of protection under the ECHR. Furthermore, the terms freedom of expression and freedom of speech are used interchangeably.

5 STRUCTURE OF THIS STUDY

The point of departure is to look for a common ground with regard to the protection of freedom of expression under English law and under the system of protection of the ECHR. In doing so a certain emphasis is put on the legislature and the judiciary. This book consists of two parts. The chapters of the first part provide a general frame of reference for the second part, where I compare in detail the aspects that determine the scope of freedom of expression. The first part of the book is divided into 4 chapters including the present introduction. The second part contains 6 chapters including the general conclusions to this study.

The contents of the chapters are as follows: chapter II contains a discussion of the Human Rights Act 1998. This chapter examines the aims of the Act and the manner in which these aims are intended to be achieved. The discussion of the Human Rights Act is general in nature: it does not merely concern the protection of freedom of expression. The provisions on the fundamental rights incorporated also concern freedom of expression. The third chapter contains an extensive treatment of English legislation and case law that touches upon freedom of expression. With regard to statute law as well as common law and equity, it is the task of the courts to determine what the law is. The scope, the restrictions and the interpretation of freedom of expression can only be ascertained by evaluating the case law of the courts. In doing so, I examine the areas of law that constitute the most significant restrictions on freedom of expression. These are the protection of public decency, the protection of reputation, the law of breach of confidence, the protection of official secrets, contempt of court law, the protection of public order and, finally, judicial review. I assess the legislation and case law of each of these areas of law with regard to their impact on the scope of freedom of expression.

The extensive examination of English law explains why chapter III is longer than the others.

In the fourth chapter I analyse the methods of protection that are applied by the European Court of Human Rights. In doing so I discuss a significant number of judgments of the Court. In the first part of the book I do not discuss the case law of the Court on freedom of expression separately. As I mentioned earlier, a number of overviews of this case law are available and I do not think it necessary to consider each of these cases separately. I wish to emphasise that in this first Part, I focus on the analysis of the *methods* of protection applied by the Court. The *manner* in which these methods are applied in the case law of the European Court of Human Rights is assessed in the second part of the book.

In chapter V, the first chapter of the second part of the book, I explore the elements of a common ground between the approach to the notion of freedom of expression in English law and under the ECHR. I discuss a common ground between English law and the ECHR regarding the methods of protection distinguished from the case law of the Court in chapters VI to VIII. Finally, I deal with the 'consideration and appreciation of facts and circumstances' in chapter IX. The preliminary conclusions of chapters V to IX, describe the common ground that existed before the entry into force of the Human Rights Act 1998, and also look at the (possible) impact of the Human Rights Act on the existence of a common ground. Chapter X contains the general conclusions regarding the existence and nature of a common ground between the protection of freedom of expression in English law and under the ECHR. I also comment on what needs to be changed in the approach of the English legislature and judiciary in order to meet the requirements of the system of protection under the ECHR and on the instruments the Human Rights Act provides to meet these requirements.

CHAPTER II
THE HUMAN RIGHTS ACT 1998

1 INTRODUCTION

Until recently the English system of human rights protection depended on domestic law before national courts. Currently, however, parts of the ECHR are about to be incorporated into English law by way of the Human Rights Act 1998.[1] The power of individual complaint under Article 25 of the Convention is extended to the possibility for citizens to invoke the rights protected under the Convention in their national courts.

The incorporation of the ECHR entails an important change from a principally non-rights based protection to a mainly rights based protection. Most relevant to the current research is that the mere fact that (part of) the Convention is incorporated does not necessarily imply that the protection of civil rights is realised to a similar degree as that provided by the European Court of Human Rights. All depends on the manner in which the protection of the incorporated rights is shaped in the Human Rights Act. The purpose of this chapter is to provide an analysis of the extent to which the ECHR is incorporated into English law by the Human Rights Act. The extent and manner of incorporation of the Convention determines the extent to which a common ground is required between the system of protection in English law and the system of protection of the ECHR, in order to meet the objectives of the Human Rights Act.

In this chapter I emphasise the changes that the Human Rights Act implies to the traditional manner in which the protection of fundamental rights is approached in English law. I first briefly discuss the aims of the Act and the sections of the Human Rights Act that have an impact on those aspects of the system of protection that are relevant to this study.

---

[1]   It should be noted that the ECHR does not impose a duty on the States to the Convention to incorporate the Convention into national law, see Martens, Incorporating the European Convention: The Role of the Judiciary, 1998, p. 5-14.

2 THE HUMAN RIGHTS ACT 1998: OBJECTIVES AND CONTOURS[2]

It was probably because the drafting of a complete new Bill would be rather time consuming, and because the rights as formulated under the ECHR made frequent appearances already in the case law of the courts, that it was decided partly to incorporate the ECHR into the UK's national law.[3] The objectives of the introducers of the Bill were to limit the time and costs of the people who wished to see their Convention rights protected, and to provide them with a possibility to invoke these rights before the national courts.[4] These arguments for incorporation of the Convention were supplemented with remarks regarding the insufficient protection of those rights under the current law of the United Kingdom, forcing people to take their cases to Strasbourg. Beside the advantage for individuals of a speedy and effective remedy for violations of their Convention rights, incorporation of the ECHR is also intended as a mechanism by way of which the legislature is forced to consider the effects of its legislation on individuals.[5]

The main concerns regarding the adoption of any Bill of Rights, including incorporation of the ECHR into English law, concerned the effect such a Bill would have on the sovereignty of Parliament, and the role the judiciary would subsequently play in protecting those rights.[6] It was feared that judges would be forced to make political choices, which were assumed to have been in the hands of Parliament until now.[7] In October 1997 the UK Government introduced the Human Rights Bill,[8]

---

2   See for a more general discussion on the background of the Bill and the extent to which the Human Rights Act meets its objectives: Bosma, A Bill of Rights for the United Kingdom, 1998, p. 107-123.

3   Bailey, Harris and Jones, Civil Liberties, cases and materials, 1995, p. 24, observe that a problem with this choice is that 'the Commission and the Court interpret the Convention for Europe as a whole'. They also comment on whether or not the ECHR covers 'all the civil and political rights one would like to see protected' and focus amongst other things on the absence of a general right to equality before the law.

4   White Paper 'Bringing Rights Home', 24 October 1997, par. 1.14-1.17. Enforcing these rights before the European Court of Human Rights was held to 'take too long and cost too much'. See also Lord Scarman, English Law – The new dimension, 1974, p. 15; Feldman, Civil Liberties and Human Rights in England and Wales, 1993, p. 78; Penner, The Canadian Experience with the Charter of Rights; Are there lessons for the United Kingdom?, 1996, 124; Lord Hope of Craighead, Devolution and Human Rights, 1998, p. 371-372.

5   HL Deb, 3 November 1997, per Lord Chancellor (Lord Irvine of Lairg) col 1228: 'So there will have to be close scrutiny of the human rights implications of all legislation before it goes forward'.

6   White Paper, 'Bringing Rights Home', 24 October 1997, par. 2.10-2.15. HL Deb, 3 November 1997, per the Lord Chancellor (Lord Irvine of Lairg), col 1228. See also Sir Nicholas Lyell, Whither Strasbourg? Why Britain Should Think Long and Hard Before Incorporating the ECHR, 1997, 132-140.

7   HL Deb, 3 November 1997, per Lord Mayhew of Twysden col 1262.

which after a number of amendments, obtained Royal Assent as the Human Rights Act 1998 on November 9 1998.[9] The Act is an attempt to achieve a number of objectives and to meet the various concerns regarding the adoption of a Bill of Rights.

The first section of the Act indicates the Convention rights that are the subject of incorporation. These are the rights protected under Articles 2 to 12 and Article 14 of the Convention as well as Articles 1 to 3 of the first protocol and Articles 1 and 2 of the sixth protocol.[10] The rights protected are therefore tied to the rights of the Convention and of the first Protocol and sixth protocol, all three of which have been ratified by the United Kingdom.[11] According to the White Paper 'Bringing Rights Home', these are the rights 'with which the people of this country are plainly comfortable'.[12]

It is not merely the text of those Articles which has been converted into statute law. The interpretation of these rights by the Court, Commission and Committee of Ministers on the basis of the Convention also has to be 'taken into account' in determining the meaning and scope of these rights. This is determined in section 2 of the Act. It should be emphasised that this section uses the phrase 'taking into account'. The courts therefore are not bound by the interpretation of the rights by the organs of the Convention.[13] This phrase indicates a certain degree of freedom for the courts to give these rights a meaning independent from the interpretation of the European Court of Human Rights.

Section 3 of the Act provides the following: 'So far as it is possible to do so, primary legislation and subordinate legislation must be read and given effect in a way which is compatible with Convention rights'. This implies that after the courts have determined the meaning of a right incorporated by the Act, they subsequently have a duty under section 3 to attempt to interpret domestic legislation in accordance with the Convention right at issue. Consequently, the courts can give restrictive legislation

---

8   HL Bill 38. The corresponding White Paper is called 'Rights Brought Home: The Human Rights Bill', Cmnd. 3782.

9   See for a discussion of the amendments proposed, adopted and rejected, Editorial, [1998] E.H.R.L.R. 665-666.

10   Clause 1 s.1 HRA 1998, adding: '... as read with Articles 16 to 18 of the Convention'. These provisions further are referred to as Convention rights.

11   Outstanding protocols, which currently are protocol 4 and 7, have not been ratified (yet).

12   White Paper 'Bringing Rights Home', par. 2.1.

13   See Singh, Privacy and the Media after the Human Rights Act, 1998, p. 723: The fact that the national courts can take the case law with regard to the Convention into consideration, but are not bound by it, opens up the possibility for the courts to provide less, but also more protection than the Court (although less protection seems unlikely, because of the possibility to for English citizens to file a complaint against their government). In other words, the Act could be used by the Courts to develop a separate Bill of Rights from the Convention.

a 'possible' meaning, as opposed to a 'reasonable' meaning.[14] This section thus offers the courts a broader power to interpret domestic legislation. Section 3 also provides that 'this section does not affect the validity, continuing operation or enforcement of any incompatible primary legislation' or 'subordinate legislation if primary legislation prevents removal of the incompatibility'.[15] Instead, section 4 provides, that if it is not possible to interpret legislation in such a way that it is consistent with the Convention, that the senior courts[16] may make a 'declaration of incompatibility'.[17] It is significant that such a declaration does not affect the validity of the legislation.[18] In other words, the courts do not have the power to strike down statutes that they consider inconsistent with the Convention. Such a declaration therefore is not binding on those parties to the proceedings with regard to which it is made.[19] The individual whose right has been violated is left the possibility to take his case to Strasbourg. The declaration of incompatibility serves as a signal to Parliament. It does not imply an obligation to the legislature to alter the legislation to make it consistent with the relevant rights. S.6 ss.6 confirms that the final say regarding the adjustment of legislation to realise consistency with the relevant Convention rights lies with Parliament. This section prevents the possibility of citizens starting an action against Parliament for not proposing or adopting such legislation.[20]

In addition to the courts, the public authorities too, have a responsibility with regard to the protection of the Convention rights. S.6 imposes on public authorities a duty 'not to act in a way which is incompatible with a Convention right'[21] unless 'as the result of one or more provisions of primary legislation, the authority could not have acted differently' or if the authority was 'acting to give effect to or enforce provisions' from subordinate legislation based on primary legislation 'that could not be read or given effect in a way which is compatible with the Convention rights'.[22] This means first of all that discretionary powers should be interpreted in accordance with the Convention rights by public authorities.[23] Moreover, in conjunction with section 7, section 6 implies that with regard to judicial review the courts also have

---

14 See Lord Lester of Herne Hill, The Art of the Possible – Interpreting Statutes under the Human Rights Act, 1998, p. 669.
15 S.3, ss.2(a) and 2(b).
16 Most relevantly the High Court, the Court of Appeal and the House of Lords.
17 S.4 ss.2-5.
18 See for the meaning of the terms primary and secondary legislation s.21 HRA.
19 S.4 ss.6.
20 See Singh, Privacy and the Media after the Human Rights Act, 1998, p. 723.
21 S.6 ss.1.
22 S.6 ss.2(a) and 2(b).
23 See Lord Lester of Hirne Hill, the Art of the Possible – Interpreting Statutes under the Human Rights Act, 1998, p. 668.

a responsibility to ensure that the Convention rights are not violated, since a violation of a Convention right offers a cause of action to individuals under section 7. It should be noted moreover, that the courts are also regarded as 'public authorities' under the Human Rights Act.[24] This implies that the courts have an obligation to apply not just statute law but also common law and equity in a manner compatible with the Convention as regards the rights incorporated.[25] Moreover, the obligation of s.6 means that the courts must act in conformity with the Convention not just when it concerns cases in which public authorities are a party, but also when a case concerns private law.[26] This is the issue of 'horizontal effect'.

'Horizontal effect' is the extent to which the Convention rights can play a role in litigation between private parties.[27] However, 'full horizontal effect' in the sense that the Convention rights can be a source of action as such in horizontal situations, is apparently not intended.[28] Violations of Convention rights in such situations can be claimed in the course of regular causes of action.[29] Specific objections were raised from the side of the press – represented by Lord Wakeham – regarding the negative effect which a right to privacy with horizontal implications might have on press freedom. In order to meet these objections, section 12 was adopted in the Act.[30] This section provides that if a court is considering granting any relief that might effect the right to freedom of expression, 'no such relief is to be granted so as to restrain publication before trial unless the court is satisfied that the applicant is likely to establish that publication should not be allowed', that 'the court must have particular regard to the importance of the Convention right to freedom of expression

---

24 S.6 ss.3(a).

25 Singh, Privacy and the Media after the Human Rights Act, 1998, p. 722.

26 HL Deb, 24 November 1997, col 783: The Lord Chancellor held that the government 'believe that it is right as a matter of principle for the courts to have the duty of acting compatible with the Convention not only in cases involving other public authorities but also in developing the common law in deciding cases between citizens'.

27 See for a more general and extensive discussion: Markesinis, Privacy, Freedom of Expression, and the horizontal effect of the Human Rights Bill: Lessons from Germany, 1999, p. 47-88; Hunt, The 'Horizontal Effect' of the Human Rights Act, 1998, p. 423-443. See also on this subject: Sir Anthony Hooper, The Impact of the Human Rights Act on Judicial Decision-making, 1998, p. 683; Professor Sir William Wade, Human Rights and the Judiciary, 1998, p. 524-525; Editorial, [1998] E.H.R.L.R. 1, p. 1.

28 This was indicated by Lord Irvine, HL Deb, 5 February 1998, col. 840: 'What the Bill does not do is to make the Convention rights themselves directly part of our domestic law in the same way that, for example, the civil wrongs of negligence, trespass or libel are part of our domestic law. Claims in those areas are all actionable in tort in cases between private individuals... We have sought to protect the human rights of individuals against the abuse of power by the State, broadly defined, rather than to protect them against each other'.

29 See Ewing, The Human Rights Act and Parliamentary Democracy, 1999, p. 89.

30 HL Deb, 24 November 1997, col 1771. Lord Wakeham is the chairman of the Press Complaints Commission.

and, where the proceedings relate to material which the respondent claims, or which appears to the court, to be journalistic, literary or artistic material (or to conduct connected with such material), to (a) the extent to which the material has, or is about to, become available to the public; or it is or would be, in the public interest for the material to be published and to (b) any relevant privacy code'. This section was especially adopted to prevent the courts from attributing insufficient weight to freedom of expression, in particular in relation to the protection of privacy.[31]

The next issue to be discussed is the impact of the Human Rights Act on the system of protection as it was prior to the moment the Act took effect.

3 THE IMPACT OF THE HUMAN RIGHTS ACT 1998 ON THE ENGLISH SYSTEM OF PROTECTION

In section 1.1 of the introductory chapter to this study I mentioned the main aspects of English law relevant to the protection of fundamental rights. As far as the sources of law are concerned, the Human Rights Act does not constitute a change. Statutory legislation, common law and equity remain the three sources of law, since the relevant rights of the Convention become part of national law through statute. With regard to the other three elements that determine the protection of fundamental rights in the English system of protection, namely the approach to fundamental rights as protecting freedom, the influence of the ECHR on English law and Parliamentary Sovereignty, however, the Human Rights Act does constitute changes in the system of protection as it functioned until the Act took effect. It is obvious that the Human Rights Act changes the traditional protection of freedom into an extensive rights-based protection of fundamental rights. The way the Act has an impact on the Convention's influence on the English system of protection and the Act's impact on Parliamentary Sovereignty requires a more extensive discussion. I engage on this in the following two sections.

3.1 Influence of the ECHR

Until such time as the Human Rights Act takes effect, the rights of the Convention cannot be directly enforced in the national courts. By way of reference to the presumption that Parliament does not intend to restrict fundamental rights and that Parliament does not intend to legislate contrary to its international obligations the courts could resolve manifest ambiguities in statutory legislation. The influence of

---

31 This section reassured the press industry: HC Deb 2 July 1998, col 541. See also Sir Anthony Hooper, The Impact of the Human Rights Act on Judicial Decision-making, 1998, p. 681; Professor William Wade, Human Rights and the Judiciary, 1998, p. 528; Ewing, The Human Rights Act and Parliamentary Democracy, 1999, p. 94.

the ECHR after the Human Rights Act becomes law takes effect in the application of legislation by the courts, and in the exercise of powers by the executive. S.2, 3 and 6 determine the impact on the application of legislation by the courts. S.2 of the Human Rights Act requires the courts to 'take account' of the meaning given to the rights by the European Court of Human Rights. This implies that the English courts have a certain discretion in the extent to which they provide protection to the Convention rights.

As I said above, the main aim of the Human Rights Act is to provide a speedy and effective remedy. If this is to be realised, however, the English courts must provide at least the degree of protection required by the Court. They can provide such protection to the extent that the text of the restrictive law makes this possible: section 3 requires the courts, as far as it is possible to do so, to interpret legislation consistent with the Convention rights.

Section 6, which determines that the courts are 'public authorities' and as such have an obligation to exercise their powers in accordance with the Convention rights, results in an obligation on the courts to interpret common law in accordance with the Convention rights, also in cases between private individuals.[32]

The possibilities of the courts to give effect to the Convention rights in English national law is in fact limited by the existence of the possibility to make a declaration of incompatibility. I already observed above that if legislation is held to be incompatible with Convention rights, the courts do not have the power to strike it down.[33] Instead they have to apply the legislation as it is. That legislation then has a meaning that is compatible with the Convention as 'far as possible'.[34]

S.6 of the Human Rights Act also brings about a change in, or at least establishes clarity with regard to, the influence of the ECHR on the exercise of powers by the executive.

Previous to the Human Rights Act, the extent of the responsibility of public authorities not to violate Convention rights was unclear. For the individuals whose rights it concerns, the most that can be said is that this responsibility existed to the extent required by the courts in exercising judicial review.[35] S.6 of the Human Rights Act incontrovertibly provides for such a responsibility.

It should also be recalled, however, that the effect of an obligation on administrative bodies to take account of the rights incorporated into national law still

---

32 S.6 ss.3(a) HRA 1998.

33 See HL Deb, 3 November 1997, col 124; HC Deb, 16 February 1998, col 772, 816

34 It must be noted that s.21 HRA 1998 provides for a particular definition of primary and subordinate legislation. A declaration of incompatibility can be given only with regard to the defined primary and subordinate legislation.

35 This responsibility existed to the extent required by the courts in exercising judicial review. Discussion of the effect of judicial review on the protection of freedom of expression takes place in section 8 of chapter III.

depends on the extent to which the realisation of this requirement can be reviewed by the courts. The English courts can review the acts of public authorities under section 6 together with section 7 of the Human Rights Act. We saw moreover that the English courts are required to interpret legislation in conformity with the Convention as far as it is possible to do so. This includes the legislation on which executive authorities base their decisions. Beside influencing the effect of the ECHR in English law, this requirement also influences the role of the judiciary in relation to the legislature. Further discussion on this aspect of the Human Rights Act takes place in the next section, where the changes brought about by the Human Rights Act with regard to Parliamentary Sovereignty are elaborated on.

3.2 Parliamentary Sovereignty

As I said above, the main aim of the Human Rights Act is to provide speedy and effective remedies to violations of the Convention rights, but, it also attempts to achieve this without significantly altering the constitutional structure of English law. As I have said before, one of the main characteristics of this law is that parliament is sovereign. It is not only sovereign regarding the judiciary and the executive, but also regarding previous parliaments. In this section I discuss the extent to which the Human Rights Act, despite assertions otherwise, changes the relation between Parliament and the judiciary and between the executive and the judiciary and the relationship with (past and) future parliaments. In other words, to what extent does the Human Rights Act change the conventional approach to Parliamentary Sovereignty?

The Human Rights Act has not included a special amendment procedure. It is no more or less difficult to amend or withdraw the Human Rights Act than other legislation. However, the courts will in future have the power to review pre- and post- Human Rights Act legislation on consistency with the Convention rights, be it pre- or post-Human Rights Act legislation.[36] To legislate inconsistently with the Convention rights, the legislature will have to use entirely unambiguous wording, because the courts will have a duty to interpret legislation in accordance with the Convention rights as far as possible. On the other hand when such interpretation of pre- or post Human Rights Act legislation cannot lead to removal of the incompatibility, enforcement of the Act lies with Parliament. The possibility to review future legislation amounts to a change in the common approach to Parliamentary Sovereignty in the sense that it concerns legislation that previously simply would have overridden the Act, because a previous parliament cannot bind a subsequent parliament. The second observation, however, may justify the statement

---

36 As was remarked by Wadham, Bringing Rights Half-way Home, 1997, p. 141: 'Ordinarily a chronologically superior Act would take precedence in the case of conflict'.

that Parliamentary Sovereignty has remained intact. Nevertheless, the method of incorporation chosen does incontestably change the position of the judiciary vis-à-vis both the legislature and the executive. I will deal with these further separately.

Judiciary and Parliament

In the Human Rights Act there are a number of specific references to the role of the judiciary, both as interpreters of legislation and in relation to judicial review. With regard to the interpretation of legislation, the courts under the Act have the authority to apply the Convention as law of the land and as such have to determine whether domestic legislation is consistent with the Convention. In fact, under section 3(1) they have a duty to interpret legislation in conformity with the ECHR 'as far as it is possible to do so'. This implies a change in the approach of national legislation where it touches upon the rights incorporated. In the present situation the courts give statutory legislation its ordinary meaning which is derived from the statutory terminology and the purpose of the statute taken as a whole.[37] Only when there is an ambiguity in the terminology of the legislation, can the courts assume that legislation is intended to be in accordance with the UK's international obligations such as the ECHR.[38] Instead of limiting themselves to assuming that Parliament intended to legislate in accordance with the United Kingdom's obligations under the ECHR when the terms of the Act are ambiguous, the courts under the Human Rights Act should seize any opportunity to interpret the legislation in such a manner that it is consistent with the Convention.[39] Only where no such possibility exists will the courts give a declaration of incompatibility.[40] Where the possibility to interpret in conformity with the Convention rights ends, and the necessity to make a declaration of incompatibility begins is unclear. Marshall justifiably remarks that if, as Lord Irvine suggested, the power to interpret legislation so as to comply with Convention rights may stretch as far as 'straining the meaning of words or reading in words which are not there', a declaration of incompatibility would never be necessary.[41] Such an approach would amount to an unintended restriction on Parliamentary Sovereignty in favour of the interpretory powers of the courts.

---

37 Loveland, Constitutional Law, a critical introduction, 1996, p. 83-90.
38 Feldman, Civil Liberties and Human Rights in England and Wales, 1993, p. 66.
39 Lord Irvine of Lairg, 'The Development of Human Rights in Britain', 1998, p. 228.
40 Lord Lester of Herne Hill, The Art of the Possible – Interpreting Statutes under the Human Rights Act, 1998, p. 670. Lord Lester emphasises that the courts are authorised to come up with a 'possible' interpretation as opposed to a 'reasonable' interpretation to which the interpretation of South African law was restricted.
41 Marshall, Two Kinds of Compatibility: more about section 3 of the Human Rights Act 1998, 1999, p. 379.

31

Judiciary and the Executive

The relevant provisions with regard to the relationship between the judiciary and the executive are section 2 and section 6 of the Act. Section 2 of the Act imposes a duty on the courts to take account of the Strasbourg case law. Section 6 contains the obligation for public authorities to act in conformity with Convention rights. Primary responsibility for living up to this obligation lies with the public authorities. This responsibility is enforced to the extent that section 7 of the Act provides that a person who claims that his rights have been violated by a public authority may 'bring proceedings against the authority under' the Human Rights Act or may 'rely on the Convention right or rights concerned in any legal proceeding'.

Similar to their task regarding statute law, the courts have the task of judging whether acts of public authorities are in accordance with the ECHR. The previous remarks about the courts' tasks regarding the interpretation of legislation are also relevant in the field of powers delegated to public authorities. Where these powers touch upon Convention rights, the courts will interpret them restrictively and as a result might sooner conclude that an act is 'ultra vires'. However, where the review concerns the compatibility of exercise of discretionary powers, the courts' reviewing tasks will remain supervisory in nature. The extent to which the courts can review the public authorities' view of what is consistent is not settled in the Act.[42] No specific references are made with regard to the closeness of the review of decisions of public authorities. The traditional approach of the courts to reviewing the acts of public authorities is one of restraint. A combination of factors, however, could support the view that the Human Rights Act provides a basis for closer scrutiny. Section 2 of the Human Rights Act determines that in a situation in which the appellant claims a breach of a right, a court must take into account the case law of the Court and Commission. Moreover, one of the aims of incorporating the ECHR was to reduce the number of convictions by the Court. The courts could understand section 6 together with section 2 to mean that they have a duty to ensure a degree of protection of the Convention rights similar to that offered by the Court. Whether or not the Act will be applied in this manner depends on the willingness of the courts to take such a large step away from their current position vis-à-vis the executive.

The Manner of Upholding the Act

From the previous discussion of the relation of the court to parliament and the executive, we saw that with regard to both there is a shift in the direction of the judiciary where the responsibility for protection of the rights of the Convention is concerned. In this section I address the manner in which the courts are required to provide protection for the rights incorporated.

---

42 See also Lord Lester of Herne Hill, The Art of the Possible – Interpreting Statutes under the Human Rights Act 1998, 1999, p. 668.

Section 3 indicates that the courts are required to 'read and give effect to' primary and secondary legislation 'in a way which is compatible with the Convention rights'.[43] By way of 'reading' and 'giving effect', the courts are required to fulfil the obligation under s.2 and s.3 of the Human Rights Act, namely to provide protection to the Convention rights taking account of the protection that they have been given by the Court.

The difference between the term 'reading' and 'giving effect' is not made clear. In my view, 'reading' can be regarded as interpretation of legislation, whereas 'giving effect' seems to refer to the application of the legislation in a particular case.

As concerns the methods of protection, that is: the manner in which competing interests are to play a role in the judgments of the courts, the Act gives no indication of the methods to be used. It should be noted that neither the Convention itself nor the Court require the states party to the Convention to protect the rights guaranteed by incorporating the Convention into national law. This implies that there is also no requirement that the manner in which the Court reaches the level of protection of the rights included in the Convention be applied in the national systems of protection. The methods of protection are therefore not as such incorporated into English law. The Human Rights Act does indicate the degree of protection that is intended to be the result of the exercise of the duty imposed on the courts: section 2 suggests that the degree of protection should be similar to that provided by the Court under the Convention. The question then is to what extent the methods of protection applied by the Court are decisive for the degree of protection provided by the Court.

Here, however, we touch upon the central issue of discussion in this study. The discussion of that issue will provide an answer to the question of the extent of the common ground between the protection of freedom of expression under English law and under the system of protection of the ECHR. It will also indicate the changes required to provide a similar level of protection to that provided by the Court. In the second part of this book I discuss the extent to which the English courts and the European Court of Human Rights already have in common the methods of review applied.

4 PRELIMINARY CONCLUSIONS

On the extent to which the Human Rights Act incorporates the ECHR a number of remarks can be made by way of preliminary conclusions. First of all the Human Rights Act incorporates a limited number of rights. These are the rights that UK citizens feel comfortable with, according to the legislature. The case law of the Court on the meaning of those rights is incorporated to the extent that the English courts

---

43   S.3 ss.1 HRA 1998.

have a duty to 'take account' of it. As to the manner in which the rights are incorporated, the Act makes clear that this is to be established by interpretation of pre- and post- Human Rights Act legislation on the part of the courts, as far as it is possible for them to do so, since they are to provide protection when they read and give effect to legislation. If it is not possible to provide protection in this manner, they can make a declaration of incompatibility and it is subsequently up to the legislature to realise the objectives of the Act. Section 6 obliges the courts not to act in way that is incompatible with the Convention rights; This obligation of the courts to protect the rights incorporated is not limited as such, and therefore extends to the application of common law, equity and judicial review.

Although the wording of the Act is not specific regarding the extent of the protection to be provided by the courts, and consequently the impact of the Act on the protection of the incorporated rights will depend on the willingness of the courts to be assertive in that respect, I have indicated that the Act does provide for a (possible) shift in location of responsibility for the protection of fundamental rights towards the judiciary, both in protecting rights that are restricted by the executive and in protecting rights that are restricted by the legislature. One of the objectives of the Act is to provide 'sufficient' protection of rights so as to avoid individuals having to take their case to Strasbourg. Whether such a change becomes reality depends, in my view, on how rigorous a change such an approach involves compared with the protection of rights before the Human Rights Act became law.

In the next chapter I discuss a number of areas of law that reveal something of the manner in which one specific right, freedom of expression, is dealt with by the English courts up to the moment that the Human Rights Act started to influence the judgments of the English courts. In the second part of this book I investigate the common ground between the protection of freedom of expression in English law and under the ECHR. In that part, the discussion of freedom of expression in English law in chapter III will also make it possible for me to make suggestions with regard to the influence I expect the Human Rights Act 1998 to have on a common ground. In the preliminary conclusions of each of the aspects I discuss in the chapters of part 2 of this study, I elaborate on this.

CHAPTER III
FREEDOM OF EXPRESSION
IN ENGLISH LAW

1 INTRODUCTION

In this chapter I examine how freedom of expression is approached under English law. I wish to stress that the purpose of this chapter is to provide a preliminary view of the manner in which freedom of expression is shaped by the English legislature and the English judiciary. An in-depth discussion of the manner in which freedom of expression is protected will take place in the second part of this book.

Till the moment the Human Rights Act takes effect, freedom of expression has not been protected by way of a positive provision in the English constitution or any other domestic law. The de facto protection of freedom of expression therefore was developed without such a provision. Before a detailed study of the protection of this freedom can be conducted effectively, I need to give some impression of the manner in which freedom of expression has been protected under English law. In order to do this, I selected seven concepts of law that have a significant impact on freedom of expression. The selected areas of law are: first of all, the protection of public decency by means of criminal libel and related offences, which includes the Obscene Publications Act 1959. I also discuss the law concerning civil libel, the law of breach of confidence, the law concerning official secrecy, emphasising the Official Secrets Act 1989, Contempt of Court law, and the protection of public order, in particular the Public Order Act 1986. Finally, I will elaborate on judicial review, in order to shed some light on the role of the judiciary in protecting freedom of expression with regard to the review of administrative action. The first six areas of law involve restrictions on freedom of expression, the concept of judicial review concerns the role of the courts with regard to restrictions imposed by (other) public authorities. I elaborate on the restrictive law itself and on its application by the English courts in order to create a picture of the approach to freedom of expression under English law. The discussion of the relevant concepts of law and the subsequent case law provides sufficient material to be able to elaborate on the existence of a common ground regarding the approach to the concept of freedom of expression, regarding the methods of review applied by the English courts and by the Court, and regarding the consideration and appreciation of facts and circumstances. As I have said before, this search for a common ground will take place in part II of this book.

I do not discuss each of the selected concepts of law in great detail. I deal only with those aspects that have the most obvious effects on freedom of expression. In each section I first discuss the relevant legislation, after which I examine the relevant case law in which the exact scope of the restriction has taken shape. In each of the sections, the emphasis will be on whether freedom of expression was considered and if so I will briefly discuss how this was done.

2 CRIMINAL LIBEL AND RELATED OFFENCES

In this section I discuss three forms of criminal libel. These are obscene libel and related offences, blasphemous libel and defamatory libel. Obscene libels in practice are governed by the Obscene Publications Act 1959. Closely related to obscene publications is the common law offence of 'outraging public decency', and the offences of 'conspiracy to outrage public decency' and 'conspiracy to corrupt public morals'. I start off the discussion of criminal libels with these last offences. First I clarify some specifics of common law relevant to the protection of freedom of expression. Then I elaborate on the law governing the offences addressed in this section. Subsequently I discuss the case law in which their scope and the consequent extent of the restriction posed on freedom of expression has been determined.

2.1 Outraging Public Decency and Related Offences

Outraging public decency, conspiracy to outrage public decency and conspiracy to corrupt public morals constitute common law offences against public morals. With regard to common law offences, it is the courts that decide whether or not a particular offence exists under common law. The courts (of first instance) also have an obligation to instruct the jury as to the meaning of the terminology of the offence. It is the jury, however, that decides whether or not the circumstances of the case complete the offence. From this it is apparent where the courts' possibilities lie in awarding freedom of expression a certain degree of protection. Once the existence of the offence has been accepted, freedom of expression can only be of influence with regard to the scope of the offence by way of instructions regarding the terminology. This may concern instructions regarding the meaning of the terms 'public' or 'outraging'. The jury subsequently applies the offence to the particular circumstances of the case, which is where the influence of the court ends.[1] One further element of common law is of relevance. This is that under common law a defence of public good is not allowed. This means that when a jury applies the offence to a case, the jury is not allowed to take account of any interests the offensive behaviour may serve. If, for instance, the behaviour concerned constitutes an offence under common law, but also forms an expression that contributes to political

---

1   See the decision of the House of Lords in the Knuller case with regard to the instructions that should be given to a jury.

discussion, this 'public good' aspect of the behaviour cannot justify or undo the offensiveness of the speech. In other words, any interest in freedom of expression cannot be considered as a defence by a jury.[2]

In this section I focus on the role freedom of expression has played in those court decisions in which the existence and scope of the offences was determined. I first give a short introduction to the content of the offences concerned.

2.1.1 The Offences

Outraging Public Decency[3]

Knuller v. DPP is the leading case on the existence of the offence of outraging public decency.[4] In this case the majority of the House of Lords held that outraging public decency constituted an offence under common law,[5] after it had been held in an earlier case that an offence was committed in public when the 'alleged outrageously indecent matter could have been seen by more than one person, even though in fact no more than one did see it'.[6] The offence was held to consist of anything said or done in public that was considered 'lewd, disgusting and offensive' by 'ordinary decent-minded people who are not likely to become corrupted or depraved'.[7] In a relatively recent decision, the scope of the offence was further determined when it was held that no proof of intent to outrage public decency was necessary in order to be able to find the offence committed.[8] Only the act itself has to be done intentional; no intent to outrage public decency was held to be required.

The most recent charges with outraging public decency were brought against people who committed sexual acts with animals in public.[9] Further examples of the

---

2   See, however, the speech of Lord Simon in the Knuller case, discussed below, in which he introduces a possibility for a jury to take account of the interest in freedom of expression when deciding whether the criteria of the offence were met. A defence of public good is available, for instance, under s.4 of the Obscene Publications Act 1959: It justifies the publication of an obscene article if it is in the interest of science, literature, art or learning, or of other objects of general concern.

3   For a more complete overview regarding the aspects of this offence see Card, Cross and Jones, Criminal Law, 1995, p. 454-456 and Feldman, Civil Liberties and Human Rights in England and Wales, 1993, p. 708-714.

4   Knuller Ltd v. DPP [1973] AC 435, HL.

5   This position was confirmed in R. v. Gibson and another [1991] 1 All ER 439, CA.

6   R. v. Mayling [1963] 1 All ER 687, CCA.

7   Knuller Ltd v. DPP [1973] AC 435, per Lord Reid at 457. The offence is not restricted to books and newspapers.

8   R. v. Gibson and another [1991] 1 All ER 439 at 445.

9   See e.g. Independent, June 27, 1990: reported on the charges brought against a man 'who was seen on a train with his trousers around his knees, rubbing himself against a grey-brown cat he was holding on his lap'.

offence are: committing other acts of sexual indecency in public,[10] publishing indecent advertisements[11] and showing indecent objects at an exhibition.[12]

Conspiracy to Outrage Public Decency and Conspiracy to Corrupt Public Morals[13]
In Shaw v. DPP, the House of Lords controversially held that conspiracy to corrupt public morals constituted an offence under common law.[14] This judgment constituted an extension of the common law as it had existed so far. It was held that when there is an agreement to say or do something that has a negative effect on the moral standards of people, then this publication corrupted public morals. The Shaw case concerned the publication of a book called the 'Ladies Directory'. This book contained information about the addresses and services of prostitutes. It was accepted that the agreement to publish this 'Ladies directory' constituted the offence of conspiracy to corrupt public morals.

The existence of this offence was confirmed in Knuller v. DPP.[15] The accused in Knuller v. DPP was also convicted for conspiracy to outrage public decency.[16] Beside conspiracy to outrage public decency, the defendant was also convicted for conspiracy to corrupt public morals. The act for which the accused was convicted was held to be a publication of advertisements encouraging homosexual acts between consenting adults in private. The majority of the House of Lords held that the offence of conspicacy to outrage public decency existed under common law. With regard to this offence also ordinary decent people had to be taken as the standard. The offence had to be committed in public in order for it to be seen by more than one person. The only difference with the offence of outraging public decency was that it had to be committed by two or more persons conspiring. To outrage was held to mean that ordinary decent people are at least disgusted by it. The behaviour concerned therefore

---

10   R. v. Mayling [1963] 1 All ER 687.
11   In the Knuller case, an advertisement was published encouraging homosexual acts between consenting adults in private.
12   In the Gibson case, freeze-dried earrings made out of human foetuses were exhibited.
13   Notice that conspiracy offences are statutory offences under s. 5(3) of the Criminal law Act 1977 in so far as conspiracies to commit the substantive offences of corrupting public morals or outraging public decency are concerned. One question concerns the extent of conspiracy offences under common law. When the conduct in question falls outside the substantive definition in the Criminal Law Act, then the conspiracy counterpart will be a common law offence. Since the statutory offence does not offer any defences which might create protection for freedom of expression, I will not go into the details of this discussion and discuss them as if common law offences. For a more complete overview of the aspects of these offenses see Card, Cross and Jones, Criminal Law, 1995, p. 508-511 and Feldman, Civil Liberties and Human Rights in England and Wales, 1993, p. 706-715.
14   Shaw v. DPP [1962] AC 220, HL.
15   Knuller v. DPP [1973] AC 435.
16   Knuller v. DPP [1973] AC 435.

does not influence their attitude as to what is morally accepted in society. This characteristic distinguishes outraging public decency from corrupting public morals.

In the judgments in the Shaw case and the Knuller case the existence of the three offences discussed in this section was accepted. After this brief introduction to the offences concerned, in the following section I elaborate on the extent to which freedom of expression was taken account of by the courts in the determination of the exact scope of these offences.

2.1.2 Influence of Freedom of Expression

In the judgments in the Shaw case and the Knuller case, freedom of expression could have influenced the courts in two ways. The first one is in relation to the extension of criminal liability under common law. The second concerns the instructions given to the jury by the judge regarding the meaning of the terminology of the offence concerned. I now discuss the extent to which these possibilities were put to use.

Existence of the Offence

The decision in Shaw v. DPP to extend criminal liability under common law to conspiracy to corrupt public morals constituted a rather serious interference with freedom of expression. The majority of the House of Lords did not consider the freedom of expression aspect of their decision. Instead the majority held that 'there is in the courts ... a residual power, where no statute has yet intervened to supersede the common law, to superintend those offences which are prejudicial to the public welfare'.[17] This consideration seemed to imply that freedom of expression may be considered, like any other freedom that may be interfered with, but that when the courts are of the opinion that the public welfare is at stake this will be of overriding interest. Moreover, the interest in public welfare seemed to legitimate the extensive interpretation of the common law.

There was no evidence of any presumption in favour of freedom of expression. For Lord Reid, who dissented, it was mainly the aspect of certainty in criminal law that led him to assert that the, to his opinion, new offence of conspiracy to corrupt public morals should not be held to exist under common law.[18]

In Knuller, it was considered whether or not the decision in Shaw should be followed. It was stressed: 'The decision in Shaw is in no way to be taken as affirming or lending any support to the doctrine that the courts have some general or residual power either to create new offences or so to widen existing offences as to make punishable conduct of a type hitherto not subject to punishment'.[19] Nevertheless it

---

17   Shaw v. DPP [1962] AC 220 per Lord Viscount at 268.
18   Shaw v. DPP [1962] A.C. 220, per Lord Reid at 281.
19   Knuller v. DPP [1973] AC 435.

was decided by the majority of the House of Lords that the Shaw decision was to be followed in order to avoid uncertainty in criminal law.[20] Only Lord Diplock considered freedom as a reason to go back on the decision of the majority of the House of Lords in the Shaw case: 'If this House in its judicial capacity has mistakenly curtailed the liberty of the citizen to do what he wants to do, by holding that if he does it he is liable to be punished by the state, it seems to me self-evident that this House should correct its mistake unless there are compelling reasons to the contrary'. The speech of Lord Diplock in the Knuller case was the only one in which there was a presumption in favour of liberty. Apart from this one example, in neither of the cases mentioned above, in which the existence of any of these common law offences was considered, was liberty explicitly mentioned as an interest to be taken into account. With regard to the issue of the existence of the offence, freedom of expression played no role of importance.

Scope of the Offence
As I observed, judges have the obligation to instruct the jury as to the content of the terminology of the offence at issue. The words 'outrage' and 'corrupt' are terms with regard to which a judge would have to instruct a jury. By way of such an instruction he influences the scope of the offence concerned and consequently the extent of the interference with freedom of expression.

In Knuller v. DPP, an appeal to the House of Lords was allowed with regard to the charge of conspiracy to corrupt public decency because the jury had not been appropriately instructed as to the principles of the offence. It was held that there had been a misdirection in relation to the meaning of the terms 'decency' and 'outrage'. For both the word 'outrage' and the word 'decency' it was determined that it had to be pointed out to a jury that they had a 'strong' meaning.[21] Consequently 'outrage' meant more than 'shocked or disgusted'.[22] This indicated that it should not be accepted too easily that certain conduct would outrage public decency.[23] It was for the jury to decide whether the conditions constituting the offence of conspiracy to outrage public decency had been fulfilled. The restrictive meaning given to the indicated terms by the House of Lords created some room for freedom of expression. Considerable room for freedom of expression was suggested by Lord Simon in his speech in the Knuller case. According to him, not only should it be emphasised that 'outrage' like 'corrupt' in the offence of corrupting public morals was a very strong

---

20 Knuller v. DPP [1973] AC 435, per Lord Reid at 455. Apparently one decision to that effect can create such certainty.
21 Knuller v. DPP [1973] AC 435, per Lord Simon of Glaisdale at 495.
22 Knuller v. DPP [1973] AC 435 at 458.
23 In the same manner it was held that anything which an ordinary decent man would find shocking, disgusting or revolting constituted indecency.

word, he went even further by stating: 'Outraging public decency goes considerably beyond offending the susceptibilities of, or even shocking reasonable people. Moreover the offence is ... concerned with recognised minimum standards of decency, which are likely to vary from time to time'. Subsequently he held that the term 'public decency' should be viewed as a whole and that 'the jury should be invited, where appropriate, to remember that they live in a plural society, with a tradition of tolerance towards minorities, and that this atmosphere of toleration is itself part of public decency'.[24]

These considerations are of interest to this study in two ways. First it was explicitly held that it requires more than shocking expressions to amount to the offence. And second, if these were in fact the instructions given to the jury, the judges were thereby inviting the members of the jury to take the value of freedom of expression into consideration. This could be perceived as an introduction of a 'public good' defence as I indicated in footnote 2 in section 1.1.1.

The common law offences discussed in this section of the paragraph exist alongside obscene publications law. The offences of outraging public decency and conspiracy to outrage public decency are not obscenity-based. Instead they are concerned with the protection of people's sensibilities.[25] Under criminal libel a specific distinction is retained between a tendency to shock and disgust and a tendency to corrupt or deprave.[26] The reason for the distinction lies in whether or not a publication or an act influences the behaviour of the public. This distinction between outraging and corrupting is acknowledged in the Obscene Publications Act 1959 which governs the limits regarding the publication of obscene articles. The Obscene Publications Act is the topic of discussion in the next section of this paragraph.

2.2 Obscene Publications Act 1959[27]

Under English law it is an offence to publish an obscene article.[28] Liability for obscenity arises out of harm done to the likely reader. The harm consists of corrupting and depraving him. Harm is not done when the likely reader is outraged

---

24 Knuller v. DPP [1973] A.C. 435, per Lord Simon of Glaisdale at 495.
25 See Feldman, Civil Liberties and Human Rights in England and Wales, 1993, p. 709 and Gardner, Freedom of Expression, 1994, p. 216.
26 Gardner, The protection of freedom of speech in constitutional and civil law, 1990, p. 377.
27 See on general information on all aspects of the Act: Feldman, Civil Liberties and Human Rights in England and Wales, 1993, p. 715-724; Bailey, Harris, Jones, Civil Liberties, cases and materials, 1995, p. 349-363; Card, Cross and Jones, Criminal Law, 1995, p. 448-452; Smith and Hogan, Criminal Law, 1992, p. 730-749.
28 S. 2(1) Obscene Publications Act 1959.

by a publication. Depending on whether the accused are tried summarily[29] or on indictment,[30] a judge or a jury consisting of twelve people has to decide whether an article meets the requirements to constitute obscenity.

Similar to the previously discussed offences, freedom of expression may be considered in determining the exact scope of the offence also in relation to obscene publications. With regard to liability for obscene publications, however, s.4 of the Obscene Publications Act offers an explicit possibility to protect freedom of expression. In the following sections, I elaborate on the behaviour held to be liable under the Obscene Publications Act 1959 Act. Also I discuss the extent to which freedom of expression has influenced the scope of the offence, be it by way of s.4 or otherwise.

2.2.1 The Offence

What constitutes an obscene publication is further defined under the Obscene Publications Act 1959 s.2(1).[31] This section determines that any person who, whether for gain or not, publishes an obscene article or who has (in his possession) such an article for publication for gain (whether gain to himself or gain to another) shall be liable. This statutory offence covers any article containing or embodying matter to be read or looked at or both, any sound record, and any film or other record of a picture or pictures.[32] An article is considered to be obscene when it tends to deprave and corrupt persons who are likely to read, see or hear the matter.[33] No

---

29 In a summary trial a judge tries accused persons without a jury. Summary trials are restricted to statutory offences, but serious crimes must be tried on indictment (see Walker, The Oxford Companion to Law, 1980, p. 1197).

30 In Walker, The Oxford Companion to Law, 1980, p. 612, indictment has been defined as: 'A written accusation, running in England in the name of the Queen, ..., against a person, charging him with serious crime triable by jury'. Currently indictment is the remedy for 'any serious crime, other than an offence over which courts of summary jurisdiction have exclusive jurisdiction'.

31 Supplemented by the Obscene Publications Act 1964, amended by the Criminal Law Act 1977, s.53 and the Broadcasting Act 1990, s.162. Furthermore, the 'Telecommunications Act 1984' makes it an offence to send 'by means of a public telecommunications system, a message or other matter that is grossly offensive or of an indecent, obscene or menacing character'.

32 Obscene Publications Act 1959 s.1(2). Regarding indecent photographs of children the offence has been further extended in the Criminal Justice and Public Order Act 1994 s.84-87.

33 The terms 'article', 'publish' and 'obscene' are defined in section 1:
(1) For the purpose of this Act an article shall be deemed to be obscene if its effect or (where the article comprises two or more distinct items) the effect of any one of its items is, if taken as a whole, such as to tend to deprave and corrupt persons who are likely, having regard to all relevant circumstances, to read, see or hear the matter contained or embodied in it.
(2) In this Act 'article' means any description of article containing or embodying matter to be read or looked at or both, any sound record, and any film or other record of a picture or pictures.
(3) For the purposes of this Act a person publishes an article who

intent to deprave and corrupt is necessary.[34]

2.2.2 Influence of Freedom of Expression

Scope of the Offence

From the definition of obscenity it becomes clear that there are two elements of obscenity that require specification. These elements are first the 'likely readers' and second the fact that the publication has to 'deprave' and 'corrupt' the persons likely to read, see or hear the matter. In determining the meaning of these elements the scope of the offence may be influenced in such a manner that the restricting effect on freedom of expression remains limited.

In relation to the offence, Barendt observed with regard to these vague terms: 'British law ... emphasises that there is no absolute test to determine obscenity: rather there is a variable standard, the application of which depends on the probable readership or audience. The significance of the harm is assessed by reference to these particular people, not ordinary people in general'.[35] In other words, there is no objective obscenity, since the likely readers will vary. The harm referred to will consist of depraving and corrupting a specific audience. Because the likely audience is variable, this might imply that also the terms 'deprave' and 'corrupt' involve a variable standard, the meaning of which is to be determined with regard to the circumstances of each case. The variable elements of the term obscenity, namely 'corrupt', 'deprave' and 'likely readership', have been specified in the case law. These specifications indicate the extent to which the offence restricts freedom of expression.

With regard to the likely readership, the Court of Appeal in R v. Calder and Boyars determined that the jury must assess whether the article tends 'to deprave and corrupt a significant proportion of those persons likely to read it'. It also stated: 'What is a significant proportion is a matter entirely for the jury to decide'.[36] However, 'a significant proportion' may be much less than half, it merely indicated that it had to be a part of the likely readers and it should be not numerically negligible.[37]

(a) distributes, circulates, sells, lets on hire, gives, or lens it, or who offers it for sale or for letting on hire; or
(b) in the case of an article containing or embodying matter to be looked at or a record, shows plays or projects it, or, where the matter is data stored electronically, transmits that data.

34 Shaw v. DPP [1962] AC 220: '... obscenity depends on the article and not upon the author.'
35 Barendt, Freedom of Speech, 1985, p. 256.
36 R v. Calder and Boyars Ltd [1968] 3 All ER 644, HL, per Lord Salmon LJ. at 648.
37 DPP v. Whyte [1972] 3 All ER 12, HL at 25.

With regard to the terms 'deprave' and 'corrupt', terms which were both considered to be ambiguous,[38] it was initially held that they were of such a nature that no definition could be provided.[39] In later cases, however, some indication as to the meaning of these words was provided. In the Knuller case the House of Lords held, as we have seen, that the words have a 'strong' meaning.[40] In another case, the House of Lords held that articles which are objectively filthy, lewd, repulsive or indecent according to the standards of the community, are not necessarily obscene.[41] Moreover, it was accepted that there may be a defence in an argument of aversion. This means that instead of tempting people to behave in the portrayed manner, the article will disgust and thus discourage them from indulging in the particular practices described.[42] These were considerations which in effect decreased the possible the impact of the offence on freedom of expression.

In DPP v. Whyte, which dealt with the sale of hard-core pornographic magazines and is the leading case on obscene publications, the House of Lords further clarified the meaning of 'deprave' and 'corrupt', moreover the case considered the scope of the term 'likely readers'.[43] The House of Lords determined that the terms referred to 'corruption of the mind' and that it was not necessary that this resulted in any behaviour indicating this effect.[44]

In the magistrate court's decision in this case, the likely readers of pornographic magazines were narrowed down to 'middle-aged men' who were regular customers of the shop that sold these magazines. The magistrate court considered these customers to be 'inadequate, pathetic, dirty-minded men seeking cheap thrills ...', whose morals were already in a state of depravity and corruption'. According to the court this consequently influenced the scope of harm done by the magazines. The court stated that it doubted if 'such minds could be open to any immoral influences which the said articles were capable of exerting'. The majority of the House of Lords, however, was not willing to follow the magistrate court's reasoning concerning the group of 'likely readers'. The shop in which the magazines were sold, sold a wide variety of magazines and had a separate corner for those with a pornographic content. It was clearly indicated that this corner was for adults only. The House of Lords determined that the likely readers in this case were all people likely to wander into the shop, consequently significantly broadening the group of 'likely readers'.

---

38 See also Gardner, Freedom of Expression, 1994, p. 216.
39 R. v. Calder and Boyars Ltd [1968] 3 All ER 644 at 647.
40 Knuller v. DPP [1973] AC 435 at 456, per Lord Reid and Lord Simon 491.
41 This was first held in R v. Anderson [1971] 3 All ER 1152, CA, and affirmed in DPP v. Whyte [1972] 3 All ER 12, HL, per Lord Salmon at 27.
42 R v. Anderson [1971] 3 All ER 1152, CA.
43 DPP v. Whyte [1972] 3 All ER 12.
44 DPP v. Whyte [1972] 3 All ER 12 per Lord Pearson at 21.

However, this approach alone was not decisive for the restrictive effect on freedom of expression, since the House of Lords also did not agree with the magistrate court's decision on the meaning of 'deprave and corrupt'. The doubts expressed by the magistrate court as to whether the regular customers' minds 'could be said to be open to any immoral influences which the said articles were capable of exerting', since the morals of the likely readers 'were already in a state of depravity and corruption', were rejected in the strongest terms. Lord Cross held that the words 'tend to deprave and corrupt' are well able to include 'maintaining in a state of depravity and corruption'. He also stated that 'it should be taken into account that it takes time for a man to become depraved'. Lord Wilberforce held that 'to propose that all these men are incapable of being depraved and corrupted because they are addicts ... is contrary to the whole basis of the Act. The Act is not merely concerned with the once for all corruption of the wholly innocent, it equally protects the less innocent from further corruption, the addict from feeding or increasing his addiction'.[45]

The variable standard as indicated by Barendt consequently was not used to the fullest extent. The likely readership is not differentiated to the greatest extent that it could be, since the House of Lords is not willing to interpret 'likely readers' in the restrictive manner proposed by the magistrate court. The same is true for the meaning of 'deprave' and 'corrupt'. As I observed, it was determined that to 'deprave and corrupt' deals with corruption of the mind. No depraved or corrupted behaviour to show the effect on the mind is necessary to be able to consider an article obscene. Finally it was decided that also when an article maintains a person in a state of depravity and corruption it can be considered to be obscene.

In none of these decisions on the scope of the offence, was freedom of expression considered. It does not appear that the possibilities offered by the formulation of the offence to establish some basic protection for freedom of expression by opting for the more restrictive definitions of the ambiguous terms in the Act, were in fact used.

Although in the previously discussed offences under criminal liability, freedom of expression was not considered of interest as a rule, at least there seemed to be some awareness of the restricting effect the offences had on freedom in general. Regarding the scope of the obscene publication offence there appears to be a complete lack of such awareness. Reasons for this might be found in the fact that obscenity is a statutory offence, the punishability of which has been decided on by the legislature, which in the legislative process should have considered the effect the Act might have on freedom. Regardless of whether or not the legislature in fact took account of the impact on freedom, the courts follow the wording and intention of the statute. A second reason might be found in the fact that the Act offers the possibility of 'internal' protection of freedom of expression under s.4, which decreases the

---

45   DPP v. Whyte [1972] 3 All ER 12 at 19.

necessity to take account of the restrictive effect on freedom with regard to the scope of the offence.

Defence – The Defence of Public Good
Unlike the situation with regard to common law offences, a defence of public good is possible under the Obscene Publications Act 1959.[46] This is provided for in s.4 of the Act. This defence does not remove the obscene nature of the article, but it provides justification for its obscenity:[47] If it is proved that publication of the article in question is justified as being for the public good on the ground that it is in the interests of science, literature, art or learning, or of other objects of general concern, a person shall not be convicted of an offence against s.2 of the Act.[48] With regard to moving picture or soundtrack the possible justification of the obscenity as being for the public good is more restricted. Here a conviction under s.2 shall not take place 'if it is proved that publication of the film or soundtrack is justified as being for the public good on the ground that it is in the interest of drama, opera, ballet or any other part, or of literature or learning'.[49] This provision lacks a general justification of 'other objects of general concern'.

This defence clearly offers protection to freedom of expression. As Barendt said: 'From the perspective of freedom of expression, the purpose of any special measure of protection for works of literary or scholarly value is to ensure that publications which do communicate ideas and information are not banned'.[50]

The degree of protection offered to freedom of expression was acknowledged by Lord Simon in his statement on the intention of the Obscene Publications Act 1959: 'The intention of the Act was ... on the one hand to enable serious literary, artistic, scientific or scholarly work to draw on the amplitude of human experience without fear of allegation that it could conceivably have a harmful effect on persons other than those to whom it was in truth directed, and on the other to enable effective action to be taken against the commercial exploitation of hard pornography – obscene articles without pretension to any literary, artistic, scientific or scholarly value'.[51]

---

46 Besides the defence of public good, another defence is available, namely the defence of excusable ignorance. This defence is provided for in s.2(5) of the Act. If the accused can prove that he had not examined the article concerned, and that he had no reasonable cause to suspect that it was obscene, he is not guilty of the offence. The offence of excusable ignorance will not be discussed further, since it does not involve balancing of interests with regard to freedom of expression.

47 See also DPP v. Jordan [1977] AC 699, HL, per Lord Wilberforce at 728.

48 Obscene Publications Act 1959 section 4(1).

49 Obscene Publications Act 1959 s. 4(1A). This section was added by the Criminal Law Act 1977, s.53.

50 Barendt, Freedom of speech, 1996, p. 269.

51 DPP v. Whyte [1972] 3 All ER per Lord Simon of Glaisdale at 23. See Feldman, Civil Liberties and Human Rights in England and Wales, 1993, p. 723: The absence of an initial protection of

Although s.4 includes the general ground of defence for articles that concern 'other objects of general concern', the possibilities of this ground to extend the protection of freedom of expression have not been used. It was held that the defence under s.4 as a whole 'deals with aspects of general concern'.[52] Consequently the defence that 'hard pornography' had therapeutic value, since it may relieve sexual tensions, was not accepted. A distinction is made between what 'conduces' to the public good and what 'concerns' the public in general.[53] In the case of DPP v. Jordan, Lord Wilberforce also specified the conditions under which the defence of s.4 could be brought forward. He stated that the words 'other objects of general concern' must be interpreted so as to fall within the same area as the areas of justification listed previous to this term in s.4, namely: literature, science, art and learning.[54] In a later case, it was determined moreover that the term 'learning' in the context of s.4(1) refers to a 'product of scholarship ... something whose inherent excellence is gained by the work of the scholar'.[55] Therefore sex education for children was not considered to be within the meaning of 'learning'.[56] This restriction of the scope of the defence is somewhat disappointing, since freedom of expression had not been considered at all when the scope of the offence was determined.

Although the scope of it is limited, still the application of the defence as such influenced the scope of freedom of expression. This can be derived from the statements of Lord Salmon in R v. Calder and Boyars on the relation between the decision on the obscenity of an article and the decision on whether this obscenity can be justified on one of the given grounds. In the case in question he held the following: '... the proper direction on a defence under s.4 in a case such as the present is that the jury must consider on the one hand the number of readers they believe would tend to be depraved and corrupted by the book, the strength and tendency to deprave and corrupt, and the nature of the depravity or corruption; on the other hand they should assess the strength of the literary, sociological or ethical merit which they consider the book to possess. They should then weigh up all these factors

---

freedom of expression, becomes apparent as well through s.3 of the 1959 Act, which provides the power to order forfeiture without a conviction. It allows magistrates to grant an order for confiscation and destruction of obscene publications.

52   DPP v. Jordan [1977] AC 699, HL, per Lord Wilberforce at 718.
53   Smith and Hogan, Criminal Law, 1992, p. 738.
54   It should be noted that contrary to the decision on whether an article is obscene, expert evidence is allowed with regard to the literary, artistic etc. value of the article. S.4(2) of the 1959 Act states that 'the opinion of experts as to the literary, artistic, scientific or other merits of an article may be admitted in any proceedings under this Act either to establish or to negative the said ground'. No evidence is allowed however to prove that the article can be considered to be for the public good.
55   A-G's Reference (No.3 of 1977) [1978] 3 All ER 1166, CA, per Lord Widgery CJ. at 1169.
56   Feldman in Civil Liberties and Human Rights in England and Wales, 1993, p. 719, is of the opinion that 'it might, perhaps, still be arguable that sex education is a matter of general concern'.

and decide whether on balance the publication is proved to be justified as being for the public good'.[57]

Consequently the jury first has to assess whether an article is obscene. If the article is found to be obscene, then the jury must consider whether the obscenity can be justified. However, publication of an obscene article is not justified merely by being, for instance, of literary value. The interest in the ground of justification has to outweigh the harm done to the likely readers in the form of depravity and corruption. This approach to the role of the defence of 'public good' is supported by the structure of the Act. It first defines the prohibited behaviour and subsequently defines possible justifications. Such a structure puts freedom of expression in arrears beforehand.

It can be concluded that the Obscene Publications Act leaves room for freedom of expression. However, the structure of the Act in combination with the manner in which the defence of public good should be applied seems to imply that information has to be of exceptional quality to avoid being prohibited. Only after it has been determined that an article is of an obscene nature, is the interest of the public in literary or other culturally elevating articles considered, and the public good should outweigh the harm done by the article. This extensive interpretation of behaviour liable under the Obscene Publications Act may become apparent in particular with regard to the possibly large area of information that is of no particular literary or artistic value, but that also cannot be considered 'hard pornography' published for commercial reasons.

Apparently, however, the Act has not been abused to ban any mention of topics such as sex or drug usage. John Gardner stated: '... it was accepted that almost any kind of redeeming social value in a publication, including its value as an exposé of depraved lifestyles, could be relied upon to support a public-good defence'.[58] There is no evidence of excessive use of the restrictive possibilities of the Obscene Publications Act 1959.[59] After the revision of the Obscene Publications Act in 1959, books such as William Burroughs's Naked Lunch and D.H. Lawrence's Lady Chatterly's Lover were permitted to be published. Still a number of publications were

---

57 R. v. Calder and Boyars [1969] 1 QB 151, CA, at 171 on Last Exit to Brooklyn (Hubert Selby).

58 Gardner, Freedom of Expression, 1994, p. 215, referring to the trial on the book American Psycho (Brett Easton Ellis). The value of an article as 'an exposé of depraved lifestyles' however was accepted as a defence against the qualification as 'corrupting and depraving', so not as a defence for the public good: Calder Boyars. See similar thought but less disapprovingly Feldman, Civil Liberties and Human Rights in England and Wales, 1993, p. 721.

59 In relation to the common law offenses discussed in the previous paragraph, it has to be noted that, although they have a different purpose, they may still be applied to the same cases. Under common law the public good defence is not available. See also Gardner, Freedom of Expression, 1994, p. 217-218, who seems of the opinion that R. v. Gibson could have been tried under the Obscene Publications Act 1959.

suppressed under the 1959 Act.[60] So, although not excessively used, the Obscene Publications Act 1959 does restrict freedom of expression in the sense that it has been used to ban books to which the audience subsequently has no access.[61] Moreover, the relatively restrictive use of the Act seems to be a result of policy, which might just as easily become more restrictive again. The Obscene Publications Act makes a change in policy possible.

2.3 Blasphemy[62]

Despite several attempts to abolish the blasphemy laws,[63] blasphemous libel remained a common law offence. This offence does not concern the outraging or insulting of people's feelings regarding decency. Instead it focuses on the outraging or insulting of their religious feelings. Freedom of expression may be restricted because of an expression's blasphemous content.

2.3.1 The Offence

As I said, there have been attempts to abolish the offence of blasphemous libel. These attempts failed, but the nature of the offence changed significantly over time. In order to be blasphemous, statements initially were required to have a 'tendency to endanger the peace'[64] irrespective of the manner in which these views were expressed. In more recent case law this criterion was relaxed considerably. As of recent decisions, statements were considered to be blasphemous if they were 'couched in indecent or offensive terms likely to shock and outrage the feelings of the general body of Christian believers in the community'.[65] Furthermore, it was held that no intent is necessary with regard to the blasphemous effects of the words.[66] It suffices to prove intent to publish.

---

60 E.g.: R. Phillip's 'Fuck'; P. Sotos' 'Pure'; J. Goad's and D. Goad's (eds.) 'Answer Me!'.

61 The Act is in principle applicable to possession of pornographic images. Possession of child pornography is charged under the Protection of Children Act 1978, also applicable to images stored on a computer: R v. Fellows, R v. Arnold [1997] 2 All ER 548, CA.

62 See for a more complete overview of the offence of blasphemy: Feldman, Civil Liberties and Human Rights in England and Wales, 1993, p. 685-698; Smith and Hogan, Criminal Law, 1995, p. 723-726.

63 Smith and Hogan, Criminal Law, 1995, p. 723.

64 Bowman v. Secular Society Ltd [1917] A.C. 406, at 466 per Lord Summer.

65 R. v. Lemon [1979] AC 617, HL. See also Smith and Hogan, Criminal Law, 1995, p. 724.

66 R. v. Lemon [1979] AC 617.

2.3.2 Influence of Freedom of Expression

Scope of the Offence

A relatively recent case of importance for the scope of the offence is R. v. Lemon.[67] This case was the first criminal prosecution for blasphemous libel to succeed in the British courts in 44 years. In relation to freedom of expression this is a most interesting case, because this freedom was explicitly considered in determining the scope of the offence.

In this case a poem describing Christ engaging in homosexual acts with his disciples was at issue. The House of Lords was asked to decide whether or not intent was necessary to constitute blasphemy. Through an in-depth study of previous cases and after considering the various opinions on the subject matter in authoritative literature, the majority of the House of Lords came to the conclusion that this was not the case. As a result the editor of the magazine in which the poem was published received a suspended prison sentence for blasphemous libel.[68] Some members of the court did not consider freedom of expression in reaching their decision. However, Lord Diplock and Lord Edmund-Davies did consider freedom of expression in their dissenting opinions. In reaction to their considerations, Lord Scarman took this aspect into account in his opinion as well. Lord Scarman stated the following regarding the reliance on freedom of expression: 'Article 10 (ECHR) provides that everyone shall have the right to freedom of expression. The exercise of this freedom "carries with it duties and responsibilities" and may be subject to such restrictions as are prescribed by law and are necessary "for the prevention of disorder or crime, for the protection of health or moral, for the protection of the reputation or rights of others ..." It would be intolerable if by allowing an author or publisher to plead the excellence of his motives and the right of free speech he could evade the penalties of the law even though his words were blasphemous in the sense of constituting an outrage upon the religious feelings of his fellow citizens'.[69] Lord Scarman emphasised the protection of the religious sensibilities of Christians. When a publication is held to outrage those feelings, the offence has been committed. It was unthinkable that protection of freedom of expression should lead to a requirement of intent in order for a publication to constitute blasphemy. The application of Article 10 in this manner is interesting. If certain behaviour is criminalised and is covered by one of the exceptions listed in the second section of Article 10 then freedom of expression as a result can no longer play a role. Consequently, the Convention is neatly fitted into the classic English approach to the protection of fundamental rights, to wit: that of freedom being residual. In reaching his conclusion, Lord Scarman did consider

---

67 R v. Lemon [1979] AC 617, (1979) 1 All ER 898.
68 The poem is still banned in England.
69 R. v. Lemon [1979] AC 617 per Lord Scarman at 665.

freedom of expression as an interest. However, it was only considered to be of interest outside the scope of the offence, and therefore could not influence its scope. In other words, first it must be determined what behaviour is prohibited. After that has been done, the behaviour that is not prohibited is the resultant freedom of expression.

Lord Edmund-Davies also undertook a thorough investigation of previous decisions on cases involving blasphemous libel and of opinions of authoritative authors on the offence of blasphemy. He, however, relied on a different decision from the one on which the majority relied.[70] In the decision referred to by Lord Edmund-Davies, an authoritative publication on blasphemy was quoted in which '... the splendid advantages which result to religion and truth from the exertions of free and unfettered minds' was considered and subsequently he quoted from this publication the following consideration: 'It is the mischievous abuse of this state of intellectual liberty which calls for penal censure. The law visits not the honest errors, but the malice of mankind'.[71] Freedom of speech was considered to be of great value to a free society. For this reason free comment on various matters and in different terms should not be restricted, when it can be considered sincere criticism. Lord Edmund-Davies concluded that the quoted consideration meant that the offence of blasphemous libel depended 'not merely on the words used but on the state of mind of the person using them'.[72]

The previous two approaches to the issue of whether intent should be an element of the offence of blasphemy have a different point of departure. Lord Edmund-Davies started with an assumption in favour of freedom of expression. He was of the opinion that expressions which insult religious feelings of Christians should be accepted as long as they are not intended to outrage or shock these feelings. The majority of the House of Lords did not follow Lord Edmund-Davies' reasoning. Criticism of the Christian religion was allowed, but a publication 'needs to be couched in decent and temperate language'.[73] In the view of the majority, the manner in which the opinion is given, as opposed to the state of mind of the defendant, influences whether it is considered blasphemous.

In the more recent case of R v. Chief Metropolitan Stipendiary Magistrate, ex p. Choudhury, the scope of the offence was considered as well. Here it was not the aspect of intent which was concerned, but the nature of the religious. It was

---

70 As formulated by Lord Coleridge C.J. in Reg. v. Bradlough, 15 Cox C.C. 217.
71 R. v. Lemon [1979] AC 617 at 652-653. Quoted from: Starkie's Slander and Libel, 4th edition, p. 599.
72 R. v. Lemon [1979] AC 617 at 653.
73 As formulated in Stephen's digest of criminal law, 1950, art 214, and as adopted by the majority of the House of Lords in R. v. Lemon and also by the divisional court in its decision in Chief Metropolitan Stipendiary Magistrate, ex p. Choudhury. This seems to be a rather harsh requirement for comments on such a possibly emotional issue, both for believers and non-believers.

confirmed that the law of blasphemy is only applicable to Christianity.[74] The court consequently found that neither the publisher nor the writer (Salman Rushdie) of 'The Satanic Verses' could be alleged to be guilty of blasphemous libel against the Islam, because of the absence of a domestic law of blasphemy relating to Islam.[75] In this regard the scope of the offence is limited.

An interesting point in this case is the use of the ECHR by both the applicant and the defendant to state their case before the courts. The applicant held that English law would be in violation of the ECHR if the offence of blasphemy were not extended to other religions beside Christianity. The applicant therefore assumed that there was a pressing social need to protect religious feelings. The defence, however, held that such an extension would lead to a violation of Article 10 of the Convention, since the common law of blasphemy was not certain with regard to the religions it concerned.[76] Moreover, the defence held that an extension was not necessary in a democratic society, because there was no pressing social need. The defence supported this argument by claiming that an extension would not serve one of the legitimate aims listed in the second paragraph of Article 10 ECHR. The court followed this reasoning in the Choudhury case, but did not specify what the legitimate aim or pressing social need served by protecting the religious feelings of Christians was.

In determining the scope of the offence of blasphemy, freedom of expression was considered, and was of decisive importance to the decision not to extend the offence to other religions beside Christianity.

---

74 R v. Chief Metropolitan Stipendiary Magistrate, ex p. Choudhury [1991] 1 All ER 306, QBD.

75 See also Feldman, Civil Liberties and Human Rights, 1993, p. 691-692.

76 In the decision of the Court, Mr Lester is quoted in relation to the question of whether an interference with freedom of speech as exercised by Salman Rushdie and the publisher of his book in England would amount to a breach of the ECHR under Article 10: 'What the applicant seeks to do, Mr Lester said, is to interfere with a well-founded right to freedom of expression, a kind of interference never at any time foreshadowed by the common law of this country. Nothing in the argument of counsel ... could bring either Mr Rushdie or Viking Penguin within one of the exceptions in art 10(2). The test of necessity, if that could be said to be relevant, requires, he contended, the existence of a pressing social need for an interference with free speech for one of those purposes'. Mr Lester thus focused on the requirement that a restriction has to be prescribed by law. Subsequently he seemed to hold that if it were, then the restriction would have to be necessary in a democratic society, which it would not be since, according to him, the restriction did not fall under one of the legitimate aims. This seems unlikely. However, if he were correct in his opinion, the question arises whether an interference with freedom of expression based on insulting the feelings of Christians could be justified and consequently could be necessary in democratic society. Is Lester of the opinion that the offence of blasphemy as such constitutes a violation of Article 10 ECHR?
In fact, the European Commission of Human Rights, in Gay News Ltd and Lemon v. United Kingdom [1983] 5 EHRR 123, held that the interference with the right to freedom of expression was justified by the public interest in protecting Mrs. Whitehouse's religious feelings.

Although blasphemy cases do not come before the courts frequently, the offence of blasphemy also exerts influence to the scope of freedom of expression under English law outside the court system. This is by way of the system of self-censorship established with regard to the publication of films and videos. If these forms of expression have a blasphemous content, this is held to have an impact on the public they may be exhibited to, and they are therefore regulated. A discussion of the (possible) impact of this system of self-censorship follows in the next section.

Application of the Offence
The system of self-censorship with regard to films and videos comprises a system in which the publishers of films and videos are required to have their product classified by the British Board of Film Classification.[77] The classification of films means that they are allowed to be exhibited to certain age-groups. The classification conferred upon a film or video is in theory advisory in nature.[78] However, the owners of video-shops and cinemas that rent, sell or show a film to viewers outside the certified age-group in fact run the risk of prosecution under, for instance, the Obscene Publications Act 1959 or the law of blasphemy. Although classification does not rule out the possibility of prosecution for such offences, in practice classification offers security as regards the legality of the film or video concerned.[79]

A recent case in which blasphemy was the centre of discussion concerned the refusal by the British Board of Film Classification (BBFC) to grant a certificate for Nigel Wingrove's video film Visions of Ecstasy.[80] This refusal was based on the blasphemous nature of the film. In it, an erotic fantasy of St. Theresa was depicted in which she had intercourse with Jesus Christ. The refusal to grant a certificate implied that Wingrove was prohibited from distributing the film.

As I have shown, the supervision as to whether films or videos are suitable for exhibition under English law, at least to start with, is not in the hands of the courts. As for videos the Video Recordings Act 1984 determines that the British Board of Film Classification (BBFC) gives videos a classification certificate which indicates the age-group for which the film is suitable. The extent to which sex and violence

---

77 Cinemas Act 1985 and Video Recordings Act 1986, which was extended in 1994 to include digital media as well.

78 But a film or video cannot be exhibited without having received a certificate of the British Board of Filmclassification. This is required by the Local Government Act 1982, the Cinemas Act 1985 s.1(3) and the Video Recordings Act 1984 s.1 and 2.

79 The Cinemas Act 1985 establishes local authorities statutory powers of censorship. Although local authorities may allow the showing of a film not categorized by the BBFC or ban the showing of one which has a BBFC certificate, in practice local authorities accept the BBFC's classification. See for an extensive discussion of the system of censorship of films and videos: Robertson and Nicol, Media Law, 1992, p. 564-593.

80 See Robertson and Nicol, Media Law, 1992, p. 591-592 and NJ 1998/359.

occur in the video will determine the classification it receives, if any. In principle all videos have to be submitted for classification. Based on s.4 of the Video Recordings Act 1984 a system of appeal to the Video Appeals Committee (VAC) against the certification or against the refusal to grant a certificate by the BBFC is established.

In the Wingrove case a certificate had been refused after the BBFC came to the conclusion that Visions of Ecstasy was likely to be held to be blasphemous by a jury. Wingrove subsequently appealed to the VAC. The appeals committee concerned itself with the question of whether the film had any historical, religious or artistic value beside its obvious (soft) pornographic content. Three of the five members of the VAC came to the conclusion that 'a reasonable and properly directed jury would be likely to convict', consequently the appeal was dismissed.[81] It is interesting that their considerations regarding any historical, religious or artistic aspects of the film imply that if the film was thought to be of some value in that respect, certification would not have been refused. The considerations of the VAC suggest that the more explicit film 'The last temptation of Christ' was certified because it had 'depth' and 'seriousness'.[82] Consequently, the artistic value of a film or video in fact functioned as ground for justification comparable to the public good defence available under Obscenity legislation. Artistic value – or any other public good – is not a defence under the common law of blasphemy, either as a justification or in terms of the definition of the offence. However, the position of the public good value of a film or video may influence the strength of the public good argument. As I have said with regard to the justifications allowed under the Obscene Publications Act 1959, if public good functions as a justification it seems that an interest in freedom of expression is taken into account only after it has been held that a publication is blasphemous in nature. In my opinion it is more difficult to overturn such a

---

81 In coming to its conclusion, the VAC explicitly discussed its perception of crucial scenes of the film and this was considered in the decision of the European Court of Human Rights (NJ 1998/359): '... the video did not as the appellant claims, explore St Theresa's struggles against her visions but exploited a devotion to Christ in purely carnal terms. Furthermore they considered that it lacked the seriousness and depth of "The last Temptation of Christ" with which the Counsel for the applicant sought to compare it. Indeed the majority took the view that the video's message was that the nun was moved not by religious ecstasy but rather by sexual ecstasy, this ecstasy being of a perverse kind – full of images of blood, sado-masochism, lesbianism (or perhaps auto erotism) and bondage. Although there was evidence of some element of repressed sexuality in St Theresa's devotion of Christ, they did not consider that this gave any ground for portraying her as taking the initiative in indulging in sexuality. They considered the overall tone and spirit of the video to be indecent and had little doubt that all the above factors, coupled with the motions of the nun whilst astride the body of Christ and the response to her kisses and the intertwining of their fingers, would outrage the feelings of Christians, who would reasonably look upon it as being contemptuous of the divinity of Christ'.

82 Note however that a certificate from the BBFC does not grant immunity from prosecution under the Obscene Publications Act or under the common law offence of blasphemy.

conclusion by way of a justification than when the public good is taken into account in deciding whether a film or video is blasphemous. This is the approach which would be taken if lack of public good is a requirement of the offence.

2.4 Criminal Defamation

The last criminal libel to be discussed in relation to freedom of expression is criminal defamation. The publication of a libel is a misdemeanour under common law.[83] 'A writing which tends to vilify a man and bring him into hatred, contempt and ridicule' constitutes such a libel.[84] In addition to this it has been determined that the libel has to be 'serious'.[85] A heavy burden of proof lies on the defendant however. Not only does he have to demonstrate that the allegations are true, but he also has to prove that it is for the public interest that the statements were published.[86]

This offence will not be discussed any further. Although as such it has an impact on freedom of expression, criminal proceeding against libel are brought so rarely that in fact its bearing on freedom of expression is limited.[87] The fact that criminal libel cases are rarely brought before the courts, may be explained by the existence of a civil counterpart under tort law.[88] Civil libel does have a significant effect on freedom of expression partly because of the number of cases brought under it and because of the large amount of damages that may be awarded if an expression is accepted to be defamatory by the courts. With regard to defamation law I focus on civil libel. The scope of the offence and the influence of freedom of expression on the scope and application of the offence are examined in the next section.

3 CIVIL LIBEL[89]

Under English law a person's reputation is protected against unjustifiable harm by the law of defamation. Defamation consists of libel, which is written, and slander, which

---

83　This has been confirmed in Goldsmith v. Pressdram Ltd [1977] All ER 557, QBD.

84　This definition was taken Smith and Hogan, Criminal Law, 1992, p. 726.

85　Gleaves v. Deakin [1979] 2 WLR 665, HL.

86　Lord Diplock in Gleaves v. Deakin (at 667, 668) is of the opinion that the misdemeanour is most likely an unjustifiable restriction on freedom of expression under Article 10 ECHR, because this heavy burden of proof cannot be considered necessary in a democratic society.

87　See also Barendt, Freedom of Speech, 1996, p. 187.

88　The offence of criminal libel was founded on the idea that it is appropriate for the state to act on behalf of the injured party and bring criminal charges against the defendant. Also because of the availability of the tort of civil libel, prosecutors rarely have much to gain from bringing criminal charges.

89　For a more a complete overview of civil libel see Markesinis and Deakin, Tort Law, 1994, p. 565-605.

is spoken. Although the influence of the idea of libel and slander on freedom of expression is similar, in practice the influence of slander on freedom of expression is limited by the fact that slander is rarely claimed before the courts.

Libel is both a crime and a tort.[90] There are three aspects of the tort of libel that are relevant to freedom of expression and that therefore require elaboration. The first concerns the scope of the offence, and relates to the issue of who is allowed to sue for libel. The second concerns the defences that are available to avoid speech being held libellous. There are four defences available: absolute privilege, qualified privilege, the defence of fair comment and the defence of justification. I address the content of each of these defences in section 3.2.2. below, in which I discuss the role of freedom of expression with regard to the manner in which these defences are applied by the courts. A third aspect of the tort of libel that is of relevance to the scope of freedom of expression concerns remedies that are available to the plaintiff in a libel action. To avoid having his or her reputation damaged, the plaintiff can ask for an interim injunction to prevent publication of the libellous material. Once someone's reputation has been damaged by a libellous publication this attracts an award of damages.

The question of who can bring an action for libel, the defences and the remedies are discussed in the first, second and third parts of section 3.2. on the influence of freedom of expression on libel law.

First, however, I elaborate on the nature of the tort of defamation and explain why I examine libel and not slander to gain insight into the approach to freedom of expression under English law.

3.1 The Tort[91]

In cases regarding civil defamation, a precise definition of defamation has not been given. Based on the formulated elements of the offence, however, it has been described as follows: 'A defamatory statement is one which injures the reputation of another by exposing him to hatred, contempt or ridicule, or which tends to lower him in the esteem of right thinking members of society'.[92] A statement injures the reputation of another if it is communicated to a third person. A letter to a third person will be defamatory, but also an open postcard to the person written about is

---

90   The definition of tort in Walker's The Oxford Companion to Law is: 'The term in common law systems for a civilly actionable harm or wrong, and for the branch of law dealing with liability for such wrongs. Analytically the law of tort is a branch of the law of obligations, where the legal obligations to refrain from harm to another and, if harm is done, to repair it or compensate for it, are imposed not by agreement, but independently of agreement by force of the general law'.

91   See footnote 90.

92   Markesinis and Deakin, Tort Law, 1994, p. 565-566.

defamatory.[93] Furthermore it has been determined that a statement refers to someone if 'reasonable persons' would think that the words referred to the plaintiff.[94] The intention of the defamer is not an element of the tort, only the fact of defamation is of interest. Defamation can consist of libel and slander.[95] In this section I focus on libel. This is because the impact of libel on freedom of expression is more significant than that of slander. Libel covers not only books, articles and newspapers, but also films, theatre and broadcasting, both on radio and television.[96] Libel originally consisted of written statements. The decisive factor now seems to be that it is stated in a 'permanent form'. This to distinguish it from the offence of slander, which consists of statements that are 'temporary and audible'.[97] Another distinction between the tort of slander and of libel is that slander is only actionable if there is proof of financial damage. This is not a requirement with regard to libel.[98]

In the next section I discuss the manner in which and the extent to which freedom of expression has influenced the application of libel law.

3.2 The Influence of Freedom of Expression

1 Scope of the Tort

As far as the scope of the tort of libel is concerned, the question of who is entitled to sue for libel is where the influence of freedom of expression is most visible. The general answer to this question used to be anyone, individuals and institutions,[99] about whom defamatory statements had been made to one or more other persons. However, in the decision in Derbyshire County Council v. Times Newspapers Ltd this approach was changed.[100] In this case, the House of Lords expressly considered that the offence of civil defamation may have a significant impact on freedom of expression, especially with regard to the press and its function concerning open debate on issues of public interest. This impact on freedom of expression was

---

93 Markesinis and Deakin, Tort Law, 1994, p. 580-581.
94 Morgan v. Odhams Press [1971] 1 WLR 1239, QBD.
95 Slander is only a tort and not a crime.
96 Defamation Act 1952 s.1.
97 See Markesinis and Deakin, Tort Law, 1994, p. 568. Not only books, newspapers or letters can constitute a libel, but also a waxwork may be libellous. By the Defamation Act 1952 s.1 theatre, broadcasting, radio and television are treated as libels.
98 Markesinis and Deakin, Tort Law, 1994, p. 569.
99 In South Hetton Coal Co. Ltd v. North Eastern New Association Ltd [1894] 1 QB 133, CA, a trading company could bring an action for libel, and in Bognor Regis UDC v. Campion [1972] 2 QB 169, the rule formulated in the 1894 case was extended to local authorities. Later, as we shall see below, this was overturned in Derbyshire County Council v. Times Newspapers Ltd.
100 Derbyshire County Council v. Times Newspapers Ltd [1993] 2 WLR 449, HL.

reflected in the view of the House of Lords on who is entitled to bring an action for damages for libel.

The Derbyshire County Council had stated that they had been defamed by two articles published in a newspaper. They brought an action for libel which was accepted in first instance. The Court of Appeal, however, denied that a local authority had a right to bring an action for libel and the House of Lords agreed with the Court of Appeal. The House of Lords took consideration of the 'distinguishing features' of a local authority. It held that 'since it was of the highest public importance that a democratically elected governmental body should be open to uninhibited public criticism, and since the threat of civil actions for defamation would place an undesirable fetter on the freedom to express such criticism, it would be contrary to the public interest for institutions of central or local government to have any right at common law to maintain an action for damages for defamation'.[101]

I observed that the Court of Appeal had previously come to the same conclusion. This court based its findings on Article 10 of the ECHR. The court was of the opinion that English law was uncertain on the point of whether a local authority could sue for libel because of the existence of two conflicting decisions on the matter. It therefore held that the effect of Article 10 could and should be considered. The considerations of the House of Lords with regard to protection of speech which has a certain public interest because it concerns public authorities, were based entirely on common law. Lord Keith explicitly found that there was no need to rely upon the European Convention. In his speech he referred to the Spycatcher decision[102] in which it was stated, with regard to the law of breach of confidence, that 'there are rights available to private citizens which institutions of central government are not in a position to exercise unless they can show that it is the public interest to do so'.[103] He extended this reasoning to local authorities and moreover stated that it would be contrary to the public interest for organs of government to bring a libel action, because 'to admit such actions would place an undesirable fetter on freedom of speech'.[104] These words could be read to mean that there is never an interest strong enough in a libel action by a governmental organ to set aside the public interest in open debate on issues of public interest, which would completely remove the right of governmental authorities to bring an action for libel.[105] Barendt

---

101 Derbyshire County Council v. Times Newspapers Ltd [1993] 2 WLR 449.

102 Attorney-General v. Guardian Newspapers Ltd (No. 2) [1990] 1 AC 109, HL.

103 Derbyshire County Council v. Times Newspapers Ltd [1993] 2 WLR 449 at 458.

104 Derbyshire County Council v. Times Newspapers Ltd [1993] 2 WLR 449 at 458.

105 Barendt in his article Libel and Freedom of Speech in English Law, 1993, p. 449-464, discussed the possibility that this may not be so absolute because of the words regarding local authorities in 'its governmental and administrative functions'. He dismissed this possibility by referring to Lord Keith's words on p. 459 of the decision where he stated that 'under the common law of England a local authority does not have the right to maintain an action of damages for defamation'.

remarked on this matter that 'the principles underlying it (the decision) surely point to its inevitable extension to individual politicians and officials'.[106] If a 'democratically elected body ... should be open to uninhibited criticism' then this would be 'equally true of comment on elected politicians and many appointed officials'. The possibility to sue for libel would also in these cases 'bring an undesirable fetter upon freedom of expression'.[107] In fact, however, the decision was not clear on whether or not a politician or a public official is entitled to sue for libel. This issue was clarified to some extent in a defamation case that came before the Queen's Bench Division of the High Court sometime after the decision of the House of Lords in the Derbyshire case.

In this case of Goldsmith v. Bhoyrul, the opinion of Lord Keith in the Derbyshire case was relied upon.[108] In his judgment, Buckley J. extended the impossibility of democratically elected governmental bodies and institutions of central or local government to sue for libel to political parties. He held: '... but it seems to me that the public interest in free speech and criticism in respect of those bodies putting themselves forward for office or to govern is also sufficiently strong to justify withholding the right to sue. Defamation actions or the threat of them would constitute a fetter on free speech at a time and on a topic when it is clearly in the public interest that there should be none'.[109] Also he said that in reaching his conclusion he took account of the fact that '(1) any individual candidate, official or other person connected with the party who was sufficiently identified could sue; (2) the party can by public announcement answer back'.[110]

Buckley J. extended the impossibility to sue to political parties under the condition that individual persons connected to the party could sue. He seemed to make a clear distinction between organisations and the individuals that are members of the organisation. This could imply that 'individual politicians and appointed officials' would be able to sue.

In fact, in Hamilton v. Al Fayed, a Member of Parliament initiated an action for libel.[111] This case concerned an action for libel against the defendant's claim that he had frequently handed cash to Mr Hamilton in order to get him to raise certain issues in the House of Commons. A report on Mr Hamilton's conduct was drawn up by Sir Gordon Downey, the Parliamentary Commissioner for Standards. After an inquiry he concluded that 'there was compelling evidence that the former M.P. had

---

106 Article Barendt, Libel and Freedom of Speech in English Law, 1993, p. 453.
107 This does not mean however that statements on governmental authorities enjoy absolute protection. There is still the possibility to sue for malicious falsehood: Derbyshire County Council v. Times Newspapers Ltd [1993] 2 WLR 449 at 460.
108 Goldsmith and another v. Bhoyrul and others [1997] 4 All ER 268, QBD.
109 Goldsmith v. Bhoyrul [1997] 4 All ER 268, per Buckley J. at 270-271.
110 Goldsmith v. Bhoyrul [1997] 4 All ER 268 per Buckley J. at 271.
111 Hamilton v. Al Fayed [1999] 3 All ER 317, CA.

received cash payments from Mr Al Fayed for lobbying services' and that this behaviour fell 'seriously and persistently' below the standards expected of M.P.s.[112] His conclusions were adopted in the report of the Committee on Standards and Privileges, and this report was approved by the House of Commons. Mr Al Fayed, however, had repeated his statements in a Channel Four TV program. Subsequently Mr Hamilton sued Mr Al Fayed for libel. The defendant claimed that this was abuse of process, since it concerned issues already settled by Parliament, and that the libel action amounted to an infringement of parliamentary privilege. In fact, the Court of Appeal acknowledged that 'the courts will not challenge or assault by any order of their own, an assertion of authority issued by Parliament pursuant to Parliament's own procedures' and that this principle 'extends to acts and decisions of Parliament which are not part of the process of enacting primary legislation'.[113] It was held, however, that this action involved 'no assertion by the court of any power to challenge the exercise of authority by Parliament'. It concerned statements made outside the House of Commons even if based on statements uttered within that House. The court emphasised, however, that this shift in the approach to the issues considered to be governed by parliamentary privilege, was induced by s.13 of the Defamation Act 1996.[114] There were no considerations by the court regarding the possibilities to comment on the behaviour of elected politicians. S.13 of the Defamation Act 1996 implies that an individual Member of Parliament can waive parliamentary privilege, such as in this case with regard to parliamentary inquiries into his conduct, in his own interest.[115] In this decision it was ruled that when statements made in Parliament were repeated outside the Houses, this meant that they could be subject of cases before the courts, and that in that respect parliamentary privilege could not be used to restrict the scope of defamation law. The issue of whether a politician could sue for libel was not explicitly addressed. I conclude therefore that although the judgments in the Derbyshire case and the Goldsmith case caused uncertainty with regard to the extent of the protection of speech of importance to public debate, still the scope of the tort was narrowed considerably. Although there is no doubt that a libel action directed against comments made on the behaviour of individual politicians has a 'chilling effect', this has not led the English courts to deny politicians the right to sue.

The scope of the tort of libel is not the only aspect with regard to which freedom

---

112 Committee on Standards and Privileges, First Report, H.C. 30 (1997-98), Vol I, p. 120-130.
113 Hamilton v. Al Fayed [1999] 3 All ER 317 at 334.
114 S.13 (1) provides: 'Where the conduct of a person in or in relation to proceedings in Parliament is in issue in defamation proceedings, he may waive for the purposes of those proceedings, so far as concerns him, the protection of any enactment or rule of law which prevents proceedings in Parliament being impeached or questioned in any court or place out of Parliament'.
115 Bradley, The courts in conflict with Parliament, 1999, p. 389.

of expression may be considered. I said in the introduction to this chapter that a number of defences are available under libel law that provide possibilities to restrict the influence of civil libel on the scope of freedom of expression. I discuss the defences in the next section.

2 Defences

If a libel action is allowed, there are a number of ways in which the defendant can prevent a decision that some publication is libellous, the granting of an injunction or an order to pay damages. In this part I discuss the manner in which freedom of expression influenced the courts with regard to the application of the defences in relation to freedom of expression. First, however, I briefly introduce the four defences available.

I observed that the four defences that can be brought forward by the defendant are absolute privilege, qualified privilege, the defence of fair comment and the defence of justification. Absolute privilege is granted, for instance, to statements made in Parliament, and statements of judges, lawyers and witnesses in the courts. Absolute privilege gives complete immunity from liability for defamatory statements. Qualified privilege is granted to comments made out of a moral or social duty.[116] Although the idea of public interest in a publication could be closely linked to the notion of qualified privilege, for instance, for the press, for a long time it was not accepted by the courts that the press had a general obligation, or social duty, to inform the public and consequently that such publications could have qualified privilege.[117] However, under influence of the fact that the Human Rights Act is about to become law, the possibilities offered by the defence of qualified privilege in that respect have been acknowledged. I elaborate on this in the next section. Qualified privilege does not provide complete immunity from liability for libellous statements. Qualified privilege gives immunity unless the comments were made with malicious intent.[118]

Fair comment is a defence that excludes 'fair comment on a matter of public interest' from being qualified as libellous. Lastly, under the defence of justification, a defendant claims that the statements he made were true; under libel law true statements are held not to damage a person's reputation.

---

116 Toogood v. Spyring (1834) 1 CM & R 181 at 193 per Baron Parke. A number of reports and statements that are privileged are specified in s. 15 Defamation Act 1996.

117 Robertson and Nicol, Media Law, 1992, p. 87-90. See also Kingshott v. Associated Kent Ltd (CA) in which it was held: 'that section 7 of the Defamation Act 1952, in permitting a newspaper to claim that a published article was a fair and accurate report of the proceedings, struck a balance between the rights of the press and the rights of individuals and, save in the clearest case, it was for the jury to hold the scales'.

118 Robertson and Nicol, Media Law, 1992, p. 86.

The expressions that attract absolute privilege are settled. The concept of absolute privilege guarantees that reporting on statements made in parliament or in the courts cannot be restricted by libel law. For the rest, this defence provides little evidence of the manner in which freedom of expression is of influence to the courts. With regard to qualified privilege, fair comment and justification, the situation is quite different. I discuss separately these last three defences and the influence of freedom of expression on the manner in which they are applied. Fair comment and justification are discussed under heading b and c of this section. I start with a discussion of qualified privilege. Here I focus on the change in approach of the courts to this offence under influence of the Human Rights Act 1998, since previously qualified privilege hardly had a function in the protection of freedom of expression.

a Qualified Privilege

As early as 1870 it had been held that there are occasions in which uninhibited discussion on factual issues should be possible, without their being restricted by the law of defamation. These occasions were held to occur under 'circumstances where a person is so situated that it becomes right in society that he should tell certain facts to another'.[119] Under such circumstances only proof of malice on the part of the defendant could make a publication qualify as libellous. I remarked above that in the past the defence of qualified privilege did not protect speech on matters of public interest in general. In the recent case of Reynolds v. Times Newspapers Ltd a.o. the courts, however, seem to have turned in that direction.[120] In this case the newspaper that was sued for libel by Reynolds, the former Taoiseach of Ireland, claimed qualified privilege for their publication. The newspaper had published an article in which it claimed that Mr Reynolds as Taoiseach had misled the Dáil (Parliament) and his cabinet by suppressing information. In the Reynolds case, however, the Court of Appeal had accepted that it should be considered whether the publication concerned should be protected by privilege in the absence of malice. It was accepted that the context of the case concerned discussion of a matter of political importance. The case of Derbyshire County Council was referred to, and it was commented that where it concerned political speech regarding organs of central or local government, the speech should be protected from all unnecessary restrictions. The majority of the House of Lords held that such an approach with regard to qualified privilege was not required in a democratic society and that in order to assess whether the publication in the Sunday Times should be protected by qualified privilege 'the nature, status and source of the material published and the circumstances of the publication' should be

---

119 Davies v. Snead (1870) L.R. 5 Q.B. 608, QBD, per Blackburn J. at 611.
120 Reynolds v. Times Newspapers Ltd and others [1998] 3 WLR 862, CA; [1999] 4 All ER 609, HL.

considered.[121] In taking this approach the House of Lords followed the Court of Appeal. In the absence of proof of malice, there were three requirements that had to be met for a publication to attract qualified privilege. First, there must be a duty to publish to the particular audience. Second, the audience must have an interest in receiving the material. And thirdly, the publication must pass the 'the circumstantial test', which was formulated by the Court of Appeal, and accepted by the House of Lords as the appropriate test.[122] The 'circumstantial test' implies a consideration of all the relevant facts and circumstances of the particular case at issue and a decision whether, taking account of those circumstances, the interest in the publication of the speech or the interest in protection of the reputation of the plaintiff should prevail.

With regard to political speech, the relevant audience is the public at large. Also it was accepted that the press has a duty to inform that audience. The Court of Appeal subsequently applied the 'circumstantial test' to the case, and held that the circumstances of the case could not satisfy its requirements. Although the subject matter was considered to be of great public interest and the newspaper was held to have a duty to inform the public of such matters, the source of the information was a member of the staff of a certain Mr Spring, one of Mr Reynold's political opponents, who could not be qualified as an 'authoritative source'. Moreover, the allegation was held to be serious and factual in nature, whereas Mr Reynolds was held not to have lied but sooner to have made an 'honest but mistaken omission'. Furthermore, Mr Reynold's own account of the situation had not been reported in the article and 'the defendants failed to resolve whether Mr Reynolds was a victim of circumstance' or 'a devious liar'. For these reasons the Court of Appeal held that the publication concerned should not be protected by privilege.[123]

The advantage of the 'circumstantial test' was held to be that it made it possible for the courts 'to have regard to all the circumstances when deciding whether the publication of particular material was privileged because of its value to the public' and subsequently 'this solution has the merit of elasticity' and 'can be applied appropriately to the particular circumstances of individual cases in their infinite variety'.[124] The objection to this approach that it would involve an unpredictable outcome was acknowledged as well: 'Hand in hand with this advantage goes the disadvantage of an element of unpredictability and uncertainty'.

It is noteworthy that the accusation that Mr Reynolds had lied to parliament was held to be a statement of fact. The consequences of that conclusion are far reaching,

---

121 Reynolds v. Times Newspapers Ltd and others [1999] 4 All ER 609, HL, per Lord Nicholls of Birkenhead.
122 Reynolds v. Times Newspapers Ltd and others [1998] 3 WLR 862, CA at 899.
123 Reynolds v. Times Newspapers Ltd and others [1998] 3 WLR 862, CA, in a unanimous decision.
124 Reynolds v. Times Newspapers Ltd and others [1999] 4 All ER 609, HL, per Lord Nicholls of Birkenhead.

since otherwise the defence of fair comment would have provided protection against the accusation that the publication was libellous. This becomes clear from the following discussion of the defence of fair comment.

b Defence of Fair Comment

With regard to a possible interlocutory injunction the defendant is allowed a defence of 'fair comment on a matter of public interest' under the Defamation Act 1952. Libel law acknowledges that there are two opposing interests, which should both be taken into consideration before deciding whether speech can be regarded as libellous.

The terms 'comment' and 'public interest' determine the scope of this defence. The scope of the term 'public interest' is rather wide.[125] Public interest has been defined by Lord Denning MR in London Artists Ltd v. Littler: 'Whenever a matter is such as to affect people at large, so that they may be legitimately interested in, or concerned at, what is going on; or what may happen to them or to others; then it is a matter of public interest on which everyone is entitled to make fair comment'.[126] From this description it becomes clear that this defence is not restricted to statements of a political nature. The case in question, for instance, dealt with the accusation of an impresario that the plaintiff had plotted against him to end a play he was running at the time. This was thought to be a matter of public interest. The defence of fair comment offers protection to comment which is honestly stated no matter how extremely formulated.[127] This defence does not provide protection if the plaintiff pleads and proves intent of malice, in which case the comment cannot be considered 'fair'.[128]

Of importance in relation to the defence of fair comment is, however, that 'fair comment' can only consist of *an opinion* on a matter of public interest, as opposed to *statements of fact*. This distinction is of great consequence for the protection of the expression concerned, because the defendant has to plead justification (proof of truth) with regard to libellous statements of fact. Whether the statement is of fact or of opinion is for the jury to decide.

The considerable impact on freedom of expression of a jury decision as to whether the statement is one of fact or of opinion was illustrated in Telnikoff v. Matusevitch.[129] In this case a Russian immigrant wrote a letter to a newspaper in reaction to an article published in this newspaper. This article had been written by

---

125 Lord Ackner (in Telnikoff v. Matusevitch [1992] 2 AC 343, HL, at 357) defined the defence as: 'the right of the citizen honestly to express his genuine opinion on a subject of public interest, however wrong or exaggerated or prejudiced that opinion may be'. He emphasised the importance of the freedom to comment on matters of public interest to a democratic society.

126 London Artists Ltd v. Littler [1969] 2 QB 375, CA, at 391.

127 See also Barendt, Freedom of Speech, 1996, p. 178-179.

128 Markesinis and Deakin, Tort Law, 1994, p. 594.

129 Telnikoff v. Matusevitch [1992] 2 AC 343, HL.

another Russian immigrant. The writer of the original article felt defamed by the letter because he was made out to be a racist. The issue to be dealt with by the House of Lords was whether the jury, in determining whether the allegations were statements of fact or of opinion, should consider the letter in relation to the article it was a reaction to, or should merely consider the letter as such. The majority of the House of Lords concluded 'that the question whether the words complained of were capable of constituting statements of fact was to be determined by the consideration of the contents of the letter alone and not in conjunction with the terms of the article in response to which it was written, since many readers of the letter would not have read the article, or if they had read it, have its terms fully in mind'.[130] In other words, the impression given to readers of the letter who had not read the article was decisive. As long as the first article was not reprinted as part of the letter, the letter itself was deemed to be factual. The role the letter plays in a discussion on matters of public interest was not taken into account by the majority of the court. The only interest considered was the reputation of the plaintiff. The impact of this approach on freedom of expression was not evaluated in the majority opinion.

Lord Ackner, however, in his dissenting opinion, implicitly did recognise that freedom of expression was at issue and was of the opinion that it should be awarded great weight. He formulated his opinion in a rather strong fashion: '... if the court is not entitled to look at the material on which it is alleged that the words complained of were commenting, it would unduly restrict the defence of fair comment. Indeed, it would diminish and impair this vitally important right, by whittling it down by a wholly unjustified legal refinement. If the criticism of an article published in a newspaper on a subject matter of public importance is to be confined to passages actually set out in the criticism, then the freedom to comment on a matter of public importance becomes, from a practical point of view, illusory or non-existent. The ability of a defendant to comment should not depend on whether or not the reader is aware of the material which is the subject of the comment ... the defence of fair comment is based on the principle that a citizen should be entitled to comment on a matter of public interest and the fact that the publication is limited does not affect the public interest'.[131]

The case of Telnikoff v. Matusevitch came before the House of Lords prior to the Derbyshire County Council case. As I observed, in the Derbyshire decision, the House of Lords acknowledged the existence of a principle of freedom of expression under common law. Barendt is of the opinion that, had Telnikoff v. Matusevitch been brought before the House of Lords after this decision, the majority opinion would most likely have been different.[132] The House of Lords then should have applied

---

130 Telnikoff v. Matusevitch [1992] 2 AC 344.
131 Telnikoff v. Matusevitch [1992] 2 AC 343 per Lord Ackner at 361.
132 See Barendt, Libel and Freedom of Speech in English Law, 1993, p. 458.

the principle in Telnikoff v. Matusevitch similar to the manner in which the Court of Appeal applied this principle in Rantzen v. Mirror Group Newspapers, a case that I discuss in the following part of this section.

It should be considered here that although it was held in the Rantzen case that Article 10 ECHR and its case law should be taken account of when judges exercise a discretionary power, the size of awarded damages was an issue that constituted an evident interference with Article 10.[133] In a decision such as the one in Telnikoff v. Matusevitch, the influence of Article 10 is less obvious, since the European Court never commented on the exact issue addressed in the Matusevitch case. In the case law of the Court, however, evidence can be found that statements or allegations should be seen in the light of the discussion of which they are part.[134] However, had freedom of expression and what constitutes a necessary restriction to it been considered, the outcome might indeed have been different. Moreover, if one examines the discussion that took place in Telnikoff v. Matusevitch, it appears that the law regarding the material that should be taken into account in order to determine whether a statement is factual in nature or constitutes an opinion, was not clear. It therefore offered ample opportunity to take account of the spirit of Article 10 ECHR to fill this gap.

Fair comment on a matter of public interest, unless induced by malice, is a defence against the accusation that statements are libellous. If a statement is held to be factual, defamation law provides for another defence. This is the defence of justification, which I discuss next.

c Defence of Justification
If statements are factual in nature and if the defendant claims he can prove the truth of his statements, he is pleading 'justification'. The statements concerned are not required to be for the public benefit in order to be justified.[135] In fact proof of truth is of importance not only potentially libellous factual statements as such: the facts on which a fair comment is based have to be true as well.[136] Proof of truth will offer

---

133 In reaching its decision in Telnikoff v. Matusevitch the Court of Appeal anticipated the decision of the European Court of Human Rights in Tolstoy Miloslavsky v. UK (1995) A.323. In this case the Court held that large libel awards could disproportionately restrict freedom of expression.

134 Lingens v. Austria, (1986) A.103; Jersild v. Denmark, (1994) A.298.

135 Feldman, Civil Liberties and Human Rights in England and Wales, 1993, p. 613 and Markesinis and Deakin, Tort Law, 1994, p. 594-595: Only fair and accurate reports of Parliamentary and judicial proceedings attract qualified privilege, which means that the publication is privileged against liability, but only so long as those responsible were not actuated by malice. Absolute privilege is a defence that award complete protection, but this is only applied to statements made in Parliament, and statements made by a judge, jury, advocates, or witnesses in any judicial or quasi-judicial proceedings.

136 Turner v. Metro-Goldwyn-Mayer Pictures Ltd [1950] 1 All ER 449, per Lord Porter at 461: If the

a complete defence to claims that statements of fact are libellous in nature. As we have seen, no proof of truth is necessary with regard to statements that are considered fair comment on matters of public interest. However, when comments are regarded as statements of fact the burden of proof lies completely on the defendant. This, together with the decision in Telnikoff v. Matusevitch, which significantly extended the situations in which statements are regarded to be factual, gives the impression that the emphasis in libel law lies on the protection of reputation. A change in this approach, according to Barendt, could be realised by way of an extension of the reasoning of the House of Lords in the Derbyshire County Council case. He extends the reasoning of the House of Lords for rejecting a libel action brought by a governmental body to the rules concerning the burden of proof. He holds that if the House of Lords believed that the possibility of a libel action by a local authority would have a 'chilling effect' on freedom of speech, because it could prevent people from commenting at all, the 'acceptance of that argument is incompatible with the presumption of falsity' with regard to other cases which concern a matter of public interest, i.e. other than those relating to who is allowed to sue for libel.[137] He said: 'Logically, it follows that the English courts should alter the rule concerning the burden of proof ...'.[138]

If the plaintiff asked for an injunction to prevent publication of the alleged libellous material and the defendant pleads one of the available defences, the courts will not grant the injunction. With this remark we touch upon the possibilities the plaintiff has to remedy the (future) damage to his reputation. As well asking for an injunction to prevent publication of allegedly libellous material, there is the possibility to ask for damages if it is too late to mend the damage done to the plaintiff's reputation. I now discuss the application of these two remedies and the role of freedom of expression in this regard.

3 Remedies

Civil law provides for remedies for individuals to whom unlawful harm has been done. Particular remedies granted by courts may be divorce, payment of debt, injunction, specific performance and pecuniary damages.[139] Regarding the particular laws discussed in this section, the most appropriate remedies are those of

---

content of the statements 'were a statement of facts, and the facts were untrue, a plea of fair comment would not avail and it is for the jury in a proper case to determine what is comment and what is fact, but a prerequisite to their right is that the words are capable of being a statement of a fact or facts'.

137 Barendt, Libel and Freedom of Speech in English Law, 1993, p. 457.
138 Barendt, Libel and Freedom of Speech in English Law, 1993, p. 457.
139 See Walker, the Oxford Companion to Law, 1980, p. 1056-1057.

injunction and damages. The injunction provides for a method to prevent (further) infringements, for instance, of the right to a good reputation or on the dissemination of confidential information. If such damage can not be prevented then the harm done can be compensated by way of damages.

a Injunction

In libel law the greatest threat to freedom of expression is the injunction, the granting of which may result in prior restraint. The plaintiff can ask for an interlocutory injunction to prevent (further) publication of allegedly libellous material. Unless there is a serious risk of prejudice to the trial of the action, the English courts will not grant an interlocutory injunction to restrain publication of an alleged libel if the defendant is asserting absolute or qualified privilege for the publication, if the defendant claims fair comment or if the defendant intends to argue at trial that the allegation is true.[140] The reason for the refusal of the interlocutory injunction is the importance of leaving free speech unfettered till the moment that it is absolutely clear that an allegation is untrue and has infringed the plaintiff's rights.[141] If the defence fails in the decision on the merits, the harm done will be compensated by way of damages. This starting point was prompted by the value placed on freedom of expression. Laws J. explained in R v. A.S.A. Ltd, Ex p. Vernons Ltd with regard to the defence of 'fair comment' that: '... there is a general principle in our law that the expression of opinion and the conveyance of information will not be restrained by the courts save on pressing grounds. Freedom of expression is as much a sinew of the common law as it is of the ECHR ... and so I must grapple with the submission that there is no pressing ground to restrain the publication which the authority intends'.[142] Similar considerations were made with regard to the defence of 'justification'.[143]

This rule against prior restraint results in the interest in publication of the information prevailing over the interest in the protection of reputation. The injunction will be granted only if the plaintiff can prove immediately that the defendant will publish untrue information. The nature of the information is not considered.

---

140 Feldman, Civil Liberties and Human Rights in England and Wales, 1993, p. 613.

141 Feldman, Civil Liberties and Human Rights in England and Wales, 1993, p. 613.

142 R. v. Advertising Standards Authority, ex p. Vernons Ltd [1992] 1 WLR 1289 at 1293.

143 Lord Denning formulated this rule against prior restraint in Fraser v. Evans [1969] 1 All ER 8, CA, as follows: 'The court will not restrain the publication of an article, even though it is defamatory, when the defendant says he intends to justify it or to make fair comment on a matter of public interest. The reason sometimes given is that the defences of justification and fair comment are for the jury, which is the constitutional tribunal, and not for the judge. But a better reason is that the truth should out. ... The right of free speech is one which it is for the public interest that individuals should possess, and, indeed, that they should exercise without impediment, so long as no wrongful act is done. There is no wrong done if it is true, or if it is fair comment on a matter of public interest. the court will not prejudice the issue by granting an injunction in advance of publication'.

b Damages

A final aspect of libel law that influences the scope of freedom of expression is the damages which are awarded after published statements are considered to be libellous. The jury determines the size of awarded damages. The courts have the possibility, however, to adjust the award if the damages awarded by a jury can be considered to be 'excessive'.[144] In Rantzen v. Mirror Group Newspapers Ltd the apparent change in attitude of the House of Lords with regard to freedom of expression in previous case law such as the Derbyshire case and A-G v. Guardian Newspapers, was referred to and extended to the manner in which the amount of damages is determined. In this case Esther Rantzen, a successful television presenter and founder and chairman of an organisation that helps sexually abused children, was said amongst other things to have helped a teacher keep secret the fact that he had abused pupils. These allegations were made in a number of articles published in 'The People' newspaper. The statements were thought to be defamatory and the jury awarded the plaintiff 250,000 pounds in damages. On appeal the defendants asked for a reduction of the damages, claiming that such a large sum of money to be paid for damages constituted a breach of article 10 ECHR.

The Court of Appeal held that the power conferred upon the Courts to reduce the award 'should be construed in a manner which was not inconsistent with article 10 of the European Convention for the Protection of Human Rights and Fundamental Freedoms; that an almost unlimited discretion in a jury to award damages for defamation did not provide a satisfactory measurement for deciding what was a necessary restriction in a democratic society on the exercise of the right to freedom of expression under article 10 to protect the reputation of others and the common law therefore required that large awards of damages by a jury should be more closely scrutinized ...'.[145] It was considered that although the Convention was not part of English domestic law, it could determine the meaning of ambiguous legislation.[146] More importantly the court went on to state: 'Where freedom of expression is at stake, however, recent authorities lend support for the proposition that article 10 has a wider role and can properly be regarded as an articulation of some of the principles underlying the common law'.[147] Since the House of Lords in the Derbyshire case accepted the existence of a principle of freedom of expression under common law, the court was of the opinion that this principle should be the starting point in applying the discretion of judges to modify the amount of damages awarded by a jury. Till recently the powers of the jury to determine the damages had been nearly limitless. The recent developments in common law with regard to the attitude to

---

144 Courts and Legal services Act 1990.
145 Rantzen v. Mirror Group Newspapers Ltd [1993] 3 WLR 954, CA.
146 Under reference to ex p. Brind [1991] 1 A.C. 696, 760.
147 Rantzen v. Mirror Group Newspapers Ltd [1993] 3 WLR 953 at 971.

freedom of expression made it necessary for the court to exercise a 'more searching scrutiny than has been customary in the past'.[148] The court subsequently applied a test of objective reasonableness and stayed close to the manner of testing of the European Court of Human Rights by interpreting reasonable as 'necessary' or 'proportionate', consequently looking at the effect of the expression concerned, and concluding that the damage done to Miss Rantzen's reputation was not sufficient to justify the large sum of damages awarded by the jury.[149]

The restriction of the discretion of the jury to award damages extended the protection of freedom of expression under English law. This restriction was realised through the power of review of the courts, as to whether the damages awarded were excessive.[150]

4 BREACH OF CONFIDENCE[151]

In the previous section we saw that proof of truth is a defence against the allegation that statements are libellous. However, when information is correct, this does not automatically mean that it can be communicated freely. The flow of information may still be restricted under confidentiality law or secrecy legislation. In section 5 below I elaborate on the possibilities to take the interest in freedom of expression into account under secrecy legislation. The subject of the present section is confidentiality law. Confidentiality law is governed by equity, which includes liability for a breach of confidence. Breach of confidence is most often relied on in the context of commercial information concerning copyright and trade secrets. However, also the publication of private information and governmental information can be prevented or can attract damages by way of an action for breach of confidence. In the first subsection below I define the obligation under equity to keep information confidential and I describe the circumstances under which a breach of confidence is held to have occurred. In this subsection I also introduce the defences that are available against an action for breach of confidence, and the remedies available to the plaintiff. In the second subsection I go on to discuss the impact of freedom of expression on the most relevant aspects of the law of breach of confidence. These aspects concern: first the scope of the obligation of confidence and the type of information that can be the

---

148 Under reference to Attorney-General v. Guardian Newspapers Ltd [1987] 1 WLR 1248 at 1296.
149 Rantzen v. Mirror Group Newspapers Ltd [1993] 3 WLR 953 at 976.
150 As applied in John v. MGN Ltd [1996] 2 All ER 35, CA.
151 See for a more extensive discussion on all aspects of breach of confidence: Gurry, Breach of Confidence, 1984. Also see: Feldman, Civil Liberties and Human Rights in England and Wales, 1993, p. 433-441 and 616-632; Bailey, Harris, Jones, Civil Liberties, cases and materials, 1995, p. 474-492 and p. 550-563; Deans, Scots Public Law, 1995, p. 218-221; Robertson and Nicol, Media Law, 1992, p. 172-212; Boyle, Freedom of expression as a public interest in English Law, 1982, p. 586-592; Gardner, Freedom of Expression, 1994, p. 222-224.

subject of an action for breach of confidence; second, the defences, being the public domain-doctrine and the public-interest exception; third the available remedies of interlocutory injunction and damages.

4.1 The Obligation

An obligation of confidence may exist under contract, but also under the law of equity.[152] In Seager v. Copydex it was held that breach of confidence relies on the broad principle of equity, that 'he who has received information in confidence shall not take unfair advantage of it'.[153] This obligation is enforceable in law by way of an action for breach of confidence. Breach of confidence has been described as 'a civil remedy affording protection against the disclosure or use of information that is not publicly known, and that has been entrusted in circumstances imposing an obligation not to disclose that information without the authority of the person who has imparted it'.[154] In accordance with this definition the three requirements that have to be satisfied for a court to accept that a breach of confidence took place, were summarised by Megarry J. in Coco v. A N Clark.[155] These requirements were that the information itself 'must have the necessary quality of confidence about it', that the information 'must have been imparted in circumstances importing an obligation of confidence', and finally 'there must be an unauthorised use of that information (by the defendant) to the detriment of the party communicating it (the plaintiff)'. In other words it is not sufficient for the information to be confidential. There must also be a duty to keep it confidential.

The three requirements formulated in Coco v. A N Clark have been clarified further in a number of cases. It has been established that information is considered confidential when it is not 'public property and public knowledge'.[156] Moreover, information is considered to be disclosed in circumstances importing an obligation of confidence whenever 'information is imparted, either explicitly or implicitly, for a limited purpose'. The circumstances under which this can be the case are discussed in the first part of the next subsection. The duty to keep the information confidential rests in the first place on the recipient of the information. The recipient, however, must be aware of the confidential nature of the information, which may be the case

---

152 As I mentioned in chapter I, legislation, common law and equity together constitute the law of England. Equity is the law which originated from the rulings of the Court of Chancery on petitions offered to the King. The distinction that is usually made between equity and law, means no more than that equity is not a part of common law. See also Williams, Learning the Law, 1973, p. 24-29.

153 Seager v. Copydex [1967] 2 All ER 415, CA.

154 Robertson and Nicol, Media Law, 1992, p. 173.

155 Coco v. A N Clark Ltd [1969] RPC 41, 47.

156 Saltman Engineering Co. Ltd v. Campbell Engineering Co. Ltd [1963] 3 All ER 413, CA, per Lord Greene at 415.

when it has been stated explicitly that the information is confidential in nature, but confidentiality may also be inherent in the relationship within which the information has been disclosed. An important element concerning the restrictive effect of the law of breach of confidence on freedom of expression is that third parties to whom the confidential information has been disclosed assume the obligation of confidence if they are aware of the circumstances under which the discloser received the information.[157] This particular aspect of the obligation may create great tension between the interest in keeping the information confidential, and the interest of the press to publish newsworthy material. Finally, concerning the three requirements that have to be satisfied before the (future) publication of information is held to constitute a breach of confidence, use of information is considered to be unauthorised when such use was for a purpose other than that for which it was imparted.[158]

A defendant can plead that the information concerned was already in the public domain. By means of the public domain doctrine, the confidentiality of the information is removed. Another defence can be found in the public interest exception, which results in the failure of the action for breach of confidence because the public interest in publication is held to be greater than the interest in keeping the information confidential.

As is the case with the law of defamation, the plaintiff can ask the courts for an injunction to prevent publication of information. Once the information has already been published by the person on whom a duty of confidence rested, the remedy of damages remains.

From this brief overview of the most important aspects of the law of breach of confidence it is clear that the findings of a breach of confidence may restrain freedom of expression considerably. As with the previously discussed areas of law, I examine the role freedom of expression played in the relevant case law of the courts with regard to the different aspects of the obligation of confidentiality.

4.2 Influence of Freedom of Expression

1 The Scope of the Obligation

a Confidential Information
I said above that information must have a quality of confidence in order to be able to be the subject of an action for breach of confidence. Such a quality may arise out of contract. Moreover, certain relationships imply an obligation to keep received information secret. Such a relationship may be the one between a doctor and a

---

157 Feldman, Civil Liberties and Human Rights in England and Wales, 1993, p. 435; Gurry, Breach of Confidence, 1984, p. 4; Fraser and Evans [1969] 1 All ER 8, CA.
158 See Gurry, Breach of Confidence, 1984, p. 4.

patient, between a solicitor and a client or between an employer and an employee. The requirement of quality of confidence has also been determined in relation to the content of the information. In this regard, this requirement gave rise to considerable discussion. I elaborate on the developments that took place with regard to the types of information that can be subject of an action for breach of confidence and I discuss the role freedom of expression played in the discussion regarding these developments. An obligation of confidence was initially applied to restrain the unauthorised use of commercial information.[159] In Saltman Engineering Co. Ltd v. Campbell Engineering Co. Ltd, breach of confidence was accepted with regard to a drawing to construct tools for the manufacture of leather punches which had been given to the defendants to make such tools in accordance with them.[160] The defendants used the drawings for their own use. Lord Greene stated that 'the obligation to respect confidence is not limited to cases where the parties are in a contractual relationship'. He then went on to consider that the defendants knew that the drawings had been 'placed in their possession for a limited purpose' and that the information, to be confidential, 'must, ..., have the necessary quality of confidence about it, namely, it must not be something which is public knowledge'.[161] This did not mean, however, that all information considered to be commercial in nature was confidential unless it was public knowledge. Whether or not the information could be considered confidential depended on the level of secrecy that was awarded to it. This became clear from Faccenda Chicken Ltd v. Fowler.[162] In this case a former employee of a company selling frozen chickens, started a similar company selling the same product and applying the same methods to do so. It was held that 'confidential information concerning an employer's business acquired by an employee in the course of his service could be used by the employee after his employment had ceased unless the information was classed as a trade secret or was so confidential that it required the same protection as a trade secret'. Such confidential information may cover 'secret processes of manufacture such as chemical formulae, or designs or special methods of construction'.[163] In general the circumstances of the case would have to be taken into account to determine whether the information amounts to a trade secret or information equivalent to that. Circumstances that might be taken into account could be the nature of the employment, the nature of the information, whether it could easily be identified as confidential in relation to the other information the employee received during his employment, and whether the confidentiality of the information had been pointed out to the employee.

---

159 See Deans, Scots Public Law, 1995, p. 218.
160 Saltman Engineering Co. Ltd v. Campbell Engineering Co. Ltd [1963] 3 All ER 413.
161 Saltman Engineering Co. Ltd v. Campbell Engineering Co. Ltd [1963] 3 All ER 413 at 414.
162 Faccenda Chicken Ltd v. Fowler a.o. [1986] 1 All ER 617, CA.
163 Faccenda Chicken Ltd v. Fowler a.o. [1986] 1 All ER 617, CA, at 625.

Only later was liability for breach of confidence applied to domestic confidences.[164] The fact that the doctrine of breach of confidence was first used in relation to information of a domestic nature, namely to prevent the publishing of drawings made of Queen Victoria on her honeymoon, may seem contrary to this development.[165] However, the doctrine had till 1965 been used to protect commercial information. In Duchess of Argyll v. Duke of Argyll, information exchanged between partners during marriage was protected as confidential information.[166] In this case, the Duchess sought an injunction against her ex-husband, the Duke of Argyll, and the publisher of the magazine, to prevent them from publishing any more articles in which the Duke disclosed information about their marriage and information obtained by the Duke during their marriage. The injunction was granted. It was held that 'confidential communications between husband and wife during coverture were within the scope of the court's protection against breach of confidence'. It was further explained that 'the confidential nature of the relationship is of its very essence and so obviously and necessarily implicit in it that there is no need for it to be expressed'.

Confidentiality of information obtained during marriage some years later was extended to confidentiality of information about a person's sexual life in general. In Stephens v. Avery, the plaintiff informed a friend of a lesbian relationship she had had.[167] This information was subsequently published in a weekly magazine. Sir Nicolas Browne-Wilkinson V.C., referring to the requirement of 'inaccessibility' which was formulated by Francis Gurry, held on the extention of the types of information on which a duty of confidence rests: 'In principle therefore, I can see no reason why information relating to that most private sector of everybody's life, namely sexual conduct, cannot be the subject matter of a legally enforceable duty of confidentiality'.

Finally in 1975 the duty of confidence was extended to governmental information.[168] In the Jonathan Cape case, the government sought to prevent publication of the diaries of a former member of the Cabinet.[169] Although the injunction was refused, the court did hold that it had 'power on the ground of public policy to restrain publication of information in breach of confidence; that, since the maintenance of the doctrine of joint responsibility within the Cabinet was in the public interest and that doctrine might be prejudiced by the premature disclosure of

---

164 See also Deans, Scots Public Law, 1995, p. 218.
165 Prince Albert v. Strange (1849) 18 LJ Ch 120.
166 Duchess of Argyll v. Duke of Argyll [1965] 1 All ER 611, Ch.D.
167 Stephens v. Avery [1988] 2 All ER 477, Ch.D.
168 Currently, confidential governmental information is protected under the Official Secrets legislation. The reason why it was thought necessary to provide for special legislation regarding governmental information and the position of freedom of expression in relation to this legislation will be discussed in the next section.
169 A-G v. Jonathan Cape Ltd a.o. [1975] 3 WLR 606, QBD.

the views of individual Ministers, opinions expressed during discussions at a Cabinet meeting were confidential until such time as their disclosure would not undermine the doctrine of joint Cabinet responsibility'.

With regard to this gradual extension of the scope of breach of confidentiality, freedom of expression was not considered. Such consideration would have been appropriate, since a consequence of the protection of confidential information is the restriction of the free circulation of information and ideas. Especially with regard to the extension of confidentiality to governmental information, consideration regarding the impact on the free flow of information would have been expected, since here the step from the protection of private information to the protection of public information was taken. Although the difference in the nature of the information was acknowledged, this was not held to be of consequence to the application of the law of breach of confidence. Lord Widgery, in the Jonathan Cape case, put it as follows: 'I cannot see why the courts should be powerless to restrain the publication of public secrets, while enjoying the Argyll powers in regard to domestic secrets. Indeed, as already pointed out, the court must have power to deal with publication which threatens national security, and the difference between such a case and the present case is one of degree rather than kind'.[170] Emphasis lies on the aim that is served with the action for breach of confidence and not on the restriction of freedom of expression.

The heart of the law of breach of confidence is that confidential information which is used for other purposes than those for which it has been disclosed can be protected by way of an action for breach of confidence.[171] It is held to be in the public interest in general to be able to restrain the publication of information disclosed in confidence.[172] Consequently, the scope of the offence is limitless as far as the nature of the information is concerned.[173] However, although this will be dealt with further below, it should be remarked here that it has been held that for an action for breach of confidence to be successful where governmental information is concerned, some additional requirements have to be satisfied. Beside the usual requirements, in order for the courts to be able to conclude a breach of confidence, it also has to be shown 'that the public interest requires that the publication be

---

170 A-G v. Jonathan Cape Ltd a.o. [1975] 3 WLR 606, QBD, at 618.

171 See also Norwich Pharmacal Co. v. Commissioners of Customs and Excise [1972] RPC 743, 766 per Lord Denning MR; [1974] AC 133, discussed in Gurry, Breach of Confidence, 1984, p. 5.

172 It is considered to be in the public interest to protect economic innovation and privacy. The extension from trade secrets to domestic secrets in Duchess of Argyll v. Duke of Argyll was done by referring to the nature of a marital relationship.

173 Feldman, Civil Liberties and Human Rights in England and Wales, 1993, p. 435 puts it as follows: 'Confidentiality is to cover any relationship within which there is a recognized public interest in fostering free exchange of information between the parties, avoiding the fear of disclosure to others which might inhibit frankness'.

restrained, and that there are no other facts of the public interest contradictory of and more compelling than that relied upon'.[174]

2 Defences

Information that by its nature would be qualified as confidential, is not qualified as such when the information is in the public domain. And even if the confidential nature of the information there is another defence that may result in the information being allowed to be published. This is when the defendant pleads the public interest exception. I elaborate on the content and the manner of application by the courts of both the public domain doctrine and the public interest exception in the next two subsections. In this discussion, I emphasise the role of freedom of expression with regard to these defences.

a Public Domain Doctrine

The 'public domain' doctrine, has been described as follows: 'Information cannot be protected from disclosure if it can be gleaned from public sources or if its originator has already circulated it to a number of outsiders'.[175] This defence corresponds to the requirement of confidentiality as formulated by Lord Greene in the Saltman case, namely that the information should not be 'public property and public knowledge'.[176] The publication of information that is publicly known cannot be restricted by way of an action for breach of confidence, because the information lacks the quality of confidentiality. Consequently, freedom of expression cannot be restricted with regard to publicly known information. The scope of freedom of expression in relation to confidential information is thus determined by the manner in which 'public domain' is interpreted.

An example of information being considered to be public property can be found in the Woodward v. Hutchins case.[177] The public domain doctrine was used to motivate the refusal of an injunction to prevent the publication of articles on the behaviour of three pop singers. A former public relations officer of the three wrote articles on their behaviour, which the Daily Mirror intended to publish. One of the reasons for refusing the injunction was that part of the information concerned could not be considered to be confidential. Lord Denning MR formulated it as follows: '... Mr Hutchins, as a press agent, might attend a dance which many others attended. Any incident which took place at the dance would be known to all present. The

---

174 See also Boyle, Freedom of Expression as a public interest in English Law, 1982, p. 590.

175 Robertson and Nicol, Media Law, 1992, p. 188-194. See also Feldman, Civil Liberties and Human Rights in England and Wales, p. 436-438.

176 Saltman Engineering Co. Ltd v. Campbel Engineering Co. Ltd [1963] 3 All ER 413 at 415.

177 Woodward v. Hutchins and others [1977] 2 All ER 751, HL.

information would be in the public domain. There could be no objection to the incidents being made known generally'.[178] Consequently, the attendants of a party or as in this case the passengers on a plane were considered to be 'the public'.

In A-G v. Guardian Newspapers, the House of Lords did not grant a permanent injunction, because the book from which excerpts were (to be) published, had been widely circulated and therefore the information could no longer be considered confidential. However, in this case the House of Lords did decide that members of the security service owed a lifelong duty of confidence.[179] As a result, when such information is in the public domain, newspapers are free to publish it, but intelligence officers are still not allowed to make their experiences public. It should be noted, however, that information is not considered to be in the public domain easily. In 'The Scotsman' case, an intelligence officer wrote a book about the service and his work for it and subsequently send a few hundred copies of it to 'friends and family', the information was not considered to be in the public domain.[180] Feldman suggests that the difference as compared to the approach in the Hutchins case may be explained from the fact that in the later case the information was merely disclosed to people selected by the person disclosing the information.[181] In my opinion the nature of the information was also relevant to the approach in 'The Scotsman' case. Where private information is concerned the passengers of a plane or the guests to a party could be 'the public'. It is uncertain whether these groups of people would suffice to constitute 'the public' if the information concerned touched upon national security, since two-hundred friends and family members, who cannot all be close and personal friends of the defendant, did not constitute 'public domain'.

The scope of freedom of expression is extended by the public domain defence, but freedom of expression does not seem to be a consideration in relation to it. The underlying reasoning is that if information is in the public domain, an injunction is not going to keep the information confidential.

With regard to the protection of freedom of expression it is necessary to note that even though the outcome of the defence might seem pre-determined once the information is available freely, in the application of the defence, the courts reasoned differently.

Schering Chemicals v. Falkman is an example of a case in which the court granted an interlocutory injunction, even though the information concerned was in

---

178 Woodward v. Hutchins and others [1977] 2 All ER 751, per Lord Denning at 754.
179 A-G v. Guardian Newspapers Ltd (No.2) [1990] 1 AC 109, HL; See also Official Secrets Act 1989, s.1. A duty of confidence of an intelligence officer which exists outside the confidentiality of the information is thought to be necessary because the government must be able to rely on the certainty that its servants will not disclose any information given to them.
180 Lord Advocate v. The Scotsman Publication Ltd [1989] 2 All ER 852, HL, at 862.
181 Feldman, Civil Liberties and Human Rights in England and Wales, 1993, p. 437.

the public domain. The case dealt with the publication of a film about a drug allegedly causing deformity in children before birth.[182] The information used in the film had been obtained by a person who agreed to keep the information confidential. However, at the time this case was dealt with, the same information was already public knowledge and the drug concerned was no longer marketed.

The majority of the Court of Appeal held that because of the defendant's duty of confidence an interlocutory injunction should be awarded. The fact that the information was also available from other sources was held to be of no importance in relation to this. The majority emphasised the duty of confidence of the defendant and, moreover, emphasised that the information concerned was merely a 'communication in a commercial context'.[183]

Lord Denning took a very different approach in this case, and supported his position by way of reference to the right to freedom of expression. He started by considering that an injunction is one of the most serious interferences with 'one of our most fundamental freedoms – the freedom of the press' because it constituted prior restraint.[184] He considered that the law of England should be in conformity with the Convention as much as possible.[185] He referred to the Sunday Times case, in which it was held that restrictions of freedom of expression must be 'necessary in a democratic society', which was the case when there was 'a social need sufficiently pressing to outweigh the public interest in freedom of expression'. This led Lord Denning to conclude that 'prior restraint is such a drastic interference with the freedom of the press that it should only be ordered when there is a substantial risk of grave injustice'.[186] Lord Denning recognised that the 'pressing social need' in this case lay in the right to privacy, which may 'take priority over freedom of the press', but 'there are other cases when the right of the press to inform the public – and the corresponding right of the public to be properly informed – takes priority over the right to privacy'.[187] In applying these considerations to the circumstances of this case he concluded: 'I am clearly of opinion that no injunction ought to be granted to prevent the publication of this information, even though it did originate in confidence. It dealt with a matter of great public interest. It contained information of which the public had a right to know. It should not be made the subject of an

---

182 Schering Chemicals Ltd v. Falkman Ltd [1981] 2 WLR 848, HL.
183 Compare this judgment to Markt Internverlag v. Germany, (1989) A.165: Commercial context seems to mean in this case that the information concerned is about a commercial company. In other cases, the Court has demonstrated, however, that it is able to look past the commercial context of an expression, as it did, for instance, in the case of Barthold v. Germany, (1985) A.90.
184 Schering Chemicals Ltd v. Falkman Ltd [1981] 2 WLR 848, HL, per Lord Denning at 859.
185 Schering Chemicals Ltd v. Falkman Ltd [1981] 2 WLR 848 at 861.
186 Schering Chemicals Ltd v. Falkman Ltd [1981] 2 WLR 848, at 866.
187 Schering Chemicals Ltd v. Falkman Ltd [1981] 2 WLR 848, at 864.

injunction'.[188] Lord Denning considered freedom of expression in relation to the restriction an injunction imposed on it and in relation to the nature of the information. It is remarkable that also Lord Denning does not refer to the uselessness of an injunction once the information is available freely.

The opinion of Lord Shaw is representative for the approach of the majority to this case. He approached the issue from the opposite direction.[189] Instead of starting his considerations by emphasising the importance of freedom of the press, he first emphasised that the defendant was under an obligation to keep the information confidential on behalf of the commercial interests of Schering Chemicals. In extraordinary circumstances, this obligation could be put overruled. Such circumstances did not exist in this case, according to Lord Shaw, since the drug had already been taken off the market. In other words, he considered that the publication of the information no longer served a purpose, instead of considering that the injunction could not serve a purpose. For Lord Shaw, under certain circumstances freedom of expression may constitute an exception to a duty of confidentiality. For Lord Denning confidentiality may under certain circumstances be an exception to freedom of expression.

In this case the difference in emphasis on the facts and circumstances of the case caused the difference in approach. The majority emphasised that it 'merely' concerned confidential information and that the interest in not publishing the information on the company in question should prevail, especially because the drug concerned was no longer available. Lord Denning held that the information was of public interest and that therefore the injunction should not be granted. With regard to the approach to the public domain doctrine, I observe that the defence is not applied consistently. The obvious conclusion that because the information was available already to the public the information lacked the necessary quality of confidence was not considered either by Lord Shaw or Lord Denning. Both used reasons other than that the information was in the public domain to argue their case.

Another example of the possibility still to consider other interests with regard to the request for an interlocutory injunction when the information is in the public domain is the above-mentioned case of A-G v. Guardian Newspapers Ltd. This case was also interesting due to the fact that it dealt with confidential governmental information.

Although in this case also the ambiguity of the term 'public domain' was of importance to the application of the law of breach of confidence, again interests other than the confidentiality of the information influenced the decisions of the judges at the interlocutory stage. In the decision on the merits, the public domain doctrine did cause the action for breach of confidence to fail. I elaborate on this case.

---

188 Schering Chemicals Ltd v. Falkman Ltd [1981] 2 WLR 848 at 865.
189 Schering Chemicals Ltd v. Falkman Ltd [1981] 2 WLR 848, per Lord Shaw at 866-869.

The case of A-G v. Guardian Newspapers dealt with the publication of a book called 'Spycatcher', which was written by a former member of the British security service. The government obtained an interlocutory injunction which restrained the publication of the book in the United Kingdom and also prevented the newspapers the Sunday Times, the Observer and the Guardian from, respectively, serialising the book and commenting on it. The British government, however, failed to obtain a similar injunction in the United States, where the book was subsequently published. Consequently the book could be brought into the UK quite easily. Eventually the interlocutory injunction was lifted and a permanent injunction refused, not because of any public interest in being informed about government actions but because the information was already thought to be in the public domain. Lord Keith actually stressed the fact that he did not consider any interests such as freedom of expression to come to his conclusion in the decision on the merits. Instead he based it on 'the view that all possible damage to the interest of the Crown has already been done by the publication of Spycatcher abroad and the ready availability of copies in this country'.[190] Because the information was already in the public domain the Crown would never be able to prove that the injunction was necessary in the public interest. The public interest represented, for instance, by confidence in the government's capability of securing the safety of the country could not be damaged even more if the book had been published in the UK, than had already been done. Lord Goff reached the same conclusion, also because the book was already in the public domain and because this fact implied that there was no public interest in keeping the information secret. So in both these opinions the public domain doctrine was applied in relation to the requirement that the government should demonstrate a public interest in confidentiality.

The most important decision with regard to freedom of expression was, however, taken at the interlocutory stage of the Spycatcher case.[191] When the information was 'news' and the English newspapers were consequently eager to publish it.

I observed in subsection 3.1, that an action for breach of confidence by the government can succeed only if the government demonstrates a public interest in keeping the information confidential. Lord Keith in A-G v. Guardian Newspapers (No.2) formulated the reasons for this additional requirement with regard to governmental information as follows: 'The Crown, however, as representing the nation as a whole, has no private life or personal feelings capable of being hurt by the disclosure of confidential information. In so far as the Crown acts to prevent such disclosure or to seek redress for it on confidentiality grounds, it must necessarily, in my opinion, be in a position to show that the disclosure is likely to damage or has

---

190 A-G v. Guardian Newspapers Ltd [1988] 3 All ER 545, HL, per Lord Keith at 643.
191 A-G v. Guardian Newspapers Ltd [1987] 3 All ER 316, HL.

damaged the public interest'.[192] The mere existence of an obligation to keep certain information confidential does not suffice to restrain the publication of the information concerned. The government has to show that there is an additional public interest in confidentiality. Only after this has been established and accepted does a defendant have to prove public interest in the disclosure of the information. These considerations touch upon the public interest exception that can be pleaded by the defendant. I discuss this defence in the next part of this section. Elaboration on it is not required here, since the only question that needed to be answered to determine whether the requested interlocutory injunction should be granted apparently was whether the government has any interest at all in keeping the information confidential. This is regardless of whether the information is in the public domain, since the fact that the book was published in the United States and subsequently imported into the United Kingdom did not cause the House of Lords to refuse the injunction at the interlocutory stage.

A three to two majority of the House of Lords was of the opinion that an interlocutory injunction should be granted. The manner in which, in both the majority and minority speeches, the decisions were reached is interesting. In all speeches the competing interests are represented by the abstract right of the public to be fully informed and the abstract public interest in the maintenance of the secrecy of the British security service. The interest in freedom of expression consequently played a role in applying the law of breach of confidence to the case. The considerations of Lord Brandon resulted in the finding that the injunctions should be maintained in order for the case to have a chance to be judged on the merits on full evidence. The positions of the two competing interests were made clear: 'If the temporary injunctions are continued until trial, and the Attorney General's claim to final injunctions then fails, the newspapers will be free to publish Mr Wright's disclosures as they please. They will certainly have been delayed in exercising rights which will, in that event, have been vindicated. Mr Wright's disclosures, however, relate not to recent events but to events many years in the past. That being so, a further delay in the exercise of the newspapers' rights will in no way be equivalent to a complete denial of those which the Attorney General might have'.[193] And since the damage to the Attorney General would be irreparable if the injunctions were lifted, the balance fell on the side of the interest in maintenance of secrecy of the security service. This reasoning results in a situation where an interlocutory injunction will always be granted since it is under any circumstance impossible to repair the damage done by publishing confidential information.

Lord Templeman held that the question to be answered was whether continuance of the injunctions was 'necessary in a democratic society', applying Article 10 ECHR

---

192 A-G v. Guardian Newspapers Ltd [1988] 3 All ER 545, per Lord Keith at 640.
193 A-G v. Guardian Newspapers Ltd [1987] 3 All ER 316, per Lord Brandon at 351.

directly to the case. The necessity of the injunction lay in the fact that the injunction could prevent 'British newspapers from profiting from the unlawful conduct of Mr Wright and in the fact that lifting the injunctions would create a precedent in that it could be held to be useful to publish confidential information abroad to circumvent a national injunction'. This opinion was supported by the remark that the press should not feel it had 'the power to evade an order of the court ...'.[194] This approach results in the situation that if there is a necessity, this automatically justifies interference with freedom of expression. The necessity moreover can be found in the aim of preventing the press from profiting from a breach of confidence of a third person, even if the information is in the public domain.

Lord Bridge on the other hand asked himself whether the remaining interest in national security after publication of the book in the United States was of 'sufficient weight to justify the massive encroachment on freedom of speech ...'. The remaining interest in national security was 'to deter other officers of the intelligence or security services from following Mr Wrights deplorable example'. This could not justify a 'total ban on discussion in the press of this country of matters of undoubted public interest and concern which the rest of the world now knows all about and can discuss freely'.[195] Lord Oliver came to the same conclusion in that he held that disclosure of the information could not be prevented by the injunctions since the information was already available. Moreover he felt that it was inappropriate to prevent the newspapers from commenting on publicly available information in order to provide an example to others. Although he did not explicitly say so, he held that the injunctions directed at these appellants were not the appropriate means to achieve the aim.[196]

The above cited judgments demonstrate that the public interest of the government could consist of the interest in discouragement of other intelligence officers, of the interest in not allowing the press to profit from a breach of confidence and even the possibility to have the case judged on the merits. Originally the injunctions had been imposed to keep the information concerned confidential. The fact that the information was in the public domain only persuaded a majority to lift the injunction when it came to the decision on the merits.

A last point of interest in relation to freedom of expression is that it was assumed in this decision that a court has the power to try and prevent future breaches of confidence, consequently exceeding the scope of the case at hand.[197] Lord Bridge

---

194 A-G v. Guardian Newspapers Ltd [1987] 3 All ER 316, per Lord Templeman at 357.
195 A-G v. Guardian Newspapers Ltd [1987] 3 All ER 316 at 346.
196 A-G v. Guardian Newspapers Ltd [1987] 3 All ER 316, per Lord Oliver 373.
197 This willingness to leave the actual case and lift it to a more general level is, I think, underlined by the extension of the injunction, without this being asked for, to the court reports of the Australian case on the Spycatcher book.

was the only member of the court who emphasised that these injunctions constituted a significant step in the direction of censorship. He was of the opinion that the government was heading straight for 'inevitable condemnation and humiliation by the European Court of Human Rights in Strasbourg'.[198] And in fact the European Court of Human Rights held the interlocutory injunctions to be in breach of the Convention once the book was published in the United States.

Before I discuss the second defence available under the law of breach of confidence, I wish to make some remarks regarding the current approach of the government to governmental information. Recently the UK government seems to be striving for more openness as regards its own acts and decisions, by way of a proposal for a Freedom of Information Bill.

The Freedom of Information Bill is intended to create a general right of access to information held by public authorities such as government departments, the armed forces, local government and the police.[199] A right of access to information, however, only exists with regard to a limited range of recorded information. Some categories of information are exempted,[200] and the public authority which is asked to disclose the information, must examine the consequences of disclosure. When there is no right of access, the public authorities have a duty to consider whether the public interest outweighs the interest in keeping the information confidential.[201] Whatever may become of this proposal and whatever its eventual effect will be on the accessibility of governmental information, if the Bill becomes law, there are still a number of Acts that enable the government to prevent disclosure of particular information.[202]

The consultation paper on the Bill that was presented to Parliament moreover mentions that the Bill is not meant to 'overturn duties of confidence which arise at common law'.[203] However, this consideration mainly benefits confidentiality of information concerning private individuals doing business with public authorities, because the decision in the A-G v. Guardian Newspapers made clear to the government that disclosure of information it wished to keep secret could not be properly prevented by way of the civil law remedy of breach of confidence. As a reaction to the findings of the House of Lords in the decision on the merits in A-G v. Guardian Newspapers, the Official Secrecy Act 1989 was enacted. And although the Freedom of Information Bill is declared to repeal some provisions of Acts that

---

198 See A-G v. Guardian Newspapers Ltd [1987] 3 All ER 316, per Lord Bridge 346-347.

199 Freedom of Information Bill, clause 8. See for a more extensive elaboration on this Bill: Le Sueur, Taking the soft option? The duty to give reasons in the draft Freedom of Information Bill, 1999, p. 419-427.

200 Including all unrecorded information.

201 Freedom of Information Bill, clause 14, commentary in Consultation paper par. 22.

202 E.g. Civil Defence Act 1948, Airports Act 1986, Radioactive Substances Act 1993.

203 Home Office, Freedom of Information: Consultation on Draft Legislation, Cm. 4355, par. 33.

provide possibilities to restrict dissemination of confidential governmental information, the Official Secrecy Act 1989 still stands as providing for the most extreme statutory prohibitions on disclosure of governmental information. I elaborate on the Official Secrecy legislation and its restrictive effect on freedom of expression in section 4.

After this extensive discussion of the 'public domain'-doctrine I turn to the second defence that is available against an action for breach of confidence. This defence is the public-interest exception.

b Public Interest Exception

The 'public domain' defence actually negates the confidentiality of the information. The public interest exception, does not remove the confidentiality, but overrules it. Information may be disclosed in breach of confidence if the public interest in publication outweighs the public interest in keeping the information confidential. As Lord Denning MR said in Fraser v. Evans: 'There are some things which may be required to be disclosed in the public interest, in which event no confidence can be prayed in aid to keep them secret'.[204]

It has to be taken into account with regard to this defence, however, that 'not to keep a confidence secret' does not automatically mean that the information can be distributed at someone's choice. Instead of, for instance, providing the press with the information, it might be more appropriate to give it to the police 'or some other responsible body', in which case an injunction will still be granted with regard to publication in a newspaper.[205]

A public interest that may overrule the confidentiality of information can be found for example in reasons of public health, or in the protection from wrongful criminal prosecution. Public health was the ground for not granting an interlocutory injunction in Hubbard v. Vosper.[206] Mr Vosper, a former member of the Church

---

204 Fraser v. Evans [1969] 1 All ER 8, CA, per Lord Denning MR at 11.

205 For example Francome v. Mirror Group Newspapers Ltd [1984] 2 All ER 408, CA, in which case a tape of a telephone conversation of a famous jockey and his wife was evidence of criminal behaviour on their part. The Court of Appeal thought that in this case the public interest would be best served if the tape was given to the police. Publication before trial would not be in the best interest of the public, a police investigation without prior publication of the subject matter would. Also see Feldman, Civil Liberties and Human Rights in England and Wales, 1993, p. 617: Here the boarder between when publication is allowed and when it would be more appropriate to approach the situation in a different manner was formulated: 'If the matter raises questions of genuine public interest, as where conversations appear to reveal serious miscarriages of justice and widespread police malpractice, it will not be inappropriate to retail the information to the public at large as well as drawing it to the attention of the authorities', as was found in Cork v. McVicar, The Times, 1 Nov. 1984. This approach is comparable to the approach to the defence of qualified privilege, available in libel cases.

206 Hubbard v. Vosper [1972] 1 All ER 1023, CA.

of Scientology, wrote a book about this Church. Mr Hubbard and Scientology brought an action against Mr Vosper claiming amongst other things breach of confidence and sought an interim injunction. The confidential information consisted amongst others of a description of a course given to members of Scientology, in which they were instructed about the specific terminology used in books in which the philosophy of Scientology was explained. This injunction was granted initially. The Court of Appeal, however, removed the interlocutory injunction because of the acceptance of a public interest exception: 'there were grounds for thinking that the courses of the Church of Scientology contained such dangerous material that it was in the public interest that it should be made known'.[207] Following this, it was considered that in fact the plaintiffs did not have a right to raise the issue of confidentiality before the courts since 'there was evidence that the plaintiffs had been protecting their secrets by deplorable means, such as was evidenced by their code of ethics, and therefore did not come to the court with clean hands in seeking to protect those secrets by the equitable remedy of an injunction'.[208] This consideration is based on one of the basic rules of equity that when a plaintiff intends to invoke an equitable right that he himself 'must come with clean hands'.[209]

In Lion Laboratories Ltd v. Evans, prevention of wrongful prosecution overruled the confidentiality of the information. It was explicitly stated that a defence of public interest 'was not limited to cases in which there had been any wrongdoing on the part of the plaintiff'.[210] In this particular case an injunction to restrain information on the 'Lion Intoximeter', which measured the alcohol concentration in the breath of drivers, was refused. This instrument was used by the police. The information concerned revealed that the instrument's readings were inaccurate, and that subsequently a substantial number of people were convicted falsely of drink-drive offences.

The previous examples illustrate that when the press is allowed to publish confidential information because of a public interest exception, the public interest in confidentiality is not usually freedom of expression as such. Only in the previously discussed Hutchins case on the three pop-singers who built up a positive image which did not match the truth, and who then sought an injunction to restrain the publication of some revealing facts concerning their lives, was this injunction refused on arguments that referred to an element of freedom of expression as such.[211] It was held: 'In the circumstances the public interest in giving publicity to the truth outweighed the public interest in protecting confidential information obtained by an

---

207 Hubbard v. Vosper [1972] 1 All ER 1023 at 1024.
208 Hubbard v. Vosper [1972] All ER 1023 at 1024.
209 Williams, Learning the Law, 1973, p. 28.
210 Lion Laboratories Ltd v. Evans [1984] 2 All ER 417, CA.
211 Woodward v. Hutchins [1977] 2 All ER 751.

employee about his employers ...'. Freedom of expression, or the right to receive and publish information, was the public interest which was weighed against the public interest in keeping information confidential. The decisive element in this case was the fact that the three pop-singers had 'sought publicity which was to their advantage' and therefore 'they could not complain if publicity were given to matters which revealed them in a less favourable light'.[212] Moreover, the information was held to be in the public domain. Nonetheless, these considerations come closest to the actual acceptance of freedom of expression as an interest in itself. The fact that there is a process of communicating information on a certain topic means that more than one party can disseminate information relevant to the subject. In the Hutchins case, unlike the Schering Chemicals case, the interests involved are raised to the general level of an interest in freedom of expression. However, this consideration, and the opinion of Lord Denning in the case of A-G v. Guardian Newspapers in which he referred to the right of the public to be informed, are the only examples of breach of confidence cases in which freedom of expression is considered at a general level.

Having discussed the possibilities to prevent an action for breach of confidence from succeeding, I now continue with a discussion of the remedies available to those who initiate an action for breach of confidence.

3 Remedies – Damages and Interlocutory Injunction[213]

The traditional remedy with regard to a breach of confidence action is the injunction. There may, however, also be a pecuniary relief.[214] With regard to damages, an account of profits serves to accomplish that the defendant does not profit from the breach of confidence. The account of profits is at the same time the measure for the amount of pecuniary relief that will be offered. The indication for this amount is the defendant's liability.[215] Since the Lord Cairns Act 1858,[216] damages have also

---

212 Woodward v. Hutchins [1977] 2 All ER 751, per Lord Denning at 754.
213 See for a more general and extensive discussion of interlocutory injunctions Gurry, Breach of Confidence, 1984, p. 376-395; Robertson and Nicol, Media Law, 1992, p. 190-194.
214 See for a general and more complete discussion on damages awarded in breach of confidence cases: Gurry, Breach of Confidence, 1984, p. 428-451.
215 Gurry, Breach of Confidence, 1984, at p. 415 explains the difference between account of profits and damages: 'Although an account of profits and damages are both remedies directed at giving a plaintiff pecuniary relief, the two are completely different in principle and in operation. An account is equity's way of measuring the defendant's liability, whereas damages are the traditional common law measure of a plaintiff's loss resulting from the defendant's wrongful acts'.
216 Which reads as follows: 'In all cases in which the Court of Chancery has jurisdiction to entertain an application for an injunction against a breach of any covenant, contract, or agreement, or against the commission or continuance of any wrongful act, or for the specific performance or any covenant, contract, or agreement, it shall be lawful for the same court, if it shall think fit, to award damages to the party injured, either in addition to or in substitution for such injunction or specific

been awarded in confidentiality cases. The discussion on whether this pecuniary relief originates in equity or in common law is still going on.[217] The acceptance of the existence of damages under equity is an extension of the relief that was offered for breach of a contractual obligation of confidentiality, in that it does not cover only past damage done to the plaintiff but also 'prospective' loss that will occur on account of the breach of confidence.[218] But beside enabling substitution of an injunction by awarding damages, the Cairns Act also made it possible for damages to be awarded in addition to an injunction.

An action for breach of confidence is aimed at preventing the (further) publication of the information concerned. The primary remedy offered therefore is a final injunction, which results in a permanent prevention of publication.[219] With regard to freedom of expression, however, the possibility of an interlocutory injunction may be of greater importance. In particular when information is of great news value and may contribute to a discussion about an issue of public interest, this remedy can restrict freedom of expression considerably.[220] The remedy of injunction is available under common law and equity. Gurry defined the remedy of interim injunction as follows: 'a discretionary remedy which will be granted when the plaintiff demonstrates that there is a serious question to be tried at the final hearing, and the court considers that it would be more convenient to restrain the alleged violation of his right pending the final hearing of the case than to allow the defendant to continue his course of allegedly wrongful conduct'.[221]

This definition reflects the application by the courts of a 'balance of convenience'. In cases concerning breach of confidence, the 'balance of convenience' test is applied thus: The plaintiff has to show that he has an 'arguable case' and that the harm done by the publication could not be sufficiently compensated by damages.[222] The defendant then has to show that if he cannot disclose the information concerned he will suffer uncompensatable loss. If the defendant or the plaintiff manages to prove that his or her loss could not be compensated by damages, then the court has to determine the 'balance of convenience' between the two interests. As the approach to the request for an interlocutory injunction in A-G v. Guardian Newspapers demonstrated, and as Robertson and Nicol say: 'In breach of confidence cases this approach favours suppression, simply because allowing publication of the secret is an irreversible step and preservation of the secret is what

performance, and such damages may be assessed in such manner as the Court shall direct'.

217 See Bailey, Harris and Jones, Civil Liberties, cases and materials, 1995, p. 562. See also Gurry, Breach of Confidence, 1984, p. 431-433.
218 See also Gurry, Breach of Confidence, 1984, p. 434.
219 For an extensive discussion of final injunctions see Gurry, Breach of Confidence, 1984, p. 398-410.
220 Robertson and Nicol, Media Law, 1992, p. 190.
221 Gurry, Breach of Confidence, 1984, p. 363.
222 Robertson and Nicol, Media Law, 1992, p. 191.

such actions are usually all about'.[223] Under such circumstances apparently a public domain defence or a public interest exception cannot overrule the claim by the plaintiff that publication of the information will cause irreparable damage. The chance of success of these defences lies in the decision on the merits.

The approach of the courts to the granting of interlocutory injunctions in breach of confidence cases is different from the approach in libel cases. As I observed in the paragraph concerning libels, in such cases the courts will not grant an interlocutory injunction if the defendant pleads justification or fair comment. Lord Denning proposed a similar approach with regard to the defence of public interest in breach of confidence cases. He did this in Hubbard v. Vosper and in doing so explicitly referred to freedom of speech: 'We never restrain a defendant in a libel action who says he is going to justify. So in a copyright action, we ought not to restrain a defendant who has a reasonable defence of fair dealing. Nor in an action for breach of confidence, if the defendant has a reasonable defence of public interest. The reason is because the defendant, if he is right, is entitled to publish it; and the law will not intervene to suppress freedom of speech except when it is abused'.[224] The approach suggested by Lord Denning has not been followed by a majority of judges in the English courts, as the much referred to Spycatcher case demonstrates. I mentioned already that after a permanent injunction was refused in that case, the government felt it should have broader possibilities to protect governmental information. The result was amendment of the Official Secrecy legislation. I discuss this legislation in the following section.

5 OFFICIAL SECRECY[225]

Although the civil law road of an action for breach of confidence eventually led to a dead end, with regard to official secrets the government had a criminal law option at its disposal to prevent publication of confidential information. This was provided for in the Official Secrets Act 1911. This Act was reformed by the Official Secrets Act 1989. Although the members of the Labour party in Parliament at the time opposed the introduction of the 1989 Act because in their opinion is was too

---

223 Robertson and Nicol, Media Law, 1992, p. 192.
224 Hubbard v. Vosper [1972] 1 All ER 1023, per Lord Denning at 1030.
225 See for general information on Official Secrecy: Card, Cross and Jones, Criminal Law, 1995, p. 387-391; Robertson and Nicol, Media Law, 1992, p. 414-432; Bailey, Harris and Jones, Civil Liberties cases and materials, 1995, p. 444-470; See for further information and opinions: Feldman, Civil Liberties and Human Rights in England and Wales, 1993, p. 607-612 and p. 638-642; Palmer, Tightening Secrecy Law; The Official Secrets Act 1989, 1990, p. 243-256; Deans, Scots Public Law, 1995, p. 215-217; Gardner, Freedom of Expression, 1994, p. 224-226; Loveland, Constitutional Law, A critical introduction, 1996, p. 575-582; Ewing and Gearty, Freedom under Thatcher, Civil Liberties in Modern Britain, 1990, p. 137-208.

restrictive, the current labour government has no plans to replace or amend the Act.[226] In the discussion of the protection of official secrets, emphasis lies on the Official Secrets Act 1989. I discuss the 1911 Act to the extent that it differed from the Official Secrets Act 1989. I first elaborate on the behaviour that is prohibited under the Official Secrets Act 1911 and the Official Secrets Act 1989. Subsequently I address the issue of the influence of these Acts on the scope of freedom of expression. With regard to the 1989 Act, I discuss the influence on freedom of expression of the scope of the offensive behaviour, as well as the defences available under the Act that influence the scope of freedom of expression. In the discussion of the defences I focus on the absence of a public interest defence under the Official Secrets Act 1989.

5.1 The Offence

S.2 of the Official Secrets Act 1911 prohibited the unauthorised passing and receiving of any official information, by anyone, if the act was committed in any part of the King's dominions. S.2 moreover penalised the disclosure of any official information to anybody 'other than a person to whom he is authorised to communicate it, or a person to whom it is in the interest of the State his duty to communicate it'.[227] British citizens were punishable for disclosing official British secrets anywhere in the world.[228] A specific aim that was to be served with the confidentiality of the information was not formulated, nor was there any public interest or public domain defence available. Freedom of expression in this regard was restricted to authorised communication of official information. S.2 therefore was also referred to as the 'catch-all provision'.

In 1989 reform of the legislation took place by means of the Official Secrets Act 1989, which repealed the 'catch-all provision' of s.2 of the Official Secrets Act 1911. The 1989 Act penalises the disclosure of six specified categories of information.[229] S.12 of the Act establishes that the main persons at whom the Act is directed are 'Crown servants and Government contractors'. In direct reaction to the case of A-G v. Guardian Newspapers, s.1 determines that a person who is or has been a member of the Security Service has a lifelong duty of confidentiality. S.5 of the 1989 Act makes it an offence to disclose information resulting from unauthorised disclosures

---

226 HL debates, 12 January 1999, Cm 75. The Minister of State held in that regard: 'We believe that the Act provides a sound basis for protecting sensitive official information'.
227 Palmer, Tightening Secrecy Law; The Official Secrets Act 1989, 1990, p. 243.
228 Official Secrets Act 1911 s.11.
229 The protected classes of information cover: S.1: Security and Intelligence; s.2: Defence; s.3: International relations; s.4: Crime and special investigation powers; s.5: Information resulting form unauthorized disclosure or entrusted in confidence; s.6: Information entrusted in confidence to other States and international organisations.

or entrusted in confidence, consequently prohibiting the press from publishing information coming from (former) members of secret security services.

5.2 Influence of Freedom of Expression

1 Official Secrets Act 1911

S.2 of the 1911 Act implied that there was a duty to disclose official information to persons to whom it was 'in the interest of the State' to communicate it. It had been determined that the duty of disclosure 'in the interest of the State' should not be understood as a public interest defence, but that the interest of the State was determined by the policies of the government of the day.[230] Juries as it turned out, however, could not be relied upon to rule in accordance with this approach in all instances. In the 1980s there were two cases in which civil servants were prosecuted under s.2 of the Official Secrets Act 1911. The first case involved a civil servant who passed information to the Guardian newspaper on the keeping of United States Cruise missiles on British air force bases.[231] The civil servant did this after Parliament had not been given a chance to question the person responsible on the subject. Although the government admitted that no national security aspect was concerned with the information itself, it was the presence of a leak as such that compromised national security. This reasoning was accepted, also by the House of Lords.[232] The dissemination of the information constituted an offence under the 1911 Act.

In the second case, Clive Ponting, an influential civil servant in the Ministry of Defence, passed on documents on the sinking of an Argentine battleship in the Falklands War to a member of Parliament, apparently because he was of the opinion that 'ministers within this department were not prepared to answer legitimate questions from a member of Parliament about a question of considerable public concern' and that the Commons were consequently being misled.[233] Here again the government admitted that the disclosed information did not pose a threat to national security. Ponting claimed that his actions were in the public interest. Because he informed a Member of Parliament, the Commons would now, as opposed to the situation before he passed on the documents, be able to form a well-informed opinion on the government's behaviour.

---

230 Chandler v. DPP [1962] 3 All ER 142, HL, also: R. v. Ponting [1985] Crim LR 318.
231 Sarah Tisdall-case, see Ewing and Gearty, Freedom under Thatcher, 1990, p. 137-142.
232 Lord Scarman and Lord Fraser apparently dissented, stating that no national security interest has been shown. See Loveland, Constitutional Law, a critical introduction, 1996, p. 576 and Ewing and Gearty, Freedom under Thatcher, 1990, p. 139-143.
233 See Ewing and Gearty, Freedom under Thatcher, 1990, p. 144.

Although the jury had been informed that the State interest was determined by the Government and its policies, which meant that since this government decided to prosecute it was not in the State's interest that the information was disclosed, the jury nevertheless did not find Clive Ponting guilty of an offence under s.2 of the 1911 Act. On which grounds they reached this verdict is not known, but it is not unreasonable to assume that Ponting's justification was accepted. Consequently, although in the first case discussed the jury had been willing to cooperate, from Ponting's case on the Official Secrets Act 1911 could no longer be considered watertight. This together with the, from the government's point of view, disappointing outcome of the Spycatcher case, left the government keen to reform the official secrets legislation. In the meantime, for different reasons, others beside the government were also in favour of a reform of the Official Secrets Act. The formulation of the so-called 'catch-all' provision of s.2 was considered to be much too broad and imprecise. All governmental information was covered by it; it was an offence to disclose and receive such information without authorisation; and everyone had a duty to keep this information secret. Although the press was rarely convicted under the Act for receiving such information,[234] still the possibility of prosecution was condemned. In reaction to the discontent with the 1911 Act, the Official Secrets Act 1989 was introduced.

In the next subsection I discuss this Act. No cases have been brought under this Act so far. In order to describe the influence of freedom of expression, I address the reasons given for its introduction and the manner in which its aims are realised in the text of the Act. In doing so I focus on the scope of the offences formulated in the Act and the possible defences and their influence on freedom of expression.

2 Official Secrets Act 1989

a Scope of the Offence

The purpose of the Official Secrets Act 1989 was said to be 'to reduce the amount of information protected by criminal sanctions to areas where disclosure would be harmful to the public interest'.[235] A number of aspects of the Act confirm that it constitutes a relaxation of the situation that existed under the 1911 Act. The scope of the offence has been restricted to six categories of information.[236] Moreover, s.12

---

234 See Robertson and Nicol, Media Law, 1992, p. 416-418. The Aitkin case and the Campbell case were two cases in which journalists were prosecuted under section 2. Both cases led to great embarrassment for the government: Aitkin was acquitted, the jury accepted his public interest defence, and Campbell's prosecution collapsed when it turned out that the information concerned came from published sources.

235 Palmer, Tightening Secrecy Law; The Official Secrets Act 1989, 1990, p. 243.

236 The protected classes of information cover: S.1: Security and Intelligence; s.2: Defence; s.3: International relations; s.4: Crime and special investigation powers; s.5: Information resulting from

seems to restrict the possible offenders to 'Crown servants and Government contractors'. On (former) members of the Security Service a lifelong duty of confidentiality is imposed. Beside the fact that not all governmental information is included in the 1989 Act and that the duty of confidentiality is primarily directed at servants of the Crown, another apparent relaxation in comparison to s.2 of the 1911 Act took place. For certain kinds of information, the disclosed information must be shown to be harmful to the public interest.[237] Moreover, under s.5 of the Act it is necessary to prove damage done by publication of the information under all circumstances. Disclosure is generally thought to be harmful if it is damaging. Per stated category of information it is indicated what constitutes damage. If one takes a closer look at the 1989 Act, however, it is doubtful that it provides an improvement compared with the situation under the 1911 Act.

First of all, s.5 of the 1989 Act makes it an offence to disclose information resulting from unauthorised disclosures or entrusted in confidence. Consequently the obligation of confidentiality of Crown servants and government contractors is extended to members of the public, including journalists.[238] A second aspect that diminishes the apparent improvement with regard to the protection of governmental information is that the 1989 Act puts an absolute ban on official information coming from members or former members of the Security Service. This in fact constitutes a tightening of official secrecy law. And although the Act does restrict the offence to certain categories of information, these categories have been formulated broadly and they cover the sort of information for which the disclosers were usually prosecuted under the old section 2.

Finally, the requirement that the government has to show harm done by the disclosure of the information seems to be an improvement. To meet this requirement the government has to prove damage. However, the extent of the harm required is unclear and the definition of damage given in relation to each category of information is imprecise. Disclosure of information relating to security and intelligence is damaging, for instance, 'if it causes damage to the work of or any part of the security service'.[239] The level of harm that is required to constitute damage will be of great importance to the impact of this act on freedom of expression. I already said that, so far, prosecutions under the 1989 Act have not taken place. The government, however, still intends to charge David Shyler with an offence under the Official Secrets Act 1989. David Shyler is a former officer of MI5. In 1997 he revealed details of

---

unauthorized disclosure or entrusted in confidence; s.6: Information entrusted in confidence to other States and international organisations.

237 Also see Palmer, Tightening Secrecy Law: The Official Secrets Act 1989, 1990, p. 244.

238 Although Robertson and Nicol, Media Law, 1992, at p. 425-426 feel that there is room for a public interest defence in the decision whether the damage done subsequently caused harm.

239 Ss.1(4)(a) Official Secrets Act 1989.

ineptitude and malpractice within the security services. He claimed he was acting in the public interest, since the shortcomings of the secret service undermined democracy. One of his disclosures concerned an attempt by MI6 to assassinate Colonel Gadaffi of Libya. The French courts rejected the UK's request to extradite Shyler, who currently resides in France. He continues to provide information on the operating of the British secret service via the internet. Prosecution under the Official Secrets Act has not taken place and it should be noted that the use of new technology seems to have overtaken the possibilities to prevent disclosure of official secrets by means of the Official Secrets Act 1989.

If prosecution is not avoided by staying out of the country, the 1989 Act provides for some defences that may decrease the restricting effect of the Act on freedom of expression. They are the subject of discussion in the next subsection.

b Defences

Generally, it is a defence for a person charged with an offence under the 1989 Act 'to prove that at the time of the alleged offence he did not know, and had no reasonable cause to believe that the information, document or article in question' related to the category concerned or 'would be damaging within the meaning of damage' of the category of information concerned. This last defence of lack of damage is not available to (former) members of the Security Service with regard to information on security and intelligence.[240] Moreover, it seems unlikely that a journalist will be able to invoke this defence successfully. A journalist will generally be aware of the nature of the information he is holding, also because he will be informed of its source.

A very significant aspect of the 1989 Act is that it does not provide for a public interest defence. The government rejected the adoption of a public interest defence, but claimed otherwise. The home office press release referred to 'specific tests of harm to the public interest'.[241] And Mr Hurd said on the subject: 'the prosecution would have to satisfy a test of harm to the public interest ... Under these proposals, where there is a harm test the defendant could argue that the disclosure caused good not harm to the public interest. It would be for the jury to decide'.[242] However, the text of the Act does not explicitly provide for possibilities to take a public interest in confidentiality or disclosure of the information into consideration. The harm referred to concerns the harm done to the categories of information. This is a deterioration in

---

240 See also Card, Cross and Jones, Criminal Law, 1995, p. 388. Information disclosed by (former) members of the Security Service does not have to be damaging for its disclosure to be unauthorised, therefore such a defence cannot be available either.
241 Frankel, The Official Secrets Bill, http://ww.cfoi.org.uk/osareform.html.
242 Frankel, The Official Secrets Bill, http://www.cfoi.org.uk/osareform.html. Mr Hurd was the Secretary of State for Home Affairs at the time.

the protection of freedom of expression compared to the situation under the 1911 Act and with regard to the situation under the law of breach of confidence. Under s.2 of the 1911 Act it was a defence to hold that the information was disclosed to someone 'to whom it is in the interest of the State to communicate it'.[243] This part of the section had been applied as a public interest defence in the Clive Ponting case. As we have seen in the section above on confidentiality law, a public interest defence is also available against accusations of breach of confidence. In the Spycatcher case, Lord Griffith accepted that the obligation of confidentiality of a member of the security service was lifelong. He also held, however, that it was not absolute. Disclosure in the public interest could, under exceptional circumstances, offer a defence.

Nevertheless, although the 1989 Act does not provide for an explicit possibility to argue the public benefit of disclosure of information, it is in fact with regard to the requirement of harm that the courts may provide some protection to freedom of expression. Although the sections of the Act do not refer to public interest, the definitions of harm and damage in several relevant sections are sufficiently vague to allow the courts to consider the public interest in disclosure of the information. Such an approach could not only be supported by the remarks of Mr Hurd referred to above, but also by the existence of the Freedom of Information Bill once it becomes law. This Bill provides for a duty of public authorities to provide information regarding their acts and decisions. As I have said above, this Bill does not repeal any provisions of the Official Secrets Act 1989 and as such the obligations stated in the Bill do not change the openness regarding governmental information protected under the Official Secrets Act. The intention the Bill is supposed to have, however, may influence courts when they determine whether the requirement of harm or damage has been satisfied.

I discussed the prevention of confidential information in the previous two sections. The areas referred to restrict freedom of expression with regard to private information as well as public information to the extent that government information is concerned. In the following section I address the restriction of information relating to active court proceedings. The regulation of dissemination of this type of information is governed by Contempt of Court law.

---

243 Also see Frankel, The Official Secrets Bill, http://www.cfoi.org.uk/osareform.html, p. 11.

6 CONTEMPT OF COURT[244]

English contempt law serves to prevent a jury or judges from being influenced by (media) attention for the case they sit on.[245] There is civil and criminal contempt of court. The purpose of civil contempt is 'to assist in the enforcement of court orders', 'it provides the ultimate sanction against a person who refuses to comply with the order of a properly constituted court'.[246] Criminal contempt aims to protect 'many of the requirements for the due administration of justice' and consists of contempt in the face of the court, scandalizing the court and prejudicing a trial.[247] Both kinds of contempt impose restrictions on freedom of expression. A more significant distinction is that between strict liability contempt and deliberate contempt. Strict liability means that intent is irrelevant to the committal of the offence. The Contempt of Court Act 1981 is governed by the strict liability rule.[248] Contempt of Court law, however, is governed by common law as well as statutory law. The common law contempt concerns deliberate contempt. Intent to influence court proceedings has to be proved by the A-G. This distinction has not led to the disappearance of the common law offence in practice, since under common law the public interest defence is unavailable.

Contempt law contains a definition of the prohibited behaviour, provides for remedies such as prior restraint; by way of an injunction, the Contempt of Court Act 1981 provides for an innocent publication defence[249] and for a public interest defence.[250] Although the Contempt of Court Act forms the most significant restriction on publication of information on court proceedings, I discuss both the relevant statutory legislation and common law. This is not only because the common law offence is still regularly invoked, but also because the common law of contempt was criticised by the European Court of Human Rights in a manner which necessitated adjustment of the law. This resulted in the Contempt of Court Act 1981. It is interesting to examine the extent to which the Act adjusted the common law of

---

244 See for general information on Contempt of Court: Miller, Contempt of Court, 1990; Feldman, Civil Liberties and Human Rights in England and Wales, 1991, p. 733-781; Bailey, Harris and Jones, Civil Liberties cases and materials, 1995, p. 373-442; Robertson and Nicol, Media Law, 1992, p. 261-304; Card, Cross and Jones, Criminal Law, 1995, p. 368-379. See for further information and opinions: Gardner, Freedom of Expression, 1994, p. 226-229; Gardner, Protection of Free Speech in Constitutional and Civil Law, 1990, p. 377-379; Boyle, Freedom of Expression as a Public Interest in English Law, 1982, p. 593-598; Leigh, United Kingdom, 1992, p. 273-275.

245 An example in which a conviction was overturned due to prejudicial media attention: R v. Cullen, McCann and Shanahan [1990] Cr. App. R. 239, CA.

246 Miller, Contempt of Court, 1990, p. 2-3.

247 Miller, Contempt of Court, 1990, p. 2.

248 Contempt of Court Act 1981, s.1.

249 Contempt of Court Act 1981, s.3.

250 Contempt of Court Act 1981, s.5.

contempt so as to realise the changes required by the decision of the European Court of Human Rights. I first discuss the nature of the offence under contempt law, subsequently I elaborate on the influence of freedom of expression first on the common law of contempt, and then on the statutory law of contempt.

6.1 The Offence

Contempt of court is originally a common law offence. It still is. Currently, however, it is primarily regulated by the Contempt of Court Act 1981. Under common law a publication constituted a contempt when it was 'calculated' or 'likely' to interfere with the course of justice.[251] The Contempt of Court Act concerns unintentional contempt, consequently intentional contempt is still regulated under common law.

The Contempt of Court Act restricts the 'strict liability' contempt to 'a publication which creates a substantial risk that the course of justice in the proceedings in question will be seriously impeded or prejudiced' (s.2(2)).[252] Furthermore, a publication can only constitute a contempt 'if proceedings in question are active within the meaning of this section at the time of the publication' (s.3(3)). Also the distributer of a publication is not liable for contempt if he 'does not know that it contains such matter and has no reason to suspect that it is likely to do so' (s.3(2)). Moreover, a 'discussion of public affairs or other matters of general public interest' cannot constitute a contempt of court as long as it is 'merely incidental to the discussion' (s.5). Finally, s.10 of the Act provides for a (limited) protection of sources of information. The combination of these provisions of the Act justify the statement by Feldman that the law of contempt of court 'recognizes the public interest in open justice and in permitting fair and accurate contemporaneous reporting of legal proceedings'.[253] Of importance to this study is not only that the courts recognise these interests but also the extent to which they do that. I elaborate on the role of freedom of expression with regard to the application of both contempt under common law and the mentioned provisions of the Contempt of Court Act 1981 in the following subsection. I start with a discussion of the common law of contempt.

---

251 See also Bailey, Harris and Jones, Civil Liberties, cases and materials, 1995, p. 383; R. v. Evening Standard Co Ltd [1954] 1 All ER 1026, QBD.
252 Noteworthy is the fact that the contempt may not only concern comments on court proceedings, but also attacks on the judiciary (although rarely used) and jury deliberations. Publications on how jurors reached their decisions are prohibited.
253 Feldman, Civil Liberties and Human Rights in England and Wales, 1993, p. 733.

6.2 Influence of Freedom of Expression

a Under Common Law

A discussion of the common law of contempt implies that I discuss intentional contempt, since liability for unintentional contempt is governed by the Contempt of Court Act 1981. In order to determine the cases that can be brought under the common law of contempt, the content of the term 'intention' is decisive.

Feldman indicates two aspects of contempt of court under common law that enlarge the extent of the offence in comparison to contempt governed by the strict liability rule.[254] The first aspect is that, contrary to contempt under the Contempt of Court Act 1981, common law contempt might apply to proceedings before they are active.[255] Secondly, common law contempt is not limited to those types of publications which create a substantial risk that active proceedings will be seriously impeded or prejudiced. Any publication 'likely' to prejudice legal proceedings will suffice to constitute contempt. Of importance beside these two aspects is that intentional contempt does not attract a public interest 'defence' like that of s.5 of the Contempt of Court Act.

With regard to prejudicing proceedings, a 1988 case gave an indication of what could be considered intentional contempt.[256] The moment at which a publication could be considered contemptuous of court proceedings was also established. The case concerned was A-G v. News Group Newspapers.[257] In this case, initially the DPP had declined to prosecute a doctor who was accused of raping an 8-year-old girl. The Sun newspaper subsequently made an offer to the mother of the child to pay for private prosecution in exchange for the exclusive story. Following this deal, the Sun published articles on the issue, in which the doctor was declared guilty of the rape and was accused of having committed other offences of that kind. These claims were supported by potential witnesses and made believable by accusing the doctor of other sexual crimes. Despite these allegations in the Sun newspaper, the doctor was eventually acquitted. The Sun was convicted for contempt of court.

In this case the scope of the offence was considerably widened when it was held that under common law comments on proceedings that were 'pending' but also comments on proceedings that were 'imminent' (prior to arrest or charge) could

---

254 Feldman, Civil Liberties and Human Rights in England and Wales, 1993, p. 751-752.
255 A person could also be liable for contempt when proceedings were 'imminent': A-G v. News Group Newspapers plc. [1988] 2 All ER 906, DC.
256 A-G v. News Group Newspapers [1988] 2 All ER 906.
257 A-G v. News Group Newspapers [1988] 2 All ER 906.

attract liability.[258] This decision posed an enormous restriction on freedom of expression. The meaning of intention was interpreted narrowly however: 'a publisher would only be liable unless he knew that proceedings were likely to follow soon enough to make prejudice likely, and intended that to happen'.[259] With regard to the circumstances of this case it was not the criticism of the DPP's prosecution policy that constituted contempt of court. It was the combination of the newspaper paying for a private prosecution and publishing articles which made the defendant seem guilty of an offence which he had not (yet) been held to have committed.[260]

In a subsequent case, the extension of liability for contempt became topic of discussion again. At a press conference, the police asked the press for help in finding the suspect in relation to the disappearance of a 15-year-old girl. The police explicitly asked the press not to print any information on the man's previous criminal record. Sport Newspaper did not receive this request directly, but was aware of the fact that the police were looking for this suspect. The next day the paper published an article mentioning the man's name and describing him as a 'vicious evil rapist' and going into detail about a previous rape for which he had been convicted. Later the suspect could be arrested and was convicted of the murder of the girl.

Bingham LJ. confirmed the decision in the previous case of A-G v. News Group Newspapers. He acknowledged that the decision in that case constituted an extension of liability for contempt under common law, but since the decision was so clear on this point he was of the opinion it should be followed: 'contempt may be committed even though proceedings are neither in existence nor imminent'.[261]

Although the differences with strict liability contempt may make it tempting to bring charges for contempt under common law, it must be reminded that the burden of proof for intent lies on the prosecution. The just discussed case of A-G v. Sports Newspapers further explained what should be proved in order to establish intent on the part of the plaintiff. Intention is not the same as 'motive or desire'. Nevertheless, 'in proving specific intent, however, although such intent could be inferred from all the circumstances, including the foreseeability of the consequences of publication, the probability of the consequences being foreseen had to be little short of overwhelming before it sufficed to establish the necessary intent and on the facts it had not been shown beyond reasonable doubt that at the date of publication the paper's editor had the specific intention to prejudice the fair conduct of proceedings, whose existence

---

258 A-G v. News Group Newspapers [1988] 2 All ER 906, per Watkins LJ. at 920. He even took it a step further by stating: 'The circumstances in which a criminal contempt at common law can be committed are not necessarily ... confined to those in which proceedings are either pending or imminent'.

259 Feldman, Civil Liberties and Human Rights in England and Wales, 1993, p. 753.

260 See also Robertson and Nicol, Media Law, 1992, p. 287.

261 A-G v. Sport Newspapers Ltd [1992] 1 All ER 503, QBD, per Bingham LJ. at 515.

he regarded at that time as being speculative and remote'. So although intentional liability offers an additional possibility to restrict freedom of expression regarding court proceedings, a possibility of particular interest when publication takes place before 'proceedings in question are active' or when there is a public interest in the publication, the effect of this restriction is not excessive because of the limited scope of the term 'intention'.[262]

The changes in contempt of court law achieved by the Contempt of Court Act 1981 were instigated by the Thalidomide case. The case confronted the way in which the English courts dealt with freedom of expression as a competing interest in relation to contempt of court, with the way the European Court of Human Rights dealt with freedom of expression and the restrictions to it.[263] The case dealt with a publication in the Sunday Times on better settlement for victims of the drug thalidomide. Children were born with severe deformities because their mothers had taken this sedative during pregnancy. While the company that marketed the drug was negotiating the amount of damages that would be paid to the parents of these children, the Sunday Times ran an article about the behaviour of the company in these negotiations, namely that it was trying to keep the damages as low as possible. The House of Lords unanimously decided that the article constituted a contempt. It was thought to put pressure on a litigant to change its behaviour in relation to the claims put forward by the parents and it was thought to prejudice the issue of negligence brought forward in the case. An injunction was granted.

It was generally accepted by the House of Lords that there existed a public interest in freedom of expression and in the right of the public to be informed.[264] However, the starting point was the public interest in a proper administration of justice. Freedom of expression could only exist outside the 'reasonable necessity' to prevent prejudice in the administration of justice.[265] Publication of the article would interfere with the trial, because it was held to prejudice the case. Furthermore, the article might discourage future litigants to use the opportunities the law offers them in settling damage claims. Whether or not a particular article dealt with a subject of particular public interest was of no influence. Lord Reid did not see 'why there should be any difference in principle between a case which is thought to have news-value and one which is not'.[266]

---

262 In relation to Spycatcher the government showed that it knew of other ways to restrict the freedom of the press through the intentional contempt by claiming that newspapers were in contempt for not acting in conformity with interim injunctions.: A-G v. Observer Ltd [1988] 1 All ER 385, Ch.D, in which merely knowing of possible prejudice to trials seemed to suffice to establish intent.

263 A-G v. Times Newspapers Ltd [1973] 3 All ER 54, HL. See also Boyle, Freedom of expression as a public interest in English law, 1982, p. 593-598.

264 Only Lord Diplock completely ignored freedom of expression as a competing interest.

265 A-G v. Times Newspapers Ltd [1973] 3 All ER 54, per Lord Reid at 60.

266 A-G v. Times Newspapers Ltd [1973] 3 All ER 54, per Lord Reid at 66.

As Boyle stated in his article 'Freedom of expression as a public interest in English law', Lord Simon was the only one who found that freedom of expression and due administration of justice were two public interests 'which are liable to conflict in particular situations'.[267] Lord Simon stated that the function of freedom of expression was that 'members of a democratic society should be sufficiently informed that they may influence intelligently the decisions which may effect themselves'.[268] He then went on to hold, however, that where the administration of justice is concerned, society has decided to base legal decisions on the law, and it has decided that these decisions are made by a judge or a jury. The separate members of society have delegated this decision-making power to them. Consequently he held 'the paramount public interest pendente lite is that the legal proceedings should progress without interference'.[269] Although Lord Simon's initial considerations seemed to indicate that 'neither interest will necessarily prevail where there is a conflict',[270] the rather restrictive way in which he interprets the function of freedom of expression, especially in relation to legal proceedings, made it hard to distinguish his point of view from that of the majority, that freedom of expression only exists outside the public interest in due administration of justice.

This approach to the role of freedom of expression re-establishes the traditional approach to freedom under English law, namely that freedom of expression is allowed as long as it is not prohibited. In this case, freedom of expression was allowed as long as it did not prejudice the case at hand and as long as a publication did not put pressure on the litigant, just as a publication should not intimidate a judge, a member of the jury or a witness.[271] These requirements were not conclusive of what constitutes contempt, however, since the aim of the law is to prevent interference in general. The extent of the restrictions imposed on freedom of expression by contempt of court law was therefore uncertain.

The Sunday Times Newspaper brought the case before the European Court of Human Rights, which held that the decision of the English courts constituted a violation of Article 10 ECHR. The principal reason for this decision was that the starting point of the House of Lords was the administration of justice, whereas the European Court of Human Rights emphasised freedom of expression. The injunction granted to protect the 'authority of the judiciary', was held to be motivated insufficiently to justify the restriction of freedom of expression. Information on a

---

267 A-G v. Times Newspapers Ltd [1973] 3 All ER 54, per Lord Simon at 81. See also Boyle, Freedom of Expression as a public interest in English Law, 1982, p. 594.
268 A-G v. Times Newspapers Ltd [1973] 3 All ER 54, per Lord Simon at 81.
269 A-G v. Times Newspapers Ltd [1973] 3 All ER 54, per Lord Simon at 81-82.
270 Boyle, Freedom of Expression as a public interest in English law, 1982, p. 594.
271 See A-G v. Times Newspapers Ltd [1973] 3 All ER 54, at 80.

matter of such great public interest could not be restrained on such a ground, especially because the matter was already a topic of discussion in the press.[272]

Quite soon after this decision of the Court its influence on English law could already be felt.[273] In A-G v. BBC, the BBC appealed against an injunction restraining the broadcasting of a programme, which touched upon matters that were part of an appeal some time later before a local valuation court.[274] The broadcast was held to constitute a contempt of court. The House of Lords, however, allowed the appeal, since a local valuation court was considered not to be a court of law. Consequently the law of contempt could not be extended to these courts. It was expressly stated that it was not the task of the courts to widen the scope of this law.[275] Viscount Dilhorne and Lord Edmund-Davies made no mention of freedom of expression. The remaining three law Lords did hold that this case 'requires the House to consider two interests of great public importance freedom of speech and the administration of justice'.[276] However, Lord Fraser commented on the relation between English law and the decisions of the European Court of Human Rights:[277] 'I agree that in deciding this appeal the House has to hold a balance between the principle of freedom of expression and the principle that the administration of justice must be kept free from outside interference. Neither principle is more important than the other, and where they come into conflict, as they do in this case, the boundary has to be drawn between the spheres in which they respectively operate. That is not the way in which the Court would approach the question',[278] after which he cited the following passage from the Sunday Times judgment of the Court: 'Whilst emphasising that it is not its function to pronounce itself on an interpretation of English law adopted in the House of Lords the Court points out that it has to take a different approach. The Court is faced not with a choice between two conflicting principles, but with a principle of freedom of expression that is subject to a number of exceptions which must be narrowly interpreted'.[279]

The idea that pending trial the administration of justice must prevail over freedom of expression remained the starting point for the English courts. However, Lord Fraser, Lord Salmon and Lord Scarman did come to the conclusion that to extend the scope of contempt of court law to local valuation courts would be 'too great a

---

272 Sunday Times v. United Kingdom, (1979) A.30
273 See also Barendt, Freedom of Speech, 1996, p. 139-140.
274 A-G v. BBC [1980] 3 WLR 109, HL.
275 A-G v. BBC [1980] 3 WLR 109, per Lord Edmund-Davies at 128.
276 A-G v. BBC [1980] 3 WLR 109, per Lord Scarman at 130, see to the same extent Lord Fraser at 128 and Lord Salmon at 117.
277 See also Miller, Contempt of Court, 1990, p. 14.
278 A-G v. BBC [1980] 3 WLR 109, per Lord Fraser at 128.
279 Sunday Times v. United Kingdom (1979) A.30.

curtailment of the right to freedom of expression'.[280] Although courts which are not courts of law often were not judges in the legal sense, and thus more susceptible to interference from a television program, still the certainty of the law was chosen over 'strict logic'.[281]

Still contempt law was too broad and too uncertain with regard to 'ordinary courts' to be in conformity with the ECHR. The law of contempt had to be adjusted to the requirements of the Convention. The English Government reformed contempt law by means of the Contempt of Court Act 1981, and it consequently claimed to have fulfilled its obligations under Article 10 ECHR. I discuss the changes brought by this Act and the extent to which it provides possibilities to take freedom of expression into account in the next section.

b Statute Law: The Contempt of Court Act 1981

Sections 2(2) and 5

Regardless of whether a publication is intended to prejudice court proceedings, under the Contempt of Court Act 1981 a publication has to create a 'substantial risk' that the course of justice will be 'seriously impeded'.[282] However, when the publication is 'merely incidental to the discussion', 'discussion of public affairs or other matters of general public interest', it will not constitute a contempt.[283]

A-G v. English was the first case to reach the House of Lords on the 1981 Act.[284] This case provided clarity on the meaning of the term 'substantial risk'. It moreover dealt with the relation between the criteria of s.2(2) and the exclusion of liability for discussion of topics of public interest. It was specified when information of public interest is considered to be 'merely incidental to the discussion'.

The case dealt with a publication during the trial of a doctor who was accused of murder by starvation of a baby suffering from Down's syndrome. A national newspaper published an article which was written in support of a pro-life candidate for parliament. In this article, the practice of doctors to end the lives of handicapped babies, amongst others by starving them, was discussed. The trial itself was not mentioned.

The first question to be answered by the House of Lords was whether the publication met the requirements of s.2(2). The risk posed by it at the time of publication was assessed. The fact that the publication did not influence the outcome

---

280 A-G v. BBC [1980] 3 WLR 109, per Lord Fraser at 129.
281 A-G v. BBC [1980] 3 WLR 109, per Lord Fraser at 129. See also Boyle, Freedom of Expression as a public interest in English law, 1982, p. 597 who saw much more in this decision.
282 Contempt of Court Act 1981 s.2(2).
283 Contempt of Court Act 1981 s.5.
284 A-G v. English and another [1982] 2 All ER 903, HL.

of the proceedings did not alter the fact that there was a contempt of court at the time of publication.[285] It was held that substantial risk was meant to 'exclude a risk that is only remote'. The word seriously was thought to be sufficiently clear, but could be substituted with the term 'real'. The risk of the article in question to prejudice the trial could be held to be 'substantial not remote' and therefore the criterion of s.2(2) had been satisfied.

Lord Diplock consequently gave a rather wide interpretation of 'substantial'. In later cases this wide interpretation seemed to be restricted somewhat.[286] In a 1983 case, it was held that a slight or trivial risk of serious prejudice was not enough to constitute a substantial risk, nor was a substantial risk of 'slight prejudice'.[287] If an article could be about one of six defendants on trial,[288] this posed no substantial risk, nor did a publication on an IRA terrorist published nine months before his trial, also because the newspaper concerned had very limited circulation.[289] The place of the trial, the nature of the proposed publication and the proximity of publication to the date of the trial were factors of considerable importance in assessing whether the criterion in s.2 were met.[290]

For publications falling outside the public discussion criteria of s.5 of the Act, fulfilment of the criteria in s.2 is sufficient to conclude that there is a contempt. S.5, however, creates room for discussion of public affairs in the following manner: 'A publication made as or part of a discussion in good faith of public affairs or other matters of general public interest is not to be treated as a contempt of court under the strict liability rule if the risk of impediment or prejudice is merely incidental to the discussion'. As I indicated, in A-G v. English not only was the meaning of the term 'substantial risk' clarified, but also the relation between s.2 and s.5 was explained: 'Section 5 does not take the form of a proviso or an exception to s.2(2). It stands on an equal footing with it'. Consequently it is not intended to serve as an exception to the rule. Like s.2(2) it indicates the type of publications that shall not attract liability for contempt of court 'despite their tendency to interfere with the course of justice in particular legal proceedings'.[291] Since s.5 was not an exception and therefore not a defence in the legal sense of the term, the burden of proof rested on the prosecution.[292]

The House of Lords in the English case held that the newspaper article considered in that case was part of a wider discussion on a matter of general public interest,

---

285 A-G v. English [1982] 2 All ER 903 per Lord Diplock at 918.
286 See Harris, Bailey and Jones, Civil Liberties cases and materials, 1995, p. 388-390.
287 A-G v. Times Newspapers Ltd, 1983, Times, 12 February, DC.
288 A-G v. Guardian Newspapers [1992] 3 All ER 38.
289 A-G v. Independent Television News Ltd and others [1995] 2 All ER 370, HL.
290 A-G v. News Group Newspapers [1986] 2 All ER 833, CA.
291 A-G v. English [1982] 2 All ER 903, per Lord Diplock at 918.
292 It does seem to me that it is the defence that has to bring up a possible applicability of s.5.

namely mercy killing. The District Court had been of the opinion that the passages of interest were not merely incidental to the discussion, since they were unnecessary; moreover they were thought to be accusations and therefore they could not be part of a 'discussion' since discussion was confined to 'the airing of views and the propounding and debating of principles and arguments'. The House of Lords adopted a much wider interpretation of both elements of s.5. It held that such a limited meaning of discussion would more or less restrict s.5 to 'academic discussions of hypothetical problems, remote from all public affairs'.[293]

With regard to the proof of the article being not 'merely incidental to the discussion', Lord Diplock stated: 'The test is not whether an article could have been written as effectively without these passages or whether some other phraseology might have been substituted for them that could have reduced the risk of prejudicing Dr. Arthur's fair trial; but it is whether the risk created by the words actually chosen by the author was "merely incidental to the discussion", which I take to mean no more than an incidental consequence of expounding its main theme'.[294] The facts of the case led the House of Lords to believe that the subject of mercy killing was 'merely incidental' to the general discussion. Reference to that topic would be necessary to make any meaningful discussion on the issue possible.[295]

Applied in this manner, the Contempt of Court Act created clarity about the type of publications that constitutes prejudicial publicity, and it created protection for publications of public interest.[296] The interpretation of s.2 seems to have been relaxed since the English case and also s.5 has not been interpreted narrowly since then. Therefore these sections were able to accomplish their goal of providing a balance between freedom of expression and the fair administration of justice.[297]

Besides the possibilities to protect freedom of expression under s.5 of the Contempt of Court Act, also s.10 of the Act provides for such a possibility. It concerns the protection of sources of information.

---

293 A-G v. English [1982] 2 All ER 903, per Lord Diplock at 920.

294 A-G v. English [1982] 2 All ER 903, per Lord Diplock at 920.

295 Its interesting to note the Sunday Times case would probably not have been considered merely incidental to the discussion, as Lord Diplock stated in the English case. The article would almost certainly have fulfilled the requirements of substantial risk of serious impediment, and therefore the newspaper would even under the new Act have been held to be in contempt.

296 For the most part the courts seem to have taken the new restrictions seriously, explicitly recognizing their importance as contributions to freedom of expression. See also A-G v. News Group Newspapers Ltd [1986] All ER 833.

297 Although s.2(2) were not meant to be balanced it does seem as if such a process takes place see English at 920 f,g.

Section 10

S.10 of the Contempt of Court Act 1981, is of particular importance to journalists, since it allows them to maintain the anonymity of their sources 'unless it be established to the satisfaction of the court that disclosure (of the source) is necessary in the interest of justice or national security or for the prevention of disorder or crime'. Unlike s.5, this provision does constitute an exception to the offence.

Three cases can be referred to with regard to this section, that give an indication of the role of freedom of expression with regard to its application. The first of these is a case which dealt with a newspaper that received and published a secret memorandum on the placement of cruise-missiles at a Royal Air Force Base.[298] Sarah Tisdall, as then unknown, had anonymously sent the memorandum to the newspaper. The government then asked for a court order ordering the newspaper to return the document, so it would be possible to study markings on it which would enable them to discover the leak. The newspaper claimed that it had a right to refuse this under s.10 of the 1981 Act. When the case came before the House of Lords, it turned out that a majority had a different opinion on this. The House of Lords reduced this case to an issue of evidence. If the Crown was able to show that it was necessary 'in the interest of national security' to know the identity of the source, then disclosure would be ordered.

The second case of importance to s.10 is X Ltd v. Morgan Grampian.[299] In this case a journalist, Mr Goodwin, got hold of a confidential report of a company, showing that this company had great financial difficulties. At the same time the firm in question was trying to obtain a considerable loan to refinance. Goodwin intended to write an article about this situation. The company managed to obtain an injunction to prevent publication of the information contained in the report. The journalist was at the same time ordered to reveal the identity of his source. To this end he had to hand over the notes he had made of a telephone conversation with the, to Goodwin as well, anonymous source. Goodwin, relying on s.10 refused and was subsequently held to be in contempt of court, because the privilege could be overridden by the interest of justice. Although freedom of expression was considered by the court when it came to its decision, the privilege awarded to the media to keep their sources secret, in the end did not in fact benefit freedom of expression when it mattered.

In the Morgan Grampian case, there was just one aspect of the case relating to the placement of cruise-missiles which Lord Bridge did not agree with, and that was Lord Diplock's interpretation of the term justice as 'the administration of justice in the course of legal proceedings in a court of law'. He considered this to be too narrow an interpretation and held that it was 'in the interest of justice ... that persons should be enabled to exercise important legal rights and to protect themselves from

---

298 Secretary of State for Defence and another v. Guardian Newspapers Ltd [1984] 3 All ER 601, HL.
299 X Ltd v. Morgan Grampian [1991] 1 AC at 1, HL.

serious legal wrongs whether or not resort to legal proceedings in a court of law will be necessary to attain these objectives'.[300] This considerably broader explanation imposed a much greater restriction on the s.10 privilege and on the room given to freedom of expression than was the case under Lord Diplock's view on the terminology of s.10.

The decision of the House of Lords in the Morgan Grampian case was held to constitute a breach of Article 10 by the European Court of Human Rights, in Goodwin v. UK. I elaborate extensively on the details of this decision in chapter VIII of this book.

The third case in which the influence of s.10 on freedom of expression was explained was the case of Camelot Group v. Centaur Ltd. This case was comparable to the Morgan Grampian case with regard to its facts. It also concerned a journalist who had been given confidential information by an employee of the prosecuting company. The information concerned a financial report of the company. In Camelot Group v. Centaur Ltd, Schiemann LJ. referred to the Morgan Grampian case and considered the interest in further disclosure of the information by the leak and the public interest in disclosure of the information given to the journalist.[301] In this case the information revealed would have been made public five days after the magazine for which the journalist worked planned to publish the information. It was considered that a court order to reveal the identity of the source might have a chilling effect on other sources considering making public material that they feel is of importance to the public interest. However, the interest of the company to prevent the leak from disseminating further information and in the good working relationships between its employees was held to justify the court order.[302] It should be noted that although the approach of the Court of Appeal to this case is similar to that of the House of Lords in the Morgan Grampian case, the Court of Appeal did consider the general impact on freedom of expression of such an order explicitly. I conclude therefore that freedom of expression is increasingly acknowledged as an opposing interest under s.10 of the Contempt of Court Act, and that the Act certainly offers sufficient possibilities to take consideration of this freedom, but that in those cases in which journalists relied on that section, the courts did not come to their aid by extending the room allowed for freedom of expression.

---

300 X Ltd v. Morgan Grampian [1991] 1 AC 1, per Lord Bridge at 43.
301 Camelot Group v. Centaur Ltd [1998] 1 All ER 251, CA.
302 Camelot Group v. Centaur Ltd [1998] 1 All ER 251, per Schiemann LJ. at 261.

7 PUBLIC ORDER ACT 1986[303]

7.1 Introduction

Beside the previously discussed areas of English law that touch upon freedom of expression, there is another aspect I wish to discuss, namely public order law. This area of law touches upon the public expression of thoughts, ideas and opinions when they are expressed by means of demonstrations or meetings. Several statutory regulations and common law provisions are important to this area of law. Under common law first of all the concept of 'breach of the peace' constitutes restrictions on freedom of expression. When there is 'reasonable apprehension of imminent danger of a breach of the peace' this brings with it a power to arrest for a police officer or a citizen.[304] It was held in Howell that 'we cannot accept that there can be a breach of the peace unless there has been an act done or threatened to be done which either actually harms a person, or in his presence his property, or is likely to cause such harm, or which puts someone in fear of such harm being done'. A requirement for a situation to constitute breach of the peace is that it involves 'immediate unlawful violence towards persons or property'.[305] Although this definition seems to indicate that a breach of the peace is not thought to occur too easily, the powers of arrest of the police have been used to such an extent that they were held to constitute a violation of Article 10 ECHR by the European Court of Human Rights.[306] The Court in Steel v. the United Kingdom determined that since it was not satisfied that the police had 'grounds reasonably to apprehend that the applicants' peaceful protest would cause a breach of the peace' the restriction of freedom of expression could not be considered 'prescribed by law'.[307] In addition

---

303 See on general information on all aspects of this Act: Card, Public Order the new law, 1987; Bailey, Harris and Jones, Civil Liberties, cases and materials, 1995, p. 166-263; Feldman, Civil Liberties and Human Rights in England and Wales, 1993, p. 802-842; Card, Cross and Jones, Criminal Law, 1995, p. 392-435.

304 R. v. Howell (1982) 1 QBR 416, QBD, at 417.

305 Also see Kistenkas, Vrije straatcommunicatie, de rol van de locale overheid bij de regulering van de uitingsvrijheid in rechtsvergelijkend perspectief, 1989, p. 120-121.

306 The broader definition of 'breach of the peace' given by Lord Denning in R. v. Chief Constable of Devon and Cornwall ex p. Central Electricity Generating Board (1982) 1 QBR 458 at 471, has not been followed in later cases. In this case he defined 'breach of the peace' as follows: 'There is a breach of the peace whenever a person who is lawfully carrying out his work is unlawfully and physically prevented by another from doing it'. Instead in Percy v. DPP (1995) 1 WLR 1382 the definition given in R. v. Howell was followed. As stated, in this case 'breach of the peace' was defined as: 'an act done or threatened to be done which actually harms a person, or in his presence his property, or is likely to cause such harm, or which puts someone in fear of such harm being done'.

307 Steel v. United Kingdom, 23 September 1998, Reports 1998-VII.

107

to the common law powers to prevent a breach of the peace there is a common law offence of public nuisance, which includes causing excessive noise and obstructing the highway. To constitute public nuisance, the misuse of a highway must amount to 'unreasonable use'.[308] This 'unreasonableness' was assumed to be established if it could be shown that passage was obstructed.[309] Consequently any blocking of passage will suffice to constitute public nuisance.

Under statute law, for example, the Highways Act 1980 criminalises the wilful obstruction of free passage along a highway. However, the most important example of public order regulation is the Public Order Act 1986.[310] This Act governs both the message and the manner in which it is delivered. It governs a very wide range of behaviour and under this Act the powers of the police to intervene in public forms of expression were extended considerably compared to the Public Order Act 1936.

This section is not intended to give a complete overview of public order law, but is meant to give an impression of the impact it may have on freedom of expression, of the manner in which the government in its legislation and the courts in applying this legislation, take consideration of this freedom in relation to the maintenance of public order. I focus on the Public Order Act 1986 to establish this. Part I of the Act criminalises six forms of conduct, namely riot, violent disorder, affray, causing fear or provocation of violence, causing intentional harassment, alarm or distress and finally causing harassment, alarm or distress. Part II of the 1986 Act deals with requirements and demands that can be made with regard to the conduct of assemblies and processions.[311] These sections require advance notice of public processions, give the possibility to prohibit public processions and create the power to impose conditions on public assemblies. The role of the police in deciding what measures will be necessary to maintain public order is remarkable. The decision whether one of the measures possible under Part II is necessary is completely in the hands of the police. They are thought to be in the best position to determine this necessity. Local authorities do not play a part in restricting freedom of expression by regulating

---

308 Bailey, Harris and Jones, Civil Liberties cases and materials, 1995, p. 183.

309 Hubbard v. Pitt [1976] 1 QB 142, CA, per Forbes J.

310 From 1980 on there was pressure to reform the law related to public order. See for a short overview Richard Card, Public Order the New Law, p. 4-5. The main reason for the call for reform was not the disorder in public order law, but a number of protests and strikes that had got severely out of hand (see Ewing and Gearty, Freedom under Thatcher, 1990, p. 113-128). The question was how public order law should be altered to be able to prevent such situations, should they occur again. A report on this matter was made and the conclusion was that 'reform was required to provide the police with adequate powers to deal with disorder, or where possible to prevent it before it occurs, in order to protect the rights and freedoms of the wider community'. The law was considered 'complex and fragmented and it was necessary to bring up to date the age-old balance between fundamental but sometimes competing rights in our society'. From: Gearty, Freedom of assembly and public order, 1994, p. 52. Gearty cited from Review of Public Order Law (The White Paper).

311 Extended by the Criminal Justice and Public Order Act 1994.

demonstrations or assemblies, with the exception of the making of banning orders on request of the chief of police.[312] Finally, part III of the Act criminalises incitement to racial hatred.

In this section I focus on the offences of the first part of the Public Order Act 1986 and on the extension of these offences to the offence of incitement to racial hatred in Part III. In general, the provisions of part II are not discussed. I make an exception, however, for the offence of trespassory assembly. The scope of this offence has been widened to an extent that the possible impact on the content of expressions is such that it justifies separate discussion.

I limit the examination of public order offences to causing fear of provocation of violence, causing intentional harassment, alarm or distress, causing harassment, alarm or distress, incitement to racial hatred and trespassory assembly. These five offences are concerned with the content of expressions. First, however, I make some remarks about violent conduct and freedom of expression. The offences of riot, violent disorder and affray, also adopted in part I of the Act, concern violent conduct. Violence may be regarded as expression, society is in general protected from this form of expression.

The question whether or not the English courts assume violence to be a form of expression has not been answered explicitly. In R. v. Caird several applicants were convicted of riot and unlawful assembly because of serious disorder that occurred at a Greek dinner held in a hotel in Cambridge. At this time the Greek government was

---

312 Although the power to make by-laws has been conferred on local governments, the subjects which the local authorities are allowed to regulate are mainly limited to issues of planning, housing, education and public health. The power to make a by-law must have explicit authority in an Act of Parliament and this power may only be used for the goal for which it was granted. Local government has a very limited role in the regulation of public order, although the rather general by-law making power conferred by section 235 of the Local Government Act 1972 does include some aspects that could be regarded as public order issues. This section enables the councils of districts and London boroughs to make by-laws 'for good rule and government of the whole or part of the district or borough, ..., and for the prevention and suppression of nuisances therein' (s. 235(1)). This by-law covers amongst others the topics of 'music near houses, churches and hospitals', 'wireless loudspeakers', 'indecent language', 'nuisances contrary to public decency', 'flags'. This section however, can probably not be used in relation to the public expression of opinion through demonstrations and assemblies. The power was not granted to the local authorities for that purpose. See also Cross and Bailey, Cross on local government law, 1986.
See also Kistenkas, Vrije straatcommunicatie, 1989, p. 117-118, where he remarks that local authorities do have some influence on freedom of expression. They have for instance the competence to grant building-licences for dishes and antennas. Such a licence could be refused because of the dish being too big or too conspicuous, consequently influencing the free reception of information. However, whether or not the refusal influences freedom of expression is not a matter of concern to the local authority in question, nor to the courts. The refusal to grant the licence was an intra vires decision as long as the local authority stayed within the powers granted to it by Act of Parliament.

unpopular in radical circles.[313] In this case, Sachs LJ. stated: 'Any suggestion that a section of the community strongly holding one set of views is justified in banding together to disrupt the lawful activities of a section that does not hold the same views so strongly or which holds different views cannot be tolerated and must unhesitatingly be rejected by the courts. When there is wanton and vicious violence of gross degree the Court is not concerned with whether it originates from gang rivalry or from political motives. It is the degree of mob violence that matters and the extent to which the public peace is being broken'.[314] This statement as such does not seem to exclude violence from the scope of freedom of expression.

This approach was confirmed in Kamara v. DPP. In this case a group of students from Sierra Leone occupied the premises in London of the High Commission of Sierra Leone with 'the object to gain publicity for their political grievances'. One member of the staff was threatened with an imitation gun and a large part of the staff was locked in a room. The students were amongst other things convicted of unlawful assembly 'with intent to carry out a common purpose in such a manner as to endanger the public peace'.[315] The important issue in this case is that it was decided that unlawful assembly could also threaten the public peace when conducted on a private premises. In this judgment freedom of expression was not explicitly considered, but the thoughts and feelings behind the action were. Lord Hailsham stated the following: 'they acted from a genuine sense of grievance. The father of at least one of them was, we were told, under sentence of death at the time of the alleged offence, and all appear genuinely to have believed that the government in power in their country, though recognised by her Majesty's Government here, was arbitrary, tyrannical and unconstitutional. We, of course, are not concerned with these matters, and, whatever the result of this appeal, it is not possible to approve their actions'.[316] Again the behaviour was not excluded from the scope of freedom of expression.

However, both cases made clear that once the scope of the offence was determined, whether or not the offence restricted freedom of expression was no longer important. Any interest in freedom of expression should have been considered by the legislature. The courts only apply the legislation that is the result of the considerations of the legislature. In Brutus v. Cozens Lord Reid formulated it as follows: 'Parliament had to solve the difficult question how far freedom of speech or behaviour must be limited in the general public interest. It would have been going much too far to prohibit all speech or conduct likely to occasion a breach of the peace because determined opponents may not shrink from organising or at least threatening

---

313 Wade and Bradley, Constitutional and Administrative Law, 1993, p. 550.
314 R. v. Caird 91970) 54 Cr App R 499, CA, at 506.
315 Kamara and others v. DPP [1974] AC 104, HL.
316 Kamara and others v. DPP [1974] AC 104 at 114.

a breach of the peace in order to silence a speaker whose views they detest. Therefore vigorous and it may be distasteful or unmannerly speech or behaviour is permitted so long as it does not go beyond any one of three limits. It must not be threatening. It must not be abusive. It must not be insulting'.[317]

The 1986 Act, in which provisions dealing with three forms of unlawful violence were adopted, does not provide for any justification which could create some room for freedom of expression with regard to the offences involving violent behaviour. As I said, a more relevant restriction on the content of freedom of expression is established by the offences of causing fear or provocation of violence, causing intentional harassment, alarm or distress, causing harassment, alarm or distress, incitement to racial hatred and trespassory assembly.

I first discuss the conduct that is prohibited by these offences. Subsequently I examine the role freedom of expression plays with regard to the provisions in the Act and the subsequent case law in the third subsection.

7.2 Offences against the Public Order

Fear or Provocation of Violence and Causing (Intentional) Harassment, Alarm or Distress

The use of threatening, abusive or insulting words or behaviour is criminalised in s.4, 4A and 5 of the Public Order Act 1986. This behaviour constitutes an offence if it causes fear or provocation of violence (s.4),[318] intentional harassment, alarm or distress (s.4A)[319] or harassment, alarm or distress (s.5),[320] These offences replaced and extended the offence under s.5 of the Public Order Act 1936, in which it was held to be an offence to use threatening, abusive or insulting words or behaviour with intent to provoke a breach of the peace or whereby a breach of the

---

317 Brutus v. Cozens [1972] 2 All ER 1297, HL, at 1299-1300.

318 S.4(1): 'A person is guilty of fear or provocation of violence if he (a) uses towards another person threatening, abusive or insulting words or behaviour, or (b) distributes or displays to another person any writing, sign or other visible representation which is threatening, abusive or insulting, with intent to cause that person to believe that immediate unlawful violence will be used against him or another by any person, or to provoke the immediate use of unlawful violence by that person or another, or whereby that person is likely to believe that such violence will be uses or it is likely that such violence will be provoked'.

319 S.4A(1): 'A person is guilty of an offence if, with intent to cause a person harassment, alarm or distress, he (a) uses threatening, abusive or insulting words or behaviour, or (b) displays any writing, sign or other visible representation which is threatening, abusive or insulting, thereby causing that or another person harassment, alarm or distress'.

320 S.5(1): 'A person is guilty of an offence if he (a) uses threatening, abusive or insulting words or behaviour, or disorderly behaviour, or (b) displays any writing, sign or other visible representation which is threatening, abusive or insulting, within the hearing or sight of a person likely to be caused harassment, alarm or distress thereby'.

peace was likely to be occasioned. Consequently 'breach of the peace' has been replaced in s.4 by 'likely to provoke violence', in s.4A by 'causing harassment, alarm or distress' and in s.5 by 'likely to cause harassment, alarm or distress'. This is a significant extension of s.5 of the 1936 Act and may form a serious restriction on freedom of expression. S.5(3) of the 1986 Act, different from the old s.5, provides for a number of defences. If the accused can prove: '(a) that he had no reason to believe that there was any person within hearing or sight who was likely to be caused harassment, alarm or distress, or (b) that he was inside a dwelling and had no reason to believe that his behaviour would be heard or seen by a person outside that or any other dwelling, or (c) that his conduct was reasonable'.

Incitement to Racial Hatred
The use of threatening, abusive and insulting words or behaviour or the display of any written material which is threatening, abusive or insulting constitutes a separate offence if it is intended to stir up racial hatred or if it is likely to stir up racial hatred.[321] In the same manner the publishing of threatening ... written material (s.19) and the possession of racially inflammatory material have been criminalised (s.23). Sections 18 and 19 replace the old s.5A of the Public Order Act 1936.[322] S.23 makes it possible to prosecute manufacturers or suppliers of racially inflammatory material. Racially inflammatory material is 'written material which is threatening, abusive or insulting, or a recording of visual images or sounds which are threatening, abusive or insulting' (s.23(1)).

Trespassory Assembly
S.14(A) of the Public Order Act 1986 provides: 'If at any time the chief officer of police reasonably believes that an assembly is intended to be held in any district at a place on land to which the public has no right of access or only a limited right of access and that the assembly (a) is likely to be held without the permission of the occupier of the land or to conduct itself in such a way as to exceed the limits of an permission of his or the public's right of access (b) may result (i) in serious disruption to the life of the community ... he may apply to the council of the district for an order prohibiting for a specified period the holding of all trespassory assemblies in the district or a part of it, as specified'. In s.14(B) the 'Offences in

---

321 Under s.31 of the Crime and Disorder Act 1998 racially aggravated offences under s.4, s.4A and s.5 of the Public Order Act 1986 have also been separately criminalized. This Act aims to ensure that high priority is given by both public authorities and the courts to the racial element of a crime, also in the sentencing. Amongst other things, it lowers the standard of proof for the prosecution to show racial motivation.

322 Inserted by s. 70 of the Race Relations Act 1976.

connection with trespassory assemblies and arrest therefore' are adopted.[323] Assembly has been defined as 'an assembly of 20 or more persons'.[324] This rather wide power of the chief officer of police primarily has great impact on freedom of expression of roadprotesters.

7.3 Influence of Freedom of Expression

Fear or Provocation of Violence and Causing (Intentional) Harassment, Alarm or Distress

The behaviour that forms the centre of all three offences is the use of 'threatening, abusive or insulting words or behaviour'. The sections of the Act do not provide for specific possibilities to consider freedom of expression. Subsequently the decisions on the behaviour that is held to constitute threatening, abusive and insulting speech is decisive for the extent of the restriction on freedom of expression. The first question to be answered now is whether freedom of expression has been taken account of in the interpretation of the wording of the offence. In Brutus v. Cozens the approach to freedom of expression in public order cases was indicated. Lord Reid in this case was of the opinion that freedom of expression was not restricted by prohibiting threatening, abusive and insulting speech.[325] In the case of Brutus v. Cozens it was held that the word 'insult' should be given its ordinary meaning.[326] In this case a tennis-match on the courts of Wimbledon was disrupted by the appellant who went on to the court when a South African player was on it. 'He blew a whistle and threw leaflets about', in protest against the apartheid policy of the South African government. The House of Lords held he was not guilty of an offence under s 5a of the Public Order Act 1936. Initially he was thought to be guilty of insulting behaviour since it had 'affronted other people, or evidenced a disrespect for their rights so as to give rise to resentment or protest on their part'. The House of Lords held, however, that behaviour that causes anger or distress is not enough to constitute an insult.

This approach did not diminish the application of these offences, although the topic of the expression might be of influence. It has been held to be an insult, for instance, when a person made homosexual advances towards another person present in a public lavatory 'by making indecent gestures and masturbating while looking at'

---

323 Trespass means to enter another person's land unlawfully, in other words without their permission.

324 S.14(A)(9) Public Order Act 1986.

325 Brutus v. Cozens [1972] 2 All ER 1297, at 1300: 'Free speech is not impaired by ruling them out', them meaning the words or behaviour within the limits set by threatening, abusive or insulting.

326 All three words 'threatening, abusive or insulting' are meant to have their ordinary meaning, that is the meaning they would have according to a reasonable member of the public; See Brutus v. Cozens [1972] 2 All ER 1297 and also Card, Cross and Jones, Criminal Law, p. 400.

the other person. The other person in this particular case was a 'plain clothes police officer'. It was held: '... as the person importuned by each appellant might have been an ordinary heterosexual person using the lavatory for normal purposes and might have been insulted by the appellants' behaviour because it was tantamount to a statement by the appellant that he believed the other person to be a homosexual, the behaviour of each appellant could fairly be regarded as being potentially insulting, and therefore constituting insulting behaviour ...'.[327]

This offence has been held to be governed by the rule that a speaker 'must take his audience as he finds it'.[328] This rule implies that the behaviour does not have to be threatening, abusive or insulting towards a person of reasonably firm character. If the audience is insulted, then the behaviour is insulting. Consequently it will be no defence to claim that the reaction of the audience was unreasonable.[329] In the above-mentioned case, the audience happened to be a police officer. Power of arrest is apparently instigated by chances of the audience being extremely susceptible to insults of a sexual kind.

The interpretation of the offences does not seem overly restrictive. This approach was confirmed with regard to the meaning of aspects of s.4. With regard to this particular offence, it has been held that it has to be likely for the person at whom the behaviour is directed to believe that 'immediate unlawful violence' will be used or provoked, instead of merely 'unlawful violence'.[330] The court came to this conclusion by referring to the section in the Law Commission's report on this offence and reasoned: 'A ... very compelling reason for our conclusion on the correct construction of this subsection is that here we are construing a penal statute, of which there are, or may be, two possible readings. It is an elementary rule of statutory construction that, in a penal statute where there are two possible readings, the meaning which limits the scope of the offence thus created is that which the court should adopt'.[331] S.4 requires that threatening, abusive or insulting behaviour be used towards another person. In Atkin v. DPP it was held that the person towards

---

327 Parkin v. Norman [1982] 2 All ER 583, QBD. See also Masterson v. Holden [1986] 3 All ER 39, DC, where two men kissing and cuddling at 2 a.m. in a street, were convicted of insulting behaviour likely to cause a breach of the peace, because two men walking by with their girlfriends reacted aggressively to their behaviour.

328 Jordan v. Burgoyne [1963] 2 All ER 225: 'for the purposes of s.5 of the Public order Act 1936, a person had to take his audience as he found them and, if the words that he used to a particular audience, or part of it, were in fact likely to provoke a breach of the peace, then he would be guilty of an offence under s.5'.

329 See Bonner and Stone, the Public Order Act 1986; steps in the wrong direction?, 1987, p. 208.

330 R. v. Horseferry Road Metropolitan Stipendiary Magistrate, ex p. Siadatan [1991] 1 All ER 324.

331 R. v. Horseferry Road Magistrate, ex p. Siadatan [1991] 1 All ER 324 at 328. These considerations were all the more interesting because the 'immediacy' requirement did not exist under s.5 of the 1936 Act.

whom the threatening behaviour was used, must also be the person who was threatened.[332] This decision seems to create some room for words said in aggravation but not meant to be taken literally.[333]

Sections 4A and 5 of the Public Order Act 1986 criminalise the same behaviour as s.4. The difference between s.4A and s.5 lies in the consequences the behaviour is required to have. Under s.4A the behaviour only has to cause harassment, alarm or distress. Under s.5 the behaviour has to be 'likely' to cause harassment alarm of distress. S.5 therefore amounts to a specification of s.4A. In the discussion I focus on s.5.

In order to constitute an offence under s.5 as compared to s.4 some important differences exist with regard to the prohibited behaviour. Firstly the threatening, abusive or insulting behaviour does not have to be used towards another person, it only has to be used 'within the hearing or sight of a person'. Secondly, not only threatening abusive or insulting behaviour is criminalised, but also disorderly behaviour.[334] And lastly instead of causing or provoking immediate unlawful violence or fear of it, it suffices for the behaviour to be within the hearing or sight of a person 'likely to be caused harassment, alarm or distress' thereby. So even

---

332 Atkin v. DPP (1989) 89 Cr App R 199. In this case two customs officers and a bailiff went to a farm to recover outstanding tax. When the defendant made clear that he would not be able to pay the tax, the officers 'informed him that the bailiff would have to enter the farmhouse to distrain on his goods'. The defendant replied: 'if the bailiff gets out of the car he's a dead un'. The officers noted a gun in the house and then informed the bailiff of the threats. The bailiff consequently did not leave the car.
It was held that although the words were threatening, the behaviour of the defendant did not constitute an offence under s.4 because 'use towards another threatening words' means that 'the person against whom the words were used must perceive with his own senses the threatening words and behaviour' in other words it means 'uses in the presence of and in the direction of another person directly'.

333 Card, Cross and Jones, Criminal Law, 1995, on p. 401 make the following comment in relation to this: 'The insertion of "to another" after "distributes or displays" would equally seem to require that the written material be distributed or displayed directly to another, rather than simply being distributed (eg by leaflets being left lying around in a shopping centre) or displayed (eg by sticking a poster on a wall in the middle of the night). If this is correct, it means that writing graffiti on a wall or wearing a badge is unlikely, however threatening, abusive or insulting it may be, to result in a conviction for an offence under s.4; generally, the written material displayed will not be displayed to another in the sense outlined above. By contrast, handing out abusive leaflets to people in the street or carrying an insulting banner during a demonstration clearly involves distributing or displaying written material to another'.

334 In Chambers and Edwards v. DPP [1995] Crim LR 896, it was held that the words disorderly behaviour 'are to be treated as words in ordinary everyday use as part of the English language and given their normal meaning'. The Brutus v. Cozens approach is to be applied to these words as well.

though the interpretation of the wording is not extremely restrictive, the prohibited behaviour under s.5 may be extremely restrictive of freedom of expression.

Disorderly behaviour that causes distress to a person within hearing or sight constitutes an offence under s.5. The question is why this sort of behaviour was thought to be such a burden on society that freedom of expression could not prevail above the interest of society to be spared such expressions of opinion. A large part of political speech that will be done publicly, will be done because of disagreement with the current policy in that respect, therefore, this speech can in most cases be qualified as disorderly behaviour since it is likely to cause distress to at least some of the bystanders, also because it is probable that the speaker will look for an audience that can be converted.

The Government named some examples of conduct which this section was intended to control. These examples consisted mainly of minor acts of Hooliganism and anti-social behaviour.[335] However, a small number of examples are available, that show that the risk of this section being used to restrict unpopular expressions was not merely hypothetical. The section has been used against people wearing obscene T-shirts and hats,[336] against a man who had a birthday party for his son in his back garden where he played loud music, against two 19 year old males for kissing in the street, and 'in the so called Madame M case against four students who were in the process of putting up a satirical poster during the last general election. It depicted the Prime Minister as a sadistic dominatrix'.[337]

More recently, anti-abortion protesters have been prosecuted under s.5. These cases constitute more examples of how s.5 interferes with more than the conduct of hooligans knocking over dustbins. Demonstrators in front of an abortionclinic in one case shouted slogans, waved banners and prevented staff and patients from entering the clinic, which distressed some of the patients,[338] and in another case shouted and talked to persons attending the clinic, displaying plastic models of human foetuses, photographs of dead foetuses and placards.[339] In the first case the conduct of the

---

335 See Bailey, Harris and Jones, Civil Liberties, cases and materials, 1995, p. 228, Ewing and Gearty, Freedom under Thatcher, 1990, p. 122 and Card, Public Order the new law, 1987, p. 47-48: The specifically mentioned examples were: Rowdy behaviour in the streets late at night which alarms local residents; someone turning out the lights in a crowded dance hall, in a way likely to cause panic; groups of youths persistently shouting abuse and obscenities or pestering people waiting to catch public transport or to enter a hall or cinema; hooligans on housing estates causing disturbances in the common parts of blocks of flats, blockading entrances, throwing things down the stairs, banging on doors, peering in at windows and knocking over dustbins (taken from White Paper, paras 3.22 and 3.25).

336 Ewing and Gearty, Freedom under Thatcher, 1990, p. 122.

337 Bailey, Harris and Jones, Civil Liberties, cases and materials, 1995, p. 229.

338 Morrow, Geach and Thomas v. DPP [1994] Crim LR 58.

339 DPP v. Fidler and Moran [1992] Crim LR 62, QBD. The actual decisions of both cases are not in my possession. The comments on these cases are based on their discussion in the Crim LR. I

demonstrators was thought to be disorderly within the meaning of s.5(1)(a) and in the second case the behaviour was thought to cause harassment, alarm or distress. Whether or not the accused in these cases were actually convicted depended on other aspects of the case, namely whether one of the possible defences could be established.

Maybe in reaction to the possible overly restrictive effect of this offence on freedom of expression, s.5(3), unlike the case with the offences under s.4, offers three defences. I recapitulate: if the accused can prove (a) that he had no reason to believe that there was any person within hearing or sight who was likely to be caused harassment, alarm or distress, or (b) that he was inside a dwelling and had no reason to believe that his behaviour (...) would be heard or seen by a person outside that or any other dwelling, or (c) that his conduct was reasonable. The defence under s.5(3)(a) that the accused had no reason to believe that there was anyone within hearing or sight who was likely to be caused harassment, alarm or distress may offer 'some protection against over-sensitivity of others'.[340] However, as soon as it has been pointed out to a person that someone within hearing or sight may be caused harassment, alarm or distress by his conduct, this defence will no longer be applicable.[341]

Under s.5(3)(c), the accused has not committed an offence under s.5 if he can prove that his conduct was reasonable. In DPP v. Clarke, Lewis, O'Connell and O'Keefe the approach to the 'reasonable behaviour' defence was specified. In this case also, the accused also demonstrated in front of an abortion-clinic. They were carrying pictures of aborted foetuses. The persons being caused alarm and distress by the display of these pictures, however, were the police officers, who had requested the demonstrators not to show the pictures. The Queen's Bench Divisional Court held that the magistrate had been correct in responding to the claim of the accused that their behaviour had been reasonable by applying an objective test (their state of mind was of no relevance) and was correct in concluding that the behaviour of the respondent had not been reasonable. In applying the reasonable test in Morrow, Geach and Thomas v. DPP it was held that 'all the circumstances which might indicate the reason for such behaviour' have to be taken into account. 'The sincerity of the appellants' views' seemed to be of importance in relation to this, however, sincerity as such did not make the conduct reasonable.[342] Some subjectivity was incorporated into the reasonableness test, but its impact was limited. Freedom of

---

assume that in the first case the behaviour is also 'likely to cause harassment, alarm or distress' and that the behaviour in the second case is also 'threatening, abusive or insulting' or can be regarded as being 'disorderly behaviour'. If it were otherwise, the 'reasonableness' issue would not have to be dealt with.

340 Feldman, Civil Liberties and Human Rights in England and Wales, 1993, p. 809.
341 Feldman, Civil Liberties and Human Rights in England and Wales, 1993, p. 809.
342 See Morrow, Geach and Thomas v. DPP [1994] Crim LR 58.

expression therefore also may have only limited influence on whether certain behaviour constitutes an offence under s.5.

One other possibility to provide some protection for freedom of expression remains. S.5, like the other offences of part I of the Public Order Act 1986, is open to the defence that if a person did not intend his conduct to be threatening, abusive or insulting or was not aware that it may be threatening, abusive or insulting, he is not guilty of an offence under s.5.[343] The 'intent' and the 'awareness' were meant subjectively. The prosecution must prove that the accused was aware of the threatening, abusive, or insulting nature of his conduct.[344] On applying a subjective test in DPP v. Clarke, Lewis, O'Connell and O'Keefe, the magistrates concluded: 'on the balance of probabilities none of the respondents intended the pictures to be threatening abusive or insulting, nor was any of them aware that they might be'.[345] Therefore the conduct could not constitute an offence under s.5. What was said in relation to the defence under s.5(3)(a) is also applicable here: 'the respondents are now aware of the insulting and abusive effect which the pictures may have on those to whom they are displayed so that, if they do it again, they may well be found to have the requisite awareness'.[346] The defences seem to offer only limited protection to freedom or expression.

The drafting of s.5 is much wider than would be necessary to guarantee the goal for which the section was drafted, namely minor acts of hooliganism by which 'the public' feels threatened or even merely annoyed. Consequently, as Ewing and Gearty said: 'It is likely that the section will be used to criminalise the unusual. ... In s.5 we have a mechanism for punishing non-violent nonconformity for the crime of being itself'.[347] Despite the scope of s.5 only limited possibilities to prevent such excessive use of the section have been provided for. Beside what this section could be used for it is interesting to see what this section is actually being used for. Research conducted during 1990 actually shows that nearly 25% of all s.5 cases involved the use of abusive or threatening words directed solely at the police.[348]

In DPP v. Orum it was decided that 'a police officer is capable of being a person likely to be caused harassment, alarm or distress by threatening, abusive or insulting words or behaviour'.[349] This made clear that if a police officer is the only person at which the threatening or abusive words are directed this may also constitute an

---

343 S.6(4) Public Order Act 1986.
344 See Feldman, Civil Liberties and Human Rights in England and Wales, 1993, p. 808.
345 DPP v. Clarke, Lewis, O'Connell and O'Keefe [1992] Crim LR 60.
346 DPP v. Clarke, Lewis, O'Connell and O'Keefe [1992] Crim LR 60, commentary.
347 Ewing and Gearty, Freedom under Thatcher, 1990, p. 123.
348 Criminalizing Disrespect, 1995, p. 98, in which Brown and Ellis, Policing low-level disorder: Police use of s.5 of the Public Order Act 1986 was discussed. This is a report of a study of the use of section 5 in six police forces during 1990.
349 DPP v. Orum [1988] 3 All ER 449, QBD.

offence under s.5. With this decision, the idea of this section protecting the public was abandoned. A significant consequence of this approach is that after issuing a warning, the police officer will have the power to arrest. In DPP v. Orum, however, the applicability of s.5 with regard to behaviour directed at police officers was differentiated: 'Very frequently, words and behaviour with which police officers will be wearily familiar will have little emotional impact on them save that of boredom'. Whether or not a police officer was actually caused harassment, alarm or distress 'is a question of fact for the magistrates to decide having regard to all the circumstances: the time, the place, the nature of the words used, who the police officers are and so on'. Judging from the results of the above mentioned study, however, police officers are apparently not easily bored.

Incitement to Racial Hatred

The use of threatening, abusive and insulting words or behaviour or the display of any written material which is threatening, abusive or insulting constitutes a separate offence under s.18 of the Public Order Act 1986, if it is intended to stir up racial hatred or if it is likely to stir up racial hatred. S.19 makes it an offence to publish or distribute material of such content.

Racial hatred is defined as 'hatred against a group of persons in Great Britain defined by reference to colour, race, nationality (including citizenship) or ethnic or national origins' (s.17) called a 'racial group'. Of importance to the extent of the offence is how the term racial group is defined. In Mandla v. Dowell Lee, 'racial group' was defined by reference to 'ethnic origins', and a group was considered to have 'ethnic origins' if it had 'a long shared history of which the group was conscious as distinguishing it form other groups, and the memory of which it kept alive and second it had to have a cultural tradition of its own, including family and social customs and manners, often but not necessarily associated with religious observance'.[350] According to this standard Sikhs were thought to constitute a racial group[351] as well as gipsies,[352] but rastafarians were not.[353] Interestingly a religious group is not automatically a racial group. However, it may be a 'racial group'. Where the offence of blasphemy does not offer protection to other than Christian believers, this offence may, if the words used are threatening, abusive or insulting and these words concern e.g. Jews or Arabs (as opposed to the Jewish or Muslim religion). In relation to this I wish to note that if racist speech does not stir up racial hatred in the meaning of part III of the Act or if the group concerned cannot

---

350 Mandla v. Dowell Lee [1983] 1 All ER 1062, HL.
351 Mandla v. Dowell Lee [1983] 1 All ER 1062.
352 Commission for Racial Equality v. Dutton [1989] 1 All ER 306, CA.
353 Dawkin v. Department of the Environment [1989] NLJ 610, CA.

be considered a 'racial group', and the words used are threatening, abusive or insulting, the previously discussed s.5 may be applicable.

It is remarkable is that it is not necessary to intend to stir up racial hatred. It suffices that the words used are likely to stir up racial hatred. The old s.5A already held that subjective intent was not a requirement to constitute an offence under that section.[354] The conduct merely had to be objectively likely to stir up racial hatred. This aspect of the offences under part III remained unchanged and forms a significant restriction on freedom of expression.

Moreover, it is prohibited to express views in a manner that may constitute the offence under s.18 in a private place, with the exception of a dwelling, even if everyone present shares these views. Similarly the publication or distribution of written material to members of an organisation to which the publisher or distributor belongs is prohibited conduct under s.19.[355] This was considered justified by the government since '... it is possible that even those who already hold racialist views may be incited or incited further to racial hatred. ... The Government sees no justification for allowing material to be circulated privately when it would be open to prosecution if circulated more generally and may have the same effect in both cases'.[356] Accordingly, such behaviour under s.18 was probably prohibited in order to prevent the people present from taking action on the ideas expressed.[357] Under the old s.5A such conduct was not prohibited. This exemption was intended to protect freedom of expression within a group holding particular views.[358] Feldman noted that these provisions constitute a serious interference with freedom of expression: 'Any attempt to give practical expression to hatred outside is likely to constitute an offence, so it is particularly draconian to impose liability at the preattempt stage on words or conduct which might not even amount to an incitement to commit an offence'.[359]

In relation to the offences of part III of the Public Order Act 1986, (subjective) intent is not required. S.19 even takes it a step further. If a person intends to incite racial hatred but his conduct is not likely to have this consequence he will still be guilty of the offence. The government made the following comments in relation to this: 'One area in which difficulties have been experienced with s.5A is where circulation of the material is to selected groups of people, such as clergymen or Members of Parliament who might be thought unlikely to be incited to racial

---

354 Card, Public Order, the new law, 1987, p. 94.
355 See Bailey, Harris and Jones, Civil Liberties, cases and materials, 1995, p. 667.
356 Bailey, Harris and Jones, Civil Liberties, cases and materials, 1995, p. 667 (from the White Paper).
357 See also Feldman, Civil Liberties and Human Rights in England and Wales, 1993, p. 811.
358 Card, Public Order, the new law, 1987, p. 105.
359 Feldman, Civil Liberties and Human Rights in England and Wales, 1993, p. 812.

hatred'.[360] This is interesting because when a person can ask his MP in reasonable terminology, for instance, by handing or sending him a pamphlet, to please take care that no more immigrants enter the country, his request will most likely not constitute an offence under s.18 or 19. If the words used are threatening abusive or insulting, however, which may relatively easily be the case with less eloquent persons, it will be an offence. The justification for criminalizing such communications seems rather far-fetched: 'The public order consideration is relevant here since the material may well find its way to other, less equable, audiences, although no directly distributed to them, and its effect may be to stir up racial hatred'. This provision constituted a change with the situation under the Public Order Act 1936. This becomes apparent from the case of R. v. Britton, in which the example of the MP in fact occurred. In this case a 17 year old boy left 5 or 6 pamphlets in and around the house of an MP. These pamphlets read: 'Blacks not wanted here'. The boy was not found guilty of incitement to racial hatred under s.6(1)(a) of the Race Relations Act 1965 since distribution of this kind could not be considered distribution to 'the public at large'. In this case the court had the following final consideration: 'Finally the court would like to say that it seems difficult to believe that Parliament ever intended that there should be any distribution within the meaning of this section by leaving a pamphlet of this sort with a member of Parliament with the object of persuading him to change his policy, and fight against allowing immigrants to come into the country'.[361] In this formulation 'the circulation of the material to selected groups of people' did not seem to be regarded as a problem but more as a possibility people should have. Under the new Act this was changed, constituting a significant restriction on freedom of expression. Similar to s.5 there is no defence available by way of which this impact could be softened.

Trespassory Assembly
Although trespassory assembly does not concern the content of freedom of expression and therefore strictly speaking has no place in the discussion of legal restrictions on freedom of expression, I still discuss the offence in this subsection. I feel its discussion is justified, because the possible application of it has recently been widened to such an extent that it no longer only constitutes a restriction on freedom of assembly. As shows from the discussion on this offence, its extent is such that it forms a significant restriction on freedom of expression as well. Under the offence of trespassory assembly, police can ban groups of 20 or more meeting in a particular area if they fear 'serious disruption to the life of the community'.[362] The exact

---

360 Bailey, Harris and Jones, Civil Liberties, cases and materials, 1995, p. 666 (citation from the White Paper).
361 R. v. Britton [1967] 1 All ER 486, CA, at 488.
362 S.14(A) Public Order Act 1986, a new offence brought in by way of the Criminal Justice and

scope of the interference with freedom of assembly but also freedom of expression became clear from the recent case of DPP v. Jones.[363] In this case an order was made under s.14(A) of the Public Order Act, prohibiting the holding of trespassory assemblies within a four-miles radius of Stonehenge from 29 May to 1 June 1995. On 1 June a group of 21 people gathered near Stonehenge to commemorate the 10th Anniversary of the 'Battle of the Beanfield' demonstration. The High Court admitted that the gathering was peaceful, that is non-violent and non-obstructive, but nonetheless such protests on public highways could be banned by the police in order to curb protests on public roads. A peaceful demonstration was held not to amount to a reasonable right of passage of the highway. Consequently the broad powers of the police under the Public Order Act can seriously affect all kinds of protest. The defendants appealed to the House of Lords which allowed the appeal. A three to two majority held that reasonable activities on the public highway 'provided that these activities are reasonable, do not involve the commission of a public or private nuisance, and do not amount to an obstruction of the highway unreasonably impeding the primary right of the general public to pass and repass, they should not constitute a trespass'.[364] Consequently the broad terms of the decision of the High Court were rejected by the House of Lords. Instead, within the conditions formulated by Lord Irvine of Lairg there is a right of peaceful assembly on the highway. Lord Hutton also allowed the appeal but emphasised that his opinion was 'based on the finding of the Crown Court that the assembly in which the appellants took place on this particular highway, the A344, at this particular time, constituted a reasonable use of the highway. I would not hold that a peaceful and non-obstructive public assembly on a highway is always a reasonable use and is therefore not a trespass'. It is for the tribunal of fact to determine whether the assembly was 'reasonable'. Subsequently, under certain circumstances, a peaceful assembly could be considered a trespassory assembly according to the House of Lords. Again, freedom of expression and the considerable impact this approach to the offence of trespassory assembly may have on it was not considered with regard to the extension of the offence. The use of the term 'reasonable' was not such that it provided for a defence in which the effect on that right could be limited.

One last concept of law requires discussion, before I can examine whether there is a common ground between the protection of freedom of expression under English law and its protection under Article 10 of the ECHR. This concept is judicial review, which I address in the next section of this chapter.

Public Order Act 1994.

363 DPP v. Jones [1997] 2 All ER 119, QBD.

364 DPP v. Jones [1999] 2 All ER 257, HL, per Lord Irvine of Lairg.

8 JUDICIAL REVIEW

8.1 Introduction

The discussion of several of the areas of law in previous sections of this chapter demonstrated that the scope of freedom of expression is greatly influenced by statutory interpretation. This occurs in relation to criminal and civil statutory law, but also with regard to administrative law, in which amongst others public authorities are granted powers that may restrict freedom of expression. Interpretation of the wording of statutory administrative law does not differ from the interpretation of civil or penal law. However, when by way of statute a discretionary decision-making power is granted, the interpretation of legislation can offer only limited protection to civil liberties. The exercise of discretionary power, however, can also be reviewed by the courts.[365] The extent of the protection of freedom of expression by the courts, depends on how they regard the task of reviewing decisions based on such powers. In this section I examine the characteristics of judicial review that are relevant to the protection of freedom of expression. Subsequently I discuss the role freedom of expression has played in the application of these characteristics by the courts.

8.2 Characteristics

Under English law, pursuant to statutory legislation certain bodies or persons are given decision-making powers. These powers are not unlimited and the courts have a function in ensuring that these 'statutory powers are not usurped, exceeded or abused, and that procedural and substantive duties owed to the public are duly performed'.[366] What is stressed in most academic writings on judicial review is that it is a supervisory jurisdiction. As opposed to appellate procedures before the courts, in exercising judicial review the courts do not substitute their opinion for that of the decision-maker. The courts do not have jurisdiction to adjudicate upon the merits of the decision, it merely reviews whether or not the manner in which the decision was reached was appropriate. In exercising judicial review the courts observe an attitude of judicial self-restraint. Besides the scope of the review also the criteria of review are limited. I elaborate on these aspects separately.

a Judicial Self-Restraint
The extent to which judicial review may offer protection to fundamental rights depends on the scope of the review. As I observed, this scope is limited because the courts apply judicial self-restraint. This means that in reviewing a decision they will

---

365 The rules regulating the powers of review of the courts are governed by common law.
366 Jones and Thompson, Garner's Administrative Law, 1996, p. 162.

not decide on the merits of a decision. The traditional test that was accepted by the English courts to review decisions of the executive based on discretionary powers, is Wednesbury review. This review is also called the test of Wednesbury unreasonableness and was formulated by Lord Greene in Associated Provincial Picture Houses Ltd v. Wednesbury Corporation, in which he said that 'although the local authorities have kept within the four corners of the matters which they ought to consider, they have nevertheless come to a conclusion so unreasonable that no reasonable authority could ever have come to it'.[367] The subsequent Wednesbury principles entail that the decision-making authority has a broad discretion regarding the facts and circumstances of the case which are taken into consideration before arriving at a decision, unless the statute formulated clear requirements regarding the factors that have to be taken into account.

The Wednesbury principles, however, do not only define the closeness of the scrutiny applied by the courts. They also formulate a substantive criterion, namely that of Wednesbury unreasonableness. This brings us to the second characteristic of judicial review, which is the grounds of review.

b Grounds of Review
Judicial review may concern itself with different aspects of the decision. Three grounds of review have been recognised. These three are: illegality, which requires the proper use of statutory powers; procedural fairness, concerning the procedural duties of the public authorities; and, finally, Wednesbury unreasonableness. Only the last one offers the courts a possibility of substantive review. It concerns the manner in which the facts and circumstances of the case are appreciated and the extent to which the courts formulate requirements as to the appreciation of the facts. This may concern the facts and circumstances that have to be considered and the weight subsequently given to them.

8.3 Influence of Freedom of Expression

I examine three cases that illustrate the manner in which the courts approach the review of the exercise of a decision-making power used in a way that restricts freedom of expression. The first of these is the case of Wheeler v. Leicester City Council.[368] In this case the Leicester council banned a local rugby club from using a recreation ground for matches and training, because three of the members of the club participated in a touring team that played in South Africa. It did this after the club had not given the desired answers to a number of questions related to the club's

---

367 Associated Provincial Picture Houses Ltd v. Wednesbury Corporation [1948] 1 KB 223, CA, at 233-234.
368 Wheeler v. Leicester City Council [1985] AC 1054, HL

position on apartheid and the efforts it would undertake to prevent its members from participating in the tour. The council felt it could exercise its discretionary powers in such a manner since it also saw as its duty the promotion of good race relations under section 71 of the Race Relations Act 1976.

The House of Lords unanimously decided that the decision to ban the club from using the recreation ground should be quashed. However, the manner in which they came to this unanimous decision differed greatly. Lord Templeman held that the Council could not use its statutory powers to punish the club 'when the club had done no wrong'.[369] Lord Roskill held: 'I greatly hesitate to differ from four learned judges on the Wednesbury issue but for myself I would have been disposed respectfully to do this and to say that the actions of the council were unreasonable in the Wednesbury sense. But even if I am wrong in this view, I am clearly of the opinion that the manner in which the council took that decision was in all the circumstances unfair ...'.[370] He held the decision of the council to be unreasonable because the club held a legitimate view yet was illegitimately pressured to make this opinion conform to that of the council through threatening sanctions. However, because the other Lords were unwilling to qualify Wednesbury unreasonableness as such, he turned his qualification of unreasonableness into a separate ground for quashing the decision by holding that 'the court should interfere because of the unfair manner in which the council set about obtaining its objective'.[371]

Lord Brown-Wilkinson, in his dissenting opinion of the case before the Court of Appeal, explicitly stated that the decision was not unreasonable on Wednesbury grounds. He called the decision a 'misuse of powers' and based his opinion directly on freedom of expression: 'The unlawfulness lies not in the basic views of the council but in their use of their powers so as to punish those who refuse to endorse those views, thereby interfering with the fundamental right of the club and its members to freedom of speech and conscience'.[372] Parliament did not expressly authorise the restriction of a fundamental right through the words of the Race Relations Act and therefore it could not be used in such a way. He consequently created protection for freedom of expression, not by reviewing the merits of the case, but by introducing the requirement of explicit restriction of freedom of expression in an Act of Parliament.

The fundamental rights aspect of this case was not explicitly mentioned by the House of Lords, although Lord Roskill came close to acknowledging that freedom of expression is a factor of influence in this case by stating that the rugby club is free (within limits) to hold a different opinion from that of the Council regarding race

---

369 Wheeler v. Leicester City Council [1985] AC 1054, at 1081.
370 Wheeler v. Leicester City Council [1985] AC 1054, per Lord Roskill at 1079.
371 Wheeler v. Leicester City Council [1985] AC 1054, at 1079.
372 Wheeler v. Leicester City Council [1985] AC 1054, per Brown-Wilkinson, CA at 1066.

relations. The House of Lords did feel that the position of the rugby club should be protected, but avoided running the risk of seriously changing the relation between the courts and decision-makers by evaluating the facts and circumstances of the case. They could have been held to have done this if they had reviewed the decision other than on Wednesbury-unreasonableness grounds. Instead concepts such as punishing without wrong and unfair means of obtaining an objective are used to quash the decision.[373] In this case the diversity of manners in which to protect freedom of expression by way of judicial review seemed to imply that the courts were looking for ways to offer protection, but that such a possibility was not provided for by law.

In the more recent Brind case, the House of Lords offered more clarity in this respect. The Brind case was an influential case in relation to the role of the courts in cases involving fundamental rights and freedom of expression in particular, because here the House of Lords was very outspoken on its attitude towards the issue of restriction of freedom of expression by way of the exercise of discretionary powers. This case dealt with the request of the Home Secretary to the independent broadcasters and the BBC to 'refrain from broadcasting any matter consisting of or including words spoken by persons appearing or being heard on programmes where such persons represented organisations proscribed under the Prevention of Terrorism Act or the Northern Ireland Act 1978 and certain other specified groups, or where the words spoken supported or invited support for such organisations'. This directive concerns amongst others Sinn Fein, Republican Sinn Fein and the Ulster Defence Association.[374] The government was of the opinion that terrorists survived by the 'oxygen of publicity' and should therefore be prevented from obtaining publication. The directives issued under the named provisions were supposed to deprive them of this oxygen.[375] The ban was issued in 1988 and was initially thought to prohibit the broadcasting of any statements from the spokesmen of terrorist organisations. As it turned out, once a commercial channel experimented with this method, the ban only prohibited the broadcasting of statements using the actual voices of the spokesmen.[376] This led to the situation that the person concerned was shown on television while the words he spoke were dubbed.

A number of journalists, among whom Brind, claimed before the courts that the issuing of the directives contravened Article 10 of the ECHR, that they conflicted with the broadcasters' duty to preserve due impartiality and that 'the directives were disproportionate to the mischief at which they were aimed, namely to prevent intimidation by or undeserved publicity and an appearance of political legitimacy for

---

373 Also see Jowell and Lester, Beyond Wednesbury: substantive principles of administrative law, 1987, p. 373.
374 Bailey, Harris and Jones, Civil Liberties, cases and materials, 1995, p. 339.
375 Robertson and Nicol, Media Law, 1992, p. 27.
376 Robertson and Nicol, Media Law, 1992, p. 27.

such organisations, and were unreasonable so as to amount to an unlawful exercise of the Secretary of State's powers'.[377] It was accepted by all Law Lords that the directive interfered with freedom of expression and that 'any restriction of the right of freedom of expression could only be justified by an important competing public interest'.[378] The House of Lords made clear, however, that it was of the opinion that its power to review the decision of the Secretary of State to issue directives under s.13(4) of the Licence and Agreement Act and s.29(3) of the Broadcasting Act 1981, was very limited.

It was emphasised that where it concerns an administrative discretion, the limits within which such a power must be exercised could not be set by the courts, let alone be held by the courts to have to be exercised within the limits set under the Convention. The position of freedom of expression was defined in relation to these considerations. Lord Bridge held: 'Thus, article 10(2) of the Convention spells out and categorises the competing public interests by reference to which the right to freedom of expression may have to be curtailed. In exercising the power of judicial review we have neither the advantage nor the disadvantages of any comparable code to which we may refer or by which we are bound. But again, this surely does not mean that in deciding whether the Secretary of State, in the exercise of his discretion, could reasonably impose the restriction he has imposed on the broadcasting organisations, we are not perfectly entitled to start from the premise that any restriction of the right to freedom of expression requires to be justified and that nothing less than an important competing public interest will be sufficient to justify it. The primary judgment as to whether the particular competing public interest justifies the particular restriction imposed falls to be made by the Secretary of State to whom Parliament has entrusted the discretion. But we are entitled to exercise a secondary judgment by asking whether a reasonable Secretary of State, on the material before him, could reasonably make that primary judgment'.[379]

Lord Templeman in his opinion also felt that a restriction of freedom of expression should be justifiable, but for the courts to determine whether this was the case he suggested to specify Wednesbury reasonableness by relying on concepts of the case law of the ECourtHR: '... the interference with freedom of expression must be necessary and proportionate to the damage which the restriction is designed to prevent'.[380] Lord Bridge rejected the possibility of applying the 'necessary in a

---

377 R. v. Secretary of State for the home department, ex p. Brind and others [1991] 1 A.C. 696, HL, at 696-697.

378 See for an extensive discussion of the Brind case: Thompson, Broadcasting and Terrorism in the House of Lords, 1991, p. 346.

379 R. Secretary of State for the Home Department ex p. Brind [1991] 1 AC 696, Lord Bridge at 748-749.

380 R. v. Secretary of State for the Home Department ex p. Brind [1991] 1 AC 696, per Lord Templeman at 751.

democratic society' test but still implicitly referred to the case law under the ECHR by requiring the decision-maker to exercise a balancing of interests. Lord Irvine of Lairg was of the opinion that if the review as suggested by Lord Bridge is exercised, this would require the decision-maker to acknowledge the fact that freedom of expression is an interest in the case at hand and then decide whether the public interest in restricting it is sufficiently important enough to justify restraint.[381]

In this case the remaining three Law Lords were not prepared to go as far as Lord Bridge but it was unanimously accepted that the directive prohibiting the use of spoken words of spokesmen of terrorist organisations interfered with freedom of expression and that 'any restriction of the right to freedom of expression could only be justified by an important competing public interest'. The substantive requirement of Wednesbury reasonableness was consequently specified, but the scope of the review of whether this requirement was met remained limited.

With regard to both the content of the requirements of review and the scope of review, the case of R. v. DPP ex p. Kebeline should also be mentioned. Although this case had no influence on freedom of expression the approach of both the Divisional Court and the House of Lords is interesting in the sense that it dealt with the discretionary power of the DPP to give his consent to a prosecution and that with regard to the review of the exercise of this power the Human Rights Act 1998 was referred to. In this case, the DPP gave such consent to charge amongst others Mr Kebeline with offences under s.16A of the Prevention of Terrorism Act 1989, which provides that 'a person is guilty of an offence if he has any article in his possession in circumstances giving rise to a reasonable suspicion that the article is in his possession for a purpose connected with the commission, preparation or instigation of acts of terrorism to which this section applies'. The respondents claimed that the exercise of this power violated Article 6 ECHR. The Divisional Court agreed under reference to the Human Rights Act 1998, which was not yet in force. The reverse legal burden on the defendants was held to violate Article 6 of the Convention, which gave rise to the legitimate expectation that the DPP would exercise his discretion in accordance with Article 6. The reason for this expectation can be found in s.6(1) of the Human Rights Act, which provides: 'It is unlawful for a public authority to act in a way which is incompatible with a Convention right'. For the DPP not to exercise his discretionary power in conformity with this obligation led to an 'abuse of power' according to the Divisional Court. A majority of the House of Lords rejected this approach however. It was held that the exceptional circumstances that need to exist to allow for judicial review of the decision of the DPP to prosecute did not exist in this case, since other legislation also has reverse legal burden provisions. Since the Human Rights Act was not yet law and even clearly showed the intention to postpone

---

381 Lord Irvine of Lairg, Judges and Decision-Makers, 1996, p. 64.

the coming into effect of the Act in s.22, it could be of no influence to the decision in this case. Moreover, it was held by Lord Hope of Craighead that on striking the balance between the general interest of the community and the protection of the fundamental rights of the individual, the reversed burden of proof is not necessarily in contradiction with the Convention. Noteworthy is that these considerations are not made with regard to the exercise of the discretionary power of the DPP, but with regard to s.6(1) of the Prevention of Terrorism Act. While the Divisional Court focused on the exercise of the power by the DPP, Lord Hope of Craighead focused on the legislation. What the approach would be towards an exercise of a discretionary power in violation of the Convention is not clear. Whether the extent of the review of the Divisional Court would be accepted after the Human Rights Act's entry into force, is not discussed.

9 PRELIMINARY CONCLUSIONS

In the previous sections, by means of discussion of a number of concepts of law, I gave an impression of the manner in which freedom of expression is shaped under English law. The scope of freedom of expression is first of all shaped by the legislation that restricts this freedom. Sometimes law implicitly takes account of freedom of expression by providing defences and exceptions that limit the scope of a restrictive law. Furthermore, the scope of the restrictive law is determined by the interpretation of it made by the courts. This concerns both the interpretation of the initially prohibited behaviour and the defences, exceptions and remedies that are provided for in relation to the offences, torts and obligations. The examination of the relevant case law shows that the courts do not only implicitly influence the scope of freedom of expression. Increasingly frequently, freedom of expression is part of their considerations in an explicit manner. Consequently, although freedom of expression is not protected by way of a defined right, the term 'protection' of freedom of expression is increasingly appropriate. It also noteworthy that, as decisions such as in the Derbyshire case, the case of A-G v. Guardian Newspapers and the Rantzen case demonstrate, the influence of the ECHR on the development of 'protection' of freedom of expression is significant.

Beside the resultant degree of protection of freedom of expression as such, it is important to note that this protection is determined mainly by the role the courts play in interpreting the legislation. With regard to the interpretation of the Public Order Act the courts were restrained in their interpretation of offences under the Act. They stuck to the meaning of the words of the offence and held that any influence by freedom of expression should have been considered by Parliament.[382] The courts

---

382 R. v. Horseferry Road Magistrate, ex p. Siadatan [1991] 1 All ER 324, QBD, at 328. See par. 6.2.

merely applied the result of those considerations. With regard to the Obscene Publications Act 1959 a similar approach was taken.[383] However, regarding the scope of civil libel[384] and the damages that could be awarded under libel law and in the application of the law governing breach of confidence, the courts were more active in their references to and taking account of Article 10 of the ECHR. Also in some recent contempt of court cases,[385] the courts allowed themselves more leeway in interpreting law in a manner more considerate of freedom of expression, which was influenced by the previous decisions in the libel and breach of confidence cases.

At this stage, I have only made a cursory mention of some examples; a more in-depth discussion takes place in part II of this book. They demonstrate, however, that the courts are starting to take a more active approach towards the protection of freedom of expression in the application of common law and equity and in their discretionary powers and that such approaches subsequently may spread to the interpretation of statutory legislation.

In this chapter, an indication was given of the approach of the courts to this freedom. The exact methods applied by the courts to take freedom of expression into consideration were not elaborated on. In that regard I wish to remind the reader that the purpose of this study was to formulate a common ground that may exist between the protection of freedom of expression under English law and under the ECHR. This implies that I search for a common ground between the approach to the notion of freedom of expression, and also between the methods of protection applied by the European Court of Human Rights and the methods applied by the English courts. In chapter III, I supplied the material for such a search in English law. I do not give a comparable account of the approach to the protection of Article 10 under the ECHR. However, in order for me to be able to give a coherent account of the search for a common ground and the conclusions of this search, I do first need to elaborate on the methods of review applied by the European Court of Human Rights. Before I am able to look for a common ground between the application of methods of protection, I first need to address the issue of the type of methods of protection applied by the Court. This issue is the subject of the next chapter.

---

383 DPP v. Whyte [1972] 3 All ER 12 at 21. See par. 1.2.2.
384 Derbyshire County Council v. Times Newspapers Ltd [1993] 2 WLR 449, at 458; Reynolds v. Times Newspapers Ltd [1999] 4 All ER 609. See also par. 2.2.
385 A-G v. English [1982] 2 all ER 903 at 920; Camelot Group v. Centaur [1998] 1 All ER 251 at 261. See also section 6.2.

CHAPTER IV
METHODS OF PROTECTION
APPLIED BY THE COURT

1 INTRODUCTION

The aim of this chapter is to distinguish the methods of protection applied in the case law of the Court. The methods of protection are the techniques the Court applies to take account of freedom of expression in its case law.

An indication of the methods of protection applied can be derived from the text of Article 10 ECHR. To determine whether a restriction amounts to a violation of Article 10 the Court evaluates whether the restriction falls within one of the legitimate aims set out in the second paragraph of the Article, and it assesses whether the restriction was 'necessary in a democratic society'. I discussed the manner in which the Court approaches this requirement in chapter I of this book. As I observed, the Court is not very critical in reviewing whether the restriction is prescribed by law and whether the legitimate aim put forward by the national authorities to justify the restriction is in fact served. The review of the Court regarding the substance of a case centres around the requirement that the interference should be 'necessary in a democratic society'. The Court has developed a number of criteria which have to be met for the restriction to be 'necessary': there has to exist a pressing social need, the measure has to be proportionate to the legitimate aim pursued and the reasons to justify the measure have to be relevant and sufficient.[1] By way of these requirements, the Court reviews whether appropriate weight was given to the facts and circumstances of a case. This review is influenced by the strictness of the scrutiny applied.

Two elements of protection by the Court should therefore be distinguished. The strictness of the scrutiny should be distinguished from the methods of protection concerning the substance of the case. In other words, the margin of appreciation allowed to a state party should be distinguished from the requirements that a measure

---

[1] Starting with the Handyside judgment this became the Court's standard formula: Handyside v. United Kingdom, (1976) A.24, par. 48-50. For instance Sunday Times v. United Kingdom (1979) A.30, par. 62: 'It now must be decided whether the "interference" complained of corresponded to a "pressing social need", whether it was "proportionate to the legitimate aim pursued", whether the reasons given by the national authorities to justify it are "relevant and sufficient under Article 10 par. 2".' See also Harris, O'Boyle and Warbrick, Law of the European Convention on Human Rights, 1995, p. 396.

should serve a pressing social need, should be proportionate to the legitimate aim pursued and that the reasons for justification should be relevant and sufficient.

I discuss the manner of application of the methods of protection in part II of this study. The function of the present chapter is not to give an extensive overview of the manner in which the methods of protection are applied by the Court. Here I merely distinguish the different methods of protection applied in order to provide a structure for the discussion in part II of this book. I first address the issue of the scope of review, which is determined by the 'margin of appreciation' (section 2). Subsequently I elaborate on the substantive methods of protection (section 3). In section 3 I make a distinction between the methods of protection the Court is held to apply according to itself and according to academic writings on this issue (section 3.1) and the methods the Court in fact applies (section 3.2).

2 MARGIN OF APPRECIATION

The Court, until recently together with the Commission, protects the rights guaranteed under the Convention.[2] The rights protected under the Convention are not absolute. It is possible for the Contracting States to restrict them. However, the meaning of the terminology which allows for restriction is not self-evident. Several terms need interpretation to determine the protection offered by the rights and freedoms adopted in the Convention. With regard to Article 10 amongst others the term 'necessary in a democratic society' needs interpretation. In relation to this the Court has determined that the interpretation of the Convention cannot be left completely to the States party to the Convention.[3] However, the Court also held that it should not impose its own views of what it considers necessary in a democratic society.[4] It does not want to 'take the place' of the national authorities, with which the initial responsibility lies to guarantee the rights adopted in the Convention.[5] Between these two extremes the Court has to determine the degree of scrutiny to which it subjects the decisions of the national authorities. To determine this degree of scrutiny the Court developed the concept of the 'margin of appreciation'. The margin of appreciation expresses the latitude allowed to States party to the Convention in their observance of the Convention. Its scope is influenced by the

---

2 Protocol 11 to the Convention and previously Art. 19 ECHR.
3 See also: Wiarda, Extensieve en restrictieve verdragstoepassing door het Europese Hof voor de Rechten van de Mens; een middenkoers?, 1981, p. 371-374.
4 Referring to: Council of Europe, Collected Edition of the 'Travaux Préparatoires' of the European Convention on Human Rights, 1975, p. 264.
5 See also: Wiarda, Extensieve en restrictieve verdragstoepassing door het Europese Hof voor de Rechten van de Mens; een middenkoers?, 1981, p. 371-374.

circumstances of the case. I address the exact manner in which the margin of appreciation is applied in chapter VI of this book.

In the following section I elaborate on the substantive methods of protection that are applied by the Court. I discuss separately the view on this topic in academic writings and the comments the Court itself has made on the issue. After this I analyze some case law of the Court in order to determine the methods actually applied.

3 SUBSTANTIVE METHODS OF PROTECTION

3.1 Academic Writings

Despite the formulation of three substantive requirements by the Court, from academic writings it seems as though proportionality is the only substantive method of protection. Feldman, for instance, argued that the requirement of the interference being necessary in a democratic society brings with it a review of proportionality.[6] Eissen is of the opinion that the requirement of necessity *necessarily* implies review of the proportionality of a measure. Moreover, according to him the requirement of 'pressing social need' apparently corresponds to that of proportionality of a limitation. He held: 'From necessity to proportionality is but a small step, since for a measure to be necessary it must surely correspond to a "pressing social need"'.[7] Under the heading 'The interpretation of the Convention', Harris, O'Boyle and Warbrick restrict themselves to a short discussion of the principle of proportionality. They specify the meaning of this concept by referring to the decision of the Court in the Soering case in which it held: 'Inherent in the whole of the Convention is a search for a fair balance between the demands of the general interest of the community and the requirements of the protection of the individual's fundamental rights'.[8] Subsequently they held that 'the achievement of such a balance necessarily requires an approach based, inter alia, upon considerations of proportionality'.

The discussion on the content of the review of proportionality is concise. Feldman does not elaborate on what the proportionality test entails.[9] Barendt, who only refers to 'necessary in a democratic society' indicates that this implies 'balancing' by the

---

6 Feldman, Civil Liberties and Human Rights in England and Wales, 1993, p. 377.
7 Eissen, The Principle of Proportionality in the Case-Law of the European Court of Human Rights, 1993, p. 127.
8 Harris, O'Boyle and Warbrick, Law of the European Convention on Human Rights, 1995, p. 11.
9 Feldman, Civil Liberties and Human Rights in England and Wales, 1993, p. 714: He restricted himself to the following comment: 'If the offence breaches the principle of proportionality, it will fail to come within the justification provided by Article 10(2)'.

Court. He does not specify how this balancing is conducted.[10] Eissen is a little more specific, but merely refers to the terminology used by the Court. He does not discuss the types of tests the Court applies when it reviews the proportionality of a measure.[11] Harris, O'Boyle and Warbrick pay more attention to this matter. They distinguish three forms of proportionality applied by the Court under the provisions of Article 8 to 10 ECHR.[12] First of all a measure is disproportionate when it is 'not necessary', which is the case when the seriousness of the restriction outweighs the interest in the legitimate aim. Second, a measure would not be proportionate 'where there is an alternative, less intrusive way of protecting the public interest'. Finally, they held that a limitation is disproportionate 'where the object cannot be achieved by the interference'.

To put the approach to proportionality in a wider perspective, it seems appropriate to take into consideration some authoritative opinions on the concept that are not specifically concerned with substantive protection by the ECHR. When looking at the approach to proportionality in this broader range of literature different opinions can be distinguished. According to Emiliou proportionality requires that 'measures adopted by public authorities should not exceed the limits of what is appropriate and necessary in order to attain the legitimate objectives in the public interest; when there is a choice between several appropriate measures recourse should be made to the least onerous, and the disadvantages caused (to the individual) should not be disproportionate to the aim pursued'.[13] De Lange on the other hand has distinguished a restricted concept of proportionality from proportionality in a wider sense. Proportionality in the wider sense encompasses according to him considerations regarding 'sharing of the burden of the decision making authorities between citizens, and the relation between the competing interests'.[14] The definition given by Emiliou

---

10 Barendt, Freedom of Speech, 1996, p. 35-36. The emphasis in this book is not on the method of review, but on the weight awarded to different kinds of speech such as the approach to prior restraint (p. 150-151) or the approach to speech in the judicial process (p. 232-233).

11 Eissen, The Principle of Proportionality in the Case-Law of the European Court of Human Rights, 1993, p. 128.

12 Harris, O'Boyle and Warbrick, Law of the European Convention of Human Rights, 1995, p. 300.

13 Emiliou, The Principle of Proportionality in European Law, 1996, p. 2. The Dutch writer De Moor-van Vugt in: De Moor-van Vugt, Maten en Gewichten, Het evenredigheidsbeginsel in Europees Perspectief, 1994, p. 13, describes proportionality in a more limited manner as regards the type of requirements that the notion of proportionality encompasses. She held that the proportionality requirement demands that restriction of freedom is only allowed to the extent necessary to achieve the aim that serves the general interest. This implies that aims may always be realised at the expense of the right restricted. In this approach it does not ever seem possible that the aim may not outweigh the interest in the restricted right.

14 De Lange, Publiekrechtelijke Rechtsvinding, 1991, p. 133: 'Het evenredigheidsbeginsel in ruime zin heeft niet alleen betrekking op de keuze van middelen, maar ook op de verdeling van de lasten van het openbaar bestuur over de burgers, en de verhouding tussen verschillende in het geding

encompasses a suitability-test, a necessity-test and a balancing exercise between means and ends. Unlike the definition given by De Lange, it excludes a balancing of interests. De Lange defined proportionality on the basis of the manner of applying the requirement of 'Verhältnismässigkeit' in case law of German courts. He concluded that the application of the principle of 'Verhältnismässigkeit' developed into an application of a 'balancing of interests', which had an independent function in the considerations of the German courts.[15] It is clear that the review of proportionality may entail different requirements that range from suitability, necessity and an appropriate balance between means and ends to an appropriate balance between the interests involved. From the comments of scholars it seems as if the Court only applies the first three tests.

In order to get a grasp of what the Court actually does when it reviews the substance of a case, the logical next step is to analyze the case law of the Court in order to deduce the substantive methods of protection.

3.2 Substantive Methods of Protection in the Case Law of the Court

3.2.1 Substantive Methods of Protection in Name

As I observed, the Court ostensibly reviews the necessity of a limitation by examining whether a restriction is proportionate to the legitimate aim pursued, whether it represents a pressing social need and whether the reasons for justification are relevant and sufficient.

The requirement of relevance and sufficiency of reasons is of limited significance to the substantive methods of protection, since the cases in which it is explicitly reviewed are rare.[16] In the cases in which this criterion was reviewed, it entailed a description of the arguments that were used to add to the importance of the interest in the 'legitimate aim'. Most often, however, the relevance and the sufficiency of arguments is implied in the review of whether there was a pressing social need and whether the restriction was proportionate to the legitimate aim pursued.[17] This

---

zijnde belangen'.

15 De Lange, Publiekrechtelijke Rechtsvinding, 1991, p. 143-146.
16 Sunday Times v. United Kingdom, par. 63 and par. 64-66; Observer and Guardian v. United Kingdom, par. 61-62 and par. 68-70. See also Schokkenbroek, Toetsing aan Vrijheidsrechten van het Europees Verdrag tot Bescherming van de Rechten van de Mens, 1996, p. 194. In the recent case of Janowski v. Poland, 21 January 1999, the Court says it will review all three requirements. In its conclusion it explicitly held that it was 'satisfied that the reasons adduced by the national authorities were 'relevant and sufficient' (par. 35).
17 See for instance the role this requirement had in the decision in Wingrove v. United Kingdom in which the Court first said it would consider the pressing social need and the proportionality of the measure (par. 53). After some considerations regarding the circumstances of the case it held that

combining of the criteria of review seems unavoidable since the relevance and sufficiency of the reasons adduced by the national authorities have to be complemented at least with the Court's assessment of the position of freedom of expression in the case at hand. The question that remains is how the Court comes to its conclusions in doing this.

The manner of formulating the review of the necessity of a limitation suggests that there remain two different substantive methods of protection, i.e. on the one hand determining whether there was a pressing social need, and on the other determining whether the restriction was proportionate to the legitimate aim pursued. In earlier case law it was suggested that the two requirements may in fact amount to different substantive methods of protection. In the Müller case the conviction of a painter and a gallery holder for exhibiting obscene paintings was held not to constitute a violation of Article 10 since it corresponded to a pressing social need. This case, together with decisions such as Jersild v. Denmark, in which the Court ostensibly reviewed the proportionality of a measure and in fact concluded that it was disproportionate, seem to confirm the idea that the two requirements are separate criteria of review.[18]

The application of the requirements is not that consistent, however. Beside the cases in which none of the requirements set out were explicitly said to be reviewed,[19] there have been cases in which the Court claimed that it was reviewing whether the restriction served a pressing social need, but concluded that the restriction was disproportionate to the legitimate aim.[20] There have also been cases in which the Court ostensibly reviewed either all three above-mentioned criteria, or both the pressing social need requirement and the proportionality requirement, but in its conclusion only referred to the proportionality of a restriction.[21] From the case

---

it had to review whether the reasons given could justify the interference and were relevant and sufficient (par. 59) after which it continued the evaluation of the facts and circumstances. The Court concluded that the decision of the national authorities to ban the video 'Visions of Ecstacy' was not arbitrary or excessive. Which considerations concerned which conclusion was unclear. See also Schokkenbroek, Toetsing aan de vrijheidsrechten van het Europees Verdrag tot Bescherming van de Rechten van de Mens, 1996, p. 195.

18 See also Barfod v. Denmark, (1989) A.149 and Jacubowski v. Germany, (1994) A.291-A. Cf. another separate review of 'pressing social need' occurs in Ahmed and Others v. United Kingdom, 2 September 1999, par. 62.

19 Instead it was reviewed whether the necessity of the restriction was 'convincingly established'. See Otto Preminger Institut v. Austria, (1995) A.295, par. 50 and Autronic v. Switzerland, (1990) A.178, par. 61. In the more recent case of De Haes and Gijssels v. Belgium, 24 February 1997, Reports 1997-I, par. 33, the Court said it would review the necessity of a measure and concluded that in this case it was not necessary, without referring to any of the requirements.

20 Informationsverein Lentia v. Austria, (1993) A.276, par. 39-42.

21 Open Door and Dublin Well Woman v. Ireland, (1992) A.246, par. 70, 80; Wingrove v. United Kingdom, 25 November 1996, Reports 1996-V, par. 53, 61; Barthold v. Germany, (1995) A.90, par. 56, 59.

law of the Court it also seems that the pressing social need requirement and the proportionality requirement are not clearly distinguished from each other. In other words, the relationship between the different requirements of necessity is unclear. The fact that the Court does not distinguish clearly between the pressing social need requirement and the proportionality requirement entails that these classifications are not appropriate to distinguish different substantive methods of protection in its case law.[22] The phenomenon that in comments on the substantive methods of protection emphasis lies on the review of proportionality, can be explained from the fact that the Court, in the conclusions of its decisions, beside using the general term 'necessity' has also often referred to the proportionality of a measure. To determine the substantive methods of protection actually applied by the Court a further inquiry into its case law is necessary.

As I just concluded, from the decisions of the Court it becomes apparent that the review applied by the Court is not identical in each case. In reviewing the necessity of a restriction the Court has on occasion specified what it intended the review of proportionality to entail. The definitions given do not amount to the same method of protection. In the Barfod case the Court described the review of proportionality as follows: 'In the present case proportionality implies that the pursuit of the aims mentioned in Article 10 par. 2 has to be weighed against the value of open discussion of topics of public concern. When striking a fair balance between these interests ...'.[23] That in other cases proportionality might mean something different became

---

22 In more recent decisions the Court has started again to state that it has to review all three requirements (namely that a measure is proportionate to the legitimate aim pursued, that it serves a pressing social need and that the reasons for its justification are relevant and sufficient) in order to determine whether there was a violation of Article 10 even suggesting that whether there was a pressing social need was something for the national authorities to determine and that, taking account of the margin of appreciation, it was for the Court to determine whether this pressing social need could outweigh the interest in freedom of expression by reviewing whether the interference was 'proportionate to the legitimate aim pursued and whether the reasons adduced by the national authorities to justify it are relevant and sufficient'. See for instance Hertel v. Switzerland, 25 August 1998, Reports 1998 VI, par. 46; Lehideux and Isorni v. France, 23 September 1998, Reports 1998-VII, par. 51; Janowski v. Poland, 21 January 1999, par. 30; Fressoz and Roire v. France, 21 January 1999, par. 45. It also did this in the case of Ahmed and others v. United Kingdom, 2 September 1999, par. 55. In this case the Court did in fact review the pressing social need requirement separately (par. 62). In general however, the presentation of the three different criteria does not imply a separate review of all three requirements.

23 Barfod v. Denmark, (1989) A.149, par. 29. See also the Groppera Radion AG v. Switzerland, (1990) A.173, par. 73, in which the Court also said that it would determine the proportionality of a measure by balancing the interests: 'In order to verify that the interference was not excessive in the instant case, the requirements of protecting the international telecommunications order as well as the rights of others must be weighed against the interest of the applicants and others in the retransmission of sound radio's programmes by cable' and in the case of Jacubowski v. Germany, A. 291-A (1994), par. 27, the Court held: 'In the instant case the requirements of protecting the

apparent from the Court's approach to this requirement in the Goodwin case when it held that 'there was no reasonable relationship of proportionality between the legitimate aim pursued by the disclosure order and the means deployed to achieve that aim'.[24] These two descriptions of proportionality amount to different methods of review. The latter one involves the relationship between the means and the end to achieve the legitimate aim, whilst the first description amounts to a balancing of interests. In the first description, the Court reviews the relation between the aim and the measure imposed to achieve that aim. These two aspects are naturally linked: any restriction will serve an end and to achieve that aim a means will be required. The second definition implies that the Court awards weight to the interest of the national authorities in restricting the right and to the interest in the exercise of freedom of expression, subsequently declaring one interest to be of greater importance than the other. Unlike the implied relation between means and ends of a restriction, the countervailing interests are not necessarily connected.

The next question I need to answer in the light of this study is whether the Court in fact applies different methods of protection. In other words, I need to analyze the character of the review applied by the Court. I do this in the next subsection.

3.2.2 Substantive Methods of Protection in Fact

From the case law of the Court it becomes clear that the methods of protection used by the Court in fact can differ in content. Three initial methods of review can be distinguished, namely suitability, less restrictive alternative and a balancing exercise. As we have seen in the discussion of the literature on substantive methods of protection, Harris, O'Boyle and Warbrick distinguish these three methods of review as ways in which the Court reviews the proportionality of a measure. In this section I demonstrate that beside these three methods of reviewing the proportionality of a measure, the Court applies another substantive method of protection. This method is 'balancing of interests'. This method of protection should be distinguished from the balancing exercise between means and ends of a restrictive measure, because it does not involve considerations regarding the means by which the aim is achieved. Instead it amounts to a balancing of the interest in restricting the right (the aim) and the interest in the right as such. Elaboration on this distinction follows. I start off with a discussion of the methods by which the Court reviews the proportionality of a measure: the suitability test, the less restrictive alternative test and balancing of means

---

reputation and rights of others must be weighed against the applicant's freedom to distribute his circular and the newspaper cuttings'. In this case the Court concluded that 'the interference with Article 10 could not be regarded as disproportionate'.

24 Goodwin v. United Kingdom, 22 February 1996, Reports 1996-II, par. 42.

and ends. Subsequently I demonstrate that 'balancing of interests' is a separate method of protection and show that it is in fact applied by the Court.

Suitability

The review of suitability is also distinguished by Harris, O'Boyle and Warbrick as a method of protection.[25] This method can be defined as reviewing whether the restriction is appropriate to achieve the aim pursued. They acknowledge that this method of protection is part of the review of proportionality. According to Schokkenbroek this method of protection is not compatible with the notion of margin of appreciation, because if the Court were to conclude that a measure is not suitable this would be too great an interference in the national authority's discretion regarding its view on the restrictions that can be considered necessary in a democratic society. This explains why this test is never applied separately from other substantive methods of protection.

The suitability of a measure cannot be said to be completely irrelevant, however.[26] In the case of Open Door Dublin Well Woman v. Ireland the Court in fact took account of the appropriateness of the restrictive measure. This case concerned a prohibition to distribute information on the possibilities of having abortions abroad. The Court held that the absolute nature of the injunction that prohibited 'the provision of information to pregnant women' led to the measure being disproportionate to the end.[27] In the injunction, no account was taken of the age or state of health or the women's reasons for seeking counselling on the termination of pregnancy. This conclusion was supported by a further extensive review of the proportionality of the injunction. The weight of the aim was assessed in that the Court observed that the information was available elsewhere, and the injunction was largely ineffective 'since it did not prevent large numbers of women from continuing to obtain abortions in Great Britain'.[28] Subsequently the seriousness of the interference was considered. It was held that the injunction created a risk 'to the health of those women who are now seeking abortions at a later stage in their pregnancy, due to lack of proper counselling, and who are availing of customary medical supervision after the abortion has taken place'.[29] The Court took these factors into account to conclude finally that the measure was disproportionate. In this case the Court came close to holding that a measure was not appropriate to achieve

---

25 Harris, O'Boyle and Warbrick, Law of the European Convention of Human Rights, 1995, p. 300. They do not elaborate on its application. See also Schokkenbroek, Toetsing aan de vrijheidsrechten van het Europees Verdrag tot Bescherming van de Rechten van de Mens, 1996, p. 197.

26 See Schokkenbroek, Toetsing aan de vrijheidsrechten van het Europees Verdrag tot Bescherming van de Rechten van de Mens, 1996, p. 198.

27 Open Door and Dublin Well Woman v. Ireland, (1992) A.246, par. 73.

28 Open Door and Dublin Well Woman v. Ireland, (1992) A.246, par. 76.

29 Open Door and Dublin Well Woman v. Ireland, (1992) A.246, par. 77.

the aim pursued. Suitability seemed to be a requirement.[30] The lack of it, however, was supported by other methods of protection before the Court concluded that there was a violation of Article 10 ECHR.

Another example of how the appropriateness of a measure influenced the importance attributed to the aim pursued can be found in the case of Observer and Guardian v. United Kingdom.[31] In this case the Court expressed doubts about whether the injunction prohibiting publication of the Spycatcher book could serve to protect national security since the information concerned already was available freely. The Court refrained from any clear rejection of the appropriateness of the measure, and instead held that it was above all the fact that the newspapers were prevented from exercising their right and duty to disseminate information on a matter of legitimate public concern which was decisive.[32] The fact that the information was already available influenced the Court's conclusion as to disproportionality of the measure.[33] So far, however, there are no judgments in which the Court clearly held that a measure was unsuitable to achieve the aim pursued; also, the Court has never held a restriction not to be necessary in a democratic society because it was unsuitable.

Less Restrictive Alternative[34]
A second, more frequently applied method of protection is the evaluation of whether a less restrictive alternative was available to achieve the aim pursued. This method of protection is distinguished by Harris, O'Boyle and Warbrick as well and was also regarded as a type of proportionality review.[35] The requirement that a less restrictive alternative is not available frequently has been applied by the Court in order to reach a conclusion on the compatibility of a measure with Article 10 ECHR. I give a few examples.

---

30 See Schokkenbroek, Toetsing aan de vrijheidsrechten van het Europees Verdrag tot bescherming van de Rechten van de Mens, 1996, p. 198.
31 Observer and Guardian v. United Kingdom, (1991) A.216.
32 Observer and Guardian v. United Kingdom, (1991) A.216, par. 69.
33 See for similar considerations: Fressoz and Roire v. France, 21 January 1999, par. 53.
34 In other systems of law this method of review is also described as reviewing the 'subsidiarity' of a measure. However, this term could lead to confusion, since in English it could also imply the requirement that the restriction be imposed at the lowest possible level. In English publications on judicial review the term referred to in order to indicate the requirement that the restriction is 'the least restrictive alternative' is 'the necessity test', See De Smith, Woolf and Jowell, Judicial review of administrative action, 1995, p. 602.
35 Harris, O'Boyle and Warbrick, Law of the European Convention of Human Rights, 1995, p. 300. See also Schokkenbroek, Toetsing aan de vrijheidsrechten van het Europees Verdrag tot Bescherming van de Rechten van de Mens, 1996, p. 199.

In the case of Informationsverein Lentia v. Austria, the Court held that it could not be argued that there are no equivalent less restrictive measures, other than a state monopoly on the broadcasting of television programmes, to achieve pluralism in the programming.[36] And in the case of Tolstoy Miloslavsky v. UK, the Court held that 'an award of damages for defamation must bear a reasonable relationship of proportionality to the injury to the reputation suffered'. The amount of damages awarded exceeded that requirement, and was therefore found to be disproportionate to the aim pursued.[37] In the Müller case the Court considered that the confiscation of the paintings was the less restrictive measure compared to destruction of them and that therefore the measure could not be considered disproportionate.[38] In this case, the fact that the measure was less restrictive than it could have been was sufficient for it to be proportionate to the aim pursued.[39] In continuation of its reasoning as regards the necessity of the scope of the restriction, the Court regularly considers the absoluteness of a restriction. When the restriction is of an absolute nature, this will enhance the chances of the restriction being found disproportionate. In the Dublin Well Woman case, which I discussed previously, the Court considered the extensiveness of the prohibition to distribute information on abortions abroad. Also in the Casado Coca case the Court reviewed whether a ban on commercials for lawyers could be considered absolute, suggesting that had if that had been the case, this would have led to the decision that there had been a violation of Article 10.[40] And although the circular to clients was the most efficient and logical way of reacting to the allegations of a former employer, the Court held in the Jacubowski case that 'the impugned court order went no further than to prohibit distribution of the circular' and that the appellant consequently 'retained the right to voice his opinions and to defend himself by any other means'.[41] The Court concluded that the injunction could not be considered disproportionate. If a restriction constitutes a complete ban, the Court apparently feels that a less restrictive measure will most likely be available.

---

36 Informationsverein Lentia v. Austria, (1993) A.276.
37 Tolstoy Miloslavsky v. United Kingdom, (1995) A.323. Unlike the case of Informationsverein Lentia v. Austria, the less restrictive alternative could be found within the same measure: the payment of damages. For the measure to be proportionate to the aim, decreasing the amount of damages is required.
38 Müller v. Switzerland, (1988) A.133, par. 41.
39 See similarly the case of Ahmed v. United Kingdom, 2 September 1998, Reports 1998-VI, par. 63, in which the Court held that '... the regulations were not designed to silence all comment on political matters ...'.
40 Casado Coca v. Spain, (1994) A.285-A, par. 52. In Wingrove v. United Kingdom the confiscation of the film did amount to a complete ban. In this case the margin of appreciation was so wide that even this could not be considered disproportionate.
41 Jacubowski v. Germany, (1994) A.291-A, par. 29.

After the discussion of these two substantive methods of protection I conclude that both the review of the suitability of a measure and the review of whether a less restrictive alternative was available amount to the review of proportionality as defined by the Court in the Goodwin case. As I observed, in this case proportionality was defined as the absence of a 'reasonable relationship between the legitimate aim pursued and the means deployed to achieve that aim'. These methods of protection occur in the judgments of the Court, but the Court does not require restrictions to be suitable or necessary in each case. There have in fact been many cases in which neither of these two methods were applied, but in which the Court nonetheless reviewed the relationship between the means and ends of an interference. In those cases the Court performed a balancing exercise between means and ends. I elaborate on this method of protection next.

Balancing of Means and Ends
That balancing of means and ends is a separate method of protection is acknowledged by Harris, O'Boyle and Warbrick. They refer to it as review of the 'necessity of a measure'.[42] According to them this entails review by the Court of whether the seriousness of the restriction outweighs the interest in realisation of the legitimate aim. Schokkenbroek also acknowledges the existence of a third substantive method of protection. He consequently concluded that the review of proportionality should be described as a weighing by the Court of the interference with the right concerned and the interest represented by the legitimate aim, in which the Court examines whether or not the relation between the two is in balance, taking account of the circumstances of the case.[43]

In fact the cases discussed under the headings 'suitability' and 'less restrictive alternatives' are all examples of this method of protection. In these cases, the suitability of a measure or the possibility of a less restrictive measure were considered, but this did not determine alone that the restrictions were compatible with the Convention or not. Instead these considerations were part of more general considerations regarding the proportionality between means and ends of an interference. I illustrate the application of such a combination of substantive methods of protection by way of a rather extensive discussion of one case.

A relatively recent example is a case in which the suitability of a restriction played a role, but was only one of several considerations on the proportionality of a measure. This is the case of Fressoz and Roire v. France.[44] In this case, the taxable income of a director of Peugeot motor company was published in the light of the

---

42 Harris, O'Boyle and Warbrick, Law of the European Convention of Human Rights, 1995, p. 300.
43 Schokkenbroek, Toetsing aan de vrijheidsrechten van het Europees Verdrag tot bescherming van de Rechten van de Mens, 1996, p. 201.
44 Fressoz and Roire v. France, 21 January 1999.

debate on the refusal to give pay rises to the workforce at this company. Fressoz and Roire obtained the information from a confidential tax file, which was in the possession of the tax authorities. According to the French government the publication amounted to a breach of confidence. The Court first established that the publication was part of a more general debate on a topic of public interest.[45] Then it appreciated the interest in the legitimate aim of protecting fiscal confidentiality: it considered that the applicants must have known that the documents were confidential and consequently that they had the responsibility not to disclose the information concerned. Subsequently the Court assessed the relation between means and ends by asking whether 'there was any need to prevent the disclosure of information that was already available to the public'.[46] Although the information was not free to be disseminated, local taxpayers did have access to a list of the people liable for tax in their municipality which also revealed their taxable income. As a consequence, a large number of people already had access to the information. The information could not be published, but it was held to be available to the public and therefore it was considered not confidential. Moreover, information on the taxable income of the management of large companies was regularly published in financial reviews. The conviction for the publication of documents which contained information available to the public could not be justified under Article 10.

These considerations illustrate that the means, namely the conviction for the publication of the information, had to be proportionate to the legitimate aim, which was the protection of fiscal confidentiality. The question asked is whether the conviction could be justified by the interest in confidentiality. However, the information concerned was part of a public debate; moreover, the information was to a large extent already available to the public. So the aim was partly a hopeless cause, and the fact that the information was of public importance meant that the interest in the aim was not sufficient to justify the restriction.

There is more however. In this balancing exercise between means and ends, also the importance attributed to the interest in freedom of expression plays a role. The importance attributed to it in the case of Fressoz and Roire v. France influenced the conclusion that the relationship between means and ends was disproportionate. It influenced the importance attached to the conviction. It could therefore be said that the review of the appropriateness of the measure was couched in more general considerations regarding the relationship between the means and ends of the restriction.[47] In this case therefore the importance attributed to freedom of expression is merely a part of the balancing of means and ends. The review by the

---

45   Fressoz and Roire v. France, 21 January 1999, par. 50.
46   Fressoz and Roire v. France, 21 January 1999, par. 53.
47   A similar kind of review can be found in the case of Hertel v. Switzerland, 25 August 1998, Reports 1998-VI, par. 47-50.

Court in this case consequently seems to support the definition given by Schokken-broek, in which the importance of freedom of expression is considered as part of the assessment of the interference with the right, in other words with the means.

Now, however, it is time to cross over to the last method of protection, namely 'balancing of interests'.

Balancing of Interests
In the case of Goodwin v. United Kingdom, the relation between the review of proportionality by way of balancing means and ends and the weighing of the interest in freedom of expression is less clear.[48] I first discuss the relevant considerations of the Court in this case. Subsequently I examine what methods of protection the Court in fact applied. The case of Goodwin v. the United Kingdom dealt with a disclosure order in which Goodwin, a journalist, was ordered to reveal the identity of the source that gave him financial information about a company called Tetra. Most importantly, the journalist was informed by the anonymous source about a significant loan the company was raising, although it had considerable financial problems. The journalist alarmed the company when he called to verify the information before he would publish it. Tetra consequently obtained an injunction which prevented not only Goodwin but all relevant periodicals from publishing the information. In addition, however, Tetra asked and obtained the disclosure order, which Goodwin held to constitute a violation of Article 10.

The government held that the aim of the order was to prevent dissemination of the confidential information. In addition the government asserted that it served to give the company an opportunity to unmask the disloyal employee, to make it possible for the company 'to bring proceedings against him for recovery of the missing document', to enable the company to apply for an 'injunction against further disclosure by the employee' and finally to enable the company to acquire 'compensation for damage'.[49] According to the Court, however, the injunction restraining publication of the information by newspapers and periodicals in general, largely 'neutralised' the potential damage to Tetra, in that it prevented dissemination of the information by the press. Consequently 'Tetra's creditors, customers, suppliers and competitors would not therefore come to learn of the information through the press'. In fact the Court reviewed whether the means was appropriate to achieve the aim and partly concluded that it was not. Review of the necessity of the order was subsequently restricted to the remaining aims, which were the possibility for the company to discover who the disloyal employee was in order to prevent further incidents like this, to recover the missing document and to obtain damages.

The question was therefore whether the additional aims provided 'sufficient

---

48 Goodwin v. United Kingdom, 22 February 1996, Reports 1996-II (X Ltd v. Morgan Grampian.)
49 Goodwin v. United Kingdom, 22 February 1996, Reports 1996-II, par. 42 and 44.

justification' for the restriction of freedom of expression.[50] The Court noted that the mere fact that Tetra would not be able to 'avert the threatened legal wrong' without knowing the identity of the source was in itself not sufficient to necessitate disclosure. To review the necessity of the measure, the Court evaluated 'the balance of competing interests': 'On the facts of the present case, the Court cannot find that Tetra's interests in eliminating, by proceedings against the source, the residual threat of damage through dissemination of the confidential information otherwise than by the press, in obtaining compensation and in unmasking a disloyal employee or collaborator were, even if considered cumulatively, sufficient to outweigh the vital public interest in the protection of the applicant journalist's source'.[51]

The relation between means and ends of the restriction led the Court to restrict the review of 'necessity' to the remaining aims. The above cited considerations of the Court show, however, that the means and ends of the restriction were not considered in determining whether the restriction was 'necessary'. The Court awarded weight to freedom of expression (of 'vital public interest' since it concerns a restriction of the press, the functioning of which is of the greatest importance to a democratic society) and it gave weight to the interest of Tetra in knowing the identity of the source, the possibility to prevent publication of the information by other means than the press, the possibility to obtain compensation and to unmask a disloyal employee who could subsequently be dismissed. The Court subsequently concluded that it did 'not therefore consider that the further purpose served by the disclosure order, when measured against the standards imposed by the Convention, amounts to an overriding requirement in the public interest'.[52] In other words, the weight awarded to the aim was not as great as that awarded to the interest in freedom of expression.

The evaluation of the importance to be attributed to the interests involved did not have any apparent function with regard to the previous suitability test which determined the scope of the interest in the restriction. In fact the review of the necessity seems to amount to a 'balancing of interests'.

Since the Court does not specify the exact methods of protection it applies, since in writings on the issue of substantive methods of protection the application of these methods is rarely elaborated on, and since the application of 'balancing of interests' as a substantive method of protection has not been a topic of discussion, the application of this method of protection needs to be addressed further.

As observed, when the methods of protection applied by the Court are discussed, they are always found to involve the evaluation of the relation between means and ends. Even the 'necessity' test as described by Harris, O'Boyle and Warbrick and the 'balancing' definition of Schokkenbroek involve such a review. However, the

---

50 Goodwin v. United Kingdom, 22 February 1996, Reports 1996-II, par. 42-43.
51 Goodwin v. United Kingdom, 22 February 1996, Reports 1996-II, par. 45.
52 Goodwin v. United Kingdom, 22 February 1996, Reports 1996-II, par. 45.

definition given by the Court in the Barfod case implied that the Court's view of proportionality might be broader than that. To recall, the Court held: 'In the present case proportionality implies that the pursuit of the aims mentioned in Article 10 par. 2 has to be weighed against the value of open discussion of topics of public concern'. The Court subsequently referred to this review as 'striking a fair balance between these interests'. From the considerations in the Goodwin case, it becomes clear that the Court may in fact balance interests to determine the 'proportionality' of a measure.

A more recent example of the application of 'balancing of interests' as a method of protection, also demonstrating that the Goodwin case was not a single instant deviation, is the case of Janowski v. Poland.

In this case Janowski, a journalist, was convicted for verbally insulting two municipal guards. The guards had insisted on street vendors leaving a square to move their stands to a nearby marketplace. The journalist intervened and correctly informed the guards 'that their actions had no legal basis', since 'the municipal authorities had not passed any resolution prohibiting the sale of merchandise on the streets'. The guards therefore had no authority to clear the square. During the incident, which took place in front of a number of bystanders, the journalist called the guards 'oafs' and 'dumb'.[53] By using the offensive words the journalist had, according to the domestic courts, exceeded the limits of freedom of expression and was subsequently convicted under Article 236 of the Polish Criminal Code, which aimed to ensure 'that civil servants were not hindered in carrying out their duties'. On appeal, an initial suspended prison sentence of eight months was quashed along with the order to pay PLZ 400,000 to charitable organisations. The applicant had to pay a fine of PLZ 1,500,000 and court costs of PLZ 150,000.

The Court held that it had to assess whether there was a pressing social need, whether the interference at issue was 'proportionate to the legitimate aim pursued' and whether the reasons adduced by the national authorities to justify it were 'relevant and sufficient'. It concluded that Article 10 ECHR had not been violated, because the national authorities had not overstepped their margin of appreciation in determining the necessity of the restriction. In evaluating the facts and circumstances of the case the Court emphasised the importance of freedom of expression to a democratic society, but it also held that the speech did not 'form part of an open discussion of matters of public concern' since Janowski had been convicted of insulting the guards, not for criticising their behaviour. Moreover the speech did not 'involve the issue of freedom of the press since the applicant, although a journalist by profession, clearly acted as a private individual on this occasion'.[54] Subsequently the Court assessed the interest in the legitimate aim pursued, namely the prevention

---

53 Janowski v. Poland, 21 January 1999, par. 8-14.
54 Janowski v. Poland, 21 January 1999, par. 32.

of disorder, in particular the prevention of offensive and abusive verbal attacks on civil servants. The Court considered that under some circumstances the limits of acceptable criticism may be wider 'with regard to civil servants exercising their powers than in relation to private individuals'. Then it went on to say: 'However, it cannot be said that civil servants knowingly lay themselves open to close scrutiny of their every word and deed to the extent to which politicians do and should therefore be treated on an equal footing with the latter when it comes to the criticism of their actions'. Moreover, the Court held that 'civil servants must enjoy public confidence in conditions free of undue perturbation if they are to be successful in performing their tasks and it may therefore prove necessary to protect them from offensive and abusive verbal attacks'.[55] The Court then brought these general considerations regarding the importance attributed to the interests involved in relation to each other and held: 'In the present case the requirements of such protection do not have to be weighed in relation to the interests of the freedom of the press or of open discussion of matters of public concern since the applicant's remarks were not uttered in such a context'.

Subsequently the Court applied the specific circumstances of the case to this starting point: 'In the Court's view, the reasons prompting the applicant's conviction were relevant ones in terms of the legitimate aim pursued. It is true that the applicant resorted to abusive language out of genuine concern for the well-being of fellow citizens in the course of a heated discussion. This language was directed at law enforcement officers who were trained how to respond to it. However, he insulted the guards in a public place, in front of a group of bystanders, while they were carrying out their duties. The actions of the guards, even though they were not based on the explicit regulations of the municipal council but on sanitary and traffic considerations, did not warrant resort to offensive and abusive verbal attacks. Consequently, even if there were some circumstances arguing the other way, sufficient grounds existed for the decision ultimately arrived at by the national courts'.[56] The facts and circumstances of the case are evaluated and in the end it was held that the national authorities were free to come to the decision that they came to.

To arrive at this conclusion, the Court attributed importance to the interests involved but did not follow up on these considerations by putting the means and the ends in relation to each other. The Court simply 'balanced' the interests involved and subsequently declared one interest to be of greater weight than the other. The mere statement that 'the resultant interference was proportionate to the legitimate aim pursued' is not sufficient to say that a means-ends test was applied. The only considerations regarding proportionality were made in relation to the sentence. After considering that the interference was proportionate the Court held: 'In this

---

55 Janowski v. Poland, 21 January 1999, par. 33.
56 Janowski v. Poland, 21 January 1999, par. 34.

connection, it is noteworthy that the applicant's sentence was substantially reduced on appeal and, most significantly, his prison sentence was quashed ...'.[57] The balancing exercise of the Court that I described above did not concern the Court's considerations regarding the sentence inflicted on Janowski.

Beside the fact that the wording of the Court indicates this ('in this connection' should be read as 'in addition to the previous considerations' and not as 'following from the previous considerations'), the aspects of the case considered in the balancing of interests are – as far as their content is concerned – detached from considerations concerning the seriousness of the sentence. The proportionality of the sentence seems to be a circumstance adding to the importance of the interest in protecting public order. The balancing of interests, independent from the proportionality considerations, led the Court to conclude that the interference was proportionate.

Keeping in mind the different definitions of proportionality given by the Court, it can be concluded that beside the review of the suitability of a measure, the review of whether a less restrictive alternative was available and the review of whether the means and ends of a restriction are in balance, another method of protection can be distinguished, namely 'balancing of interests'. According to the Court all of these methods of protection amount to the review of the proportionality of an interference.

4 PRELIMINARY CONCLUSIONS

The Court applies two different sorts of methods of protection. The first concerns the scope of the review and is governed by the doctrine of the 'margin of appreciation'. The Court applies a margin of appreciation to each case. The other kind of method of protection concerns the review of the substance of the case. On the substantive methods of review applied by the Court some unclarities exist. The requirements formulated by the Court with regard to the substance of a case – a restriction has to serve a pressing social need, has to be proportionate to the legitimate aim pursued and the reasons for it have to be relevant and sufficient – do not each represent a different substantive method of review. The proportionality requirement is applied regularly and in fact appears in three forms: suitability (referring to the appropriateness of a restrictive measure), less restrictive alternative and necessity (referring to an appropriate balance between means and ends of a restriction). The Court does not apply the same substantive method of protection in each case. Indeed, as is observed by Harris, O'Boyle and Warbrick, sometimes considerations regarding the necessity or suitability of a measure are most relevant to the decision, and sometimes general considerations regarding the relationship between the means and ends of a restriction lead the Court to conclude as to compatibility with Article 10 ECHR. Of the first two

---

57 Also note the requirement of proportional use of freedom of expression.

forms of proportionality it can be said that they are applied regularly, but they are never sufficient on their own to lead to conclusions on the compatibility of a restriction. The method of 'balancing means and ends' is a tool which also allows the Court to take account of the interests involved in the case at hand in its considerations. The assessment of these interests then appear to be a pre-consideration to a proportionality test in the sense of reviewing whether the relationship between means and ends can be considered proportionate. This occurred in the Goodwin judgment. However, the considerations of the Court in the Janowski case show that the balancing of the interest of freedom of expression and the interest in the legitimate aim is sometimes an independent method of protection: an imbalance, independent of any considerations regarding proportionality, may lead to the conclusion that there has or has not been a violation of Article 10 of the Convention. In such cases the method of protection applied is 'balancing of interests', which I consider to be a method of protection separate from the review of proportionality. There is a fundamental difference in the review of the relationship between means and ends, and the review of the balance between the interests involved. The means and ends of a restriction are indissolubly connected: without the one there is no other. The countervailing interests exist separately, except that the pursuit of the aim restricts the right. Because of this difference I am not convinced that 'balancing of interests' can be considered to be a type of proportionality test. Apart from these considerations, the least that can be said is that on occasion the Court's concept of proportionality includes proportionality in the wider sense as distinguished by De Lange.

The Court usually does not give any explanation as to the specific method(s) of protection applied in its decisions. From the case law of the Court generally the choices of substantive method of protection seem arbitrary, but I assume that the choice of method is a conscious one. The question remaining is what the consequences are of the application of 'balancing of interests' as a method of protection.

It would go too far at this point to make statements on the extent to which 'balancing of interests' compared to the review of proportionality interferes with the competence of the national authorities to determine the restrictions that are necessary in a democratic society. What can be said is that the review of proportionality is inherent to the task of a judge in a constitutional court. A constitutional court has the competence to review the constitutionality of legislation as such. Balancing of interests on the other hand seems to imply incidental review of the application of legislation. In other words it is a method of protection that seems more suitable for review of an individual case. The occurrence of balancing of interests in the case law of the Court could be explained by the fact that the Court in principle maintains a reserved attitude towards the review of legislation. The Court prefers concrete to abstract review. If a balancing of interests results in the conclusion that there has been a violation of the Convention, this will usually not require the national authorities to adjust their restrictive regulations. They will merely be required to adjust the application of the legislation in cases that are similar as to the circumstances, and they will have to pay damages to the individual whose right was violated in the case at hand.

This chapter completes the framework on the basis of which I examine the existence and scope of a common ground between the protection of freedom of expression in English law and under the ECHR. In chapter II, I examined the requirements set out by the Human Rights Act with regard to the protection of fundamental rights in English law. These requirements mainly concern the level of protection. Although the Act is not specific on the degree of protection required, from the objectives of the Act it seems obvious that the level of protection should at least meet the level provided by the European Court of Human Rights. In chapter III, I described the approach to the protection of freedom of expression of the English legislature and judiciary in some detail. This discussion provided a first view on the scope of freedom of expression and on the manner in which it has been approached under English law before the Human Rights Act comes into force. In chapter IV, the current chapter, I concluded that there are four methods of protection that can be distinguished in the case law of the European Court of Human Rights. In part II, I use the material of these three chapters to search for a common ground among the three aspects that I considered relevant to the protection of freedom of expression. These are: the approach to the notion of freedom of expression; the methods of protection; and the consideration and appreciation of facts and circumstances. I structure part II according to this division. In chapter V I elaborate on a common ground between the approaches to the concept of freedom of expression. In chapter VI, VII and VIII a common ground between the methods of protection is examined. I search for a common ground between the application of a margin of appreciation, the review of proportionality and balancing of interests, in that order. Finally, in chapter IX, I deliberate on a common ground regarding the consideration and appreciation of facts and circumstances. Separate discussion of each of these methods of protection is justified, because only then the influence on the protection of freedom of expression of each of them can become clear.

I realise that not all methods of protection applied by the Court, in particular the margin of appreciation, can be legitimately transferred to national systems of protection. In the chapters that concern these methods of protection I elaborate on the extent to which a search for a common ground between them in the different systems of protection is justified.

PART II
COMMON GROUND

1 INTRODUCTION

A common ground should be established with regard to the approach to the notion of freedom of expression before the search for a common ground can be extended to the other factors that determine the protection of freedom of expression. I can only effectively search for a common ground between the other aspects of protection once I determine the extent to which both systems of protection are considering the same notion when they speak of freedom of expression. In section 1 of this chapter I consider the extent to which freedom of expression is acknowledged to exist. Because of Article 10 ECHR, it is evident that this freedom is acknowledged under the system of protection of the ECHR. In this section I therefore focus on English law. Subsequently I divide the discussion of the approach to the notion of freedom of expression into three subjects. First in section 2, I discuss the nature of types of expression that are covered by a right to freedom of expression. This concerns who is allowed freedom of expression and the kind of expression covered by it. Second, I address the extent to which horizontal effect of freedom of expression is possible (in section 3). Finally, in section 4 I deal with the issue of whether prior restraint is accepted under the systems of protection. In each of these four sections I first discuss the relevant aspect with regard to the ECHR and subsequently I address English law. At the end of each section I comment on the common ground that exists with regard to the particular aspect at discussion. In section 5, I draw preliminary conclusions concerning a common ground between the approaches to the notion of freedom of expression under the ECHR and English law. In that paragraph I also consider the changes implied by the Human Rights Act with regard to the English approach to the notion of freedom of expression, and its implications for a common ground in that regard.

2 ACKNOWLEDGEMENT OF THE EXISTENCE OF FREEDOM OF EXPRESSION

The existence of freedom of expression is recognised under the ECHR, since it is adopted under Article 10 of that treaty. The answer to the question concerning the approach to the notion of freedom of expression under English law, is less obvious due to the residual nature of this freedom. Scholars regularly discuss freedom of expression. The considerations on freedom of expression usually refer to the role freedom of expression may play when legislation that restricts this freedom is applied. It is even assumed that freedom of expression is more than just a residual liberty. Such considerations imply that the existence of freedom of expression is acknowledged under English law. Feldman, amongst others, holds that since it has been accepted as a principle it entitles the courts to interpret legislation in accordance with the UK's international obligations.[1] Gardner says that it serves to justify narrow readings of statutes and common law rules which threaten to inhibit expression and it also serves to outweigh various countervailing considerations which would otherwise justify censorship.[2] And Barendt states: 'Surely it is now clear that freedom of speech constitutes a legal principle in Dworkin's understanding of the term, that is, a standard which courts are under an obligation to take into account when appropriate'.[3]

Freedom of expression is, in fact, frequently referred to in the case law of the courts. The fact that freedom of expression is referred to explicitly means no more than that the court specifies which area of freedom is dealt with. And for now it suffices to demonstrate that freedom of expression is in fact referred to by the English courts. The following considerations show this.

In the early 1970s, there were a few cases in which freedom of expression was recognised as a specific interest. One of the first of these cases was Hubbard v. Vosper in which Lord Denning stated: '... and the law will not intervene to suppress freedom of speech except when it is abused'.[4] In a public order case that was ruled a year later, Lord Reid said on s.5 of the Public Order Act 1936: 'Parliament had to solve the difficult question how far freedom of speech or behaviour must be limited in the general public interest'.[5] In the famous Times Newspaper case Lord Reid held that 'freedom of speech should not be limited to any greater extent than is necessary ...'.[6] In this last case it was generally accepted by all Law Lords that there was a public interest in freedom of expression, although not all of them formulated this so explicitly.

From these cases on, it became customary for the courts to refer explicitly to the freedom of expression interest of a case. In a number of cases, freedom of expression was not mentioned as such, but the reasoning used in several of the opinions did very clearly point in the direction of freedom of expression or an aspect of it. For example Lord Ackner, in the A-G v. Guardian Newspapers case at the interlocutory stage,

---

1   Feldman, Civil Liberties and Human Rights in England and Wales, 1993, p. 66; Gardner, Freedom of Expression, 1994, p. 214.
2   Gardner, Freedom of Expression, 1994, p. 214.
3   Barendt, Libel and Freedom of Speech in English Law, 1993, p. 461.
4   Hubbard v. Vosper [1972] 1 All ER 1023, CA, 1030.
5   Brutus v. Cozens [1972] 2 All ER 1297, 1299.
6   A-G v. Times Newspapers Ltd [1973] 3 All ER 54 at 60.

spoke of 'the right of the public to be fully informed by the press'. In earlier cases Lord Diplock wrote about the very general 'curtailed liberty of the citizen' and Lord Ackner, in Telnikoff v. Matusevitch, spoke of 'the freedom to comment on a matter of public importance'.

However, from the moment it was held in the decision on the merits in A-G v. Guardian Newspapers that freedom of expression finds similar protection under common law as it finds under the ECHR, the courts no longer feel inhibited about using the term 'freedom of expression' as such. And as a consequence of this judgement,[7] in the case of Rantzen v. Mirror Group Newspapers Ltd it was held that there exists a principle of freedom of expression under common law.[8]

It should be noted that the terms freedom of expression and freedom of speech are used interchangeably and appear to refer to the same principle. Again, the fact that the right to freedom of expression is acknowledged as a principle under common law, may indicate that the influence of this right has increased. However, the mere mention of freedom of expression supplies no information on the degree of protection of this right. This is an issue of method of protection, discussed in the following three chapters.

First, however, I further elaborate on the notion of freedom of expression under English law in comparison to that of Article 10 of the ECHR. As I said, I successively discuss the nature of freedom of expression, horizontal effect, and prior restraint as aspects of the notion of freedom of expression.

3 NATURE OF FREEDOM OF EXPRESSION

Under Article 10 ECHR, the protection of freedom of expression is allowed to 'everyone', meaning all citizens no matter their occupation.[9] Moreover, not only political speech,[10] but also commercial speech[11] and artistic expressions[12] are protected. The manner of expression, including choice of wording and means of expression, come within the scope of freedom of expression as well. The Court has often held, referring to requirements of 'pluralism, tolerance and broad-mindedness without which there is no democratic society', that Article 10 is not only applicable

---

7   The Court of Appeal also referred to the Spycatcher decision (A-G v. Guardian Newspapers Ltd) in the Derbyshire County Council case.
8   Rantzen v. Mirror Group Newspapers Ltd [1993] 3 WLR 953 at 971: '... that article 10 has a wider role and can properly be regarded as an articulation of some of the principles underlying the common law'.
9   Including soldiers and civil servants.
10   E.g. Lingens v. Austria, (1992) A.103; Castells v. Spain, (1992) A.236.
11   E.g. Markt Intern Verlag GmbH and Klaus Beerman v. Germany, (1989) A.165; Casado Coca v. Spain, (1994) A.285-A.
12   E.g. Müller v. Switzerland, (1988) A.133.

to information and ideas that are 'favourably received or regarded as inoffensive or as a matter of indifference, but also to those that offend, shock or disturb'.[13] The Court applies a broad notion of freedom of expression and focuses on the assessment of the necessity of restrictions of this freedom.

As we have seen in the previous section freedom of expression has not been formulated as a right under English law. There is no specified definition that could be compared to Article 10 ECHR. Under English law the issue of the notion of freedom of expression and the necessity of restrictions to it are not separate issues. However, from the available sources some indication can be given of the approach to the notion of freedom of expression. In academic writings no real discussion as to the meaning of freedom of expression has taken place. John Gardner formulated his own idea of how freedom of expression should be protected. He stated that there is a moral right to freedom of expression which covers 'all activities which are conventionally understood to have a primarily expressive or communicative function'.[14] The freedom does not only cover 'informative communications', but also 'reflections and portrayals of people's experiences and ways of life'. Activities like talking, writing, publishing and broadcasting are always protected, but all conduct that is considered to communicate a message is covered, so also, for instance, the wearing of a uniform[15] if this is generally accepted to communicate a message.

Gardner is an exception however. In general, the authors tend to deal with the different philosophies behind freedom of expression, and leave open the question what expressions are covered by this freedom.[16] Gardner's broad definition of

---

13 E.g. Handyside v. United Kingdom, (1976) A.24; The Observer and Guardian v. United Kingdom, (1991) A.216; Sürek v. Turkey (No. 2), 8 July 1999.

14 Gardner, Freedom of Expression, 1994, p. 209.

15 Considered in reaction to O'Moran v. DPP [1975] QB 864.

16 Barendt and Feldman are examples of this, although Barendt, more or less without discussion, assumes that the wearing of political uniforms is part of freedom of expression because 'the wearing of these uniforms is clearly appreciated as conveying a message, but also because the object of the relevant legislation is to prevent ideological offence to the majority of people'. He thus formulates his own idea of what is covered by freedom of expression but does not follow up on that. He generally discusses the scope of freedom of expression in the different national legal systems discussed in his book 'Freedom of Speech'.

Mungo Deans says that freedom of expression is a 'fundamental value of a democratic society' and that it is 'essential to any informed debate and allows conflicting ideas to be exchanged, criticised and, where appropriate, empirically tested as widely as possible in order to ascertain whether a particular idea is useful or otherwise of value'. This is a rather restricted view of the meaning and scope of freedom expression and seems to suggest that its protection focuses on political speech.

Alan Boyle completely identifies with the English courts by saying about freedom of expression that 'its scope in English law can be determined only by reference to the general content of English law and to the circumstances in which judges have referred to it'.

All these opinions are mere statements, which shows that a real discussion on why certain forms of speech should or should not be covered by freedom of expression has not taken place.

freedom of expression fits in with the impression one gets of the approach to the nature of this freedom of English law. Although the terms 'freedom of speech' and 'freedom of expression' were used frequently in the relevant case law, the meaning of these terms has rarely been elaborated on. A few exceptions can be found however. In the Sunday Times case, Lord Simon in his opinion explicitly stated what the function of freedom of expression was, namely that 'members of a democratic society should be sufficiently informed that they may influence intelligently the decisions which may effect themselves'.[17] And in the Derbyshire County Council case the House of Lords said that 'it was of the highest public importance that a democratically elected governmental body should be open to uninhibited public criticism' and a civil defamation action from a local government body 'would place an undesirable fetter on the freedom to express such criticism'.[18] The right to impart and receive[19] information in these opinions is related to the functioning of democracy and this seems to suggest that it is restricted to 'political speech'. The protection of freedom of expression under English legislation and subsequent case law is wider than these opinions suggest however. First of all s.4 of the Obscene Publications Act offers a defence of public good. If a publication is considered to be of sufficient literary, artistic, or scholarly value, publication shall not be prohibited despite the obscene nature of the article.[20] Secondly, in relation to an action for defamation it is a defence to argue 'fair comment on a matter of public interest'.[21] And, finally, information may be disclosed in breach of confidence if the public interest in publication outweighs the public interest in keeping the information confidential.[22] This does seem to indicate a general protection of the communication of ideas and thoughts, with an emphasis on information of public interest, but it is not restricted to this.[23] This view of the notion of freedom of expression as

---

17 A-G v. Times Newspapers Ltd [1973] 3 All ER 54 at 81.

18 Derbyshire County Council v. Times Newspapers Ltd [1993] 2 WLR 449.

19 That also the right to be informed is protected was confirmed by Lord Simon of Glaisdale in A-G v. Times Newspaper Ltd [1973] 3 All ER 54, at 77: 'The first public interest involved is that of freedom of discussion in a democratic society. People cannot adequately influence the decisions which affect their lives unless they can be adequately informed on facts and arguments relevant to the decisions'.

20 The defence under s.4 was held to 'deal with aspects of general concern': DPP v. Jordan [1977] AC 699, per Lord Wilberforce at 718.

21 Public interest was in the case-law defined as: 'Whenever a matter is such as to effect people at large, so that they may be legitimately interested in, or concerned at, what is going on; or what may happen to them or to others' (London Artists Ltd v. Littler [1969] 2 QB 375, per Lord Denning at 391). In practice this defence has not been restricted to statements of a political nature.

22 As I observed, these interests may consist of, for instance, public health or wrongful criminal prosecution.

23 See also X Ltd v. Morgan Grampian [1991] 1 AC 1, in which the speech concerned was held to be of a commercial nature and freedom of expression was considered in relation to it.

communication and ideas in general is also apparent from the fact that it has been accepted that commercial information is protected by freedom of expression as well.[24]

The information concerned may be exchanged in different ways. First of all, through spoken or written (or printed) word, also through tape, video or film, broadcast on television[25] and probably also by way of art. 'Physical manifestations of support for an opinion' seem to be excluded as a form of expression,[26] although it seems difficult to draw a distinction between 'conduct' and 'expression'.[27]

The profession of the person expressing himself also does not seem to be a reason for assuming that freedom of expression cannot play a role in a case.[28] It can be assumed that everyone has a right to freedom of expression, except where this right has been restricted.[29]

---

24 R. v. Radio Authority, ex p. Bull [1995] 3 WLR 572 – Reviewed on Wednesbury reasonableness of the decision of the Radio Authority. See further Barendt, Freedom of Speech, p. 54: 'Not surprisingly the theoretical issues have never been discussed in Britain, where advertising is subject to a battery of tort and administrative remedies, as well as to possible criminal prosecution under the Trade Descriptions Act 1968 or other legislation. Commercial advertising is further controlled informally and extra-legally by an Advertising Standards Authority, which attempts to enforce a code of practice prescribing false and misleading claims (Under the Code of Practice, an advertisement must be legal, decent, honest and truthful. The Code goes well beyond legal controls. For example, in forbidding advertisement which cause grave or widespread offence) ... some restrictions on professional advertising ... On the other hand, thee do not seem to be any restrictions in Britain on publicizing the availability of advice about contraception or abortion facilities. It is further illegal to publish an advertisement on behalf of a parent wishing to have a child adopted or for a prospective adoptive parent (Adoption Act 1976, s.58)'.

25 R. v. Secretary for the Home Department ex p. Brind [1991] 1 AC 696; Lord Denning explicitly in Schering Chemicals Ltd v. Falkman Ltd [1981] 2 WLR 848 at 851.

26 See Feldman, Civil Liberties and Human Rights in England and Wales, 1993, p. 560. He discusses meetings and processions separately under freedom of demonstration or protest. Barendt, Freedom of Speech, 1996, p. 88-91, on the other hand includes meetings and processions in the discussion of freedom of expression.

27 Barendt, Freedom of Speech, 1996, p. 43: 'In Hubbard v. Pitt, for example, where the plaintiffs secured an injunction to restrain a picket outside their offices, Lord Denning MR in his dissent considered the right to demonstrate and protest in this way so closely analogous to the exercise of free speech that the judicial prior restraint was inappropriate ([1976] 1 QB 142, 178-9). In essence the plaintiffs were complaining about the contents of the defendants' placards and leaflets. The majority of the Court of Appeal, however, took the view that the nuisance aspect of the defendants' activity was more important than its communicative effect which was merely incidental'.

28 I would use the Spycatcher litigation as an example. It should be recalled, however, that it was not the right of the government official that was at stake in these decisions, but the right of the newspapers to publish the book written by the government official.

29 This does not only include government officials and people in a special relation to the government, but also the government itself, which also enjoys freedom of expression unless restricted by law. From the Derbyshire County Council case it was recognized that the position of the government is different from that of its citizens in that it was held that 'there are rights available to private

According to Barendt, although there are, as was shown, a number of possibilities to protect the exchange of information, in particular that of general public interest in situations where information cannot be freely communicated, this protection is not generally available but restricted to those areas of English law that create an explicit possibility for such protection.[30] This warning is still appropriate in relation to statute-law. However, in relation to common law, the acknowledgement of a general principle of freedom of expression implies that it is possible for the English courts to take account of freedom of expression in all common law cases that interfere with that freedom. The rules of interpretation of legislation are also governed by common law. As a result, freedom of expression can also be considered when the scope of restricting legislation is determined.[31] Barendt's warning is only appropriate with regard to the application of the law once its scope has been determined.

Regarding the approach to the nature of freedom of expression, I conclude that the approach to the notion of freedom of expression is similar to the approach of the Court to freedom of expression under Article 10 of the ECHR.[32] Freedom of expression in both systems of protection entails the free communication of information and ideas in general, the manner in which this information and these ideas are exchanged is also covered by freedom of expression, and everyone is assumed to have a right to this freedom.

4 HORIZONTAL EFFECT OF FREEDOM OF EXPRESSION

In this paragraph I discuss whether or not freedom of expression is applied in horizontal situations. The term 'horizontal' refers to communications of private citizens about private citizens. Fundamental rights were originally adopted in the

---

citizens which institutions of central government are not in a position to exercise unless they can show that it is in the public interest to do so'. This is still a very different approach from that assumed in the ECHR and in non-common law countries in whose constitutions a Bill of Rights was adopted. In these instances the beneficiaries of the rights are the citizens and they can exercise these rights against the government and under certain circumstances the rights can be exercised against other citizens. The governments, however, are never the beneficiaries of these fundamental rights.

30 See also Barendt, Libel and Freedom of Speech in English Law, 1993, p. 462.

31 See Rantzen v. Mirror Group Newspapers Ltd [1993] 3 W.L.R. 954.; Derbyshire County Council v. Times Newspapers Ltd [1993] 2 W.L.R. 449.

32 Lord Keith in A-G v. Guardian Newspapers Ltd (No.2) [1988] 3 All ER 545, at 640: 'The general rule is that anyone is entitled to communicate anything he pleases to anyone else, by speech or in writing or in any other way'. Moreover it could be said that the protection of freedom of expression under English law was influenced by the ECHR. To what extent cannot be indicated exactly, since the House of Lords does refer to Article 10 of the Convention, but also emphasises that common law offers any kind of protection to freedom of expression that this Article offers (A-G v. Guardian Newspapers Ltd (No.2) and in Derbyshire County Council).

Magna Carta and in the Constitutions of non-common law countries to offer protection to citizens against their government. This was also the initial purpose of the ECHR. This vertical point of departure has been upheld – except, as explained above, if governments are held responsible for legislation or lack of legislation which allows the rights of citizens to be infringed by others. In such cases, a citizen of a State party to the ECHR cannot complain before the Court about another citizen infringing his rights. However, a citizen can complain about his government not providing (proper) legislation enabling him to protect his freedom to communicate thoughts and ideas on other private individuals.[33] This is of particular interest with regard to civil law actions. An interesting recent example is the Tolstoy Miloslavsky case, in which the Court held the national government responsible for not providing 'adequate and effective safeguards against a disproportionately large award' of damages in a libel case between two private citizens.[34]

In cases in which the dispute originated in a horizontal relationship, the Court has not considered this 'horizontal' background of the case. As I observed, the complaints were against the government and the nature of the original conflict was not considered. What can be concluded, however, is that it is not a strict requirement that the case dealt with an issue between a citizen and his government. This implies that the rights of the Convention can have horizontal effect, in the sense that the national authorities are held responsible for the legislation or absence of legislation that enables private individuals to exercise the rights guaranteed under the ECHR.

Horizontal effect of fundamental rights was not an issue of discussion in English literature until the Human Rights Act came about. Section 5 of this chapter deals with the effect of the Human Rights Act on the notion of freedom of expression and I return to the subject of horizontal effect and the discussion that took place on it there. Here, however, I concentrate on the current state of affairs regarding horizontal effect of freedom of expression. In English case law the role freedom of expression can play in cases of a horizontal nature is not an issue of discussion. Of the various types of law restricting the free communication of information, the action for defamation and the action for breach of confidence are the most likely to result in cases between citizens, and therefore these cases are the most likely to contain issues of whether or not freedom of expression is applicable. In a few opinions, it was implicitly accepted that freedom of expression was applicable to horizontal situations. The first of these

---

33   See Bartold v. Germany, (1983) A.90; Markt Intern Verlag v. Germany, (1987) A.165; Jacubowski v. Germany, (1994) A.291-A. In these cases the obligation of the State to provide protection for freedom of expression was implied. Although Fuentes Bobo, 29 February 2000, was decided by the Court later than the date after which no new data would be included in this study, I feel it is justified to refer to this decision. In Fuentes Bobo v. Spain, the Court explicitly held that the States party to the Convention have a positive obligation to provide protection for freedom of expression in horizontal situations.

34   Tolstoy Miloslavsky v. United Kingdom, (1995) A.323, par. 50.

was Lord Denning's dissenting opinion in Hubbard v. Vosper.[35] This case dealt with an action for breach of confidence against a former member of the Church of Scientology who wrote a book about this organization. Lord Denning proposed in his opinion to apply a similar approach to the defence of public interest under an action for breach of confidence as the approach to this defence under a civil libel action. When a defendant says in a libel action that he is going to justify, the publication concerned will not be restrained. Lord Denning stated: 'The reason is because the defendant, if he is right, is entitled to publish it; and the law will not intervene to suppress freedom of speech except when it is abused'.[36] Consequently he explicitly applied freedom of expression to a case between citizens. Lord Denning did not go into the reasons why he felt that in this case freedom of expression was applicable.

In Schering Chemicals v. Falkman the defendant received information in confidence and subsequently published this information, which revealed that a drug manufactured by Schering Chemicals could cause deformities in unborn children. With regard to this case Lord Denning again referred to 'freedom of the press'.[37] The more recent civil libel case of Telnikoff v. Matusevitch concerned a Russian immigrant who reacted to an article written by another Russian immigrant by sending a letter to a newspaper in which he accused the writer of the original article of being a racist.[38] The issue to be dealt with by the House of Lords was whether the jury, in determining whether the allegations were statements of fact or of opinion, should consider the letter in relation to the article to which it was a reaction, or should merely consider the letter as such. Lord Ackner in his dissenting opinion held that whether or not the letter defamed the writer of the previous article, should not be considered solely in relation to the letter, because if this were not done this would diminish 'the freedom to comment on a matter of public importance', which he calls 'fundamental to a democratic society'.[39]

And, finally, in Rantzen v. Mirror Group News Papers it was held by the Court of Appeal, with specific reference to Article 10 ECHR, that damages to be awarded in civil libel cases should be reduced to an amount that would not be 'inconsistent with article 10 ECHR', thus applying freedom of expression in a civil libel case between a television presenter and a newspaper.[40] Freedom of expression as protected under art. 10 ECHR led to the result in English law of a moderation of the amount of damages in cases of a horizontal nature. In the Rantzen case the court

---

35 Hubbard v. Vosper [1972] 1 All ER 1023.
36 Hubbard v. Vosper [1972] 1 All ER 1023 at 1030.
37 Schering Chemicals v. Falkman Ltd [1981] 2 WLR 848 at 861.
38 Telnikoff v. Matusevitch [1992] 2 AC 343.
39 Telnikoff v. Matusevitch [1992] 2 AC 343 at 361.
40 Rantzen v. Mirror Group Newspapers Ltd [1993] 3 WLR 954.

unanimously applied freedom of expression and thus unanimously applied it to a 'horizontal' case.

As a whole, it can be said that both under English law and under the ECHR communications between private individuals are protected by means of a right to freedom of expression. Under the ECHR this is established by means of government responsibility for the relevant legislation, or absence of it. In English law, by way of legal responsibilities or rights under statutory law, common law or equity. In English law the horizontal effect of the right does not work trough a system of government responsibility. This is a significant difference between the English system of protection and the system of protection of the ECHR. This difference, however, lies in the approach to fundamental rights and might be explained from the residual freedom approach traditional to the English system of protection. Residual freedom not only implies a non-interfering government, but also non-interfering private individuals. However, due to the degree of horizontal effect of the Convention rights, this difference in approach does not as such result in protection of speech under English law that is not also protected under the ECHR.

5 PRIOR RESTRAINT

One last issue that should be discussed in relation to the general notion of freedom of expression is that of prior restraint. Prior restraint is the restriction of an expression before it has been issued.[41] As in the previous sections, I first discuss the issue of prior restraint under the ECHR and subsequently the approach to that aspect of the notion of freedom of expression under English law.

Section 1 of Article 10 allows for a licensing system for 'broadcasting, television or cinema enterprises' and section 2 contains the words 'prevention' and 'preventing'. Consequently the text of Article 10 suggests that prior restraint is not prohibited as such.

In the Sunday Times case and the Markt Intern Verlag case the Court implicitly confirmed that prior restraint is not in principle rejected under Article 10 ECHR. In the Observer and Guardian case, the Court explicitly went into this particular aspect of restricting freedom of expression. It said '... that Art. 10 of the Convention does not in terms prohibit the imposition of prior restraints on publication as such'.[42] The words 'conditions' and 'restrictions', and 'prevention' and 'preventing' in the second paragraph of Article 10 were to be read in that light. In the Spycatcher case, the Court did state, however, that prior restraint is a serious interference with freedom

---

41 In this respect I understand the term 'issued' to mean 'disseminated'. In other words, I speak of prior restraint when the publication is prevented before it reaches its audience. This also seems to be the approach of both the Court and the English courts.

42 Observer and Guardian v. the United Kingdom, (1991) A.216, par. 60.

of expression: '... the dangers inherent in prior restraint are such that they call for the most careful scrutiny on the part of the Court'[43] and it went on to say: 'This is especially so as far as the press is concerned, for news is a perishable commodity and to delay its publication, even for a short period, may well deprive it of all its value and interest'.[44] After the book was published in the US, the Court held that the book, from that moment on, was freely available and as a consequence the prohibition of publication of information from the book in the United Kingdom could no longer be thought to be 'necessary in a democratic society'. Under the ECHR, prior restraint is an acceptable restriction on freedom of expression, but it is regarded as a particularly serious restriction on freedom of expression.

In English law, there are a number of areas of law that offer the possibility of prior restraint.[45] Apart from a few exceptions, the prior restraint aspect of these areas of law are not a point of discussion in English literature.[46] Before I discuss the approach to prior restraint under English law, I set out the areas of law that provide for possibilities of prior restraint.

The first two areas of law are libel law, and breach of confidence. As part of an action under these areas of law, an appellant can ask the courts to grant an interim injunction that may allow for prior restraint of the information concerned. Interesting in relation to this is that because governmental information can be the subject of an action for breach of confidence, it is possible for the government to commence an action for an injunction to restrain publication of confidential governmental information. An injunction is a remedy in civil law cases, which is not available in criminal law cases.[47] Therefore if the government is trying to prevent publication of certain information it has the best possibility of success by commencing an action for breach of confidence.

A third area of English law in which a possibility of prior restraint is provided for is contempt of court law. There are 'restrictions on the reporting of cases where justice cannot effectively be done in public',[48] just as there are 'several restrictions which affect reporting of hearings held in public'.[49] The most controversial

---

43 Confirmed in Wingrove v. United Kingdom, 25 November 1996, Reports 1996-V, par. 52.

44 Observer and Guardian v. United Kingdom, (1991) A.215, par.60.

45 See Feldman, Civil Liberties and Human Rights in England and Wales, 1993, p. 636-637 for an explanation of the 'special evil of prior restraint'.

46 The exceptions are Robertson and Nicol, Media Law, 1992, p. 67-70; Feldman, Civil Liberties and Human Rights in England and Wales, 1993, p. 642-668 and especially Barendt, Freedom of Speech, 1996, p. 114-144.

47 Although the Attorney General has the possibility 'to commence an action for an injunction if he deems it to be in the public interest', this in the light of his task to maintain compliance with criminal law – see Feldman p. 642.

48 See Feldman, Civil Liberties and Human Rights in England and Wales, 1993, p. 765-771.

49 See Feldman, Civil Liberties and Human Rights in England and Wales, 1993, p. 771-781.

restriction in this last category is the possibility of a 'postponement' of reporting on a case when there is 'substantial risk of prejudice to the administration of justice'.[50] The common law variant of this power, that was operative before this Act was adopted, was the matter in dispute in the notorious Sunday-Times case.[51] I return to this case when I elaborate on the approach to prior restraint in English law.

Finally the system of film-censorship is of importance to the issue of prior restraint. This is an interesting category, because in this area of law the restriction is not imposed by the courts and the censorship appears to be partly of a voluntary nature. As I described in the first section of chapter III of this book, the British Board of Film Classification applies a system of classification to films shown in the cinema. Film-makers can voluntarily subject their products to this system, but in practice, without a classification certificate they do not have much chance of their film being run in the cinemas. Local councils that license the cinemas in practice apply their powers to prohibit the showing of films[52] in accordance with the certificate given to a film by the BBFC. In order to be able to reach a larger audience (in most instances for reasons of profit), the film-maker in practice is inclined to cut scenes from the film as suggested by the BBFC, in order to obtain, for instance, an 18 instead of an 18 R certificate.[53] A comparable rating system also applies in relation to videos, a system also governed by the BBFC. It is noteworthy that film-makers hardly ever object to the classification given to their product by the BBFC, the one exception being in the Visions of Ecstasy case, which at the same time demonstrated the serious consequences of the prior restraint effect of the licensing system. As I said above, this case dealt with a video of some 20 minutes showing St. Theresa in an erotic scene with Jesus Christ. The BBFC rejected the film for certification 'on the grounds that it was likely to be convicted of blasphemy by a jury'.[54] The Video Appeals Committee[55] was divided on the question of whether a jury would actually hold the video to be blasphemous, but upheld the ban. This construction of certification prevented the legal system of criminal law from ever finding out whether this would be the case or not, since a consequence of the rejection of a certificate meant in practice that the film was banned and would therefore never be available for showing.

The courts' influence on restrictions prior to publication with regard to film censorship are limited. They are more likely to influence prior restraint by means of

---

50 Contempt of Court Act 1981, section 4(2).
51 See Feldman, Civil Liberties and Human Rights in England and Wales, 1993, p. 776-778.
52 Cinemas Act 1985.
53 See Robertson and Nicol, Media Law, 1992, p. 568 for an overview of the possible certificates granted by the BBFC.
54 Robertson and Nicol, Media Law, 1992, p. 589.
55 Video Recordings Act, S.4.

orders to postpone publication under the Contempt of Court Act, and the granting of injunctions in relation to actions for defamation and breach of confidence. In relation to defamation cases, the courts will not usually grant an injunction. As Lord Denning in Fraser v. Evans said: 'the court will not restrain the publication of an article, even though it is defamatory, when the defendant says he intends to justify it or to make fair comment on a matter of public interest'.[56] He substantiated this by referring to the right to free speech that should not be restricted 'so long as no wrongful act is done', and no wrong is done 'if it is true, or if it is fair comment on a matter of public interest' and stated: 'The court will not prejudice the issue by granting an injunction in advance of publication'.[57] He consequently implied that prior restraint is also rejected in English law in principle. However, such an approach to prior restraint can only be found in civil libel cases. In breach of confidence cases, for instance, such a rule does not apply, although Lord Denning did propose this in Hubbard v. Vosper.[58] In these cases an injunction will usually be granted when asked for. According to Barendt this can be explained by the fact that if confidential information is published, no sanction can undo such a disclosure.[59]

An important point with regard to prior restraint in breach of confidence cases is that there does exist a rule that protects freedom of expression from prior restraint in effect. This rule is that if the confidential information is of public interest, an injunction to prevent publication will not be granted.[60] The balance between confidentiality and the public interest involved, however, is not easily held to lead to a necessity to publish. In Lion Laboratories Ltd v. Evans no injunction was granted to restrain information on the 'Lion Intoximeter', which measured the alcohol concentration in the breath of drivers. This instrument was used by the police. The information concerned revealed that the readings of it were inaccurate and that subsequently a large number of people were falsely convicted of drink-drive offences. The public interest in publication in this case should prevail. However, the case of X v. Y illustrates that the courts will not easily come to the conclusion that the information should be published.

---

56 Fraser v. Evans [1969] 1 QB 349, per Lord Denning at 360.
57 Fraser v. Evans [1969] 1 QB 349, per Lord Denning at 360. The general rule formulated in this case by Lord Denning originated from Bonnard v. Perryman [1891] 2 Ch 269.
58 Hubbard v. Vosper [1972] 1 All ER 1023, per Lord Denning at 1030: 'We never restrain a defendant in a libel action who says he is going to justify. So in a copyright action, we ought not to restrain a defendant who has a reasonable defence of fair dealing. Nor in an action for breach of confidence, if the defendant has a reasonable defence of public interest. The reason is because the defendant, if he is right, is entitled to publish it; and the law will not intervene to suppress freedom of speech except when it is abused'.
59 Barendt, Freedom of Speech, 1996, p. 131.
60 See for example: Woodward v. Hutchins [1977] 2 All ER 751; Lion Laboratories Ltd v. Evans [1984] 2 All ER 417; Hubbard v. Vosper [1992] 1 All ER 1023.

This case dealt with the request for an injunction preventing a newspaper from publishing the identity of two practising doctors infected with HIV, information which was obtained from confidential hospital records. In this case, according to Rose J., the public interest in freedom of expression and in free debate were 'substantially outweighed when measured against the public interest in relation to loyalty and confidentiality both generally and with particular reference to AIDS patients' hospital records'.[61] The interest in confidentiality was also thought to be a public interest, because measures were taken to ensure that HIV infected people were 'monitored and counselled', which amongst other things would prevent them from infecting other people.[62] The public interest in this case was sought in the informed public debate on AIDS and not in the interest of possible patients to know that they were being treated by doctors infected with HIV.[63] The public interest that was referred to could not outweigh the interest in confidentiality.

Another differentiation with regard to the prevention of prior restraint by means of a public interest defence is that an injunction in a breach of confidence case will be more readily granted in respect of private information than in respect of public information.[64] This is particularly of interest in relation to confidential governmental information, especially since such information can be said to be of public interest of its very nature.[65] The courts recognise this special position of governmental information. Lord Keith in A-G v. Guardian Newspapers (No.2) formulated it as follows: 'The Crown, however, as representing the nation as a whole, has no private life or personal feelings capable of being hurt by the disclosure of confidential information ...'.[66] As a consequence, the court formulated a requirement that the Crown would have to fulfil before publication of such information could be restrained: 'In so far as the Crown acts to prevent such disclosure or to seek redress for it on confidentiality grounds, it must necessarily, in my opinion, be in a position to show that the disclosure is likely to damage or has damaged the public interest'.[67] Only after a public interest in confidentiality has been established, does the defendant have to prove an overriding public interest in the disclosure of the information. However, that there is a public interest in restriction turned out to be an easy

---

61 X v. Y [1988] 2 All ER 648, at 661.
62 In this case freedom of expression is an interest as such, but still seen in relation to its function in a public debate on a public health issue. This debate was thought still to be possible, even without the information on the identity of the two doctors.
63 See X v. Y [1988] 2 All ER 648 at 655.
64 See also Feldman, Civil Liberties and Human Rights, 1993, p. 618.
65 To protect sensitive governmental information the Official Secrets Act 1989 offers the possibility of subsequent restraint. An action for breach of confidence offers the possibility of prior restraint through an interim injunction.
66 A-G v. Guardian Newspapers Ltd [1988] 3 All ER 545, at 640, per Lord Keith (HL).
67 A-G v. Guardian Newspapers Ltd [1988] 3 All ER 545, per Lord Keith at 640.

requirement to fulfil in the A-G v. Guardian Newspapers cases, consequently in fact not offering much of a guarantee against prior restraint.

Finally with regard to prior restraint in the area of contempt of court law, the courts seem to lack any awareness of the restrictive effect prior restraint has on freedom of expression. With regard to this area of law, there have been two cases in which prior restraint was at issue. These were, first, the Sunday Times case and, second, the case of A-G v. the BBC.[68] In neither case was the prior restraint aspect considered. Under the Contempt of Court Act 1981, section 5 was adopted, which creates some protection for freedom of expression in that it creates room for discussion of public affairs. Although this section also restricts the scope of prior restraint, there is no evidence that this section is used to take consideration of the particularly restrictive effect prior restraint has. If an article is held to prejudice litigation, publication will be prevented by way of an injunction. The fact that this prohibition to publish amounts to prior restraint cannot affect the prejudicial nature of the article.

In conclusion it can be said that under English law prior restraint is an accepted method by way of which the aims of the restrictive legislation can be realised. The courts have in particular instances recognised the impact prior restraint has on freedom of expression. However, this is only in relation to defamation cases. In confidentiality cases, the starting point is that the information should be kept confidential, unless a public interest in the information overrides the interest in confidentiality. Prior restraint is accepted as a means by which the interest in confidentiality can be protected. In relation to contempt of court law, emphasis is on protection of the correct functioning of the judiciary. Freedom of expression is protected in that discussion of issues of public interest in which any mention of cases pending is incidental to the discussion, is allowed. Such discussion cannot be constrained. This approach of the courts to prior restraint together with their lack of influence on the licensing system makes clear that the English courts do not regard it as their task in general to review whether or not freedom of expression is justifiably restricted when it comes to prior restraint.

With regard to a common ground between the ECHR and English law regarding prior restraint I conclude that under both systems of protection prior restraint is an accepted method by way of which the aims pursued can be realised. The degree to which it is accepted differs somewhat. The European Court of Human Rights is in general of the opinion that prior restraint is a serious restriction on freedom of expression. It subsequently adjusts the requirements that have to be satisfied before the restriction can be held 'necessary in a democratic society'. However, the possible

---

68 Lord Fraser, Lord Salmon and Lord Scarman came to the conclusion that extending the scope of contempt of court to local valuation courts would be 'to great a curtailment of the right to freedom of expression': A-G v. BBC [1980] 3 WLR 109, per Lord Fraser at 128.

strict review under 'necessary in a democratic society' is not applied under all circumstances where prior restraint is at issue. In those areas where the Court usually leaves a wide margin of appreciation, such as national security and morals,[69] prior restraint will not be subject to any closer scrutiny than usual.[70] With these remarks I anticipate the discussion of the application of the margin of appreciation by the Court in chapter V. This, however, is necessary for me to be able to compare the approach to prior restraint under the English system of protection and that of the ECHR.

The Court's attitude in cases with these kind of circumstances – government and confidential information – is comparable to that of the English courts: if the appellant can show he has a reasonable case, confidentiality will prevail. The sort of information involved does not seem to play much of a role and the Court is not inclined to doubt the national authorities' interpretation of the facts and its explanation of why the information should be kept confidential. In the Spycatcher litigation it became clear that, in English law, an extra safeguard is the obligation on the government to indicate what the public interest in confidentiality of the information concerned actually is. This is also comparable to the approach of European Court of Human Rights. The national authorities are required to indicate a legitimate aim for keeping the information confidential and if this aim is national security the European Court will leave a very wide margin of appreciation, thus not applying the close scrutiny which in principle is applicable in cases that involve prior restraint.[71] However, if the information is in the public domain, confidentiality is in principle no longer necessary in a democratic society, in which case a narrow margin of appreciation is applied, including close scrutiny of the facts and circumstances of the case. For the English judge, at least in a confidentiality case, when the information is in the public domain, confidentiality needs no longer be guarded through an interim injunction. However, as was demonstrated in A-G v. Guardian Newspapers and in the Schering Chemicals case, even if the information is in the public domain the circumstances of the case may still justify an injunction. In protecting the impartiality of the judiciary, the European Court of Human Rights accepts prior restraint less easily, as the Sunday Times judgment of the Court illustrated.

---

69 Wingrove v. United Kingdom, 25 November 1996, Reports 1996-V, par. 52.

70 See Observer and Guardian v. United Kingdom, (1991) A.216, par. 62-63.

71 See Wingrove v. the United Kingdom, 25 November 1996, Reports 1996-V, par. 58: 'Moreover the fact that the present case involves prior restraint calls for special scrutiny by the court'. It has to be noted however that extra motivation for the restriction was not required since 'a wide margin of appreciation is usually available ... in relation to matters liable to offend intimate personal convictions within the sphere of morals or, especially, religion'. Moreover the test applied was rather marginal in nature since the Court concluded that 'the decisions by the national authorities cannot be said to be arbitrary or excessive' and in fulfilling these requirements they were thus 'necessary in a democratic society'.

The approach to prior restraint with regard to defamation cases and confidential governmental information of the English courts is comparable, in result, to that of the European Court of Human Rights. Whether it is so with regard to contempt of court law remains to be seen, since the Contempt of Court Act still provides for far-reaching possibilities for prior restraint, without any explicit reference to the view of the European Court of Human Rights that courts cannot function in a vacuum and should therefore accept discussion of matters of public concern while a trial is going on. In fact, the Contempt of Court Act 1981 does not contain provisions that guarantee that a case such as the Sunday Times case would be decided differently under this Act. In that regard, there are still some uncertainties as to the compatibility of English law with the protection provided for freedom of expression under the ECHR.

6 COMMON GROUND AND THE INFLUENCE OF THE HUMAN RIGHTS ACT 1998

Common Ground before the Human Rights Act 1998
The approach to the notion of freedom of expression is largely comparable. The manner in which the Court approaches the notion of freedom of expression under paragraph 1 of Article 10 is comparable to the areas of law in which the English courts have referred to freedom of expression. Under both systems of protection, moreover, freedom of expression may have horizontal effect and prior restraint is an accepted manner of restricting freedom of expression.

The reserved attitude towards prior restraint of the Court can also be found under English law, at least with regard to defamation cases. With regard to confidential information there is a different approach, but due to the restrictive review of the Court with regard to confidential information, at least where it concerns governmental information, this difference in approach will not easily lead to the Court concluding that a restriction is not necessary. This is different with regard to the protection of the impartiality of the judiciary. As the Sunday Times judgment demonstrated, with regard to this aim the scope of the review of the Court could in future cases lead to the conclusion that there has been a violation of Article 10. Such a conclusion would then be caused by the different approach to prior restraint.

Influence of the Human Rights Act on a Common Ground
The introduction of the Human Rights Act will influence English law not so much with regard to the approach to the nature of freedom of expression, but rather with regard to the horizontal effect of the rights incorporated and with regard to the English approach to prior restraint.

In English law, both the application of freedom of expression in horizontal situations and the application of prior restraint are usually not subjects of discussion, but they occur frequently. With the introduction of the Human Rights Act, horizontal

169

effect of freedom of expression has become an issue of debate, since s.6 of the Human Rights Act implies a horizontal effect of the rights adopted.[72] As I mentioned in chapter II of this book, s.6 ss.1 of the Human Rights Act imposes on public authorities a duty 'not to act in a way which is incompatible with a Convention right'. Beside the regular decision-making authorities, the courts are also regarded as 'public authorities' under the Act.[73] This means, first of all, that not only with regard to statute law, but also regarding common law, the courts have an obligation to apply that law in a manner compatible with the ECHR.[74] A second implication is that this obligation does not only concern public law, but also private law.[75] However, 'full horizontal effect' in the sense that the Convention rights can be a source of action as such in cases originating from a dispute between private individuals, is not intended. In other words, in horizontal cases a breach of a convention right cannot be claimed in a separate action. A breach of a Convention right can only be claimed by way of regular sources of action.[76] In my opinion, the change instigated by these provisions lies in the area of consistency. Although the English courts have already referred to freedom of expression in horizontal situations, in particular in relation to press freedom and the possible restriction as a result of a right to privacy (including reputation), the Human Rights Act could increase the consistency in applying Convention rights in cases originating in disputes between private citizens.

S.2 of the Human Rights Act is relevant for the approach of the English courts to prior restraint. This section determines, as I observed, that not only the text of the Convention is incorporated, but also that the relevant case law of the Court should be taken into account. Although this section speaks of 'taking into account', and the English courts are therefore not necessarily bound by the interpretation of the rights by the European Court of Human Rights,[77] s.2 together with s.3 provides the courts

---

72 See for a more general and extensive discussion: Markesinis, Privacy, Freedom of Expression, and the horizontal effect of the Human Rights Bill: Lessons from Germany, 1999, p. 47-88; Hunt, The 'Horizontal Effect' of the Human Rights Act, 1998, p. 423-443. See also on this subject: Hooper, The impact of the Human Rights Act on Judicial Decision-making, 1998, p. 683; Wade, Human Rights and the Judiciary, 1998, p. 524-525; Editorial, [1998] E.H.R.L.R. 1, p. 1.

73 S. 6 ss. 3(a) HRA 1998.

74 Singh, Privacy and the Media after the Human Rights Act, 1998, p. 722.

75 HL Deb vol 583, 24 November 1997: The Lord Chancellor held that the government 'believe that it is a right as a matter of principle for the courts to have the duty of acting compatible with the Convention not only in cases involving other public authorities but also in developing the common law in deciding cases between citizens'.

76 See Ewing, The Human Rights Act and Parliamentary Democracy, 1999, p. 89.

77 See Singh, Privacy and the Media after the Human Rights Act, 1998, p. 723: The fact that the national courts can take the case-law with regard to the Convention into consideration, but are not bound by it, opens up the possibility for the courts to provide less, but also more protection than the Court.

with a possibility to apply prior restraint in conformity with the approach of the Court. S.3 provides: 'So far as it is possible to do so, primary legislation and subordinate legislation must be read and given effect in a way which is compatible with Convention rights'. The effect of the Human Rights Act with regard to prior restraint will most likely lie in the area of contempt of court law, where the English courts seem to be inclined to apply prior restraint and where the European Court of Human Rights is inclined to let freedom of expression prevail.

It is important to recall that the mere fact that these aspects are common to both systems of protection does not supply information on the extent of the protection of freedom of expression. I elucidate on that. When freedom of expression is applied in horizontal situations there seems no evidence that this affects the weight given to freedom of expression. And in the section on prior restraint under English law, I noted that freedom of expression is usually not subject to prior restraint when a request for an interlocutory injunction to prevent publication in a libel case is concerned. However, when a similar action regarding breach of confidence is concerned, the injunction will usually be granted. This approach under English law, at least for defamation cases and confidential governmental information, is compatible with the requirements the Court formulated with regard to Article 10 ECHR as regards the result of the protection of freedom of expression. I am interested, further, in the extent to which a common ground between the English and ECHR systems exists as to the role freedom of expression played in achieving that result. What these issues in fact refer to is the question of what methods of protection are applied when freedom of expression is a matter of concern, and how they are applied. I elaborate on the methods of protection in the following three chapters.

I wish to observe, however, that less protection seems unlikely, because of the possibility for English citizens to file a complaint against their government in Strasbourg. The observations of Singh do illustrate that the Act could be used by the courts to develop protection of rights at a different level from the Convention, thus treating the Convention as a separate catalogue of rights.

CHAPTER VI
MARGIN OF APPRECIATION

1 INTRODUCTION

We saw in chapter IV that the term 'margin of appreciation' as used by the Court refers to the room left to the national authorities of the States party to the Convention to determine the restrictions that are 'necessary in a democratic society'. The application of the margin of appreciation by the Court does not impose any duty on the national authorities to apply a margin of appreciation (as such). The search for a common ground between the application of a margin of appreciation as applied by the Court and the application of a margin of appreciation by the English courts requires clarification.

A consequence of the application of the margin of appreciation by the Court is that it influences the degree of protection that the national authorities are required to provide for a particular fundamental right. When the margin of appreciation is wide, the national authorities are left a significant amount of room to decide on the necessity of a restriction. Under such circumstances the Court merely formulates the outer boundaries of the necessity of a restriction. When the margin of appreciation is narrow, the Court itself formulates the required protection. The degree of protection required is the result of the application of the margin of appreciation and of the application of the substantial methods of review.

The resultant degree of required protection should be achieved in all areas of domestic law, be it civil law, penal law or administrative law. The margin of appreciation is part of the manner in which the Court realises protection of freedom of expression, and as such it is relevant to the search for a common ground.

The protection of freedom of expression in civil law and penal law takes place under the English courts' appellate jurisdiction. This implies that the required degree of protection that is the result of the margin of appreciation applied by the Court, in these areas of domestic law can be achieved only by way of substantial methods of review. This is so, because with regard to civil and penal law, the courts are the only institutions that have authority regarding its meaning when law of this type is part of a dispute.

I discuss the substantial methods of review in chapter VII and VIII. With regard to administrative law, however, the situation is different. Restrictions of freedom of expression under administrative law occur also by way of application of legislation. With regard to administrative law, however, it is not the courts but the executive that have the authority to determine the meaning of law in first instance. The courts can only provide protection to freedom of expression by way of judicial review of the decisions of the executive. The approach of the English courts to this task is discussed in section 3 of this chapter. Suffice it to say here that due to the division of powers under English law, the English courts leave the decision-making authorities room to apply the powers given to them in the way they see fit. In other words, the English courts leave the executive a margin of appreciation to determine the manner in which the powers granted should be applied. I said in chapter I that the English executive is not inclined to consider the fundamental rights aspects of its decisions. In fact, the protection of fundamental rights is left to the courts in administrative law as well. Consequently, the scope of the review of the English courts of the decisions of the decision-making authorities has implications for the extent to which the English courts succeed in providing the degree of protection required by the Court. Beside a common ground with regard to substantial methods of review, it is justified therefore to search for a common ground between the margin of appreciation left by the Court to the States party to the Convention and the margin of appreciation left by the English courts to the national decision-making authorities.

In section 2 of this chapter I elaborate on the application of the margin of appreciation by the Court. I continue with a discussion of the application of a margin of appreciation by the English courts in section 3. Finally, in the fourth section, I elaborate on a common ground between the scope of review applied by the courts of the two systems of protection and on the influence the Human Rights Act will have on a common ground with regard to the margin of appreciation.

2 MARGIN OF APPRECIATION UNDER ARTICLE 10 ECHR

In discussing the scope of the margin of appreciation applied by the Court in the first part of this section, I first give a definition of the concept of margin of appreciation. I then elaborate on the development of the scope of the review applied by the Court and finally I address the current state of affairs concerning the scope of the margin of appreciation. In the second part of this section I discuss the factors that influence the scope of the margin of appreciation applied under Article 10 ECHR. And in part 3 I draw some conclusions with regard to the application of the margin of appreciation by the Court.

2.1 Scope of the Margin of Appreciation

The margin of appreciation reflects the latitude the Court allows States party to the Convention in the observance of the Convention. It is used by the Court to determine the degree of scrutiny with which it will review the justification of interferences with rights protected under the Convention. The Court and the Commission started out by allowing the national authorities a very wide margin of appreciation, because of the rather reserved attitude towards interfering with the national authorities' policy regarding the restrictions that can be considered 'necessary in a democratic society'.

An example of the Court's reserved attitude can be found in Engel and Others v. the Netherlands. In this case the Court held that Article 10 also applied to members of the military, but that it had to take account of the margin of appreciation that Article 10 par. 2 leaves to the contracting states. The case concerned the publication of a number of articles. Because this had taken place at a 'tense time', the Court held that 'the Supreme Military Court may have had well-founded reasons for considering that they (the men, red.) had attempted to undermine military discipline and that it was necessary for the prevention of disorder to impose the penalty inflicted'.[1] Up to and including the Engel case, the margin of appreciation was always wide, continuing the Court's reserved attitude. In all that time, the Court never elaborated on the responsibilities in a positive sense, regarding the protection of the rights adopted in the Convention.

In the Handyside case, which came before the Court a few months after the Engel case, the Court provided more clarity in this respect.[2] In this case, the issue was the seizure, confiscation and destruction of copies of the 'little red schoolbook'. It concerned an educational book directed towards 'young adults'. It was mainly the section on sex education that the English authorities objected to. An action was brought against the publisher of the book in England under the Obscene Publications Act 1959. The purpose of the action was the protection of morals.

The Court again applied the margin of appreciation, this time, however, it made two statements about its reviewing task: 'Art. 10 para. 2 does not give the Contracting States an unlimited power of appreciation. The Court is empowered to give the final ruling on whether a "restriction" or "penalty" is reconcilable with ... Art. 10. The domestic margin of appreciation thus goes hand in hand with a European supervision'.[3] Although the Court reviewed the decisions made by the national authorities taking account of their margin of appreciation, it subsequently held that 'it must view them (the restrictive decisions) in the light of the case as a whole ... it must decide on the different data available'. Here the Court implied that the margin of appreciation is not unlimited. In other words, under certain circumstances, it could conclude that there was a breach of the Convention.

With regard to its supervisory role the Court indicated that it took account of the 'principles characterising a democratic society'. Freedom of speech was considered to be of fundamental importance to such a society. However, the Court also held that with regard to morals a European standard could not be found since 'the protection

---

1   Engel & Others v. The Netherlands, (1976) A.22, par. 101.
2   Handyside v. United Kingdom, (1976) A.24.
3   Handyside v. United Kingdom, (1976) A.24, par. 49.

of morals varies from time to time and from place to place' and consequently the domestic courts should be granted a lot of freedom to decide on these matters 'taking into account domestic social, cultural and religious attitudes'.[4] Subsequently the Court applied a wide margin of appreciation and concluded that the national authorities were 'entitled to think' that the measure taken was 'necessary in democratic society'. The scope of the review of the national courts' decisions left the national authorities a lot of discretionary power regarding the restriction of Article 10. In this case, however, the Court indicated that the scope of the margin of appreciation was variable and that there were specific factors that influenced the scope of the margin of appreciation.

Although in the Handyside case, the margin of appreciation was wide and the strictness of the review adapted accordingly, already the dissenters included one judge who felt that the Court was taking its task too lightly. He felt that a more extensive research of the facts of the case should have led to the conclusion that Article 10 had been violated.[5]

In the Sunday Times case, the Court with the smallest possible majority accepted this broader perception of its reviewing task. As I indicated in chapter III section 5 of this book, this case dealt with an injunction which had been granted by the English courts to prevent the publication of an article on a drug which caused deformities in the unborn children of pregnant women taking the drug. In reviewing whether the injunction was necessary in a democratic society the Court first determined the margin of appreciation to be allowed to the United Kingdom. The Court confirmed that 'the domestic margin of appreciation ... goes hand in hand with a European supervision'. And in this case the Court was even more specific about its supervisory power when it stated that it was 'not limited to ascertaining whether a respondent state exercised its discretion reasonably, carefully and in good faith'. The requirements that had to be satisfied were 'whether the interference complained of corresponded to a pressing social need, whether it was proportionate to the legitimate aim pursued, whether the reasons given by the national authorities to justify it are relevant and sufficient under Article 10 para. 2'.[6]

In applying these requirements the Court again mentioned the fundamental value of freedom of expression to a democratic society. This value was of decisive importance in this case. The press was said to have an important task in providing the public with information which it had a right to receive, particularly since information on the Thalidomide disaster was of great public interest. Also the aim of the State

---

4   Handyside v. United Kingdom, (1976) A.24, par. 48. However, the Court did not specify what its reasons were for holding that where morals are concerned no European standard exists. This would be of interest, since the book was freely available in most Member States of the Convention.

5   Handyside v. United Kingdom, (1976) A.24, dissenting opinion of Judge Mosler, par. 2 and 3.

6   Sunday Times v. United Kingdom, (1979) A.30, par. 48-49.

party, to avoid prejudicing the administration of justice was thought to allow for a more narrow margin of appreciation.

The Court subsequently reviewed whether the threat to the 'authority of the judiciary' was 'absolutely certain'. The Court then undertook its own evaluation of the facts and circumstances of the case and added to its considerations that the 'very breadth (of the injunction) calls for a particularly close scrutiny of its necessity'.[7] It consequently considered the importance of the speech involved. The Court moreover took account of the fact that the Court unlike the national courts 'is faced not with a choice between two conflicting principles but with a principle of freedom of expression that is subject to a number of exceptions which must be narrowly interpreted'. The Court in this case subsequently held that the reasons given could not be considered sufficient to justify the restriction.[8] The interpretation and application of the legislation and all other facts and circumstances were considered and appreciated independently by the Court. In this process there seemed not much left of the margin of appreciation the national authorities should have. Instead, the approach of the Court resulted in a full review of the case. From the dissenting opinions, it became apparent that this new strict approach met with some resistance within the Court. In a joint dissenting opinion it was suggested that the review should examine 'whether the national authorities have acted in good faith, with due care and in a reasonable manner when evaluating those facts and circumstances' and the scope of the supervision of the Court should go no further than to review whether the national authorities were 'entitled to think' that the restriction of the right concerned was necessary in a democratic society.[9] A majority of the Court in this case, however, abandoned the 'presumption in favour of the State' and demonstrated that it felt competent to examine the facts and circumstances of a case independent from the perception of the national authorities of the matter.[10]

After the Sunday Times judgment, the Court approached a considerable number of cases in a similar manner. These decisions demonstrated that the Court is prepared to conduct a full review in all but name, requiring that the necessity of the restriction of Article 10 was 'absolutely certain'.[11] However, the Court also regularly applied a wide margin of appreciation, requiring only that the restriction 'could be justified' to achieve the legitimate aim,[12] or that it was 'justifiable in principle and

---

7   Sunday Times v. United Kingdom, (1979) A.30, par. 63.
8   Sunday Times v. United Kingdom, (1979) A.30, par. 65.
9   Sunday Times v. United Kingdom, (1979) A.30, dissenting opinion, par. 8.
10   Sunday Times v. United Kingdom, (1979) A.30, par. 67.
11   Sunday Times v. United Kingdom, (1979) A.30, par. 65.
12   Chorherr v. Austria, (1993) A.266-B, par. 32.

proportionate'.[13] It has even on occasion been satisfied with the restriction being not 'unreasonable and disproportionate' to the aim pursued.[14]

This changeable application of the margin of appreciation illustrates that it is variable in nature. The discussion of the development of the margin of appreciation by way of reference to the Handyside case and the Sunday Times case moreover demonstrated that the scope of the margin of appreciation determines the degree of scrutiny of the facts and circumstances of a case by the Court. The narrower the margin of appreciation, the stricter the test applied, the less the Court will be inclined merely to follow the national authorities' reasoning. When a narrow margin is applied the Court reviews whether the necessity of a restriction is 'absolutely certain', whereas with a wide margin of appreciation it will suffice if the State was 'entitled to think' that a measure was necessary, or if it was 'not unreasonable' for the State to assume that the interference with Article 10 was necessary in a democratic society.

Van Dijk and Van Hoof divide the three categories into the narrow approach, the reasonable test and the not-unreasonable test.[15] The first category is closest to a full review of a case. The reasonable test leaves the State a wide margin of appreciation. The difference with the not-unreasonable test, which leaves the State the widest margin, is that in the latter case, the burden of proof lies not with the State but with the applicant or the Court itself.[16]

The frequent application of the margin of appreciation and consistencies in the manner in which it is applied have led scholars to refer to the 'margin of appreciation-doctrine'. However, the Court itself has not elucidated on the content of such a doctrine, it has merely held that 'the scope of the margin of appreciation will vary according to the circumstances, the subject-matter and its background'.[17] Otherwise, the Court has not been inclined to provide clarity as to the role played by the margin of appreciation in the reasoning which leads to the decision, or to indicate what 'principles or standards' determine the scope of the margin of appreciation.[18]

Even though it is mainly the particular facts and circumstances of individual cases which determine the scope of the margin of appreciation, some general principles regarding the application of the margin of appreciation can and have been derived from the decisions of the Court. I discuss the factors that are of influence to the scope of the margin of appreciation in the following subsection.

---

13 Markt Intern Verlag v. Germany, (1989) A.165, Groppera Radio AG & Others v. Switzerland, (1990) A.173.
14 Casado Coca v. Spain, (1994) A.285-A.
15 Van Dijk and Van Hoof, The European Convention in Theory and Practice, 1990, p. 418.
16 This last approach was applied in Jacubowski v. Germany, (1994) A.291-A, par. 25.
17 Rasmussen v. Denmark, (1984) A.87, par. 40.
18 Brems, The Margin of Appreciation Doctrine in the Case-Law of the European Court of Human Rights, 1996, p. 240; Lavender, The Problem of the Margin of Appreciation, 1997, p. 380.

2.2 Factors Influencing the Scope of the Margin of Appreciation[19]

The Court, as I said above, has never formulated clear criteria determining the scope of the margin of appreciation. Rather, it has developed a relatively consistent application of the margin of appreciation case-by-case. From the body of case law of the Court, a number of aspects can be derived that influence the scope of the margin of appreciation in the same manner in each case. Regarding Article 10, four main factors can be distinguished. These are first the nature of the expression concerned, second the possible common ground that can be found among the States Party to the Convention on the law involved, thirdly the legitimate aim advanced by the national authorities and, finally, the seriousness of the interference.[20] I discuss each of these factors separately. I elaborate in particular on the manner in which they influence the margin of appreciation.

---

19 See for a more elaborate discussion of the case law of the Court: Schokkenbroek, Toetsing aan de vrijheidsrechten van het EVRM, 1996.

20 The factors of influence discussed in this section coincide more or less with those enumerated by Schokkenbroek, De Margin of Appreciation-doctrine in de Jurisprudentie van het Europese Hof, 1990, p. 55-56, which he later dealt with in more detail in his thesis 'Toetsing aan de vrijheidsrechten van het Europees Verdrag tot Bescherming van de Rechten van de Mens'. He identified as factors of influence the Consensus Principle, which is the common ground that can be found in the law of the Member States, the legitimate aim invoked, the value to a democratic society of the right interfered with, which is similar to the nature of the expression restricted, and finally to the nature and seriousness of the interference.

These factors had been referred to in a less extensive manner by MacDonald, The Margin of Appreciation in the Jurisprudence of the European Court of Human Rights, 1987, p. 203, in which he referred to the legitimate aim, the existence of a consensus in the law of the States party to the Convention and the question of whether the right interfered with was fundamental to a democratic society. These factors, in a slightly different form returned as being of influence to the scope of the margin of appreciation in 'The margin of appreciation', 1993, p. 87-98, in which, in addition to discussing the influence of the aim being the protection of morals or the protection of the reputation and rights of others, he again referred to the nature of the speech as a factor of influence when he discussed the scope of the margin of appreciation applied when the speech concerned is held to be of a commercial nature. More recently Brems distinguished a larger number of factors of influence in The Margin of Appreciation Doctrine in: The Case-Law of the European Court of Human Rights, 1996, p. 256-293. Her enumeration amounts to an elaboration of the factors of influence discussed here. O'Donnell, in an earlier article The Margin of Appreciation Doctrine: Standards in the Jurisprudence of the European Court of Human Rights, 1982, p. 479-484, referred to the consensus principle and the fundamental value of a right to a democratic society as being aspects of a case that would influence the extent of the margin of appreciation.

a Nature of the Expression

With regard to the scope of the margin of appreciation the Court has developed two different approaches to two kinds of expressions. First there are expressions which are held to contribute to the public debate, and second expressions of a commercial nature. I elaborate on the manner in which these types of expressions influence the scope of the margin of appreciation under separate headings.

Public Debate

As indicated, the first case in which a narrow margin of appreciation was applied was in the Sunday Times case.[21] The Court in its decision repeated its standpoint from the Handyside case by stressing the fundamental value of freedom of expression to a democratic society. This value was of decisive importance in this case, since it was the press that was restricted in publishing an article. The press was held to have an important task in providing the public information which it has a right to receive, particularly since information on the Thalidomide disaster was considered to be of great public interest. The content of the speech and the fact that the injunction restricted the functioning of the press together led to the application of a narrow margin of appreciation.

The notion that freedom of expression is of fundamental value to a democratic society, particularly when the content of the expression is of public interest, was maintained in a majority of cases.[22] Moreover, unlike other aspects of influence to the scope of the margin of appreciation, the Court will consider in almost all cases whether the expression concerned can be considered to be of general interest to society.[23]

In several of these cases, moreover, it was confirmed that if the press is restricted, this enhances the seriousness of the interference.[24] In the Lingens case, the Court took a very clear stand on the restriction of speech that is of public interest.[25] Lingens was an Austrian journalist who published two articles in a magazine, which were critical of the Austrian Chancellor Mr Kreisky. Lingens accused Kreisky of protecting former SS-members for political reasons and of facilitating their participation in Austrian politics. The chancellor brought private prosecutions and Lingens was convicted for

---

21 Sunday Times v. United Kingdom, (1979) A.30.
22 Karatas v. Turkey, 8 July 1999; Arslan v. Turkey, 8 July 1999; Ceylan v. Turkey, 8 July 1999; Bowman v. the United Kingdom, 19 February 1998, Reports 1998-I; Barthold v. Germany, (1985) A.90.
23 See also Fressoz and Roire v. France, 21 January 1999, which demonstrates that this aspect is not only considered when the Court finds that the expression is of public interest to society.
24 See also e.g. Gerger v. Turkey, 8 July 1999; Erdogdu and Ince v. Turkey, 8 July 1999; Sürek and Özdemir v. Turkey, 8 July 1999.
25 Lingens v. Austria, (1986) A.103.

defamation and fined, and issues of the magazine were confiscated. In this case the Court repeated its general statements on the role of freedom of expression in society and on the specific task the press had in providing the public with information it had a right to receive. The Court then went on to specify the reason why it felt freedom of expression to be of fundamental value: 'Freedom of the press furthermore affords the public one of the best means of discovering and forming an opinion of the ideas and attitudes of political leaders. More generally freedom of political debate is at the very core of the concept of a democratic society which prevails throughout the Convention. The limits of acceptable criticism are accordingly wider as regards a politician as such than as regards a private individual. Unlike the latter the former inevitably and knowingly lays himself open to close scrutiny of his every word and deed to both journalists and the public at large, and he must consequently display a greater degree of tolerance'.[26] The Court thus distinguished between speech regarding a public person and regarding a private person. The margin of appreciation will be narrower where a public person is concerned. Although even politicians are not completely deprived of protection of their reputation, 'the requirements of such protection have to be weighed in relation to the interests of open discussion of political issues'.[27]

Three aspects of the nature of the speech seemed of importance in this case. First, the political nature of the speech made it of great importance to a democratic society, second, account was taken of the fact that it was a journalist who was fined for expressing his opinion and that this was 'liable to hamper the press in performing its task as purveyor of information and public watchdog'.[28] And finally the Court distinguished between facts and value-judgements. The fact that the Austrian courts asked Lingens to prove the truth of value-judgements as such seemed to form an infringement on Article 10. The Court stated: 'The existence of facts can be demonstrated, whereas the truth of value-judgements is not susceptible of proof ... as regards value-judgements this requirement is impossible of fulfilment and it infringes freedom of opinion itself, which is a fundamental part of the right secured by Art.10 ECHR'.[29] In a later judgment the Court indicated that it does not easily accept that a statement is of a factual nature.[30]

In a number of decisions taken in the 1990s, the Court confirmed the line of thought developed in its case law on public speech, consequently applying a narrow margin of appreciation and extending its approach to defamatory speech concerning politicians to a number of other people in the public eye. A member of parliament

---

26 Lingens v. Austria, (1986) A.103, par. 42.
27 Lingens v. Austria, (1986) A.103, par. 42.
28 Lingens v. Austria, (1986) A.103, par. 44.
29 Lingens v. Austria, (1986) A.103, par. 46.
30 Oberschlick v. Austria, (1991) A.204, par. 63.

was considered to be a public person;[31] and criticism of the police was thought to be a matter of public concern.[32] In the latter case, the Court pointed out that it does not distinguish between political discussion and discussion on other matters of public interest.

On speech concerning the functioning of a court, or regarding judges in general, the Court deviated from the line of thought developed in Lingens and the later cases concerning expressions of public interest. The Court distinguished between comment on the functioning of judges, and attacks on judges personally. In the Barfod case, two lay judges were accused of being biased, in an article in a newspaper.[33] The applicant was convicted and instead of applying the expected narrow margin of appreciation, the Court applied a wide one. The Court held that the applicant's possibility to participate in the public debate on the composition of the court was not restricted by the conviction. He was only kept from attacking the two lay judges personally through the verdict, and this did not restrict his right to participate in a discussion. Consequently, the Court felt that the accusation of partiality had to be proved. In a more recent case, the Court added to these considerations, that regard had to be taken of the limited possibilities a judge has to react to criticism of this kind, taking into account the role of a judge as 'guarantor of justice'.[34] I wish to note that in the light of the Court's previous case law, instead of holding that a judge should have the trust of the public and should therefore be protected against unfounded criticism, it could also be argued that because of this special responsibility a judge should accept criticism. Where in previously discussed cases the requirement to prove a value-judgement seemed as such enough to establish a violation of Article 10, in the Barfod case, proof of truth could be required. In this case, the Court found the restriction of Article 10 necessary, because Barfod could participate in the discussion on the functioning of the national court without attacking the person of the judges.

The protection of judges provided in the Barfod judgment, however, is not unlimited. This is illustrated by the more recent case of De Haes and Gijsels v. Belgium. This case concerned an article written by two journalists on the manner in which a Belgian judge dealt with a case in which two children were put in the care of their father, although in a professional report he had been held to have sexually abused his children. Circumstances such as the position of the father in society and his personal relationship with the judge in question were said to have influenced the decision of the Belgian judge in this case. Before the national courts the article in question was held to contain defamatory statements. The Court accepted that this

---

31 Castells v. Spain, (1992) A.236, par. 47.
32 Thorgeir Thorgeirson v. Iceland, (1992) A.239.
33 Barfod v. Denmark, (1989) A.149.
34 Prager and Oberschlick v. Austria, (1995) A.313, par. 34.

article was part of a general discussion on the manner in which the Belgian judiciary dealt with problems such as these. In this judgment, the seriousness of the allegations made against the judges was thought to justify the immoderate terms in which they were formulated, thus allowing attacks on the person of judges to be part of expressing an opinion.[35] In this case, the nature of the accusation was thought proportionate to the seriousness of the allegations. It was probably the nature of the accusation that led the Court to apply an almost full review, although the Court did mention that the national authorities had a margin of appreciation.

The fact that an issue of public debate was discussed not in the written press but on television did not make a difference for the Court with regard to the scope of the margin of appreciation. This was demonstrated in the Jersild judgment.[36] The Court held that the conviction of a journalist for advocating racism after holding an interview on a television program with extreme right-wing youths, who made discriminatory statements on television, constituted a breach of Article 10. The Court explicitly stated that the general principles with regard to the press also apply to the 'audio-visual media' and that Article 10 protects the content of the idea as well as 'the form in which it is conveyed'. The margin of appreciation remains a narrow one. Although a television journalist has special 'duties and responsibilities' in this case that did not influence the margin of appreciation.

Commercial Speech

From the case law I discussed so far, it has become clear that when speech is thought to be part of the public debate, this often leads to the application of a narrow margin of appreciation. But what about speech of a commercial nature? In the first case brought before it on this matter, namely Barthold v. Germany, the Court indicated that it did not assume too easily that speech is not part of a public debate.[37] When a veterinarian in the course of an interview criticised the policy of nightshifts of veterinarian clinics and mentioned his name and his own clinic in a positive manner in relation to this issue, then the commercial aspect was of secondary importance. Consequently, the commercial aspect of his comments was held to justify ordering him not to give interviews of the same tenor again.[38] The commercial speech aspect was considered secondary to the public speech aspect of the case and the Court approached this case as it did the Lingens case. A narrow margin of appreciation was applied and the commercial interest of others was not thought to be a sufficient reason to restrict speech of public interest.

In 1989, a second case involving German competition law was brought before the

---

35 De Haes and Gijsels v. Belgium, 24 February 1997, Reports 1997-I, par. 48.
36 Jersild v. Denmark, (1994) A.298.
37 Barthold v. Germany, (1985) A.90.
38 Barthold v. Germany, (1985) A.90, par. 58.

Court.[39] In this case, however, the Court took a different approach. The publisher and the editor of a trade magazine were the applicants in this case. They had published an article about a 'mail order cosmetic club', that on four occasions had failed to fulfil its obligations under contract. The article reported these cases and subsequently the readers of the magazine were asked if they were aware of any further incidents of this kind. Based on this information, it would be possible to draw conclusions as to the policy of the mail-order company. This company sought and obtained an injunction ordering not to publish this information, because it was in breach of the competition law. Where as in the Barthold case the Court examined whether or not the speech involved was of a commercial nature, and only after this was considered did it decide on the scope of the margin of appreciation, in this case it simply accepted that the expression was of a commercial nature and that consequently a wide margin of appreciation had to be applied. It held: 'Such a margin of appreciation is essential in commercial matters and, in particular, in an area as complex and fluctuating as that of unfair competition ... the Court must confine its review to the question whether the measures taken on the national level are justifiable in principle and proportionate'.[40] The Court considered that even true statements can be steered into implying something by way of their formulation. Whether such speech is permitted under national law is for the national courts to decide. The task of the Court in this case is confined to reviewing 'whether the measures taken are justifiable in principle and proportionate'.[41] The fundamental value to a democratic society of freedom of expression was not considered. The public interest of the speech was recognised, but in this case this did not result in decreasing the scope of the margin of appreciation. Consequently, the Court took a step back from its approach in the Barthold case concerning the degree to which it wished to interfere with the national authorities' approach to what they considered necessary restrictions on freedom of expression. Although this decision was supported by the smallest possible majority of the Court, further decisions in the Casado Coca case and the case of Jacubowski v. Germany showed that this was not a one-off deviation from the Barthold approach.

In the Casado Coca case, the Court determined that as with speech concerning unfair competition also with regard to advertising the margin of appreciation was a wide one. The Court reviewed whether the measure taken 'could not be considered unreasonable and disproportionate to the aim pursued'.[42] And also in Jacubowski v. Germany, the qualification of the speech was of decisive importance. This case concerned a former employee of a company who sent out a circular in reaction to negative information that his former employers sent out to their customers about him.

---

39 Markt Intern Verlag GmbH & Klaus Beermann v. Germany, (1989) A.165.
40 Markt Intern Verlag GmbH & Klaus Beermann, (1989) A.165, par. 33.
41 Markt Intern Verlag GmbH & Klaus Beermann, (1989) A.165, par. 33.
42 Casado Coca v. Spain, (1994) A.285-A, par. 56.

He wanted to rectify this. At the time of sending the circular to those customers he also planned to set up a company in the same line of business. Consequently he was thought to have violated German Competition law, because he tried to get a business advantage through this circular. The Court relied completely on the assessments of the German courts and looked for aspects of the case that confirmed that they could have come to the conclusion that they did. The wide margin of appreciation was also applied to the qualification of the speech involved.

The case of Goodwin v. the United Kingdom, on the other hand, illustrates that nevertheless not any commercial aspect of a publication will suffice to qualify the publication as commercial speech. The publication of confidential information on the deplorable financial position of a company was qualified as speech that was of public interest.[43] The difference with the previous cases in which negative information on companies was disseminated may lie in the fact that this case concerned a publication by a journalist and not by another company or person (formerly) attached to the company concerned.[44]

In this section I discussed the manner in which the nature of the speech concerned influenced the margin of appreciation. In the next section of I elaborate on the manner in which the traditions that exist among the States party to the Convention with regard to the protection of freedom of expression influence the scope of the margin of appreciation.

b Common Ground

The common ground, that is the consensus or lack of it that exists among the contracting states with regard to the acceptance of specific restrictive regulations, is a frequently returning argument. I refer to chapter I section 4 for an explanation of the difference between the use of this term by the Court and the use of this term in this study. The common ground argument as applied by the Court has a significant influence on the scope of the margin of appreciation. Its influence may be either to widen or narrow the scope of the margin of appreciation, depending on whether or not a consensus is held to exist.

In the Handyside case, the Court held that with regard to morals a European standard could not be found.[45] Consequently the Court did not feel it could replace its opinion for that of the national courts. The Court did not explain why it felt that a European standard did not exist on morals. Such an explanation would seem to have been appropriate, since 'the little red schoolbook', issues of which were seized, confiscated and destroyed, was freely available in most States party to the

---

43 Goodwin v. the United Kingdom, 22 February 1996, Reports 1996-II.
44 Although the source of the information in this case was an employee of the company concerned.
45 Handyside v. United Kingdom, (1976) A.24.

Convention. In this case the common ground argument was used to motivate the application of a wide margin of appreciation.

This approach was followed in the Otto Preminger case, in which the hurt religious feelings of 'others' were the protected interest that should justify the restraint of freedom of expression.[46] The Court used the common ground argument in a similar manner to that in the Handyside case: 'As in the case of morals, ..., it is not possible to discern throughout Europe a uniform conception of the significance of religion in society', subsequently applying a wide margin of appreciation.[47] Also in a case concerning commercial speech, the common ground argument has led to the application of a wide margin of appreciation. In the case of Casado Coca v. Spain, the Court held that the rules regarding advertisements by lawyers for their professional activities were different in each Party State. Again, as a result a wide margin of appreciation was allowed.

In the cases I just discussed, the lack of common ground led to the application of a wide margin of appreciation. The common ground argument may also have the opposite effect, namely when the Court assumes that there is a common ground. In the Sunday Times case, the common ground argument was used to motivate the application of a narrow margin of appreciation. In this case, the Court held that a European standard did exist, and it considered that 'there is a general recognition of the fact that courts cannot operate in a vacuum. Whilst they are the forum for the settlement of disputes, this does not mean that there can be no prior discussion of disputes elsewhere, be it in special journals in the general press or amongst the public at large'.[48]

In two broadcasting cases, the common ground argument had the same function. In Autronic v. Switzerland the Court referred to the European Convention on Transfrontier Television and the fact that several other States party to the Convention allow the reception of uncoded television broadcast and subsequently applied a narrow margin of appreciation. And in the case of Informationsverein Lentia v. Austria, the Court also compared the maintenance of a State broadcasting monopoly within the country involved with the situation in the rest of Europe. Because of the large number of foreign programmes lawfully broadcasted on cable, several other States party to the Convention did not find a comparable monopoly necessary.

It should be noted that the Court may find a common ground not only in the domestic law of 'other Member States' or, more limited, in 'states of comparable size', but it may also use the existence of other European Conventions or UN Conventions to conclude that there exists a common ground.[49]

---

46 Otto Preminger v. Austria, (1995) A.295, par. 50.
47 Otto Preminger v. Austria, (1995) A.295, par. 50.
48 Sunday Times v. United Kingdom, (1979) A.30, par. 65.
49 See Jersild v. Denmark, (1994) A.298, in which the Court referred to the 1966 Convention on the

The Court does not conduct an in-depth research of the possible common ground that may exist.[50] And, I wish to emphasise, the Court does not systematically review in each case whether a common ground exists.[51] Therefore, it cannot be said that in every case in which the Court applies a narrow margin of appreciation, it felt that there was a consensus among the Party States on the protection of a right under those circumstances. For instance, its approach to the protection of political speech in the press, leaves the Party States hardly any margin of appreciation. A better explanation of this approach seems to be the Court's role as a guardian of fundamental rights. In this role the Court feels that the role of the press as a public watchdog is of fundamental value to a democratic society, even if there is no European consensus on the extent to which the press should be protected. This could lead to the conclusion that when the Court considers that there is no uniform conception on morals (even if looked at more closely, there is),[52] it accepts differences between the contracting states.[53]

Beside the existence of a common ground there is another factor that is not directly related to the speech concerned that influences the scope of the margin of appreciation. That factor is the legitimate aim the national authorities claim to pursue with the restriction of freedom of expression.

c Legitimate Aim

In the Sunday Times decision the Court itself held that 'the scope of the margin of appreciation is not identical in respect of each of the aims justifying restrictions' of a right.[54] As early as the Handyside judgment, the Court determined that in relation

---

Elimination of All forms of Racial Discrimination and Autronic AG v. Switzerland in which the Court referred to the International Telecommunication Convention. Also see Brems, The Margin of Appreciation Doctrine in the Case-Law of the European Court of Human Rights, 1996, p. 284. In relation to Article 1 of the first protocol (James and others, A.98 (1986), par. 40) the Court found a common ground in 'other democratic countries', subsequently referring to a judgement of the United States Supreme Court.

50 Mahoney, Judicial activism and judicial self-restraint in the European Court of Human Rights: two sides of the same coin, 1990, p. 75; Van Dijk and Van Hoof, Theory and Practice of the European Convention on Human Rights, 1998, p. 603.

51 See Lehideux and Isorni v. France, 23 September 1998, in which such considerations would seem appropriate, as it concerns the manner in which national authorities deal with expressions of an extreme right-wing nature. Such considerations could have contributed to the cogency of the judgment.

52 Cf. Handyside v. United Kingdom, (1976) A.24, since the little red schoolbook was freely available in a majority of the other Member States.

53 Heringa, The 'Consensus Principle', The role of the 'common law' in the ECHR case law, 1996, p. 115.

54 Sunday Times v. United Kingdom, (1979) A.30, par. 59.

to morals, the national authorities were in a better position than the Court to determine what restrictions were necessary to protect them.[55] The aim of protection of national security seems to widen the scope of the margin of appreciation as well. A clear example is the Hadjianastasiou case, in which the conviction for disclosure of confidential information by an officer of the army was held to be justified, even though the information concerned was of limited significance.[56] Also, the prevention of disorder is an aim with regard to which the Court takes a reserved attitude. In the Chorherr case, the applicant was arrested for holding a peaceful demonstration against the purchase of fighter aircraft by the Austrian government. He displayed his disapproval by walking around with a placard and handing out pamphlets.[57] At the same time and place, a military parade was in progress. The Court accepted that Mr Chorherr's freedom of expression was interfered with for the legitimate aim of preventing disorder, because he could have blocked the view of the other spectators, even though he was expressing his opinion in a public place on a matter of public concern. Considering the Court's 'Lingens case law', in a situation like this the Court would be expected to apply a narrow margin of appreciation and consequently conduct a full assessment of the circumstances of the case. Instead, the Court applied a wide margin of appreciation which was illustrated by the consideration that it reviewed whether the arrest 'could be justified to increase safety measures'.[58] The Court subsequently accepted that the applicant's conduct 'might' have led to a disturbance. When prevention of disorder comes into play the aim brought forward by the national authorities seems decisive for the Court, not the effect of the restriction. This approach could be explained by a desire of the Court to leave the national authorities a considerable amount of freedom in cases that require 'ad hoc' decisions.[59] The aim of maintaining the authority and impartiality of the judiciary, at issue in the Sunday Times case, was referred to in the context of the existence of a 'fairly broad measure of common ground', which led the Court to apply a narrow margin of appreciation. The Court elaborated on the scope of this common ground in Sunday Times v. the United Kingdom by considering that 'there is a general recognition of the fact that courts cannot operate in a vacuum. Whilst they are the forum for the settlement of disputes, this does not mean that there cannot be prior

---

55 Handyside v. United Kingdom, (1976) A.24 and confirmed in Müller v. Switzerland, (1988) A.133.

56 Hadjianastassiou v. Greece, (1992) A.252. See also Observer and Guardian v. United Kingdom, the decision on whether or not there was a breach of Article 10 before the 'Spycatcher' book had been published in the United States and was subsequently held to be freely available.

57 Chorherr v. Austria, (1993) A.266-B.

58 Chorherr v. Austria, (1993) A.266-B, par. 32.

59 Schokkenbroek, Toetsing aan de Vrijheidsrechten van het Europees Verdrag tot bescherming van de Rechten van de Mens, 1996, p. 160.

discussion of disputes elsewhere, be it in special journals, in the general press or amongst the public at large'.[60]

At this moment I wish to repeat the comments I made in section 4 of the first chapter of this book. The Court uses the term 'common ground' in a material context. 'Common ground' as applied by the Court refers to the resultant degree of protection of freedom of expression common to the states party to the Convention. The manner in which this standard was realised by way of interaction between the legislature and the judiciary is not part of this common ground. The use of the term common ground elsewhere in this study does include that aspect of the protection of freedom of expression.

Finally, I discuss the last factor of influence to the scope of the margin of appreciation applied by the Court, which is the seriousness of the interference.

d Seriousness of the Interference

In the first case in which the Court applied a narrow margin of appreciation, also the seriousness of the interference was considered to motivate the close scrutiny of the Court. In this Sunday Times case it was the fact that the injunction more or less blocked any form of comment on a matter of great public concern that contributed to the application of a narrow margin of appreciation.[61] The case of Observer and Guardian v. the United Kingdom (Spycatcher) also concerned the granting of an injunction. In this case, the English courts granted an injunction to restrain the publication of confidential governmental information, the exposure of which could endanger national security. The Court explicitly considered the prior restraint aspect of the injunction. As I observed in chapter V, in this case the Court explicitly stated that the words 'conditions', 'restrictions', 'preventing' and 'prevention' prove that prior restraint is possible within the meaning of Article 10.[62] But it also stressed that such prior restraint constituted a serious restriction of freedom of expression that calls for close scrutiny. In fact, this did not lead to the application of a narrow margin of appreciation. Close scrutiny on the part of the Court only took place after the information was freely available in the United States. The seriousness of an interference that amounted to prior restraint seemed to result in the application of a narrow margin of appreciation only after the importance of the aim of the protection of national security was reduced by this development.[63]

In other cases, the seriousness of the restriction did seem decisive as to the margin

---

60 Sunday Times v. United Kingdom, (1979) A.30, par. 65.
61 Sunday Times v. United Kingdom, (1979) A.30, par. 65.
62 Observer and Guardian v. United Kingdom, (1991) A.216, par. 60; Also: Markt Intern Verlag GmbH & Klaus Beermann v. Germany, (1989) A.165, par. 67.
63 See the discussion of the influence of the legitimate aim pursued in part C of this section.

of appreciation applied. In the Open Door and Dublin Well Woman case, the Court concluded that Article 10 ECHR was violated, mainly because of the absolute nature of the prohibition to spread information on abortion abroad. The interference did not differentiate as to the age or health of the women concerned and the danger to the women's health that was consequently present. A narrow margin of appreciation was applied, even though the protection of morals was the legitimate aim pursued.[64] And in the Casado Coca case, as well as in the Jacubowski case, two cases involving speech of a commercial nature, the fact that the restriction of freedom of expression was not an absolute one contributed to the application of a wide margin of appreciation.[65] The public, according to the Court, had other possibilities to gain access to the information.

Finally, in the case of Informationsverein Lentia v. Austria, a State broadcasting monopoly was held to be a serious restriction on freedom of expression, which contributed to the application of a narrow margin of appreciation.[66]

2.3 Concluding Remarks on the Margin of Appreciation as Developed by the Court

In reviewing cases, the Court basically applies three levels of intensity of the review. With regard to a narrow margin of appreciation the necessity of a restriction has to be 'absolutely certain', with regard to a wide margin of appreciation the State has to be 'entitled to think' that the restriction was necessary, or thirdly it had to be 'not unreasonable' for the State to assume that the interference with Article 10 was necessary in a democratic society. The scrutiny by the Court consequently varies from an almost full review of a case to a very marginal review, in which the Court is inclined to go along with the national courts' reasoning. Even though the Court claims that the limitations to the rights protected must be interpreted narrowly, as a consequence to the above described attitude, the protection offered to the fundamental rights adopted in the Convention also varies.

I distinguished four factors that influence the scope of the margin of appreciation applied by the Court. These are: the nature of the expression, the common ground-argument, the legitimate aim invoked and the seriousness of the interference. It should be kept in mind that none of the four factors discussed above are consistently applied by the Court, either regarding their occurrence in the judgments of the Court or in the manner in which they influence the margin of appreciation. And as can be noted from a number of cases returning in two or more parts of this section, the factors tend to overlap and influence each other. The argument of the seriousness of

---

64 Open Door and Dublin Well Woman v. Ireland, (1992) A.246, par. 60.
65 Casado Coca v. Spain, (1994) A.285-A, par. 52; Jacubowski v. Germany, (1994) A.291-A, par. 25.
66 Informationsverein Lentia & others v. Austria, (1993) A.276, par. 39.

the restriction usually tends to be supported by other arguments which together lead to the application of a narrow margin of appreciation. In the Sunday Times decision, the nature of the speech, namely that it concerns an issue of public interest, was strengthened by the argument that there existed a common ground in relation to the maintaining of the authority and impartiality of the judiciary. From the Chorherr case, on the other hand, it seemed apparent that when prevention of disorder comes into play, the aim brought forward by the national authorities was decisive for the Court, not the nature of the expression that was restricted. The Open Door and Dublin Well Woman case, concerned the protection of morals. Consequently it would be expected that the Court would apply a wide margin of appreciation.[67] However, the review that followed was extremely thorough. A violation of Article 10 was concluded, mainly because of the absolute nature of the prohibition to spread information on abortion abroad. As I observed, the national authorities were held not to have differentiated with regard to the age or health of the women concerned and to have taken insufficient regard of the consequent danger to the health of the women. A final interesting example of overlap, reciprocal influencing and inconsistent application is the case of Otto Preminger. In this case both 'the protection of rights of others' and 'the prevention of disorder' were accepted as legitimate aims. The rights of others in this case concerned freedom of religion. The Court stated that 'as in the case of morals – a concept linked to the "the rights of others" – it is not possible to discern throughout Europe a uniform conception of the significance of religion in society'. The Court nonetheless held that 'the supervision must be strict because of the importance of the freedoms in question', which one could be led to believe implies the application of a narrow margin of appreciation.[68] The margin applied, however, was a very wide one and the Court merely observed that the Austrian courts' approach to the case was acceptable. The strict review that was announced apparently concerned the expression and not the restriction, since the Court held that the expression should 'contribute to any form of public debate capable of furthering the progress of human affairs'.[69] This requirement removed a large part of the protection thought to have been guaranteed by the Court's previous case law. The influence of the particular facts and circumstances of the individual case on the scope of the margin of appreciation, and the fact that the Court does not explain why a certain factor outweighs another also does not promote the transparency of its judgments.[70]

---

67 Open Door and Dublin Well Woman v. Ireland, (1992) A.246, par. 67.
68 Otto Preminger v. Austria, (1995) A.295, par. 50.
69 Otto Preminger v. Austria, (1995) A.295, par. 47.
70 The Court will set out a structure for its reasoning after the factors it explicitly holds to be present in a case. It does not follow that structure or restrict itself to considerations regarding those factors however. See Lavender, The problem of the Margin of Appreciation, 1997, p. 385.

At all events, it can be concluded, that the margin of appreciation is variable in nature, that it can vary from a very wide margin to an almost full review by the Court and that the factors of influence provide a certain probability as to the scope of the margin of appreciation the Court will apply in cases brought before it. In short, this amounts to a situation in which political speech or other speech of interest to the public, in particular when disseminated by the press, will almost certainly lead to the application of a narrow margin of appreciation. Only when the particular aim protected is national security or public order will a wide margin be applied. The public interest in commercial speech or artistic speech also does not lead to the application of a narrow margin of appreciation when it is restricted in order to protect morals. The aim of the protection of reputations of others and the protection of the functioning of the judiciary will not lead to a widening of the margin of appreciation. The existence of a common ground among the traditions of the states party to the Convention and the seriousness of the restriction are most often referred to in support of the other two factors of influence. The seriousness of the interference, however, sometimes also serves as a ground to adjust the scope of the margin of appreciation based on the first two factors of influence.

In the next section of this chapter I elaborate on the margin of appreciation of the English executive that is recognised by the English courts. In the first part of section 3 I discuss the existence and location of the application of a margin of appreciation under English law. In the second part I discuss the scope of the margin of appreciation. Finally, in the third part of the next section I examine the factors that influence the scope of the margin of appreciation.

3 MARGIN OF APPRECIATION UNDER ENGLISH LAW

3.1 Existence of a Margin of Appreciation

In many cases, the English courts refer to the margin of appreciation applied by the European Court of Human Rights. On some occasions explicitly, such as in the Derbyshire case before the High Court, in which it was held that 'the English law of defamation is within the margin of appreciation' allowed to a Party State.[71] More often the courts do not explicitly refer to the margin of appreciation but refer to the requirements set by the Court in its case law, consequently taking account of the margin of appreciation applied. In A-G v. Associated Newspapers, Lord Lowry took account of the requirements of the Convention when he held: '... if it is legitimate on the ground that disclosure by a juror will be harmful to the authority and impartiality of the court system, to enact, "in response to a pressing social need" an absolute

---

71 Derbyshire County Council v. Times Newspapers Ltd [1991] 4 All ER 795 at 806 per Morland J.
   More recently: Holley v. Smith [1998] QB 726 at 734 per Staughton LJ.

prohibition against such disclosure, I do not see how it can be wrong also to prohibit a potentially more harmful further disclosure by way of publication'.[72] These examples demonstrate that the English courts do not apply a margin of appreciation themselves when dealing with fundamental rights protected under the Convention when they apply private or penal law. As I held in the introduction to this chapter, these areas of law come under the courts' appellate jurisdiction.[73] The possibilities of the national courts to provide the level of protection required by the Court in judicial review cases, however, differ from the possibilities under appellate jurisdiction. In judicial review cases, the English courts are obliged to allow the decision-making authorities leeway in exercising discretionary powers. This can be regarded as the application of a margin of appreciation.

As concerns the location of the application of a margin of appreciation, I wish to note that under English law a distinction is made between judicial review of the interpretation of vague legal terms and decisions made in the exercise of a discretionary power. Where the interpretation of vague legal terms is concerned, the courts do not observe judicial self-restraint. In such cases the courts seem to apply a full review. In fact it has been held that 'the words of a statute are to be read restrictively when they limit fundamental rights'.[74] Similarly, it was held that if the

---

72 A-G v. Associated Newspapers [1994] 2 W.L.R. 277, per Lord Lowry at 288-289. See also Home Office v. Harman [1982] 2 WLR 338, per Lord Scarman at 357-358; Dobson v. Hastings [1992] 2 WLR 414, per Sir Donald Nickolls V-C at 423; here also a recent case, not concerning freedom of expression should be mentioned, since it explicitly refers to the manner in which English courts may deal with the standards set by the Court when it applies a wide margin of appreciation: in R. v. Khan [1997] AC 558, which concerned admissibility of illegally obtained evidence and Article 8 ECHR, Lord Nolan at 581 held that 'what is significant to my mind is the court's acceptance of the proposition that the admissibility of evidence is primarily a matter for regulation under national law, and its rejection of the proposition that unlawfully obtained evidence is necessarily inadmissible'.

73 An exception is the Privy Council's jurisdiction to decide on appeals from decisions of courts of other common law jurisdictions. In those decisions the Privy Council will leave the national courts a margin of appreciation and it in fact compares its position to that of the Court; it has held that the local courts are in a better position to judge the facts and circumstances of a case. See Ming Pao Newspapers Ltd v. A-G of Hong Kong [1996] 3 WLR 272. Eventually it held that it had to determine the question of whether the restriction of Article 10 ECHR was 'necessary to preserve the integrity of investigation of the corruption in Hong Kong or whether it is disproportionate to that aim' (at 279).

74 R. v. Radio Authority, ex p. Bull [1998] QB 294, per Lord Woolf MR at 306. The RA has the power to refuse public television advertisements 'wholly or mainly' political in nature. Lord Woolf held that 'the ambiguous words "wholly or mainly" should be construed restrictively. By that I mean they should be construed in a way which limits the application of the restriction to bodies whose objects are substantially or primarily political'. He concluded that the advertisement of Amnesty International focusing attention on and stimulating protest against the human rights situation in a particular context met that requirement and could therefore be refused.

common law recognises a right, such as freedom of expression or access to the courts, 'in respect of justiciable issues' that right 'is not to be denied save by clear words in a statute'.[75] By way of this consideration, restrictions that are the result of overinclusive interpretation of legal terms are held to be ultra vires. So, if possible, statutes are interpreted in such a manner that their application does not restrict fundamental rights. If, however, by way of statutory legislation a discretionary decision-making power is granted, the situation is different. Under these circumstances restrictive interpretation does not provide a possibility to protect fundamental rights. Also with regard to the review of decisions made in the exercise of a discretionary power, the courts' approach is different. In these cases, it is stressed that in exercising judicial review, the courts do not substitute their opinion for that of the decision-maker. The courts do not have jurisdiction to adjudicate upon the merits of the decision. Instead, in such cases they merely review whether the manner in which the decision was reached was appropriate. In other words, the courts observe an attitude of judicial self-restraint.[76] On the other hand the powers granted are not unlimited. The courts have a function in ensuring that these 'statutory powers are not usurped, exceeded or abused, and that procedural and substantive duties owed to the public are duly performed'.[77] The European Court of Human Rights in its review of national decisions confines itself to the review of the substance of a decision. Judicial review of the substance of a case by the English courts takes place on the ground of 'irrationality', also referred to as unreasonableness. I wish to emphasise that reasonableness is the criterion of substantial review, comparable to the criterion of proportionality for instance. It is, however, the strictness of the review of the reasonableness of the decision that determines the scope of the margin of appreciation applied by the English courts. Just as it is the strictness of the review of the proportionality or balance between the right and the opposing interest that constitutes the margin of appreciation applied by the Court. Methods of substantial review are the subject of following chapters. In this section I focus on the scope of

---

75 R. v. Lord Chancellor, ex p. Witham [1998] QB 575, per Laws J. at 585, referring to A-G v. Guardian Newspapers Ltd [1987] 1 WLR 1248, per Lord Templeman at 1296-1297, A-G v. Guardian Newspapers Ltd (No.2) [1990] 1 AC 109, per Lord Goff of Chieveley at 283-284, and Derbyshire County Council v. Times Newspapers Ltd [1993] AC 534, per Lord Keith of Kinkel at 551 in which it was held that common law provides no lesser protection to freedom of expression that the ECHR. Laws J. determined in this case that the right to access to justice is not a lesser right and therefore should be approached in a similar manner, concluding that the decision of the Lord Chancellor to prescribe fees under s. 130 Supreme Court Act was ultra vires: 'Access to the courts is a constitutional right; it can only be denied by the government if it persuades Parliament to pass legislation which specifically – in effect by express provision – permits the executive to turn people away from the court door'. Compare also the speech of Lord Brown-Wilkinson in Wheeler v. Leicester City Council [1985] AC 1054, 1066 per Lord Brown-Wilkinson (CA).

76 The rules regulating the powers of review of the courts are governed by common law.

77 Jones and Thompson, Garner's Administrative Law, 1996, p. 162.

deference allowed to the decision-making authorities by the English courts when they review the irrationality of a decision, and the factors that influence the scope of deference. For the purpose of this study I refer to the scope of the deference left by the domestic courts as margin of appreciation. Due to the restricted amount of judicial review cases that concern freedom of expression, in this paragraph I do not restrict myself to examining cases concerning freedom of expression. I do emphasise the cases that concern freedom of expression.

3.2 Scope of the Margin of Appreciation

Irrationality is the ground on which the merits of a decision can be reviewed by the courts. Irrationality is also called 'unreasonableness' or 'Wednesbury unreasonableness' and the traditional test that was accepted by the English courts to review decisions of the executive based on discretionary powers is called Wednesbury review, after the case in which this ground of review was defined. The Wednesbury unreasonableness-test was formulated by Lord Greene in Associated Provincial Picture Houses Ltd v. Wednesbury Corporation, where he said that 'although the local authority have kept within the four corners of the matters which they ought to consider, they have nevertheless come to a conclusion so unreasonable that no reasonable authority could ever have come to it'.[78] This definition determined the scope of the 'margin of appreciation' left by the English courts to public authorities in the exercise of discretionary decision-making powers regarding the merits of their decision. The Wednesbury review as described here is based on the notion of judicial self-restraint,[79] which amounts to a wide margin of appreciation. The fact that a decision is considered to be unreasonable only when 'no reasonable authority could have come to it' demonstrates that the margin applied is very wide. This broad discretion is allowed with regard to the weight awarded to the facts and circumstances that were considered relevant to the case. Another consequence of this Wednesbury-test is that the decision-making authorities also have a broad discretion regarding the facts and circumstances of the case which are taken into consideration before arriving at a decision, unless the statute allowing the power formulated clear requirements regarding the factors that have to be taken into account.[80]

---

78 Associated Provincial Picture Houses Ltd v. Wednesbury Corporation [1948] 1 KB 223 at 233-234.
79 Lord Greene in Associated Provincial Picture Houses Ltd v. Wednesbury Corporation [1948] 1 KB 223 at 230 emphasised that a decision is unreasonable when no reasonable body could have come to it, and that this question is very different from what the court considers to be unreasonable, thus emphasising that the court does not replace the opinion of the authority with its own.
80 See [1948] 1 KB 223 per Lord Greene at 230.

The margin of appreciation consequently allowed under English law seemed rather wide and it appears to be constant, also in cases involving a restriction of a fundamental right. The English courts, however, have attempted to provide some protection to fundamental rights by way of judicial review, including some adjustment of the scope of the margin of appreciation. I elaborate on this development.

Constant Margin of Appreciation
In the Wheeler case the Leicester council banned a local rugby club from using a recreation ground for matches and training, because three of the members of the club participated in a touring team that played in South Africa. It did this after the club had not given the desired answers to a number of questions related to the club's position on apartheid and the efforts it would undertake to prevent its members from participating in the tour. The council felt it could exercise its discretionary powers in such a manner since it also regarded as its duty the promotion of good race relations based on s.71 of the Race Relations Act 1976.[81]

The House of Lords unanimously decided that the decision to ban the club from using the recreation ground should be quashed. In this case it was not the margin of appreciation as established under Wednesbury that was varied to create some protection for freedom of expression. In fact, the Lords carefully avoided changing the level of strictness under the Wednesbury unreasonableness test.

The careful formulation of Lord Roskill's opinion illustrated the refusal even to take the risk of reducing the strictness of the Wednesbury test: 'I greatly hesitate to differ from four learned judges on the Wednesbury issue but for myself I would have been disposed respectfully to do this and to say that the actions of the council were unreasonable in the Wednesbury sense. But even if I am wrong in this view, I am clearly of the opinion that the manner in which the council took that decision was in all the circumstances unfair ...'.[82] He held the decision of the council to be unreasonable because the club held a legitimate view yet was illegitimately pressured into making this opinion conform to that of the council through threatening sanctions. However, because the other Lords were unwilling to qualify Wednesbury unreasonableness as such, he turned his qualification of unreasonableness into a separate ground for quashing the decision by holding that 'the court should interfere because of the unfair manner in which the council set about obtaining its objective'.[83]

Lord Brown-Wilkinson, in his dissenting opinion in the case before the Court of Appeal, explicitly stated that the decision was not unreasonable on Wednesbury grounds. He called the decision a 'misuse of powers' and based his opinion directly

---

81 Wheeler v. Leicester City Council [1985] A.C. 1054.
82 Wheeler v. Leicester City Council [1985] A.C. 1054, per Lord Roskill at 1079.
83 Wheeler v. Leicester City Council [1985] A.C. 1054, at 1079.

on freedom of expression: 'The unlawfulness lies not in the basic views of the council but in their use of their powers so as to punish those who refuse to endorse those views, thereby interfering with the fundamental right of the club and its members to freedom of speech and conscience'.[84] In other words, Parliament had not expressly authorised the restriction of a fundamental right by way of the wording of the Act and therefore it could not be used in that manner. Consequently Lord Brown-Wilkinson created protection for freedom of expression, also not by way of reviewing the merits of the case, but by introducing the requirement of explicit restriction of freedom of expression in an Act of Parliament.

The fundamental rights aspect of this case was not explicitly mentioned by the House of Lords, although Lord Roskill came close to recognising that freedom of expression is a factor in this case by stating that the rugby club is free (within limits) to be of a different opinion from the Council regarding race relations. The House of Lords did feel that the position of the rugby club should be protected, but avoided running the risk of seriously changing the division of powers between the courts and decision-makers in evaluating the facts and circumstances of the case under closer review than Wednesbury unreasonableness. Instead, procedural concepts such as punishing without wrong and unfair means of obtaining an objective were used to quash the decision.[85]

The approach to this case illustrates that at the time of that decision the margin of appreciation was not considered to be variable. Consequently Wednesbury review did not offer the possibility of closer scrutiny of cases involving the restriction of fundamental rights. However, considering the constructions developed to offer protection to freedom of expression or interests inherent in it, it is fair to assume that the courts did feel that in cases in which freedom of expression was restricted, it should be offered some additional protection.

A Variable Margin of Appreciation

I observed that in the Wheeler case the House of Lords found ways to protect freedom of expression, without narrowing the margin of appreciation allowed under Wednesbury reasonableness. If in this case a narrower margin of appreciation was applied, this was not made visible. Arguments such as 'punishment without wrong' and 'unfair means of obtaining an objective' seemed to have been developed especially to avoid applying a stricter Wednesbury review.

From the end of the 1980s, a number of scholars have pointed out the possibilities that judicial review could offer to the protection of fundamental rights. Lord Irvine of Lairg is of the opinion that decisions involving fundamental rights contain political

---

84   Wheeler v. Leicester City Council [1985] A.C. 1054, per Brown-Wilkinson (CA) at 1066.
85   Also see Jowell and Lester, Beyond Wednesbury: substantive principles of administrative law, 1987, p. 373.

and philosophical aspects that would justify a less strict test.[86] Various writers, however, advocate stricter review of decisions restricting these rights. As early as 1987, Jowell and Lester feel that the Wednesbury unreasonableness test cannot meet 'the need for stricter scrutiny of administrative discretion where fundamental human rights are at stake' and 'the need to protect those rights'.[87] Therefore they hold the Wednesbury unreasonableness test 'unsatisfactory'. They advocate review by means of the use of general principles of law, one of these being the principle of proportionality. They assume that review of administrative action by way of general principles of law implies a stricter review. I think, however, that this is not automatically the case. A wide margin of appreciation combined with such general principles still leaves the courts powerless to protect civil liberties. Laws J. in his lecture to the Administrative Law Bar Association in 1992 holds that a stronger protection of fundamental rights could be realised by applying the Wednesbury reasonableness-test. He suggested that the courts adopt, in ECHR terms, a variable margin of appreciation in judicial review (without incorporating the ECHR). He uses the term 'differential standards in judicial review' and describes this concept as follows: 'The greater the intrusion proposed by a body possessing public power over the citizen into an area where his fundamental rights are at stake, the greater must be the justification which the public authority must demonstrate.'[88] The test applied would be executed like the Wednesbury principles test, it would just 'bring forward a more exacting standard' and this would amount to 'in principle a different exercise'.

These scholars do not only advocate a stricter approach. They bring forward evidence of a development towards stricter review of administrative action in the case law of the courts. Jowell and Lester noticed an inclination towards stricter scrutiny of cases involving fundamental rights. The most significant indication could be found in an immigration case[89] in which Lord Bridge had held, referring to the right to life, that the courts were entitled 'to subject an administrative decision to a more rigorous examination, to ensure that it is in no way flawed, according to the gravity of the issue which the decision determines'. Lord Templeman in the same case joined this view by stating: 'where the result of a flawed decision may imperil life or liberty a special responsibility lies on the court in the examination of the decision-making

---

86   Lord Irvine of Lairg, Judges and Decision-Makers, [1996] PL 65.
87   Jowell and Lester, Beyond Wednesbury: substantive principles of administrative law, 1987, p. 368.
88   Laws, Is the High Court the Guardian of Fundamental Constitutional Rights?, 1993, p. 69. This as he calls it 'significant refinement' of Wednesbury unreasonableness, would have to be based on a development of the common law in the direction of giving priority to fundamental rights (such as those protected under the ECHR) in a similar manner as done by the House of Lords in the Derbyshire case.
89   Bugdacay v. Secretary of State for the Home Department [1987] 1 All ER 940.

process'. According to Jowell and Lester, this attitude 'has great potential significance for the development of the public law'.[90]

According to Laws J. his suggested approach of 'differential standards in judicial review' was introduced already by the House of Lords referring to the immigration case that Jowell and Lester relied on. However, another case which gives evidence of the application of the concept was the Brind case, in which Lord Bridge held that the courts in exercising judicial review were entitled to determine whether a reasonable Secretary of State could reasonably think that a particular competing public interest justified a particular restriction.[91] Murray Hunt also found the development in the direction of stricter judicial review confirmed in the Brind case, and described the consequences of it as follows: '... at the same time as appearing to slam the door firmly shut on domestic use of international human rights law in public law other than where domestic law is ambiguous, the House of Lords sanctioned what amounts to an evolution of the common law of judicial review, by approving a more rigorous scrutiny of decisions affecting fundamental rights'.[92]

Apparently the controversial case of R v. Secretary of State for the Home Department, ex p. Brind is of great significance to determining the role of the courts in reviewing decisions restricting civil liberties and their future role in offering protection by way of reviewing such cases.

The Brind case is indeed important in relation to the role of the courts in cases involving fundamental rights, and freedom of expression in particular, because here the House of Lords was very outspoken in its attitude towards cases involving freedom of expression. I disagree, however, with the claims that in the Brind case a variable margin of appreciation was introduced. The consequences this decision is said to have by the above cited writers, and my disagreement with them, justifies an extensive analysis of this case. In arguing that in the Brind case a stricter Wednesbury review was applied, the writers mainly rely on the opinion of Lord Bridge, who held: 'Thus, article 10(2) of the Convention spells out and categorises the competing public interests by reference to which the right to freedom of expression may have to be curtailed. In exercising the power of judicial review we have neither the advantage nor the disadvantages of any comparable code to which we may refer or by which we are bound. But again, this surely does not mean that in deciding whether the Secretary of State, in the exercise of his discretion, could reasonably impose the

90 Jowell and Lester, Beyond Wednesbury: substantive principles of administrative law, 1987, p. 368-381.

91 Lord Irvine of Lairg was of a different opinion regarding the significance of the Brind case. Lord Irvine of Lairg, Judges and Decision-Makers: The Theory and Practice of Wednesbury Review, 1996, p. 65: 'The approach adopted in Brind, which states conclusively that the Wednesbury threshold or unreasonableness is not lowered in fundamental rights cases, must prevail'.

92 Hunt, Human Rights Law in English Courts, 1989, p. 163.

restriction he has imposed on the broadcasting organisations, we are not perfectly entitled to start from the premise that any restriction of the right to freedom of expression requires to be justified and that nothing less than an important competing public interest will be sufficient to justify it. The primary judgment as to whether the particular competing public interest justifies the particular restriction imposed falls to be made by the Secretary of State to whom Parliament has entrusted the discretion. But we are entitled to exercise a secondary judgment by asking whether a reasonable Secretary of State, on the material before him, could reasonably make that primary judgment'.[93] Lord Templeman in his opinion also felt that a restriction of freedom of expression should be justifiable. For the courts to determine whether this was the case, he suggested specifying Wednesbury reasonableness by relying on concepts of the case law of the European Court of Human Rights: '... the interference with freedom of expression must be necessary and proportionate to the damage which the restriction is designed to prevent'.[94] The remaining three Law Lords were not prepared to follow Lord Bridge's opinion. It was unanimously accepted, however, that the directive prohibiting the use of spoken words of spokesmen of terrorist organisations interfered with freedom of expression and that 'any restriction of the right to freedom of expression could only be justified by an important competing public interest'. Lord Irvine of Lairg commented that if the review as suggested by Lord Bridge was exercised, this would require the decision maker to acknowledge the fact that freedom of expression is an interest in the case at hand. Subsequently he would have to decide whether the public interest in restricting freedom of expression was sufficiently important to justify restraint.[95]

Under English law, the obligation of the public authority to take into account all relevant matters of a case already existed. The determination that freedom of expression should be an explicitly mentioned relevant matter would be a new development, as would be a full review of this requirement.[96] However, the obligation to mention freedom of expression explicitly as an interest was not formulated in the Brind case. It appears that the mere mention of a restricted interest is sufficient so

---

93 R. v. Secretary of State for the Home Department, ex p. Brind and others [1991] 1 AC 696, per Lord Bridge at 748-749.

94 R. v. Secretary of State for the Home Department ex p. Brind [1991] 1 A.C. 696, per Lord Templeman at 751.

95 Lord Irvine of Lairg, Judges and Decision-Makers: the Theory and Practice of Wednesbury Review, 1996, p. 64.

96 The requirement that all relevant matters are considered by the public authority in it decision is also subject to the Wednesbury reasonableness-test: Slade LJ. in Reg. v. Secretary of State for Transport, ex p. de Rothschild [1989] 1 All ER 933 in a case concerning the 'peaceful enjoyment of one's possessions' and as brought forward by Lord Ackner in the Brind case at 757 emphasised 'the Secretary of State's obligation to identify the factors which had motivated his decision so as to ensure that he had overlooked none which a reasonable Secretary of State should have considered'.

long as this restriction is motivated by an 'important competing public interest'. The extent to which this is a new development apart from the already existing procedural requirement that all relevant matters are considered is unclear. The requirements of justifiability and the mention of a competing interest as such are merely specifications of reasonableness as a substantial method of review.

Whether a narrower margin of appreciation was applied depends solely on whether the courts applied the traditional Wednesbury reasonableness test to the two aspects of the Wednesbury-test that were specified in the Brind case. As I just said, these are first whether the restriction is justifiable and second whether the restriction is justified by a sufficiently important competing public interest. Whether the restriction was justified was reviewed under the traditional Wednesbury reasonableness test by all five Law Lords. Lord Bridge reviewed whether 'a reasonable Secretary of State could not reasonably conclude that the restriction was justified by the important public interest of combating terrorism'.[97] This test was formulated in such a way that the reasonableness-test could be applicable only to the justifiability of the restriction. Subsequently, this could imply that the issue whether the restriction was justified by an 'important competing public interest' was not subject to the reasonableness-test. In reviewing the importance of the competing public interest the decision of Lord Bridge could be read as applying a full review, since he did not conclude that the combating of terrorism could reasonably be judged to be important by a reasonable Secretary of State, but concluded that 'in any civilised and law-abiding society the defeat of the terrorist is a public interest of the first importance'. Lord Bridge did seem to evaluate the merits of a decision.

However, the other law lords did not follow this approach. Lord Ackner explicitly avoided the suggestion that the evaluation the importance of the reason for justification was open to full review. He held: 'In a field which concerns a fundamental human right – namely that of free speech – close scrutiny must be given to the reasons provided as justification for interference with that right', but emphasised that this scrutiny is limited by the traditional Wednesbury reasonableness-test by citing Slade LJ. in a different case: 'The Secretary of State's obligation to identify the factors which had motivated his decision so as to ensure that he had overlooked none which a reasonable Secretary of State should have considered'.[98]

The specification of the Wednesbury reasonableness-test for cases involving the restriction of a fundamental rights, together with Lord Bridge's apparently progressive application of the test, indicated a willingness to offer more protection to fundamental rights in judicial review. In my opinion, the approach of Lord Bridge demonstrated that at the time of the Brind case, a variable margin of appreciation came within the scope of judicial review, and tended to be the solution opted for to

---

97 R. v. Secretary of State for the Home Department ex p. Brind [1991] 1 AC 696 at 749.
98 R. v. Secretary of State for the Home Department ex p. Brind [1991] 1 AC 696 at 757.

provide such further protection. The Brind case seemed to indicate a transitional period between a period of constant application of a wide margin of appreciation and a period where closer scrutiny may be applied in cases involving fundamental rights. This conclusion is influenced, however, by the recent developments in the area of judicial review of human rights cases. Any conclusive remarks with regard to the scope of the margin of appreciation applied by the English courts cannot be made on the basis of the Brind decision alone.

Since the decision in the Brind case, it can be said, however, that closer scrutiny has been applied by the courts. An additional issue is whether this closer review takes place under Wednesbury-review, or under a separate ground of review.

For some, the development of such a separate ground seemed to provide the possibility of a closer review.[99] The considerations of De Smith, Woolf and Jowell illustrate this: 'The intensity of review under the principle of proportionality need not necessarily eliminate or even reduce the reserve under the Wednesbury test in relation to the interference with the merits of an official decision. The so-called "margin of appreciation" is not, in many cases, obviously different from the threshold under the Wednesbury formulation. Outside the field of human rights, proportionality should normally only be applied if the means are manifestly or grossly out of balance in relation to the end sought'.[100] Consequently they imply that the application of proportionality takes place separately from Wednesbury review, but on occasion is applied with similar deference. This distinction was followed up by Kennedy LJ. in R v. Chief Constable, ex p. International Trader's Ferry, in which he held that because the test of illegality differs in content from the proportionality test, the proportionality test, can under some circumstances, be a more exacting test.[101] It should be noted that this decision concerned EU law. It could be that the opinion that proportionality is required as a separate ground of review to enable the courts to apply stricter scrutiny, was inspired by the fact that the English courts apply review on grounds of proportionality in cases regarding EU law. Because of the direct effect of this law, under certain circumstances the English courts are required to apply a full review, to live up to its standards. If the review of proportionality in this case had

---

99 See for instance R. v. Chief Constable, ex p. International Trader's Ferry Ltd [1998] Q.B. 477, per Kennedy LJ. at 495 in a decision regarding the review of proportionality in relation to EU law: 'I accept that in the light of the decision of the House of Lords in R. v. Secretary of State for the Home Department, ex p. Brind [1991] 1 AC 696 proportionality and Wednesbury irrationality cannot be regarded as simply coterminous. Proportionality requires the court to judge the necessity of the action taken as well as whether it was within the range of courses of action that could reasonably be followed. Proportionality can therefore be a more exacting test in some circumstances'.

100 See De Smith, Woolf and Jowell, Judicial Review of Administrative Action, 1995, p. 605.

101 R. v. Chief Constable, ex p. I.T.F. Ltd [1998] Q.B. 477, per Kennedy LJ. at 495. See note 99.

taken place in the context of Wednesbury review, this would have implied the application of a narrower margin of appreciation than usually applied under this test.

Also in cases that did not concern EU law, but that did concern the restriction of fundamental rights other than freedom of expression, a closer scrutiny than the usual scope of review under the Wednesbury-test has taken place. In the case of R. v. Secretary of State for the Home department, ex p. Leech, Steyn LJ. reviewed whether there was a 'self-evident and pressing need' for prison authorities to restrict a prisoner's right to access to the courts.[102] He did not review whether a reasonable Secretary could have reasonably held the view that the restriction was 'self-evident and pressing'. In this case, a separate ground of review seemed to have been applied with a wider margin of appreciation than the one applied under Wednesbury review. However, in the later case of R. v. Ministry of Defence ex p. Smith, which dealt with sexual orientation discrimination, the Court of Appeal stayed close to the reasoning of the House of Lords in Brind when it held that when fundamental rights are restricted 'the Court would require proportionately greater justification before being satisfied that the decision was within the range of responses open to a reasonable decision-maker, according to the seriousness of the interference with those rights'.[103] In this case closer scrutiny was applied by narrowing the margin of appreciation of the Wednesbury test. It was held that the Wednesbury test was 'sufficiently flexible to cover all situations'. And finally in R. v. Secretary of State, ex p. Hargreaves, the court reviewed the decision of prison authorities to restrict prisoners' possibilities to apply for home leave. Although Hirst LJ. held that Wednesbury review provided 'the correct test', after close scrutiny he held that a pressing social need had been shown and that the restriction was proportionate to the legitimate aim pursued, which seemed a full review. Whether this amounted to the application of a separate ground of review or the application of a narrow margin of appreciation under Wednesbury is unclear.

In the International Trader's Ferry case, the review of proportionality was considered to be broader in substance than the Wednesbury-test. In this case, the application of a proportionality test implied the possibility to apply a closer review. Although it was recognised that often the margin of appreciation in the two tests is similar, still the fact that proportionality in content is held to be broader in scope led to the application of two different grounds of review. Another ground of substantial review subsequently created the possibility of a varying degree of scrutiny under English administrative law.

Also in cases that do not concern EU law, there is an obvious development of extended protection of fundamental rights under judicial review regarding the review on the merits of the case. Whether the ground for closer scrutiny is found under an

---

102 R. v. Secretary of State for the Home Department ex p. Leech [1994] QB 198.
103 R. v. Ministry of Defence ex p. Smith [1996] 1 All ER 256.

extended Wednesbury test, or in a separate ground for review under which a narrow margin of appreciation is allowed has not been determined yet. The approach varies per case. The considerations of De Smith, Woolf and Jowell and the approach in the International Trader's Ferry case therefore cannot, as such, be held to constitute the new rule with regard to the application of a variable scope of review under English law.

I conclude on the application of a margin of appreciation by the English courts, whether it is applied under Wednesbury reasonableness or a different test, that it is variable and that its scope can be narrower than the Wednesbury reasonableness test formulated in the Wednesbury case. A subsequent relevant issue is what the factors are that influence the scope of the margin of appreciation applied by the English courts.

3.3 Factors Influencing the Scope of the Margin of Appreciation

Under the case law of the Court, factors such as the nature of the expression, the existence of a common ground, the legitimate aim invoked and the seriousness of the restriction influence the scope of the margin of appreciation. Under English law the existence of a variable margin of appreciation is controversial, even though there are indications that the climate in this respect is changing. One ground for varying the margin of appreciation, that is for applying a narrower margin of appreciation, is the restriction of a fundamental right. The decisions of the European Court of Human Rights always concern the restriction of a fundamental right and in such cases the margin of appreciation varies. The English courts are not solely dealing with cases in which a fundamental right is at issue.

It was, however, the restriction of a fundamental right, namely freedom of speech, that led the English courts to search for ways to offer more protection to fundamental rights when conducting judicial review. In the Wheeler case it was a political expression that made the House of Lords look for alternative ways of protection, and in the Brind case it was political speech that made the House of Lords adjust the formulation of the Wednesbury reasonableness-test for cases involving fundamental rights, thus opening the door to the application of a variable margin of appreciation.

The factors that will determine the scope of the margin of appreciation if its flexibility is developed further in future, are unclear. However, it can be expected that such factors as the nature of the speech, the aim of the restriction and the seriousness of the interference will influence the margin applied by the English courts as well. I conclude this from the fact that the last two factors were already referred to as being of influence to the scope of the scrutiny in the ex p. Smith case. In this case, it was first considered that the seriousness of the interference would influence the level of justification required for the interference with the right. Subsequently, after considering that the Wednesbury test was 'sufficiently flexible to cover all situations', the court indicated that the aim of the restriction affected the scope of the review when it held that it would 'show greater caution where the nature of the decision was exoteric, policy-laden or security based'.

4 COMMON GROUND AND THE INFLUENCE OF THE HUMAN RIGHTS ACT 1998

Common Ground before the Human Rights Act 1998 Became Law
When freedom of expression is restricted, the Court reviews whether the interference is 'necessary in a democratic society'. This requirement encompasses a review of the substance of a case. In deciding on the necessity of a restriction, the Court leaves the national authorities a margin of appreciation. Depending on the circumstances of the case, this margin of appreciation may vary in scope. Under English law, when a fundamental right is restricted by an administrative decision, the courts review the substance of the decision by determining whether a reasonable decision-maker could have come to the that decision. In deciding on the reasonableness of the decision, the English courts leave the decision-making authorities a margin of appreciation. The question is whether the degree of protection that can subsequently be provided by the English courts is sufficient to meet the requirements the Court has set in its case law after having applied the margin of appreciation. If the margin of appreciation left to the decision-making authorities by the English courts is broad to the extent that it results in a violation of the Convention, a solution would be for the English courts to narrow the margin of appreciation, which would enable them to review administrative action to the extent that they could provide a level of protection similar to that of the Court.[104]

---

104 'Judges have acknowledged that even the more rigorous versions of Wednesbury review recently developed in human rights cases fall short of the level of scrutiny applied by the Strasbourg Court'. R. V. Secretary of State for the Environment, ex p. NALGO (1993) 5 Admin.L.R. 785 at 800; R. v. Ministry of Defence, ex p. Smith [1996] Q.B. 517 (DC) at 536C-538C (Simon Brown LJ. and in the CA at 558E-559A (Bingham M.R.); 564A-F (Henry LJ.; and 565C (Thorpe LJ.). Neill LJ. at 801 in NALGO: The constitutional balance in this country between the courts and the executive is a delicate one. The principle of proportionality allows the decision maker 'a margin of appreciation', but I do not understand that this 'margin of appreciation' covers so many degrees of latitude as that afforded by the traditional Wednesbury doctrine.
R. v. Ministry of Defence, ex p. Smith (DC): Simon Brown LJ. at 538: In short, I respectfully conclude with Neill LJ. that even where fundamental human rights are being restricted, 'the threshold of unreasonableness' is not lowered. On the other hand, the minister on judicial review will need to show that there is an important competing public interest which he could reasonably judge sufficient to justify the restriction and he must expect his reasons to be closely scrutinised. Even that approach, therefore, involves a more intensive review process and a greater readiness to intervene than would ordinarily characterise a judicial review challenge ...
Henry LJ. at 564: If the Convention were part of our law, then, as Simon Brown LJ. said in the DC, the primary judgement on this issue would be for the judges. But Parliament has not given us

The English courts are trying to offer increased protection to fundamental rights by way of varying the strictness of scrutiny, be it by means of a varying margin within the Wednesbury reasonableness[105] or by means of a separate criterion of review. In other words, the English courts, like the European Court of Human Rights, apply a varying margin of appreciation. The margin of appreciation as applied by the Court is a variable one, in which the nature of the expression, a possible common ground between the traditions of the states party to the Convention, the legitimate aim pursued and the seriousness of the restriction together or separately determine the scope of the margin of appreciation. Under English law, it is the fact that a fundamental right is restricted that leads to the application of a narrower margin of appreciation. However, it does seem that similar factors influence whether an English court feels that the right restricted was so valuable that the necessity of the restriction requires closer scrutiny. The public interest in speech or the aim pursued with a restriction have led the courts to apply closer scrutiny. Consequently between the application of the margin of appreciation by the European Court of Human Rights and by the English courts, a common ground can be found to the extent that in those cases in which the Court would most certainly leave a wide margin of appreciation, most likely also the English courts would not be inclined to apply closer scrutiny. In those instances in which English law and the decisions based on it are likely to constitute a violation of the Convention, English courts should be able to apply a margin of appreciation similar to the one applied by the Court under those circumstances, in order to be able to provide protection that may prevent a conviction for breach of the Convention. The question then is whether the strictness of the scrutiny of the English courts can provide sufficient protection.

I observed that the scope of the margin of appreciation under the case law of the Court varies from reviewing whether a restriction was 'absolutely certain' in a democratic society to whether a Party State was 'entitled to think' that a restriction was necessary or that it was not unreasonable for the State to think that the measure was necessary, in a democratic society. These requirements are also called the 'narrow approach', the 'reasonable-test' and the 'not unreasonable-test'. The 'not unreasonable-test' allows the national authorities a similar deference to the 'Wednesbury'-test. It is the 'reasonable-test' and the 'narrow approach' in relation to which problems are most likely to arise.

The review suggested by the House of Lords in the Brind case, namely that the

---

that primary jurisdiction on this issue. Our present constitutional role was correctly identified by Simon Brown LJ. as exercising a secondary or reviewing judgment. As it is, in relation to the Convention, the only primary judicial role lies with the European Court of Human Rights at Strasbourg.

105 As Laws J. suggested: lowering the Wednesbury threshold of unreasonableness and 'bringing forward a more exacting standard' of review.

decision will only be 'Wednesbury reasonable' when the restriction of the rights has been sufficiently justified by a competing public interest, seems comparable to the 'reasonable-test' in which the Court determines whether the decision-making authority could reasonably have come to its conclusion on the facts available.[106] Until now the narrow margin of appreciation has not been applied under English law,[107] although Steyn LJ. in the Leech case came a long way when he held that a less restrictive power would have been available than the censoring of all mail to and from prisoners in order to regulate and manage prisons. The fact that he held the power to be 'extravagantly wide' indicated that it could not be thought reasonable to decide to execute such a restriction. In cases in which the Court would (probably) apply a narrow margin of appreciation, even the strictest scrutiny applied by the English courts falls short of the degree of scrutiny applied by the Court. A common ground with regard to the scope of the margin of appreciation extends at most to the not-unreasonable-test.

The next issue of discussion is whether the Human Rights Act 1998 provides the English courts with a possibility to review acts of the executive to the extent that the Court reviews decisions of the English authorities when it applies a narrow margin of appreciation.

Influence of the Human Rights Act 1998 on a Common Ground
Whether or not the extent to which the Human Rights Act influences the scope of the margin of appreciation applied by the English courts depends on whether the Act influences the relation between the judiciary and the legislature and between the judiciary and the executive, because it is this relation that determines the scope of review. In the Human Rights Act there are a number of specific references to the role of the judiciary, both in relation to their task as interpreters of legislation and in relation to judicial review. With regard to the interpretation of legislation, the courts under the Act have the authority to apply the Convention as law of the land and as such have to determine whether domestic legislation is consistent with the Convention. In fact, under s.3(1) they have a duty to interpret legislation consistently with the ECHR 'as far as it is possible to do so'. As I observed in chapter II of this book, this implies a significant change in the approach to national legislation where it touches upon the rights incorporated. Instead of assuming that Parliament intended to legislate in accordance with the United Kingdom's obligations under the ECHR

---

106 The traditional Wednesbury review would correspond with the 'not unreasonable' test.
107 An indication is the fact that Hirst LJ. in R. v. Secretary of State for the Home Department, ex p. Hargreaves [1997] 1 All ER 397, considered that the restriction of a right to family life was not an absolute restriction. He did not consider whether the measure was maybe too restrictive, even though the restriction was not absolute. This consideration will be discussed further in the section on the review of the proportionality of measures.

when the Act is ambiguous, the courts under the Human Rights Act will take any opportunity to interpret the legislation in such a manner that it is consistent with the Convention. Only where such a possibility does not exist will the courts give a declaration of incompatibility.[108] This implies that the English courts, in cases in which this is relevant, are obliged to consider the interest in freedom of expression.[109]

Similarly, the courts have a task in judging whether acts of public authorities are in accordance with the ECHR. The previous remarks about the courts' tasks regarding the interpretation of legislation are relevant to public law, especially regarding the powers granted to public authorities. Where these touch upon Convention rights, the courts will interpret these restrictively and as a result might sooner conclude that an act is 'ultra vires'. However, where the review concerns the compatibility of exercise of discretionary powers, the courts' reviewing tasks will remain supervisory in nature. This means that the courts must protect the Convention rights by means of judicial review, implying at least a certain 'margin of appreciation', and the interpreting of legislation.

The Act does indicate the degree of protection that is intended to be the result of the exercise of the duty imposed on the courts: s.2 suggests that the degree of protection should be similar to the degree provided by the Court under the Convention. But the Act does not specify the methods of protection to be used. The relevant issue in this chapter is: if the degree of protection is to be similar to that provided by the Court, what does that presuppose in relation to the margin of appreciation applied in judicial review cases?

The relevant provisions with regard to the relationship between the judiciary and the executive are, beside s.2, s.6 and 7 of the Act. S.6 contains the obligation for public authorities to act in conformity with Convention rights. Primary responsibility for living up to this obligation therefore lies with the decision-making authorities. Looking at the Brind case, for instance, in which a broad discretionary power was granted, the public authority under the Human Rights Act has a duty to interpret that power in accordance with the Convention, which is an improvement as compared to the previous situation. However, to what extent the courts can review the public authorities' view of what is consistent is not settled in the Act.[110] S.7 of the Act provides that a person who claims that his rights have been violated by a public

---

108 Lord Lester of Herne Hill, The Art of the Possible – Interpreting Statutes under the Human Rights Act, 1998, p. 670. Lord Lester emphasises that the courts are authorised to come up with a 'possible' interpretation as opposed to a 'reasonable' interpretation, to which the interpretation of South African law was restricted.

109 See also Woolf, Judicial Review – The tension between the Executive and the Judiciary, 1998, p. 592.

110 See also Lord Lester of Herne Hill, The Art of the Possible – Interpreting Statutes under the Human Rights Act, 1998, p. 668.

authority may 'bring proceedings against the authority under' the Human Rights Act or may 'rely on the Convention right or rights concerned in any legal proceeding'. No specific references are made with regard to the closeness of the review of the decisions of the decision-making authorities. A combination of factors, however, could support the stance that the Human Rights Act provides a basis for closer scrutiny. S.2 of the Human Rights Act determines that a court in a situation in which the appellant claims a breach of a right must take into account the case law of the Court and Commission. Moreover, one of the aims of incorporating the ECHR was to reduce the number of convictions by the Court. The courts could understand s.6 together with s.2 to mean that they have a duty to ensure a degree of protection of the Convention rights similar to that offered by the Court, because s.6 includes the courts in the term 'public authority'. These two sections could be held to imply that the courts have to narrow the margin of appreciation allowed to the public authorities substantially. In that case, closer scrutiny is required at least in those cases in which the facts and circumstances would lead the Court to apply a 'reasonable-test' or a narrow margin of appreciation. This is required only in those circumstances, because the obligation on the English courts to take account of the case law of the Court refers to the level of protection provided by the Court. In cases in which the Court would allow a wider margin of appreciation, the domestic courts are left more room for an independent decision on the kind of restrictions that can be considered necessary in a democratic society. As the margin of appreciation gets narrower, the domestic courts will increasingly be obliged to follow the Court's approach to such cases in order to achieve a similar level of protection. In those situations in which the protection of the courts prior to entry into force of the Human Rights Act is less than the degree of protection provided by the Court, the English courts will be obliged to adjust their approach to that of the Court. An implication of the application of a narrow margin of appreciation is that the courts are forced to develop an independent view on the consideration and appreciation of the merits of a case in order to determine the necessity of a restriction.

Although s.6 of the Act suggests that the initial responsibility for the protection of Convention rights lies with the decision-making authority, s.2 provides a clear possibility for the courts to apply close scrutiny in order to attain a sufficient degree of protection. This would prevent appellants still having to take their case to Strasbourg to see their rights protected. Whether or not the Act will be applied in this manner depends on the willingness of the courts to take such a large step away from their current position with respect to the executive. The case of R. v. DPP, ex p. Kebeline suggests that there does exist such a willingness to come to an extensive change in attitude.[111] This case dealt with the Prevention of Terrorism Act, which

---

111 R. v. DPP ex p. Kebeline [1999] 3 WLR 175, CA; 28 October 1999, HL.

requires the defendant to prove that he did not intent a terrorist act when he behaved in a way which led to the assumption that he did. In this case, s.6 was used to state that public authorities, imposing that obligation on a person, act contradictory to Article 6 of the Convention and that this constituted 'abuse of power'. Although the House of Lords did not condone this approach, their decision does demonstrate that the courts may regard the Act as containing a general duty to protect the Convention rights, which would lead to a significant change in the relation between the executive and the judiciary.

Whether the courts will dare to apply a margin of appreciation narrow enough to offer similar protection to the Convention rights as the Court, remains to be seen, especially in those cases in which the Court comes to its closest review.[112] In those instances in which the Court leaves a narrow margin of appreciation, close scrutiny by the English courts is required by s.2.

It has been suggested that the margin of appreciation doctrine is not something that can be applied in the protection of rights in a national context, and that thus it is possible to provide much more protection than the Court does, since the margin of appreciation no longer plays a role once the Convention is incorporated.[113] The fact that s.2 speaks of 'taking account of' the case law of the Court was thought to support that approach. Again, this expectation could be realised under the Act. However, when one thinks of the level of protection given to freedom of expression by the English courts before the Human Rights Act became law, this seems an unlikely development. The English courts, in my opinion, will be most likely to offer just enough protection to freedom of expression to meet the requirements of the Court, and these requirements are influenced by the margin of appreciation left to the States party to the Convention.

I conclude that although the Act is not explicit about the methods of protection applied, it will most likely influence the common ground regarding the application of the margin of appreciation. It encourages the existing development towards a narrower margin of appreciation. This most likely also implies the incorporation of the factors that influence the scope of the margin of appreciation as applied by the European Court of Human Rights.

---

112 Hunt in Human Rights in English Courts, 1998, p. 184, remarked that this whole development does not 'constitute dramatic new departures for the common law'. In reviewing discretionary powers the courts were accustomed to attaching greater weight to some interests that were thought to be of great value 'such as the right to property and other economic interests'.

113 Singh, Hunt and Demetriou, Is there a role for the 'Margin of Appreciation' in National Law after the Human Rights Act?, 1999, p. 17.

CHAPTER VII
PROPORTIONALITY

1 INTRODUCTION

In the present chapter I continue the search for a common ground between the methods of protection applied by the Court and the methods of protection applied by the English courts. In this chapter and the following chapter I turn to the substantive methods of protection. The margin of appreciation as method of protection concerned the closeness of the scrutiny applied by the Court and the English courts. The substantive methods of protection concern the content of the requirements that restrictions of fundamental rights have to meet. I concluded in chapter IV that the Court applies two substantive methods of protection. These are the review of proportionality and balancing of interests. The topic of this chapter is the review of proportionality, which implies that there must be an acceptable relation between the means and ends of a restrictive measure. At this point I wish to emphasise that it is not the principle of proportionality that is discussed, but rather the requirements formulated by the courts with regard to restrictions of freedom of expression as a result of the existence of such a principle.

To start with, review of proportionality of a measure under English law occurs with regard to damages awarded in libel cases. The amount of damages in libel cases is determined by the jury that sits on the case. The Courts and Legal Services Act 1990, however, provides that judges can adjust the amount of damages if they consider the amount to be excessive. S.8(1) of the Courts and Legal Services Act specifies the circumstances under which this discretionary power can be exercised, namely if 'the award was so unreasonable that it could not have been made by sensible people and must have been arrived at capriciously, unconscionably or irrationally'. This power was rarely used by the courts, until the European Court of Human Rights held damages of 1.5 million pounds for an article in which the principal of a school was accused of causing the execution of 70000 people at the end of the second world war, to constitute a violation of Article 10 ECHR. The Court came to this conclusion 'having regard to the size of the award in the applicant's case in conjunction with the lack of adequate and effective safeguards at the relevant time against a disproportionately large award'.[1] Anticipating on this judgment of the Court, however, the Court of Appeal adjusted the English law with regard to the

---

1   Tolstoy Miloslavskey v. United Kingdom, (1995) A.323, par. 51.

application of s.8 of the Courts and Legal Services Act. It did this in the case of Rantzen v. Mirror Group Newspapers Ltd.[2] I elaborated on this case in section 3 of chapter III of this study. The case concerned the publication of defamatory articles concerning the television presenter Esther Rantzen. She was awarded 250,000 pounds damages. In this case the defendants, on appeal, also asked for a reduction of the damages, claiming that such a large amount of damages constituted a breach of Article 10 ECHR. The Court of Appeal then held that the power conferred upon the courts to reduce the award 'should be construed in a manner which was not inconsistent with Article 10 of the European Convention for the Protection of Human Rights and Fundamental Freedoms; that an almost unlimited discretion in a jury to award damages for defamation did not provide a satisfactory measurement for deciding what was a necessary restriction in a democratic society on the exercise of the right to freedom of expression under Article 10 to protect the reputation of others and the common law therefore required that large awards of damages by a jury should be more closely scrutinized ...'.[3] The Court of Appeal went on to specify the term 'excessive' in s.8 of the Courts and Legal Services Act. It subsequently held that it would apply an 'objective standard of reasonable compensation', and held that reasonable could also mean 'necessary' or 'proportional'. It concluded that according to this standard the amount of damages was excessive.[4] The Court of Appeal consequently made it possible for judges to apply the doctrine of proportionality in exercising a judicial discretion.

Apart from the award of damages, review of proportionality seems an appropriate means of adjusting the impact of interlocutory injunctions on freedom of expression. My discussion of the remedy of an interim injunction in libel law, in section 2 of chapter III, illustrates that an interim injunction in libel cases will only be granted if there is a serious risk of prejudice to the trial of action. I demonstrated moreover that the English courts will not grant interim relief to restrain publication of an alleged libel if the defendant is pleading fair comment or justification, because of the importance of leaving free speech unfettered until it is clear that an allegation is untrue and has infringed the plaintiff's rights.[5] This approach seems to entail a balancing of interests rather than a proportionality test, since the means – prevention of publication – is not considered in relation to the ends of protecting the plaintiff's reputation. Until the time it is clear that the plaintiff's reputation has been damaged, freedom of expression should prevail. Once it is clear that his reputation has been damaged, further publication of the material will be prohibited.

---

2   Rantzen v. Mirror Group Newspapers Ltd [1993] 3 WLR 953.
3   Rantzen v. Mirror Group Newspapers Ltd [1993] 3 WLR 953 at 971.
4   Rantzen v. Mirror Group Newspapers Ltd [1993] 3 WLR 953 at 976.
5   Feldman, Civil Liberties and Human Rights in England and Wales, 1993, p. 613.

I also observed in chapter III that in cases concerning breach of confidence the 'balance of convenience' test determines whether an interim injunction should be granted. This test is applied as such: The plaintiff has to show that he has an 'arguable case' and that the harm done by the publication could not be sufficiently compensated in damages. The defendant then has to show that if he cannot disclose the information concerned he will suffer uncompensatable loss. If defendant or plaintiff manage to prove that their loss could not be compensated by damages, then the court has to determine the 'balance of convenience' between the two interests.[6] This approach indicates that if the damage is irreparable, then either the restraint of the information or the making public of the information is disproportionate to the right to freedom of expression or to the damage to the reputation of the person about whom a secret is revealed. This opens up the possibility of a proportionality test. However, I already held in section 4 of chapter III that the right not to have confidential information made public will automatically prevail, because the importance of publishing material when it is news is not usually considered 'irreparable damage', whereas the disclosure of confidential information is considered irreversible. No consideration is given to the injunction as a means to the end, as such. The application of a balancing of interests at an abstract level removes the possibility of the application of a proportionality-test in individual cases. In libel cases there is also no evidence of the review of proportionality of a restrictive measure.

Whether or not a proportionality-test is applied with regard to damages or with regard to the granting of interim injunctions does not raise much discussion, however. In such cases proportionality considerations concern acts of the courts. Under English administrative law this is different. In administrative law cases, if the courts review the proportionality of a measure, this concerns acts of the decision-making authorities. In such cases the executive is the first to apply the law to the facts and circumstances of the case. The review of proportionality of a decision would involve the courts in considerations regarding the merits of a case, which is considered a step too far on the territory of the executive. Under English law, consequently, the very existence of the test is controversial outside the scope of directly effective Community law.[7] The discussion does not end with that conclusion however. Both in the case law of the courts and in academic writings a discussion has been taking place as to whether the proportionality of restrictive measures by the executive can be and even are being reviewed by the English courts. An additional issue of interest is that the courts and the scholars who take part in the discussion on the application of a proportionality test each have their own ideas on what the notion of

---

6   Robertson and Nicol, Media Law, 1992, p. 191.
7   See De Búrca, Proportionality and Wednesbury Unreasonableness: The Influence of European Legal Concepts on UK Law, 1997, p. 564.

proportionality entails. For me it is time therefore to determine the nature and place of the notion of proportionality under English administrative law in order to formulate a common ground between the English approach to review of proportionality and the approach of the Court. In doing so I first recapitulate the findings of chapter IV on the approach of the European Court of Human Rights to the review of proportionality in section 2. I discuss proportionality under English administrative law in section 3. In that section I first discuss what the English courts say explicitly on the application of a proportionality test. In the second part of that section I elaborate on the review that the courts in fact apply, despite what has been stated explicitly on the application of a proportionality test. In this section I also discuss the comments of a number of scholars on whether or not a review of proportionality is conducted by the English courts and, if so, the manner in which that occurs. I particularly address the perceptions these scholars have of the definition of proportionality. Because of the limited amount of case law available on the restriction of freedom of expression in judicial review cases, I also examine cases that concern the restriction of rights other than freedom of expression. In section 4 I draw conclusions on the existence of a common ground with regard to the application of the proportionality-test and I elaborate on the influence the Human Rights Act 1998 has on such a common ground.

2 PROPORTIONALITY UNDER THE ECHR

I observed in chapter IV of this book that proportionality is applied by the Court as a method of substantive protection. The Court often explicitly indicates that it will review the proportionality of a measure and it often explicitly concludes that a restriction can or cannot be regarded as proportionate to the legitimate aim pursued. Interestingly the Court gives different definitions of the proportionality test. Sometimes it will take the common approach and state that it has reviewed the relationship between the aim and the means to achieve it, but in other instances it will claim to strike a balance between the interest of the state in restricting the right and the interest of the person whose right has been restricted. I held in chapter IV that these two approaches to proportionality amount to different methods of protection. In what it says, the Court indicates that there are different methods of substantive protection, in fact the review of proportionality of a measure differs in each case. The review of proportionality can amount to a means and end test, realised by a review of whether the measure was appropriate to achieve the aim, by review of whether a less restrictive alternative was available, or by a balancing of means and ends. Beside these forms of proportionality test, the review of the Court may in fact also amount to a balancing of interests, in which case the interest in the right and the interest in the restriction are considered.

3 PROPORTIONALITY IN ENGLISH ADMINISTRATIVE LAW

3.1 Proportionality in Name

I indicated in the introduction to this chapter that the English courts are not unfamiliar with the review of proportionality, because they apply such a test when they review measures on their compatibility with directly effective Community law. Their task with regard to the application of Community law is strictly separated from their jurisdiction in other judicial review cases. In a case from 1985, Lord Diplock suggested, however, that in due time the grounds on which a decision is subject to judicial control may develop in such a way that 'a further ground' is added, being '... particularly the possible adoption in the future of the principle of proportionality ...'.[8] That time had not come yet and in this case the proportionality of the decision was not reviewed. In R v. Secretary of State for the Home Department, ex p. Brind the term proportionality again appeared. The possibility to apply the doctrine of proportionality was explicitly rejected however.[9] The fact that proportionality might be a future ground for review was again mentioned in R. v. Secretary of State for the Environment, ex p. NALGO, but also in this case it was not a reason to declare the test applicable.[10]

Occasionally, the language used by the European Court of Human Rights to indicate the review of proportionality is referred to in English case law. This might imply the application of a proportionality test. In the case of R. v. Advertising Standards Authority, ex p. Vernons Organisation Ltd Laws J. reviewed whether there existed 'a pressing ground' to justify a decision to prevent publication of a critical report on misleading advertisements.[11] And in the more recent Leech case, the Court of Appeal assessed whether there was a 'self-evident and pressing social need' for the interference with prisoners' mail.[12]

For some, the rejection of the proportionality test in the Brind case and the lack of any decisions to the contrary subsequently meant that a principle of proportionality

---

8   C.C.S.U. v. Minister for Civil Service [1985] 374, per Lord Diplock at 410 (also known as the GCHQ-case).

9   R v. Secretary of State for the Home Department ex p. Brind [1991] 1 AC 696. With the exception of Lord Templeman who stated: '... the interference with freedom of expression must be necessary and proportionate to the damage which the restriction is designed to prevent' (at 751).

10 R. v. Secretary of State for the Environment, ex p. NALGO (1993) 5 Admin. LR 785, per Neill LJ.

11 R. v. ASA Ltd ex p. Vernons Organisation Ltd [1992] 1 WLR 1289 at 1293-1294.

12 R. v. Secretary of State for the Home Department, ex p. Leech (No.2) [1994] Q.B. 198, per Steyn LJ. at 212.

under English law does not exist.[13] However, the considerations claiming that English courts cannot review the proportionality of a measure do not settle the question of whether the courts perform a review that in fact amounts to such a test. In a number of comments, it has been held that proportionality is part of English law 'in all but name'.[14] Furthermore there are some early cases in which the proportionality of a measure did seem to have been reviewed. In Webb v. Minister of Housing and Local Government, the Government was thought to have purchased more land than was necessary for coast protection works. The purchase was not thought to be disproportionate, but the compulsory purchase order was thought to be not within the powers conferred by the Coast Protection Act. A means-ends test was applied by Davies J. who held: 'The present compulsory purchase order in my judgement extends to and embraces land not required by the council for the purpose of carrying out coast protection work as defined' and only after this test he then held that 'in any event the proposed access way was neither coast protection work nor work of maintenance or repair'.[15] After close scrutiny of the necessity of the broad compulsory purchase order it was not concluded that a less restrictive measure would have been appropriate. Instead it was concluded that the order was not necessary for coastal protection work and therefore the order fell outside the powers granted by the Coast Protection Act. In R. v. Barnsley M.B.C, ex p. Hook not only the proportionality of the restrictive measure was explicitly reviewed, the disproportionality of the measure did lead directly to the quashing of the restrictive decision. In this case Lord Denning held that the suspension of a stallholder's licence for urinating in public and using offensive language was 'out of proportion to the occasion' also because 'there had been other cases where men had urinated in a side street near the market and no such punishment had been inflicted'.[16]

These cases necessitate a closer look at English case law to assess the extent to which reviews such as the ones described above can be found under English law.

---

13 Boyron, Proportionality in English administrative law: A Faulty translation?, 1992, p. 238. Interestingly, she held: 'On the facts however, the Lords were unable to justify the use of Proportionality: they emphasized that the restrictions imposed had been of very limited scope'. Does this consideration not answer the question of whether or not the measure taken was suitable to achieve the aim pursued. Such a question may be said to amount to application of the concept of proportionality.

14 Jowell and Lester, Proportionality; neither novel nor dangerous, 1988, p. 51; Jowell and Lester, Beyond Wednesbury: substantive principles of administrative law, 1987, p. 375-376; Jowell, Is Proportionality an Alien Concept?, 1996, p. 406-411; De Smith, Woolf and Jowell, Judicial review of administrative action, 1995, p. 594; Hunt, Using Human Rights Law in English Courts, 1998, p. 212; Lord Irvine, Judges and Decision-makers, 1996, p. 74, who opposes this development. De Búrca, Proportionality and Wednesbury Unreasonableness: The Influence of European Legal Concepts on UK law, 1997, p. 564 a.o.

15 Webb v. Minister of Housing and Local Government [1965] 1 WLR 755, at 784.

16 R. v. Barnsley M.B.C., ex p. Hook [1976] 1 WLR 1052 at 1057.

3.2 Proportionality in Fact

In a number of recent cases the courts in fact gave evidence of the ability to review the proportionality of a measure without calling it that. A number of scholars moreover took note of this development. I successively discuss the cases concerned and the comments that were made with regard to the application of a proportionality test.

a Proportionality under English Case Law

The first case to be discussed is Wheeler v. Leicester City Council. I referred to this case in section 7 of chapter III and in chapter VI. In this section, however, the case is examined with regard to the method of substantive protection that was applied in it. The Wheeler case was the case that concerned the banning of a local rugby club from a recreation ground by the Leicester City Council, because members of the team had played in South Africa. This case can be regarded as the first case in which the House of Lords accepted a review of the relation between means and ends of a measure. Lord Templeman held that the Council could not use its statutory powers to punish the club 'when the club had done no wrong'.[17] Lord Roskill held that 'the manner in which the council took that decision was in all the circumstances unfair ...'.[18] He held the decision of the Council to be unreasonable because the club held a legitimate view yet was illegitimately pressured to make this opinion conform to that of the Council through threatening sanctions. However, because the other Lords were unwilling to qualify Wednesbury unreasonableness as such, he turned his qualification of unreasonableness into a separate ground for quashing the decision by holding that 'the court should interfere because of the unfair manner in which the council set about obtaining its objective'.[19] Whether or not these considerations mean that the court thought the punishment to be excessive[20] or not suitable to obtain the objective of promoting good race relations, the court clearly did not want to accept the absence of a balance between the means and ends of the measure.[21]

After this case, more cases came before the courts in which pressure on the courts increased to apply closer scrutiny regarding substantive review. In the Brind case, the appellants claimed that the disputed measure was not suitable for achieving the aim. This case dealt with the directive issued by the Home Secretary under s.10(3) of the

---

17 Wheeler v. Leicester City Council [1985] AC 1054 at 1081.
18 Wheeler v. Leicester City Council [1985] AC 1054 at 1079.
19 Wheeler v. Leicester City Council [1985] AC 1054 at 1079.
20 According to Jowell in Is proportionality an alien concept?, 1996, p. 406-411, this case is an example of the necessity-test.
21 The measure was not held to be unreasonable on these grounds.

Broadcasting Act 1990. By way of this so called 'veto power', the Home Secretary requested the independent broadcasters and the BBC to 'refrain from broadcasting any matter consisting of or including words spoken by persons appearing or being heard on programmes where such persons represented organisations proscribed under the Prevention of Terrorism Act or the Northern Ireland Act 1978 and certain other specified groups, or where the word spoken supported or invited support for such organisations'.[22] The government was of the opinion that terrorists survived by the 'oxygen of publicity'. The directives issued under the cited provisions were supposed to deprive them of this oxygen.[23] The ban was issued in 1988 and was initially thought to prohibit the broadcasting of any statements from the spokesmen of 'terrorist' organisations. As it turned out, once a commercial channel experimented with this method, the ban only prohibited the broadcasting of statements using the actual voices of the spokesmen.[24] A spokesman could be shown on television while the words he spoke were dubbed. A number of journalists, among whom Brind, claimed before the courts that the issuing of the directives contravened article 10 of the ECHR and claimed amongst others that 'the directives were disproportionate to the mischief at which they were aimed, namely to prevent intimidation by or undeserved publicity and an appearance of political legitimacy for, such organisations, and were unreasonable so as to amount to an unlawful exercise of the Secretary of State's powers'.[25] As I already said, the term proportionality was used in this case, but the court explicitly rejected the possibility of applying a proportionality test. Lord Bridge as well as Lord Roskill both accepted that proportionality may be a part of the Wednesbury unreasonableness, but were as yet not prepared to accept it as a separate ground of challenge. They therefore confirmed Lord Diplock's opinion in the GCHQ case. Lord Bridge considered: 'I should add that I do not see how reliance on the doctrine of "proportionality" can here advance the applicants case'.[26] He did review proportionality in fact, however, by stating that 'what is perhaps surprising is that the restriction imposed is of such limited scope' and then he goes on to evaluate the merits of the case by saying: 'There is no restriction at all on the matter which may be broadcast, only on the manner of its presentation ... I will understand the broadcast journalist's complaint that to put him through the trouble of dubbing the voice of the speaker he has interviewed before the television camera is an irritant which the difference in effect between the speaker's voice and the actor's voice hardly justifies. I well understand the political complaint

---

22 See also Bailey, Harris and Jones, Civil Liberties, cases and materials, 1995, p. 339.
23 Robertson and Nicol, Media Law, 1992, p. 27.
24 Robertson and Nicol, Media Law, 1992, p. 27.
25 R. v. Secretary of State for the Home Department, ex p. Brind [1991] 1 AC 696 at 696-697.
26 See also R. v. Secretary of State for the Home Department, ex p. Brind [1991] 1 AC 696, per Lord Roskill at 750.

that the restriction may be counter productive in the sense that the adverse criticism it provokes outweighs any benefit it achieves'. He, however, continued to apply the system of judicial review under Wednesbury unreasonableness: 'These complaints fall very far short of demonstrating that a reasonable Secretary of State could not reasonably conclude that the restriction was justified by the important public interest of combating terrorism'.[27] The scope of the margin of appreciation remains a wide one, but these considerations still amount to a proportionality test in which the serious aim of combatting terrorism is considered in relation to the means, which is valued as only a light interference. The considerations in fact indicate, that disproportionality of a measure, if serious enough, can lead to Wednesbury unreasonableness. De Smith, Woolf and Jowell found that the suitability test that was required had not been performed. Indeed, it was not considered whether the ban was an appropriate measure to achieve the aim pursued, but the means was weighed against the ends, implying a proportionality test, balancing means and ends.[28]

In the earlier mentioned cases of Webb and Hook, the apparent review of the proportionality of a measure was not based on Wednesbury review. In the Brind case Wednesbury unreasonableness seemed to form the basis for a possible application of a proportionality test; in fact, Lord Bridge applied proportionality under the ground of review described by Lord Diplock as irrationality in the GCHQ case. I now continue to discuss cases in which proportionality was in fact applied. I comment further on the location of the review of proportionality at the end of this section.

In the case of R. v. Advertising Standards Authority Ltd, ex p. Vernons organisation Ltd proportionality was also reviewed in fact. In this case, the applicant sought an order of certiorari to bring up and quash the decision of the ASA finding the applicant in breach of the British Code of Advertising, by producing a misleading advertisement about the amounts of money that could 'easily' be won by entering a competition. Moreover, the applicant requested a stay in the publication of the report in which this decision appeared. Laws J. held that the request for an order of certiorari was comparable to a request for an injunction, except that the ASA was a public body and that therefore judicial review could offer a remedy. It was held that there was a 'general principle that the courts would not restrain the expression of opinion and conveyance of information whether by a private individual or a public body, save on pressing grounds ...'.[29] An important consideration in concluding that such pressing grounds did not exist was that 'publication would not cause damage to the applicant which was so irreparable or past recall as to give rise to a pressing

27 R. v. Secretary of State for the Home Department, ex p. Brind [1991] 1 AC 696, at 749.

28 See also De Búrca, Proportionality and Wednesbury Unreasonableness: The Influence of European Legal Concepts on UK Law, 1997, p. 576.

29 R. v. ASA Ltd, ex p. Vernons Organisation Ltd [1992] 1 WLR 1289.

ground or social need to restrain publication'.[30] In this case, the requirement of a pressing social need was thought to imply that there should not be a disproportionate effect if the restriction (i.e. stay in publication) was not granted. In this case, the publishing of the report would not cause irreparable damage and the exercise of freedom of expression would therefore not be disproportional. The means to restrict the exercise of freedom of expression is not disproportional to the end of exposing misleading advertising because the damage is not irreparable.

Also in the case of R. v. Secretary of State for the Home Department, ex p. Leech a proportionality test was applied.[31] In this case, the power of prison authorities to censor a prisoner's correspondence, including mail between a prisoner and his legal adviser concerning future legal proceedings, was challenged. This power was thought to restrict the right of the prisoner to access to the courts. Steyn J. reviewed whether there was a 'self-evident and pressing need' for an unrestricted power to read letters between a prisoner and a solicitor and a power to stop such letters on the ground of prolixity and objectionability. S.47 (1) of the statute that was the basis for this power was thought not to authorise 'the stopping of letters on the ground of prolixity nor was there any objective justification for an unrestricted power to stop such letters on the ground of objectionability'. The power was therefore thought to be ultra vires. The power was thought to be 'extravagantly wide' for the purpose of regulating and managing prisons. A less restrictive power would have sufficed to achieve this aim. Steyn LJ. held that 'it ought to be noted that ... the practice is only to examine letters purportedly passing between a prisoner and a solicitor if there is reason to doubt that it is genuine correspondence between a solicitor and a client'.[32] The court formed its own opinion on what could be considered necessary and considered the negative effects which a far-reaching power could have on the prisoner in exercising his right of access to the courts. To assess whether correspondence between a prisoner and his lawyer is 'in truth bonafide' does not require such a wide power. In this case the proportionality of the restriction on the rights was reviewed although the ground of challenge was that the power was ultra vires. The term proportionality was not used, but the proportionality of the measure was reviewed in order to determine whether the power granted had a basis in statute law. Steyn LJ. concluded that a less restrictive alternative would have been available.

---

30 R. v. ASA Ltd, ex p. Vernons Organisation Ltd [1992] 1 WLR 1289. See per Laws J. at 1294: 'I do not consider that the effects of that publication are damaging to the applicant in a manner which would be so irreparable, so past recall as to amount to a pressing ground, in the language of Strasbourg, a pressing social need, to restrain this public body from carrying out its function in the ordinary way'.

31 R. v. Secretary of State for the Home Department, ex p. Leech [1994] Q.B. 198.

32 R. v. Secretary of State for the Home Department, ex p. Leech [1994] Q.B. 198 at 214.

In the case of R. v. Secretary of State for the Home department, ex p. Chahal, the Court of Appeal explicitly referred to proportionality, but also seemed to indicate that the courts could not review the decision on that ground. In this case a deportation order was made against an Indian national, who was a member of a Sikh movement in the United Kingdom, because his presence posed a threat to national security. The appellant claimed that he had to fear for his life if he were to return to India. These claims were supported by evidence of torture during a previous visit to India. Staughten LJ. stated: 'I do not find it at all surprising that international lawyers consider the doctrine of proportionality relevant. ... it would seem to me quite wrong that some trivial danger to national security should allow expulsion or return in a case where there was a present threat to the life of the refugee if that took place'.[33] However, since the regulation on which the Home Secretary based his decision was not available for review for reasons of national security, the court could not 'balance the threat on the one hand against the risk on the other'. Staughten LJ. continued: 'What we can do, ..., is to consider the evidence of the threat to Mr Chahal's life or freedom and whether the Secretary of State's assessment of that risk was irrational or perverse'.[34] Consequently the question remained how such irrationality is determined. The suggestion in this case seems to be that this cannot be by assessing the proportionality of the measure in the circumstances of the particular case. However, had the decision been available for review, the suggestion is that review of proportionality would amount to a balancing of the threat on the one hand against the risk on the other. In other words, the court would have conducted a balancing of interests. Finally, in R. v. Secretary of State, ex p. Hargreaves, a case dealing with the decision to restrict the possibilities of prisoners to apply for home leave, a proportionality test was applied in fact.[35] Hirst LJ. started by holding that 'on matters of substance Wednesbury provides the correct test'.[36] Subsequently he stated: 'In my judgment the fundamental interference with respect to family life in the present case is brought about by the lawful sentences of the court. Of course home visits are an important feature, but it must be borne in mind that there is no suggestion that any applicant was cut from his family altogether, since prison visits continued as usual'.[37] Thus he reviewed whether the restriction was an absolute one, suggesting that if it were absolute he would have allowed the appeal.[38] Moreover, he explicitly stated that he thought that the measure met the requirement of 'pressing

---

33 R. v. Home Secretary, ex p. Chahal [1995] 1 WLR 526 at 533.
34 R. v. Home Secretary, ex p. Chahal [1995] 1 WLR 526 at 535.
35 R. v. Secretary of State, ex p. Hargreaves [1997] 1 All ER 397.
36 R. v. Secretary of State, ex p. Hargreaves [1997] 1 All ER 397 at 412.
37 R. v. Secretary of State, ex p. Hargreaves [1997] 1 All ER 397 at 413.
38 See also De Búrca, Proportionality and Wednesbury Unreasonableness: The Influence of European Legal Concepts on UK Law, 1997, p. 575.

social need' and that it was 'proportionate to the legitimate aim pursued'. Consequently, according to him article 8 had not been infringed.

Different forms of the proportionality test are consequently already being applied. With the tide of this development, the courts have also searched for the most appropriate location of such review. This search seems to be inspired by the idea that the scrutiny should be closer where it concerns the review of the proportionality of a measure. In the Brind case, where irrationality was reviewed, Lord Bridge, who applied the proportionality test, did this by way of reviewing Wednesbury reasonableness. If proportionality were to play a role in the review of the banning order it would be by determining whether a reasonable decision-maker could have come to the conclusion that the measure was necessary. Also, Lord Templeman in this case held that if proportionality were to be considered it would be by applying the Wednesbury test.[39] In the earlier cases of Webb and Hook, the review of proportionality was not based on Wednesbury review. I assess now whether in the most recent cases in which proportionality has been reviewed, this is done by way of Wednesbury review, or whether in these cases the courts felt the time right to approach proportionality as a separate ground of review, as Lord Diplock suggested might be possible in the GCHQ case.

In R. v. Advertising standards authority Ltd, proportionality seemed to be reviewed as a separate ground. Freedom of expression would not be restricted, 'save on pressing grounds'.[40] The proportionality test was not undertaken in Wednesbury reasonable terms and Laws J. felt that this was a request for an injunction in disguise, since he held that 'if a private individual will not be restrained from expressing his opinion save on pressing grounds I see no reason why a public body having a duty ... to express its opinion should be subject to any less rigid rules'. Although this case concerned review of application of libel law, in other 'pure' judicial review cases, a close review of proportionality has also taken place. In the Leech case, proportionality was reviewed when the ground of challenge was that the power was ultra vires. Steyn J. undertook a rather extensive appreciation of the merits of the case and the review of proportionality did not appear to be marginal in the Wednesbury sense either. Formulations such as that 'there was no objective justification for an unrestricted power' and that the power 'was extravagantly wide', instead of arguing that in all reasonableness there was no objective justification and that the scope of the power could be considered extravagantly wide illustrate that Steyn J. did not attempt to be careful in his rejection of the application of the provision. In the Chahal case, the speech of Staughten LJ. suggested that review of the substance of a decision

---

39 'The courts must ask themselves whether a reasonable Home Secretary could reasonably conclude that the interference with freedom of expression was justifiable', for this the restriction would have to be 'necessary and proportionate to the damage which (it) is designed to prevent'.

40 R. v. ASA Ltd, ex p. Vernons Organisation Ltd [1992] 1 WLR 1289.

could only take place under Wednesbury review, since he again used the term 'irrational'.[41] In the Hargreaves case, on the other hand, again a much closer review was applied in which Hirst LJ. considered and evaluated the facts and circumstances of the case himself when he held that the limited possibilities for home leave restricted the right to family life, but that they were the result of 'lawful sentences' and 'there was no suggestion that any applicant was cut from his family altogether, since prison visits continued as usual'.[42] Before he applied this test, he had held that 'on matters of substance Wednesbury provides the correct test'.[43] Consequently he seems to imply that Wednesbury review not only allows for the review of proportionality, but also that it allows for closer scrutiny than the reasonable test that is usually accepted.

The review of the proportionality of a measure is gradually becoming closer. Because of this shift in the strictness of the scrutiny where the proportionality of a measure is concerned, clarity on whether this review takes place under a narrower margin of appreciation within Wednesbury review or under a separate ground of review would be desirable. So far, the position of proportionality under judicial review remains confusing.

It can be concluded that substantive review is an area of law where the courts are still determining their limits, and it can no longer be said that proportionality is not a part of the substantive grounds for judicial review, even if the review applied is not labelled as a proportionality test. In fact the courts do not elaborate on what they understand a review of proportionality to entail, but they apply different types of proportionality. As already indicated, a number of academic comments are aimed at demonstrating that a proportionality test is already applied under English case law. I will take a closer look at these comments to see what they understand the notion of proportionality to be and to examine where they found the test under English law. I also elaborate on the types of proportionality I think occur in judicial review cases.

b Comments

Definition of Proportionality

Jowell and Lester are of the opinion that the notions of 'unfair manner of obtaining the objective' and 'punishing where no wrong has been done', as applied by respectively Lord Roskill and Lord Templeman in the Wheeler case, came close to a proportionality test.[44] Hunt held that the test formulated in Brind that 'nothing less than an important competing public interest will be sufficient to justify' a restriction,

---

41 R. v. Home Secretary, ex p. Chahal [1995] 1 WLR 526 at 535.

42 R. v. Secretary of State, ex p. Hargreaves [1997] 1 All ER 397 at 413.

43 R. v. Secretary of State, ex p. Hargreaves [1997] 1 All ER 397 at 412.

44 Jowell and Lester, Beyond Wednesbury: substantive principles of administrative law, 1987, p. 373.

in fact already amounts to the acceptance by the courts of the application of the principle of proportionality: 'The unavoidable relativity of the concepts of "importance" and "sufficiency" import an evaluative dimension into the reviewing court's role which, even if present in practice before, has never been so explicitly acknowledged'.[45] These writers assume a meaning of proportionality that might differ from the one I assumed, i.e. entailing a means ends test. In chapter IV section 3.1. I discussed the definition of proportionality proposed by scholars in relation to the meaning proportionality was held to have by the European Court of Human Rights. In this section I elaborate on the definition of proportionality of those scholars that participated in the discussion on the application of proportionality under English law.

Jowell and Lester, after considering the relevant case law, come to the following definition: 'Proportionality is a principle that requires a reasonable relationship between a decision, its objectives and the circumstances of a given case. It requires the pursuit of legitimate ends by means that are not oppressively excessive. It looks therefore largely to the substance of decisions rather than the way they are reached, but it also requires the decision-maker not manifestly to ignore significant alternatives or interests'.[46]

Hunt, however, defined proportionality more broadly: the reviewing court 'must carry out an exercise which involves assessing the importance of the right, the seriousness of the interference and the weight of the competing public interest before it can reach a sensible view as to the sufficiency of the justification offered'.[47] As Hunt said, this will involve the courts in a balancing or weighing exercise.

De Smith, Woolf and Jowell, in a manner similar to that of Jowell and Lester, defined three ways in which the proportionality test is exercised in a European context, thus implying that that is what they understand proportionality to be. They say that when applied in a European context it may take the form of a 'balancing test' or of a 'necessity test' and occasionally it takes the form of a 'suitability test'.[48] According to these writers, the balancing test 'requires a balancing of the ends which an official decision attempts to achieve against the means applied to achieve them'. The necessity test means that 'where a particular objective can be achieved by more than one available means, the least harmful of these means should be adopted to achieve a particular objective' and finally the suitability test 'requires authorities to employ means which are appropriate to the accomplishment of a given law, and which are not in themselves incapable of implementation or unlawful'.

---

45 Hunt, Human Rights Law in English courts, 1998, p. 217.
46 Jowell and Lester, Proportionality; neither novel nor dangerous, 1988, p 67.
47 Hunt, Human Rights Law in English courts, 1998, p. 217.
48 De Smith, Woolf and Jowell, Judicial Review of Administrative Action, 1995, p. 595-597.

This notion of proportionality differs from that of Hunt. In Hunt's view, a reviewing court may assess 'the weight of the right, the seriousness of the interference and the importance of the competing public interest', it may perform a general balancing of interests also involving the assessment of the value of the right that is being restricted. This review seems broader than the 'balancing test' of De Smith, Woolf and Jowell, which only involves a balancing of the interference with the public interest for which the right is being interfered with.

Hunt's definition of proportionality seems to imply a general balancing of interests, in which one interest will be declared to be of greater weight than the other. The definition used by Hunt does not correspond with my definition of proportionality either. On the other hand Hunt's definition includes balancing of interests in the proportionality test just as the European Court of Human Rights in fact seems to do.

Application under English Law

In this part I examine the extent to which the above-cited scholars think the types of proportionality they distinguish can be found in the case law of the courts, and the extent to which I think these types of proportionality occur in judicial review cases. The types of proportionality distinguished are the 'balancing test', referring to a balancing of means and ends, the 'necessity test', and the 'suitability test'. Finally Hunt distinguishes 'balancing of interests' as a type of review of proportionality.

As I observed, Hunt noted that his idea of a proportionality test had been applied in the Brind case. This was apparent from the consideration that 'nothing less than an important competing public interest will be sufficient to justify a restriction'. The notion of justification and sufficiency must involve the court in weighing the facts of the case.[49] I agree that the requirement of justification must lead to a balancing of interests. However, these considerations do not automatically imply the application of a proportionality test in the sense of considering the means and ends of a restriction. From the discussion of the Brind case above, it has become clear that a balancing of means and ends was in fact exercised by Lord Bridge. Lord Templeman said that an interference must be necessary and proportionate to the damage which the restriction is designed to prevent'.[50] However, he merely concluded, without discussing the facts of the case, that 'the interference with freedom of expression was minimal and the reasons given by the Home Secretary are compelling'. In saying this he did imply that he had considered the weight of the means (minimal interference) and the weight of the end.

According to De Smith, Woolf and Jowell, their 'balancing test' between means

---

49   Hunt, Human Rights Law in English courts, 1998, p. 217.
50   R. v. Secretary of State for the Home Department, ex p. Brind [1991] 1 AC 696 at 751.

and ends has been applied in cases involving review of the substance of a case.[51] Lord Denning had called the suspension of a stallholder's licence for urinating in public and using offensive language 'out of proportion to the occasion'.[52] Moreover, in that decision he had relied on an older case that showed that if a punishment is excessive and out of proportion 'the court can interfere by certiorari'.[53] In more recent cases, the courts have quashed decisions on the basis of disproportionality of the administrative penalty, in cases involving banning a person from a local authority's property[54] and in cases involving the payments of non-domestic rates.[55] De Smith, Woolf and Jowell say that in the Brind case, the appellants claimed that the measure taken was disproportionate to the aim, and that since the ban was not thought to be disproportionate, the suitability test is not applied under English law. It is true that the appellants claimed that the measure was not suitable for achieving the aim, however, as I concluded in the first part of this section, a proportionality test was applied by Lord Bridge. He did not review whether the measure was appropriate. However, in my opinion, the test he used is also an example of the 'balancing test' between means and ends. The interference was thought to be of limited scope even if the dubbing of voices is 'an irritant', and is therefore proportionate to the 'serious aim of combating terrorism'.[56]

Regarding the balancing test, I also wish to refer to the case of R. v. Advertising Standards Authority Ltd. Even though in this case instead of reviewing whether the means of the interference were proportionate to the ends, Laws J. reviewed whether the speech would not have a disproportionate effect on the person seeking the restriction, the application of this proportionality test still amounts to an example of the balancing approach. The damage of the report would not be irreparable and therefore the publication and the fact that the ASA could 'carry out its function in the

---

51 See De Smith, Woolf and Jowell, Judicial Review of Administrative Action, 1995, p. 601-602. See also Jowell and Lester, Proportionality; neither novel nor dangerous, 1988, p. 60-61 according to whom 'Proportionality is most obviously applied where a punishment bears a disproportionate relationship to an offence'. In relation to this they referred to the Wheeler v. Leicester City Council case, saying that Lord Templeman (punishing the Club where it had done no wrong) and Lord Roskill (unfair means of obtaining an end) implicitly applied the doctrine of proportionality, since these opinions entailed the refusal 'to countenance the achievement of a legitimate end by disproportionate means'.

52 R. v. Barnsley M.B.C., ex p. Hook [1976] 1 WLR 1052 at 1057.

53 R. v. Barnley M.B.C., ex p. Hook [1976] 1 WLR 1052 at 1057.

54 R. v. Brent L.B.C., ex p. Assegai (1987) 151 L.G.R. 891.

55 In relation to freedom of expression but outside the area of judicial review this is comparable to Neill LJ.'s opinion in the Rantzen v. Mirror Group Newspapers case where he held that juries in libel action should make sure that the damages awarded were proportionate to the harm suffered by the plaintiff.

56 R. v. Secretary of State for the Home Department, ex p. Brind [1991] 1 AC 696 at 749.

ordinary way' should outweigh the damage done by the report.[57] Also in the Chahal case, Staughten LJ. suggested a proportionality test amounting to a balancing test when he held that if the relevant information had been available for review he would have balanced the 'threat on the one hand against the risk on the other'.[58]

The necessity test, which reviews whether no less restrictive alternative was available, could be found in the early case of Webb v. Minister of Housing and Local Government in which the government was thought to have purchased more land than was necessary for coast protection works. The court came to the conclusion that the compulsory purchase order was not within the powers conferred by the Coast Protection Act. However, as I have said before, Davies J. held: 'The present compulsory purchase order in my judgment extends to and embraces land not required by the council for the purpose of carrying out coast protection work as defined ... and in any event the proposed access way was neither coast protection work nor work of maintenance or repair'.[59] Close scrutiny is applied and leads to an independent application of a necessity test. The fact that the order was disproportionate to the aim, did not, however, lead to declaring the compulsory purchase order invalid. Jowell in an earlier comment had already argued that the Wheeler case also involved a proportionality test, since 'the court refused to countenance the achievement of a legitimate end (i.e. in this case the promotion of good race relations) by means which were excessive (where the individual had done no legal wrong)'.[60] To me it seems these considerations could also be considered as the application of a suitability test, since punishment by denying a club the possibility to play on the local rugby grounds where this club had done no wrong, was thought not to be an appropriate means to achieve the goal of good race relations.

However, the more recent Leech case constituted an application of the necessity test.[61] The 'extravagantly wide' powers of the prison authorities to censor the correspondence of the prisoners with their lawyers was thought to be disproportionate to the aim of regulating and managing prisons. In other prisons only correspondence suspected to be not 'bona fide' correspondence between client and lawyer was examined. Thus the court held that a less restrictive measure would have sufficed to achieve the same aim.

Also in the case of R. v. Secretary of State, ex p. Hargreaves the court applied the necessity test. It held that although it had become more difficult for prisoners to apply

---

57   R. v. ASA Ltd, ex p. Vernons Organisation Ltd [1992] 1 WLR 1289 at 1293-1294.
58   R. v. Home Secretary, ex p. Chahal [1995] 1 WLR 526 at 535.
59   Webb v. Minister of Housing and Local Government [1965] 1 WLR 755.
60   Jowell, Is Proportionality an Alien Concept?, 1996, p. 407.
61   R. v. Secretary of State for the Home Department, ex p. Leech [1994] Q.B. 198 at 217-218 per Steyn LJ. (CA). See De Smith Woolf and Jowell, Judicial review of administrative action, 1995, p. 604 and also De Búrca, Proportionality and Wednesbury Unreasonableness: The influence of European Legal Concepts on UK law, 1997, p. 575.

for home leave, 'there is no suggestion that any applicant was cut from his family altogether'. This measure is not restrictive in any absolute sense. A marginal necessity test was applied by the court by reviewing whether the restriction was an absolute one.

Although, as said above, the Wheeler case might be an example of an application of the suitability test, in that the punishment without wrong having been done was not accepted as a means to accomplish good race relations, no other examples of the suitability test seem available under English law.[62]

In order to draw conclusions on a common ground between the application of the principle of proportionality in English law and in the case law of the Court, I compare the findings of the previous sections of this chapter, and with regard to the case law of the Court I refer to the considerations in chapter IV in which I elaborated on the application of the principle of proportionality by the Court.

4 COMMON GROUND BETWEEN THE APPROACH TO REVIEW OF PROPORTIONALITY

Before the Human Rights Act 1998
Proportionality as used by the Court may entail a balancing of interests and may entail considerations regarding the relationship between means and ends. It is only this last type of review which I understand to be review of proportionality. In applying the proportionality test the Court applies two methods of review. It might review whether a less restrictive measure would be available to achieve the aim, and it might review whether the means and end are in balance. It does not apply the proportionality test by reviewing the suitability of a measure. The two methods of review correspond with the 'necessity test' and the 'balancing test' as distinguished by De Smith, Woolf and Jowell. The third method they distinguish is the suitability test, no examples of which can be found either in English case law nor in the case law of the Court. The proportionality test under English law usually amounts to a balancing of means and ends, although also in English law the test is sometimes reduced to the question of whether a less restrictive measure is available.

The necessity test was applied by the European Court of Human Rights in, for example, the Informationsverein Lentia case in which it held that 'there are no equivalent less restrictive measures ...' to achieve the aim pursued. Similar to this reasoning, in R. v. Secretary of State for the Home Department, ex p. Leech, it was implied that less restrictive powers than the censoring of all prison mail must be available, because in other prisons only mail suspected to be not 'bona fide' mail between lawyer and client is examined. However, the considerations of the Court

---

62 See also De Smith, Woolf and Jowell, Judicial review of administrative action, 1995, p. 604.

regarding the absoluteness of the interference with the right have also recently been applied in English case law. Just as the Court in, for instance, the Casado Coca case considered that the ban on advertisement could not be considered absolute, Hirst LJ. in the Hargreaves case held that the restriction on the right to family life was not absolute since none of the applicants was 'cut from his family altogether'. In both cases it was suggested that a total ban would have led to, respectively, the measure not being necessary in a democratic society and the measure not being reasonable in the Wednesbury sense.

It seems that both in the case law of the Court and in English courts the notion of proportionality is concerned with the balance between means and ends of a restriction. Under English law, the review of proportionality is not concerned with a balancing of interests between the aim and the right restricted, in which case the importance of the right concerned in a particular case is considered in relation to the interest in the aim. This observation is interesting in relation to Hunt's approach to proportionality. He is of the opinion that the test as advocated by Lord Bridge in the Brind case, namely that 'nothing less than an important competing public interest will be sufficient to justify a restriction' implied the application of the proportionality test, because the court would have to 'carry out an exercise which involves assessing the importance of the right, seriousness of the interference and the weight of the competing public interest before it can reach a sensible view as to the sufficiency of the justification offered'. This definition of proportionality, as I said, is broader than a means-ends test. However, his assessment of the proportionality test does coincide with the review carried out by the Court in the Jersild case, and which led it to conclude that the means were disproportionate to the end. If on occasion a balancing of interests may serve to determine whether or not a restriction is proportionate to the aim pursued, it could be said that Hunt is at least correct in holding that proportionality may involve a balancing of all interests involved.

As we have seen, the notion of proportionality, defined as a review of the relation between the measures to achieve an aim and the aim as such, can also be found under English case law. With regard to the search for a common ground it should be noted, however, that review of proportionality is not a frequently occurring ground of review under English law. At the moment, the notion of proportionality is developing under English law. An example of this is the move from the application of the proportionality test under marginal Wednesbury review to its application as a separate ground of review. The review of proportionality as a separate ground of review might open up possibilities of a full review of the proportionality of a measure, instead of the marginal approach that still seems to be inherent in the Wednesbury reasonableness test. Whether the courts will continue on this path, and in what cases the courts will feel authorised to undertake a full review cannot be said, but it seems unlikely that the courts will return to a situation in which they refrain from reviewing proportionality completely in cases that involve an infringement of a fundamental right.

Impact of the Human Right Act 1998

The development of the proportionality test in English case law, took place without the 'threat' of incorporation of the ECHR into English domestic law. Now that the Human Rights Act is becoming law, the question is to what extent this influences the application of proportionality by the English courts.

In the conclusion to the previous chapter I remarked that the primary responsibility regarding the protection of the Convention rights lies with the decision-making authorities,[63] but that this only can be realised if the courts have the power to control the protection of Convention rights by the executive. I also observed that the Act indicates the degree of protection that is intended to be the result of the exercise of the duty imposed on the courts to protect the Convention rights. S.2 implies that this degree of protection should be similar to the degree provided by the Court under the Convention. Moreover, neither the Court nor the Act requires the courts to apply the methods of protection that are used by the Court. Consequently, if the level of protection is to be similar to the one provided by the Court, the question is what that presupposes with regard to the review of proportionality in judicial review cases.

The test currently applied to review the appreciation of the substance of a case by the executive, is the Wednesbury unreasonableness test. I observed that the English courts are already applying a proportionality test under that review, and that they have also explored the review of proportionality by applying it as a separate ground of review. It should be noted that the courts increasingly use terminology from the case law of the Court as a basis for this review. Instead of referring to reasonableness, they review whether there is a 'pressing ground' for restricting a right. Apparently, reasonableness does not provide the courts with a possibility to review proportionality, although this development also seems to be instigated by a need to come to closer scrutiny of the merits of a case. The application of this method of review is controversial, however, and consequently the courts do not review the proportionality of decisions consistently. The objections regarding the review of proportionality mainly concern the extent to which, in judicial review cases, the courts can review the merits of a decision.

Feldman convincingly held, however, that if the English courts were to refrain from using proportionality as a method of review, this 'would lead to too wide a rift between the interpretation of Convention rights in the UK and their interpretation under the ECHR, and would undermine the main purpose of the Bill'.[64] And if the Act is intended to offer protection similar to that offered by the Court, any restriction on fundamental rights such as freedom of expression will have to be necessary in a democratic society. The Court determines this necessity by reviewing the

---

63 Human Rights Act 1998, s.6.
64 See Feldman, Proportionality and the Human Rights Act 1998, 1999, p. 121.

proportionality of a measure or even by balancing the interests involved. So although the Human Rights Act does not explicitly state that the methods of protection of the Court should be adopted, s.2 of the Act, just as it offers the possibility to come to a narrower margin of appreciation, provides a possibility for the courts to adopt proportionality as a method of protection. Although the fact that s.2 speaks of 'taking into account', which implies that the courts are not bound by the Strasbourg case law, they could read this section as implying that this method of protection should be applied in order to determine whether a restriction on a Convention right was justified. In doing so, this approach might introduce different forms of proportionality into the review by the English courts, depending on the extent to which the courts are prepared to follow Strasbourg case law.

I wish to remark at this point that, as I said in the chapter IV, the degree of protection offered by the review of proportionality also depends on the margin of appreciation left to the decision-making authorities. In other words, the additional protection the consistent review of proportionality could provide also depends on the willingness of the courts to overcome their traditional reluctance of strict scrutiny of administrative decisions.[65]

---

[65] See Feldman, Proportionality and the Human Rights Act 1998, 1999, p. 122. Although in my opinion Feldman seems to confuse proportionality and the closeness of review.

Chapter VIII
Balancing of Interests

1 Introduction

In chapter IV, beside the review of proportionality, I distinguished another substantive method of protection. This is the method of balancing of interests. In chapter IV, I described the case of Janowski v. Poland to illustrate the existence of balancing of interests as a separate method of protection in the case law of the Court.[1] When the Court applies balancing of interests, it evaluates the importance of the competing interests, resulting in a decision as to the interest that should prevail. In the case law of the Court this method of protection is one of the methods to determine the necessity of a restriction. Under English law, both with regard to restrictive laws and with regard to judgments of courts in their appellate jurisdiction, considerations regarding the interest in freedom of expression could give evidence of the application of a balancing of interests. In this chapter I search for a common ground between balancing of interests as applied by the Court and balancing of interests under English law.

I first elaborate on the application of balancing of interests by the European Court of Human Rights. On the basis of some further examples of the application of balancing of interests, I discuss the character of this method of protection in the case of law of the Court. The character of balancing of interests concerns the manner in which the Court applies this method of protection and the moment at which it applies this method when it reviews a particular case. 'Moment' refers to the issue of whether the balancing of interests occurs at an abstract or at a concrete level. In the third section I then turn to balancing of interests under English law. I elaborate on evidence of balancing of interests in restrictive laws in the first section. Then I discuss the occurrence and character of balancing of interests in English case law.

2 Character of Balancing of Interests in the Case Law of the Court

2.1 Manner of Application of Balancing of Interests

As I stated in the introduction to this chapter, balancing of interests implies that the Court evaluates the opposing interests involved in cases in which freedom of

---

1   Janowski v. Poland, 21 January 1999.

expression is restricted. Beside the case of Janowski v. Poland, a number of other examples of the application of balancing of interests are available. I discuss these judgments in order to be able to comment further on the character of balancing of interests as a method of review.

An early case in which the Court applied balancing of interests as a separate method of review was the case of Markt Intern Verlag v. Germany.[2] This case concerned the publication of an article about a 'mail order cosmetic club', which on four occasions had failed to fulfil its obligations under contract. The article reported these cases and the readers of the magazine were asked if they were aware of any further incidents of this kind. Based on this information it would then be possible to draw conclusions as to the policy of the mail order company. This latter company subsequently sought and obtained an injunction preventing publication, because it was in defiance of competition law. In chapter VI I remarked that the Court attributed importance to freedom of expression by holding that the article was written in a commercial context. The Court also held that although it contained some true statements, it also 'expressed doubts about the reliability of the Club'. Furthermore the applicants should have known that the criticisms in the article should only have been expressed after 'further clarification' had been sought. The interest in the protection of the rights of 'The Club' was determined by following the German Federal Court's opinion of the case. The Court held that the applicants 'should have taken into consideration that any such premature publication of the incident was bound to have adverse effects on the Club's business because it gave the specialised retailers an effective argument capable of being used against the Club with their customers, and one which could be used even if the incident should turn out to be an isolated mishap from which no conclusion could be drawn as to the Club's business policy'.[3] Consequently the Court concluded that the national authorities did not go beyond their margin of appreciation. The Court in this case explicitly did not consider the means applied to achieve the ends when it held in relation to the granting of an injunction to prevent publication of information on the Club, 'it is obvious that opinions may differ as to whether the Federal Courts's reaction was appropriate ...'.[4] The application of a wide margin of appreciation made it unnecessary to consider the means-ends relation. The Court applied a very wide margin of appreciation and consequently closely followed the reasoning of the national courts. The Court determined that 'the national courts did weigh the competing interests at stake' and then repeated the national courts' considerations. The margin of appreciation was so

---

2   Markt Intern Verlag GmbH and Klaus Beerman, (1989) A.165, par. 36.
3   Markt Intern Verlag GmbH and Klaus Beerman, (1989) A.165, par. 36.
4   Markt Intern Verlag GmbH and Klaus Beerman, (1989) A.165, par. 37.

wide that apparently the mere fact that the competing interests were considered, sufficed to conclude that there had been no breach of Article 10.

The Court applied the balancing of interests in a similar manner in the Otto Preminger case, which concerned the prohibition to show and seizure of a film which was considered to be blasphemous. Also in this case, the Court applied a wide margin of appreciation, as a result of which the Court was inclined to follow the balancing of interests as carried out by the domestic courts. The Court then commented on the decisions of the national courts: 'They did not consider that its merit as a work of art or as a contribution to public debate in Austrian society outweighed those features which made it essentially offensive to the general public within their jurisdiction. The trial courts, after viewing the film, noted the provocative portrayal of God the Father, the Virgin Mary and Jesus Christ. The content of the film cannot be said to be incapable of grounding the conclusion arrived at by the Austrian courts'.[5] The national courts did not come to a balancing of interests. But the Court is nonetheless of the opinion that the interest in freedom of expression, which lies in the film's value as a work of art and its contribution to public debate, could be considered to be outweighed by the interest in protecting public order. The Court did not elaborate on the public interest in the expression concerned.

In both the Markt Intern Verlag case and the Otto Preminger case, the Court closely followed the reasoning of the decisions of the national courts. In applying a balancing of interest the Court subsequently pays little attention to the interest in freedom of expression. Instead it tends mainly to refer to the interest in restricting freedom of expression. Moreover, it will not come to an independent consideration of the facts and circumstances.

However, in Oberschlick v. Austria, concerning defamation of a politician, the margin of appreciation is a narrow one.[6] This case dealt with the conviction of a journalist for publishing a defamatory article in the form of a 'wanted' notice. In this case, the Court also reviewed the decision of the national authorities by balancing the interests involved. First the general principles regarding the value of freedom of expression to a democratic society, especially where the press is concerned, were summed up. The Court then applied these principles to the circumstances of the case. It attributed importance to freedom of expression: 'The Court agrees with the Commission that the insertion of the text of the said information ... contributed to a public debate on a political question of general importance. In particular, the issue of different treatment of nationals and foreigners in the social field has given rise to considerable discussion not only in Austria but also in other Member States of the Council of Europe. Mr Oberschlick's criticisms, as the Commission pointed out,

---

5   Otto Preminger v. Austria, (1995) A.295, par. 56.
6   Oberschlick v. Austria, (1991) A.204.

sought to draw the public's attention in a provocative manner to a proposal made by a politician which was likely to shock many people'. Subsequently the interest of the politician in protecting his reputation was attributed importance: 'A politician who expressed himself in such terms exposes himself to a strong reaction on the part of journalists and the public'.[7] Subsequently the Court concluded that the relevant restriction of Article 10 was not necessary in a democratic society in the interest of protecting the reputation of others. Also in this case the means by which freedom of expression had been restricted were not considered. The balancing considerations constituted an independent review of the national courts' decision, since these courts had not considered freedom of expression as a competing interest. The balancing of interests amounted to an extensive consideration of the interest in freedom of expression.

However, in the case of Schöpfer v. Switzerland, the Court said that it was applying a wide margin of appreciation, but did not leave the evaluation of the facts completely to the national authorities.[8] In this case, the Court determined that 'Mr Schöpfer first publicly criticised the administration of justice in Hockdorf and then exercised a legal remedy which proved effective with regard to the complaint in question. In so doing his conduct was scarcely compatible with the contribution it is legitimate to expect lawyers to make to maintaining public confidence in the judicial authorities. The above finding is reinforced by the seriousness and general nature of the criticism made by the applicant and the tone in which he chose to make them'.[9] These considerations were taken into account in the balancing of interests. The Court in fact explicitly held it was going to apply a balancing of interests: 'It also goes without saying that freedom of expression is secured to lawyers too, who are certainly entitled to comment in public on the administration of justice, but their criticism must not overstep certain bounds. In that connection, account must be taken of the need to strike the right balance between the various interests involved, which include the public's right to receive information about questions arising from judicial decisions, the requirements of the proper administration of justice and the dignity of the legal profession'.[10] This in fact is a very clear example of a case in which a balancing of interests was the sole method of protection applied. The Court paid a lot of attention to the interest in freedom of expression: it considered the nature of Mr Schöpfer's speech and the responsibility lawyers have when they discuss the behaviour of the judicial authorities.

In my view the outcome of this last case was not obvious to the Court, also because the aim pursued was the maintenance of the authority of the judiciary. The

---

7   Oberschlick v. Austria, (1991) A.204, par. 61.
8   Schöpfer v. Switzerland, 20 May 1998, Reports 1998-III.
9   Schöpfer v. Switzerland, 20 May 1998, Reports 1998-III, par. 31-32.
10   Schöpfer v. Switzerland, 20 May 1998, Reports 1998-III, par. 33.

balancing of interests in this case involved a thorough evaluation of aspects of both opposing interests.

Depending on different characteristics of the case, such as the nature of the speech and the aim pursued, the Court seems to have an indication of the outcome of a case. In Markt Intern Verlag, the speech was held to be of a commercial nature and the Otto Preminger case concerned the protection of public order. Both these aspects cause the Court to adopt a reserved attitude to interference with the national authorities' approach to the case. In such cases freedom of expression will not be extensively considered. In a case where political speech is restricted, the Court is inclined to attribute much weight to the interest in freedom of expression, which is illustrated by extensive considerations regarding that aspect of the case. However, when the circumstances of the case would at first sight lead one to assume that there will be a close review, despite some considerations to the contrary, such as in the Schöpfer case, but the outcome of the case is that the restriction is considered necessary in a democratic society, further elaboration on how the Court came to its decision is required. This results in an extensive consideration of both competing interests.

When the margin of appreciation allowed by the Court is evident from the case, the balancing of interests will emphasise the prevailing interest. If the circumstances of the case are less obvious with regard to the scope of the review, depending on the outcome of the case,[11] the Court will consider all interests involved.[12] However, both competing interests will at least always be considered by the Court when it applies a balancing of interests.

2.2 Moment of Balancing of Interests

Under the case law of the Court, considerations in relation to a balancing of interests may take place at an abstract level and at a concrete level. The moment of protection will influence the protection offered to freedom of expression. The Court does make abstract statements, but they never imply a certainty in outcome regarding the protection of freedom of expression in a particular case. The case of Schöpfer v. Switzerland is an example of this approach. The Court held, on an abstract level, that lawyers have 'a central position in the administration of justice as intermediaries

---

11 It appears to me that the Court is somewhat inclined to reason in the direction of the outcome of the case.

12 See also Goodwin v. UK, 22 February 1996, Reports 1996-II, in which the outcome of the case was less obvious and the Court felt obliged to argue the conclusion that there had been a violation of Article 10 in great detail. The Court completely reconsidered the interest of the UK in restricting the speech concerned, conducting a complete balancing of interests, before concluding that Article 10 had been violated.

between the public and the courts', which explained 'the usual restrictions on the conduct of members of the Bar'.[13] With regard to the position of the courts, it held that they, as 'the guarantors of justice, whose role is fundamental in a State based on the rule of law – must enjoy public confidence', and that 'regard being had to the key role of lawyers in this field, it is legitimate to expect them to contribute to the proper administration of justice, and thus to maintain public confidence therein'.[14] These considerations, however, do not imply that criticism of the administration of justice by a lawyer may always be prohibited. The circumstances of the case determine whether in the particular instance the restriction is allowed. So, although lawyers also have freedom of expression and Article 10 also protects the manner in which people choose to express themselves, criticism of the administration of justice in this case occurred while a legal remedy was still available and later proved to be effective. This meant together with the seriousness and the tone of the criticism, that the restriction was allowed.[15] In other words, abstract considerations will always have to be followed up by a balancing of interests at the concrete level, to determine whether in the case at issue the abstract considerations in fact lead to the acceptability of the restriction on freedom of expression. This balancing of interests will differ in emphasis, as influenced by the abstract statements. However, the impression given by the abstract considerations on whether the interest in freedom of expression or in the opposing interest should prevail does not always correspond to the outcome of the concrete considerations. This is also illustrated by the case of De Haes and Gijsels, which concerned accusations of friendly relations between the judges on a case and one of the parties involved, which were such as to influence the decision awarding custody of children to an allegedly abusive parent.

In this case, the abstract considerations were similar to those in Schöpfer v. Switzerland. However, in this instance the criticisms were held to be justified and of such a serious nature that a restriction of the expression was held to be a violation of Article 10 ECHR.[16]

---

13 Schöpfer v. Switzerland, 20 May 1998, Reports 1998-III, par. 29.
14 Schöpfer v. Switzerland, 20 May 1998, Reports 1998-III, par. 29.
15 See also the considerations in Castells v. Spain, (1992) A.236 I described above, in which the considerations at the concrete level emphasised the interest in freedom of expression instead of the reasons why it could be restricted.
16 In this case the freedom of expression of journalists had been restricted, which, on an abstract level, obtains additional protection from the Court; although it is doubtful whether this circumstance was decisive to the Courts decision, it did play a role.

3 BALANCING OF INTERESTS UNDER ENGLISH LAW

3.1 Balancing of Interests in English Legislation

The traditional approach to the protection of freedom of expression is that it is protected to the extent to which it is not restricted. Law, statutory as well as common law and equity, is therefore the first level of protection of freedom of expression. The restrictions that exist establish the sphere of protection around freedom of expression. In this section I give an account of the extent to which the restrictive areas of law discussed in chapter III give evidence of the interest in freedom of expression that is taken into account, and the extent to which this amounts to possibilities for the courts to take freedom of expression into consideration and to come to a balancing of interests.

Often Parliament, as the legislature, has given evidence of the fact that it took account of the interest in freedom of expression to some extent. This is indicated first of all by the formulation of the offence and, secondly, by the defences or exceptions adopted in the restrictive legislation. Under the Obscene Publications Act 1959 it is prohibited to publish an article which tends to deprave and corrupt persons who are likely to read, see or hear it. To provide a balance with the restrictive effect this would have on freedom of expression, under s.4 of the Act the legislature provided for a public good defence: if the article is in the interest of science, literature, art or learning, or of other objects of general concern the obscenity is justified. Under the Official Secrets Act 1989, there is an obligation of confidentiality of government information. This obligation is absolute for members and former members of the Security Service. Furthermore, a less absolute but still extensive obligation extends to Crown Servants, government contractors and members of the public, including journalists. The range of information is broad. Some balance in relation to the impact on freedom of expression is present in the Act. First of all, in relation to the last categories of persons, i.e. government contractors and members of the public, it is, with regard to certain kinds of information, necessary for the government to show that disclosure is harmful to the public interest. Moreover, it is a defence to prove that the offender had no reasonable cause to believe that the information would be 'damaging within the meaning of damage'. A public good defence has not been provided for, however. Under the Contempt of Court Act 1981, as far as an unintended contempt is concerned, a publication that causes a 'substantial risk' that the course of justice will be seriously impeded is prohibited. In this Act there is also a balance vis-à-vis freedom of expression in the formulation of the offence, since the risk has to be 'substantial' and the impediment has to be 'serious'. Beside this, s.5 of the Act provides that if the publication is 'merely incidental to the discussion' it will not constitute a contempt. Finally, s.10 offers the possibility for journalists to keep the identity of their sources secret. However, this section provides for a balance

239

regarding the interest in the administration of justice, since it determines that the identity of sources has to be revealed if a court holds that disclosure is 'necessary in the interest of justice or national security or for the prevention of disorder or crime'. Finally, the Public Order Act 1986 criminalises a wide range of behaviour that constitutes the use of threatening, abusive or insulting words or behaviour which causes fear or provocation of violence, intentional harassment, alarm or distress or which is likely to cause harassment, alarm or distress, or if it is intended to stir up or likely to stir up racial hatred. S.5 of the Act goes so far as to criminalise disorderly behaviour within hearing or sight of a person which is likely to cause harassment, alarm or distress. This may restrict freedom of expression to a very large extent. Under s.5, however, it is a defence for the accused to show that the behaviour in question was reasonable.

A substantial number of the restrictive laws did not come from Parliament, but stems from common law and equity. As I observed, this law has been developed by the courts. In relation to this law, the acceptance of the existence of offences and the formulation of the offences had an important impact on freedom of expression. And, as under statute law, defences may be provided for that constitute a balance between the interest in the restrictive law and the interest in freedom of expression. Under common law, however, no defence of public good is available unless provided for by Parliament. As for outraging public decency, conspiracy to outrage public decency and conspiracy to corrupt public morals, and also regarding the offence of blasphemy, no defences have been formulated. Under libel law there are four defences that provide a balance vis-à-vis freedom of expression. These defences are absolute privilege, qualified privilege and justification. Finally, with regard to defamation law, a statutory defence has been provided for under the Defamation Act 1959. Under this Act it is a defence to plead fair comment on a matter of public interest. The law of breach of confidence, under equity, provides for a defence and an exception that create room for freedom of expression. These are successively the public domain-doctrine and the public interest exception.

Within the restricting legislation there are a number of instances in which freedom of expression is offered a certain degree of protection. Sections such as s.4 of the Obscene Publications Act and s.5 of the Official Secrets Act even appear to be the result of a balancing of interests by the legislature. However, the courts are never explicitly required to apply a balancing of interests. In theory, it is possible for the courts to apply the law literally, without considering the interest in freedom of expression. Consequently they may leave the protection of freedom of expression with regard to the areas of speech covered by statute law, completely to the legislature, only considering those aspects of a case that concern the interest the legislation is intended to serve. The approach of the courts to existing common law may be similar to their approach to statutory law. Once the existence of an offence has been acknowledged, the law is applied without any further consideration of freedom of expression, except to the extent allowed by exceptions and defences.

However, even if courts merely define the wording of law, their decisions will have an impact on freedom of expression, whether they consider it as such or not. And although the meaning of some of the wording may be evident, the formulation of many provisions in the statutes is so vague that the extent of the restriction is to a large extent up to the courts. A good example is the formulation of the offence under the Official Secrets Act: the disclosure of the information is held to be harmful if it is damaging, but the definitions given of damage in relation to several categories of information are so vague that the extent of the damage required may vary considerably in scope, depending on the decisions of the courts.

A literal application of law is often impossible. And although a certain balance between freedom of expression and the competing interests can be detected in the legislation as such, it is to a significant extent up to the courts to determine the exact scope of the restriction on freedom of expression. I examine the methods of protection applied by the English courts. In doing so, I focus on the occurrence of balancing of interests in English case law, and on the character of balancing of interests as applied by the courts.

3.2 Balancing of Interests by the English Courts

3.2.1 The Traditional Approach

In the traditional English approach, in which freedom of expression is a residual freedom, there is in principle no room for considerations regarding freedom of expression. This fact is deemed to exclude the possibility for the courts to perform a balancing of interests in order to determine the scope of restrictive law. In a number of early judgments of the English courts, this approach was confirmed. In Brutus v. Cozens, which dealt with public order law, Lord Reid formulated it as follows: 'Parliament had to solve the difficult question how far freedom of speech or behaviour must be limited in the general public interest. It would have been going much too far to prohibit all speech or conduct likely to occasion a breach of the peace because determined opponents may not shrink from organising or at least threatening a breach of the peace in order to silence a speaker whose views they detest. Therefore vigorous and it may be distasteful or unmannerly speech or behaviour is permitted so long as it does not go beyond any one of three limits. It must not be threatening. It must not be abusive. It must not be insulting'.[17] And then he continued: 'Free

---

17   Brutus v. Cozens [1972] 2 All ER 1297 at 1300.

speech is not impaired by ruling [such behaviour] out'.[18] Lord Reid was of the opinion that freedom of expression was not restricted by prohibiting threatening, abusive and insulting speech. There is freedom of expression beyond the behaviour that is prohibited by law. Similar considerations can be found in an early decision concerning Contempt of Court law. In the case of A-G v. Times Newspapers Ltd it was held that freedom of expression could only exist beyond the 'reasonable necessity' to prevent prejudice in the administration of justice.[19] And even if contempt of court law touched upon freedom of expression, the power to decide what is necessary to protect the administration of justice had been delegated to a judge or jury and therefore 'the paramount public interest pendente lite is that the legal proceedings should progress without interference'.[20] This decision resulted in a conviction for breach of Article 10 ECHR. But even after the UK realised that being a Party to the Convention brought with it obligations to protect the rights adopted therein, there were cases in which judges persisted in the traditional approach to the protection of freedom of expression. Lord Scarman, in his opinion in Whitehouse v. Gay News Ltd and Lemon, emphasised that it would be intolerable if the author of a blasphemous article could defend himself by calling upon freedom of expression. If the publication constituted 'an outrage upon the religious feelings of his fellow citizens' then the author should be sentenced according to law. And according to Lord Scarman, Article 10 of the Convention confirmed that approach since the exercise of freedom of expression carried with it 'duties and responsibilities' and could be restricted if prescribed by law and necessary for the protection of one of the listed aims. By applying Article 10 ECHR in this manner, it is fitted neatly into the residual liberty approach: if certain behaviour is criminalised and is covered by one of the exceptions summed up in the second section of Article 10, then freedom of speech can no longer play a role.

In line with this approach, the English courts regularly determine the scope of freedom of expression – even if they do not do so explicitly – by specifying the scope of the restricting legislation. They do this by clarifying the wording of legislation. In relation to some aspects of areas of law freedom of expression is not considered in this process.

This is the approach taken to the offences contained in the Public Order Act. In relation to public order offences, the courts seem inclined to rely on any balancing of interests having taken place in Parliament. This is, first of all, the case regarding riot, violent disorder and affray. Although these types of conduct were never actually excluded from the protection of freedom of expression, this could be of no relevance

---

18   Brutus v. Cozens [1972] 2 All ER 1297 at 1300.
19   A-G v. Times Newspapers Ltd [1973] 3 All ER 54, per Lord Reid.
20   A-G v. Times Newspapers Ltd [1973] 3 All ER 54, per Lord Simon at 81-82.

to the courts. The cases of R. v. Caird and Kamara v. DPP both made clear that freedom of expression was, or should have been, considered when it was decided what conduct was prohibited in order to protect public order. The courts should only interpret the wording of the legislation, which became apparent when it was held in R. v. Caird: 'It is the degree of mob violence that matters and the extent to which the public peace is being broken'.[21] But it is not only in relation to these types of conduct that the English courts opt for this approach. Threatening, abusive or insulting behaviour is to have 'its ordinary meaning'. The provision of s.5(3)(c) of the Public Order Act, which offers a defence for reasonable conduct, which could have been used as a foothold for some further protection of freedom of expression against rather restrictive legislation, has also been approached in this manner. The offence under the Obscene Publications Act has been dealt with similarly. In determining what publications tend to deprave and corrupt and who are likely readers of depraving and corrupting publications, it appears that on the whole no consideration was taken of freedom of expression. However, also in relation to provisions where Parliament did intend to offer some protection to freedom of expression, this did not automatically mean that the courts would carry out a balancing of interests of some sort. Evidence of this can be found, for instance, in the application of s.2 of the Contempt of Court Act. The risk of impediment to a trial should, for instance, be 'substantial'. In defining this term, freedom of expression was not considered.

In these decisions, freedom of expression was not considered explicitly as such or by way of an interest representing freedom of expression. In my opinion this approach cannot be qualified as a method of protection. From the discussion in chapter III of the different areas of English law that touch upon freedom of expression, however, it already became apparent that the English courts did not persist in this approach. As we saw in that chapter, there are a significant number of decisions in which freedom of expression was explicitly considered. These considerations amount to a balancing of interests.

In the next section I first briefly discuss the role freedom of expression is said to play in those considerations. Subsequently I elaborate on the manner in which the English courts did in fact consider freedom of expression, which is the first aspect of the character of balancing of interests. Finally I address the second aspect of the character of balancing of interests, which is the moment at which the balancing of interests occurs.

---

21 R. v. Caird (1970) 54 Cr App R 499 at 506.

3.2.2 Balancing of Interests in Name

Usually under English law balancing of interests is not explicitly mentioned as a method of offering protection to freedom of expression. A unique example is offered by Lord Bridge in his opinion in the case of X Ltd v. Morgan Grampian, in which he explicitly announced that he was going to balance the interests involved when he held: 'In estimating the weight to be attached to the importance of disclosure in the interests of justice on the one hand and that of protection from disclosure on pursuance of the policy which underlies s.10 on the other hand, many factors will be relevant on both sides of the scale'. The character of the balancing of interests is not elaborated on. In fact, Lord Bridge continued his considerations by saying: 'It would be foolish to attempt to give comprehensive guidance as to how this exercise should be carried out'.[22] References to the method of protection applied are rare, even though the courts regularly refer to freedom of expression or an interest inherent to that freedom. These references imply that methods of protection are in fact applied. Two manners of balancing of interests can be distinguished in the areas of English law discussed in chapter III of this study. These are: implied balancing of interests and full balancing of interests. I elaborate on this.

3.2.3 Character of Balancing of Interests in English Case Law

3.2.3.1 Manner of Application of Balancing of Interests by the English Courts

a Implied Balancing of Interests
When the English courts apply this method of protection, they take freedom of expression, or an aspect of it, into consideration. However, the extent of its importance and the role it plays in relation to the opposing interest is unclear.

An example of the application of this method of protection derives from the fact that the existence of an obligation to keep governmental information secret does not suffice to establish a breach of confidence. It was held by the House of Lords, in A-G v. Guardian Newspapers, that the government has to show an additional public interest in the confidentiality of the information. This requirement might be the result of a balancing of interests, but it was not made visible as such. The protection of freedom of expression is embodied in the extension of the law of breach of confidence to the requirement of a public interest in the protection of confidentiality of governmental information. It is also interesting that, in fact, the requirement was the existence of an 'overriding public interest'. The application of such a requirement suggests a balancing of interests. However, no balancing of competing interests took

---

22   X Ltd v. Morgan Grampian [1990] 1 AC 1, per Lord Bridge at 43-44.

place regarding its application. Instead, the government merely had to present an interest and the House of Lords accepted that the requirement was fulfilled. The requirement was applied literally. This type of implied balancing of interests is an exception. In this case, the requirement of public interest in keeping the information confidential is merely stated. None of the interests involved is elaborated on.

The other examples of an implied balancing of interests all entail a rather extensive discussion of the interest in freedom of expression. These considerations do not amount to a balancing of interests, because consideration of the interest in the restrictive legislation is not made visible. A number of examples are available. The first of these is in the case of Telnikoff v. Matusevitch, in the opinion of Lord Ackner. This case dealt with the application of the defence of fair comment in a libel action. The interest in freedom of expression lay in the availability of the defence of fair comment. In relation to this defence, Lord Ackner had held that a jury, when it had to determine whether it was dealing with statements of opinion or fact in a libel case, should be able to consider these statements in the context in which they were made. He held this because 'if the criticism of an article published in a newspaper on a subject matter of public importance is to be confined to passages actually set out in the criticism, then the freedom to comment on matter of public importance becomes, from a practical point of view, illusory or non-existent'. He clearly wished to offer freedom of expression a certain degree of protection, and in fact attributed importance to it. The only interest considered is freedom of expression.

Another example can be found in the case of R v. Chief Metropolitan Stipendiary Magistrate. In this case it was decided that the scope of the offence of blasphemy should not be extended to other religions beside Christianity. Freedom of expression was explicitly considered and an attempt was even made to come to an application of Article 10 ECHR, even though it was emphasised that the Convention was not a part of English domestic law. The court held that there was no pressing social need for an extension of blasphemy law to other religions, because it did not serve a legitimate aim. A balancing of interests must have taken place in order to come to the application of Article 10. But again, this was not made visible in the considerations of the court. A visible balancing of interests was avoided by approaching the requirements of the second paragraph of Article 10 as if it concerned terms that merely had to be filled in, which, as I established, the courts often do in relation to domestic law. It is noteworthy also that it was assumed that there is a pressing social need when there is a legitimate aim for the restriction. A similar approach can also be derived from the case of Derbyshire County Council. Local authorities were not allowed to start a libel action, because they 'should be open to uninhibited public criticism' and a libel action would pose an undesirable fetter upon freedom of expression. In coming to its decision, the courts did not come to a balancing of interests in which both interests involved were considered. The only interest that was attributed importance seemed to be freedom of expression. The protection of freedom of expression under libel law in relation to the granting of an interim injunction is also comparable. If a defence of fair comment is pleaded, an injunction will most likely not be granted because 'freedom of expression will not be restricted as long as "no wrongful act is done"'. Again, there is no visible balancing of interests, but it is clear that this approach provides protection to freedom of expression.

In my view, the application of an implied balancing of interests in these instances can be explained by the fact that the competing interest is represented in the law at issue in the case at hand. Extensive elaboration on that interest is therefore not required. The interest in freedom of expression does require further discussion, because it is not implied in the restrictive law, be it statutory law, common law or equity.

b Full Balancing of Interests

As I observed, until quite recently, the approach to the offence of Contempt of Court under common law was the traditional one.[23] The scope of the offence of Contempt of Court was initially determined without balancing the interests involved, even though the interest in freedom of expression was acknowledged. This approach was illustrated by the decision of the House of Lords in A-G v. Times Newspapers Ltd.[24] It could even be said that Lord Simon applied an implicit balancing of interests when he recognised that freedom of expression was restricted, and that the interest in proper administration of justice and in freedom of expression were equally important. He then held, however, that the interest in the proper administration of justice should prevail since the courts had the task to realise this.[25] The interests on both sides were pointed out, but only one was considered, namely the interest in the proper administration of justice.

In later cases, after a violation of Article 10 had been found by the Court, freedom of expression was attributed importance in the considerations regarding the scope of the offence, e.g. in the case of A-G v. the BBC: a person could not be in contempt with regard to local valuation courts, because this would restrict freedom of expression too much. In this last case the court did come to its conclusion by way of a balancing of interests. Legal certainty was held to outweigh the interest in due administration of justice despite the fact that the judges on a local valuation court were not professionally trained and were therefore more likely to be influenced. The interest in legal certainty seemed to be influenced by the fact that an extension of the law would restrict freedom of expression. And this brings us to the second method of review, namely full balancing of interests. A number of examples are available in

---

23   Comparable also Whitehouse v. Gay News Ltd and Lemon [1979] AC 617.
24   A-G v. Times Newspapers Ltd [1973] 3 All ER 54.
25   A-G v. Times Newspapers Ltd [1973] 3 All ER 54, per Lord Simon at 81-82.

which freedom of expression and the opposing interest represented by the restricting law were both considered.

In relation to the offence of 'outraging public decency' for example, Lord Simon asked the jury to 'remember that they live in a plural society, with a tradition of tolerance towards minorities, and that this atmosphere of toleration is itself part of public decency'. Consequently he asked the jury to apply a balancing of interests. In a similar manner, in relation to the public good defence under the Obscene Publications Act, the jury was asked to 'weigh up' the literary, sociological or ethical value of a publication and its 'strength and tendency to deprave and corrupt'. In these two cases, the courts asked the jury to apply a balancing of interests.

In relation to the offence of blasphemy, Lord Edmund-Davies, in a minority opinion, emphasised the value of free discussion on religious matters and held that therefore only abuse of the freedom to comment should be punished: only if freedom of expression was abused should the religious sensibilities of others prevail. Furthermore, the application of the public interest exception under breach of confidence law amounts to a full balancing of interests. The public interest exception was held to provide protection only if the public interest in publication 'outweighed' the interest in confidentiality.[26] In deciding whether an interim injunction should be granted, however, a balance of convenience is applied.

As I observed, under defamation law if a defence of fair comment is pleaded, in principle an injunction will not be granted. This is because then there is 'no pressing ground to restrain the publication'[27] and because 'freedom of speech will not be restricted as long as "no wrongful act is done"'. This approach is very different from the balance of convenience applied in relation to breach of confidence law. In this balance of convenience, purely on the level of the interests of the parties concerned, the court considers the harm done by publication and the harm done by restricting the publication. This approach can be said to amount to full balancing of interests, since both interests involved are considered.

However, Lord Denning in Hubbard v. Vosper, criticised this approach to the granting of interim injunctions in confidential information. According to him, referring to the approach in libel law cases, the law 'will not suppress freedom of speech except when it is abused'.

The restricting effect of the balance of convenience became clear in A-G v. Guardian Newspapers Ltd. In this case, although the information concerned was already in the public domain, the interest of the A-G to have the case judged on the merits was sufficiently important to grant an interim injunction. The balance of

---

26 Balancing of interests in Hubbard v. Vosper [1972] 1 All ER 1023, Lion Laboratories Ltd v. Evans [1984] 2 All ER 417, and Woodward v. Hutchins [1977] 2 All ER 751.

27 R. v. Advertising Standards Authority, ex p. Vernons Ltd [1992] 1 WLR 1289, per Laws J. at 1293.

convenience led to a balancing of interests. Lord Brandon balanced the damage done to freedom of expression if the injunction continued against the damage done to the interest in maintenance of secrecy of the British security service. Since freedom of expression could be freely exercised if the injunctions were lifted at trial and the damage to the A-G would be irreparable if the injunction was lifted, the latter interest was held to prevail over the interest in freedom of expression. In the dissenting opinion of Lord Bridge, freedom of expression was held to prevail. The method of protection applied appeared to be a proportionality test instead of a balancing of interests.

In relation to the protection of confidentiality of governmental information, a similar method of protection was applied. The fact that the information was already in the public domain did not automatically mean that an injunction would be refused. Instead a full balancing of interests was applied, in which the right of the public to be protected by a security service was weighed against the right of the public to be fully informed. The interest in freedom of expression was not particularly emphasised, but it was considered.

An interesting point is that the public domain-doctrine in combination with the balance of convenience resulted in a balancing of interests in the case of Schering Chemicals v. Falkman, which also concerned breach of confidence law. Under the law of breach of confidence there is a public domain defence. However, when an injunction is requested in order to prevent publication of the information, the fact that the information is in the public domain is not decisive with regard to the decision, as was apparent from the Schering Chemicals case. In Schering Chemicals v. Falkman, the Court of Appeal granted an injunction because the information concerned was of a commercial nature and the defendant had a duty of confidence. That the information was available from other sources was of no importance. Lord Denning dissented and held that in this case the right to privacy could not outweigh the right to freedom of expression, because an injunction constituted prior restraint, which was one of the most serious interferences with freedom of expression. In his opinion it was the public interest in the information that was decisive. The weight of the right to privacy was reduced by the fact that the information was publicly available, and the drug concerned was no longer on the market. Lord Denning's balancing of interests was the most complete one, but also the majority applied a balancing of interests in coming to its decision. The evaluation of the facts and circumstances of the case explains the outcome.

Initially, s.10 of the Contempt of Court Act, which allows for the protection of the identity of sources, was also approached in this manner. However, some developments have taken place recently in relation to this section and as a consequence the courts have used balancing of interests as a method of protection, when the necessity of disclosure was to be found in 'the interest of justice'. First the meaning of the term 'justice' was extended to legal proceedings beyond those in a court of law. Consequently, apparently to compensate the restricting effect on freedom of expression, Lord Bridge applied a balancing of interests. Since the mere interest of an employer to be able to identify a disloyal employee was not as such thought to suffice to prove necessity of disclosure, the circumstances of the case would have to show whether the free flow of information or 'justice' should prevail. Despite the result of this case, and the fact that this decision was subsequently held to constitute a violation of Article 10, balancing of interests was the method used to consider freedom of expression. The influence of the conviction under Article 10 was felt in Camelot Group v. Centaur Ltd, in which case the chilling effect on freedom of expression of a court order to reveal the identity of a source was explicitly considered on the side of the interest in a free flow of information. However, the method of protection remained the same.

A full balancing of interests seems to constitute a kind of compensation for the protection which would have seemed to be available from other defences, whereas these were not applied in such a way as to grant that protection – the Schering Chemicals case and the Morgan Grampian case are clear examples.

The traditional approach to the protection of freedom of expression was that it could only play a role outside the scope of the restricting law.[28] It is still sometimes held that the scope of offences and obligations is determined by the legislature, such as with the Public Order Act 1986. However, in relation to a number of other concepts of law, the courts increasingly felt they could exert some influence on the scope of the restriction by taking account of freedom of expression. The manner in which freedom of expression was considered developed over time: at first, the interest in freedom of expression was represented by interests inherent in that freedom, such as literary value or freedom of discussion, but gradually freedom of expression was referred to as an interest as such, illustrated by recent cases such as the Derbyshire case and the Morgan Grampian case. This development seemed to be the result of a general growing consciousness of fundamental rights protection, encouraged by the increasing influence of the ECHR.[29]

3.2.3.2 Moment of Protection

The second aspect of the character of balancing of interests in English case law is the moment at which it occurs. As I said in the introduction to this chapter, the 'moment'

---

28 See for instance A-G v. Times Newspapers Ltd [1973] 3 All ER 54, in which it was held that freedom of expression could only exist outside the 'reasonable necessity' to prevent prejudice in the administration of justice. This approach is supported in R. v. Lemon [1979] AC 617, per Lord Scarman at 665.

29 See for a extensive discussion of this topic: Hunt, Using Human Rights Law in English Courts, 1998.

actually refers to the distinction between an abstract or concrete balancing of interests. Abstract application means that balancing of interests is conducted in order to determine the meaning of the law or an aspect of it, in detachment from the particular case. Concrete application means that the balancing of interests takes place at the level of the facts and circumstances of the individual case. I elaborate on the moment of application of balancing of interests by the English courts in this section.

a Balancing of Interests at an Abstract Level

The English courts have found moments in the process of applying law in which to carry out a balancing of interests. These moments concern the determining of the meaning of the terminology of the offence or obligation or of a defence or exception, but also the granting of interlocutory injunctions and who is allowed an action with regard to an area of law.

Lord Ackner held that to determine whether statements are of fact or of opinion, the material on which to determine this should not be restricted to the publication in which the statements were made, but should be considered in relation to the statements to which they were a comment. In relation to Contempt of Court law, it was held that an extension of that law to local valuation courts would be 'too great a curtailment of the right to freedom of expression', despite the fact that judges of these courts were more likely to be influenced that judges of ordinary courts. Furthermore, if under defamation law a defence of fair comment is pleaded, in principle an injunction will not be granted. As observed, this is because then there is 'no pressing ground to restrain the publication'[30] and because 'freedom of speech will not be restricted as long as "no wrongful act is done"'. And in relation to the scope of the offence of blasphemy, it was held that it was only applicable to Christianity.[31]

In these examples a level of protection was offered to freedom of expression, but not by way of a full balancing of interests. In all examples except the decision not to extend Contempt of Court law to local valuation courts, the balancing of interests is implied: only the interest in freedom of expression was explicitly discussed. In all examples, the balancing of interests took place at an abstract level. On those occasions where freedom of expression is protected by the decision at the abstract level and the balancing of interests takes place at that level, the choice of that moment for the consideration of freedom of expression was not accounted for. This is all the more surprising since the choice of moment influences the level of protection offered to freedom of expression, and there are sufficient possibilities to

---

30 R. v. Advertising Standards Authority, ex p. Vernons Ltd [1992] 1 WLR 1289, per Laws J. at 1293.
31 R. v. Chief Metropolitan Stipendiary Magistrate, ex p. Choudhury [1991] 1 All ER 306.

come to a balancing of interests at a concrete level. A concrete balancing of interests creates the possibility to come to a new balancing of interests in each individual case. It enables a more differentiated approach to the protection of freedom of expression.

The influence of the moment at which this method of protection is applied might be explained by looking at the Derbyshire County Council case in relation to the case of Reynolds v. Times Newspapers.[32] I observed that the main decision in the Derbyshire case was that local authorities were not allowed to initiate a libel action. The House of Lords refused local authorities this right, since they should be open to 'uninhibited public criticism' and the threat of a libel action would pose an 'undesirable fetter on the freedom to express such criticism'. The consequence of this approach is that the protection is generalised to all public authorities under all circumstances. It is not possible to see whether, after the specific circumstances of a case are considered, protection of reputation might be required. I wish to note that English libel law does offer the possibility to come to such a balancing of interests by way of the defence of fair comment on a matter of public interest or by way of qualified privilege. The case of Reynolds v. Times Newspapers illustrates this with regard to the defence of qualified privilege. In this case a full balancing of interests at the concrete level takes place concerning the alleged defamation of a politician. This judgment, which was influenced by the Human Rights Act, explains that the advantage of balancing of interests at an abstract level is that such an approach provides legal certainty. I assume that this is the reason for application of a balancing of interests at an abstract level in all instances in which this occurred.

b Balancing of Interests at a Concrete Level

As I observed, there are a number of occasions under English law where defences and exceptions are provided for, that offer a certain level of protection to freedom of expression. These occasions appear to be good opportunities to come a balancing of interests. However, they are not always approached as such. Under libel law, the defences of fair comment and of justification are available which seem excellent opportunities to carry out a balancing of interests. As we have seen, they are not approached in that manner. The same holds for the public domain doctrine, available under the law of breach of confidence, and to a large extent the exception of s.10 of the Contempt of Court Act.

An example of encouragement to carry out balancing of interests at the concrete level concerned the defence under s.4 of the Obscene Publications Act. This section provides justification against the obscene nature of a publication if it is in the interest

---

32 Similar in Goldsmith v. Bhoyrul [1997] 4 All ER 268, in which political parties were withheld the right to sue for libel, except that in this case some indication was given of the fact that a party could have an interest in protecting its reputation when it was considered that 'the party can by public announcement answer back'.

of science, literature, art or learning, or of other objects of general concern. As such, this defence protects freedom of expression to the extent that works of literary and scholarly value are protected. However, this defence provided the bases for a method of protection that differed from the traditional mere application of the wording of the law. It was implied that the courts have a more independent role from the legislature besides that of determining whether a book is of literary value, when it was held that a jury should consider the extent to which the publication has a tendency to deprave and corrupt and the extent of the 'literary, sociological or ethical' value of the publication, and subsequently the weight of these elements should be balanced to determine whether the publication can be considered to be for the public good.

However, there are examples of defences and exceptions where the opportunity to balance the interests involved is used and applied by a court. An example is the above-mentioned s.10 of the Contempt of Court Act. Although initially no balancing of interests was applied in relation to this section, in the Morgan Grampian case this was changed when the interest which was claimed to necessitate disclosure of the identity of a source was the interest in justice. In this case, the interest of freedom of expression in keeping the identity of the source secret was weighed rather extensively against the interest of justice in revealing the identity. A full balancing of interests took place at a concrete level.

Another example of a balancing of interests at a concrete level has been the public interest exception allowed under breach of confidence law. This defence has not been interpreted to mean that if information is in the public interest, disclosure cannot be restricted by way of an action for breach of confidence. Instead it has explicitly been held to require a balancing of interests: Confidential information may be disclosed if the interest in publication outweighs the interest in keeping the information secret.

Beside these examples, on one unexpected occasion a balancing of interests was applied. This was in relation to the offence of blasphemy. I observed that blasphemy is an offence under common law, under which a public good defence is not available. Blasphemy, however, also plays a role in the system of self-censorship as established under the Video Recordings Act 1984. If publication of a video is thought likely to lead to a conviction under blasphemy law, a certificate will be refused. However, in applying blasphemy law the VAC does seem to allow for an exception or defence of public good, since the historical, religious or artistic value influences the decision on whether or not to grant a certificate. The offence of blasphemy is weighed against the interest in freedom of expression, which in this case would lie in historical, religious or artistic value of the film. So where videos and films intended for the cinema (which are covered by a similar system of censorship) are concerned, a balancing of interests at the concrete level takes place. This would not be possible in the same way under the common law offence of blasphemy.

As I observed, however, the circumstances under which the courts came to a balancing of interests at a concrete level are noteworthy. In each of the available examples the balancing of interests took place after the court had, at an abstract level, interpreted the phrasing of the law in such a manner that it constituted an additional restriction to freedom of expression. In the Schering Chemicals case, the mere application of the public domain-doctrine would have meant that dissemination of the information concerned could never have constituted a breach of confidence, since it was freely available from other sources. The court did not simply apply the doctrine, but rather decided that the interests involved should be balanced. Freedom of expression was considered, but since it concerned commercial information and since there was no danger for public health because the medication concerned was no longer on the market, it could not outweigh the interest in keeping the information confidential. A balancing of interests in this case offered less protection than consistent application of the public domain doctrine would have done. Similarly in A-G v. Guardian Newspapers, where the information was also freely available, but it was still held necessary to come to a balancing of interests to determine whether the interest in freedom of expression could prevail over the interest in prohibiting publication of the book and commenting on it in newspapers. All of this was also in the light of an action for breach of confidence. A similar situation occurred in the Morgan Grampian case. The court balanced the interests concerned at a concrete level, where it was in the interest of the administration of justice to reveal the identity of a source, but only after it had extended the scope of 'interest in the administration of justice' from proceedings before a court of law to all judicial proceedings. After the Morgan Grampian decision was held to be in violation of the Convention, it is true that the same balancing approach was adopted in a subsequent case, Camelot Group v. Centaur Ltd. The VAC decided that a jury would hold the film to be blasphemous, although prosecution and subsequent conviction for blasphemy were rare. It seemed to apply a balancing of interests to justify that approach. That at the concrete level a full balancing of interests occurs is to be expected. When the circumstances of a particular case are considered, it is unlikely that only the interest in freedom of expression would be considered.

Freedom of expression is increasingly taken into account by the English courts. I cannot say, however, that full balancing of interests is the next step in the development of the character of balancing of interests. Both implied balancing of interests and full balancing of interests seem to amount to the same method of protection. They only appear to be different, because different aspects of a case are considered. This, however, is not caused by the method of review applied, but by the moment at which the method is applied, namely at an abstract or concrete level. It does seem that the courts feel more free to attribute importance to freedom of expression in relation to some subjects than others, but this is something to be considered in chapter IX on evaluation of facts and circumstances. Although it might be expected that the courts would take a more active stands regarding the protection of freedom of expression in relation to common law compared to statute law, the case law does not give evidence of such a difference in approach.

4 A COMMON GROUND AND THE IMPACT OF THE HUMAN RIGHTS ACT 1998

The English courts are increasingly taking account of freedom of expression in their decisions. In the previous paragraphs on the application of balancing of interests by the English courts and the Court a number of aspects of the application of this method of protection were described in relation to which a common ground can be formulated. This is the character of balancing of interests, which, as I said, refers to the manner in which the interests involved in the case are considered and to the moment at which they are considered.

4.1 Before the Human Rights Act 1998

4.1.1 Manner of Protection

In the considerations of the Court, a balancing of interests always involves considerations regarding the different opposing interests. In English law, we saw examples of an implied balancing of interests, i.e. where the considerations of the court only secifically referred to one interest, that being freedom of expression. A remarkable example was the Derbyshire County Council case. The character of such a balancing of interests is comparable to the manner in which the Court would offer protection to freedom of expression in such a case. After the Court had set out its line of thinking regarding political speech in the Lingens case, its elaborations on the particular circumstances of the case became less extensive in later cases. The method of protection applied in, for instance, Castells v. Spain is similar to that applied by the English courts in the Derbyshire case. In the case of Castells, an MP criticised the government and was subsequently prosecuted for criminal defamation. The abstract considerations emphasise the interest in freedom expression. The Court considered amongst others: 'The limits of permissible criticism are wider with regard to the Government than in relation to a private citizen, or even a politician. In a democratic system the actions or omissions of the Government must be subject to the close scrutiny not only of the legislative and judicial authorities, but also of the press and public opinion'.[33]

From the considerations of the Court, it is evident that at an abstract level politicians or the government should be open to public criticism, and that in principle a restriction on such criticism is undesirable. However, the considerations of the

---

33   Castells v. Spain, (1992) A.236, par. 46.

Court do not stop at freedom of expression. At an abstract level the Court also determined: 'Furthermore, the dominant position which the Government occupies makes it necessary to display restraint in resorting to criminal proceedings, particularly where other means are available for replying to the unjustified attacks and criticisms of its adversaries or the media'.[34] Although this consideration does not imply the taking into account of the interest of the government in undertaking criminal proceedings against the MP, it does imply that, even though it won't be easy to outweigh the interest in freedom of expression, still the concrete circumstances of the case will have to be taken into account. Also the application of these considerations to the circumstances of the case emphasise freedom of expression, but still the interest of the government is considered.

The implied balancing of interests by the English courts is similar to that of the Court, to the extent to which freedom of expression is considered on both sides. As I have already remarked, the fact that it is only freedom of expression which is considered by the English courts and not the opposing interest may be explained by the fact that the opposing interest is already represented in the national law that forms the restriction on freedom of expression. Continuing that reasoning, it could be said that the common ground between implied balancing of interests by the English courts and balancing of interests by the Court, goes even further. The opposing interest is represented by the very fact that the action concerned came before the courts. The problem remains that the abstract considerations of the European Court of Human Rights do not as such determine that freedom of expression should prevail. No matter what the importance attributed to the competing interest is, it is always considered.

Under English law there are examples in which a full balancing of interests takes place. It is remarkable that this method of review is applied in cases in which the legislation itself could provide for significant protection of freedom of expression. The balancing exercise seems to be undertaken to neutralise the effect of the defence or exception. In the Schering Chemicals case, the application of the public domain-doctrine would have led to the conclusion that there was no breach of confidence. Instead the court applied a rather extensive balancing of interests, which led to the conclusion that there had been a breach of confidence. As I said, the balancing of interests in this case was extensive and concerned both the interest of the firm, the interest in freedom of expression, including the interest of society to know about the information concerned. Similarly in X Ltd v. Morgan Grampian, all interests concerned were considered. Lord Bridge said that the question was whether he could be 'satisfied that disclosure of the source of this information is necessary to serve this interest'. He explicitly stated that this required a balancing exercise. He started off with the following abstract considerations: 'First, that the protection of sources is

---

34   Castells v. Spain, (1992) A.236, par. 46.

itself a matter of high pubic importance, secondly, that nothing less than necessity will suffice to override it, thirdly, that the necessity can only arise out of concern for another matter of high public importance ...'.[35] These abstract considerations are comparable to those of the Court except that they do not specifically pay attention to the importance of journalists to freedom of expression in a democratic society, which the Court did consider at the abstract level. The considerations of Lord Bridge do require consideration of the circumstances of the case at issue. And although the requirement of necessity does not necessarily imply a balancing of interests he did continue by stating: 'The question whether disclosure is necessary in the interest of justice gives rise to the more difficult problem of weighing one public interest against another'.[36] Subsequently he balanced the interests at a concrete level: on the one hand, the damage done to business and the consequences for the livelihood of employees and on the other, a public interest in the information concerned, the weight of which was decreased by the fact that the information had been illegally obtained. Subsequently it was held that a court order was necessary. In the case of Camelot Group v. Centaur Ltd also a balancing of interests was carried out; however, in this case the Court of Appeal, by Schiemann L, considered the 'chilling effect on the willingness of other sources to disclose the material which is important'. This was after the Court had held the decision in the Morgan Grampian case to be in breach of Article 10, considering an aspect that had not been taken into account in the Morgan Grampian case.

The method of protection in the Morgan Grampian case was the same: a balancing of interests, in which both the interest in freedom of expression and the interest in the protection of the administration of justice were considered. The only difference lies in the circumstances that were considered and the weight awarded to them. The appreciation of the facts and circumstances of the case is discussed in the following section.

In the cases in which the courts consider freedom of expression or an interest inherent to it, they apply a balancing of interests. At an abstract level they are inclined to consider the interest in freedom of expression only. The difference in character between this balancing of interests and the balancing of interests of the Court is that only one aspect is explicitly considered and the particular circumstances of the case are not considered. This last difference is a direct consequence of the moment of protection.

A full balancing of interests at an abstract level is only different in the last manner. A full balancing of interests at a concrete level has also been applied. In character and moment this is similar to the balancing of interests as applied by the

---

35 X Ltd v. Morgan Grampian [1991] 1 AC 1, at 41.
36 X Ltd v. Morgan Grampian [1991] 1 AC 1, at 43.

Court. The difference between this full balancing of interests by the English courts and the balancing of interests by the Court is that the English cases lack a balancing of interests at the abstract level, at which moment in all of these cases a restrictive decision was made, as I said, without taking consideration of freedom of expression. In the case law of the Court, a balancing of interests first takes place at an abstract level. Subsequently these considerations are followed by concrete deliberations on the individual case.

4.1.2 Moment of Protection

If, as was the case in the Derbyshire case, the balancing of interests takes place at the abstract level only, this means that there is no room for a more differentiated approach to the protection of freedom of expression. The one interest will prevail over the other at all times, as long as the decisive abstract element is present. This implies that the particular circumstances of the case cannot influence the decision. The consequence of abstract protection in this case was that the protection by the English courts went beyond the protection that would have been offered by the Court in Strasbourg. The English courts used the scope of the offence to come to an abstract protection of freedom of expression, by excluding local authorities. The reasoning of the English courts is partly comparable to the reasoning the Court would use. Free criticism of local authorities would be important to a democratic society etc. However, it is unlikely that the Court would exclude local authorities, or political parties for that matter, from libel actions completely in order to protect freedom of expression. It would be more likely that the Court would keep open the possibility and reconsider its standpoint in each individual case. It would thus retain the possibility to consider the interest of a local authority or a political party to protect its reputation.

In the Derbyshire example, the protection established by coming to a balancing of interests at an abstract level exceeded the protection offered by the Court. The opposite might also happen. In such instances the protection would be structurally less than the protection offered by the Court. However, the cases in which that happened were discussed under the heading of 'balancing of interests at a concrete level': in the restrictive decision, the court did not apply a balancing of interest, instead compensation for the restriction was offered by way of a balancing of interests at a concrete level.

The decision in the case of Goldsmith v. Bhoyrul suggested that individual members of a political party can sue for libel. So far, in such cases there seems to be little room for the protection of the expression of information on politicians, unless it can be seen as fair comment or unless the expression is true. This decision was taken to justify the exclusion of political parties from the possibility to sue for libel.

Therefore it is unclear whether in such a case a balancing of interests would take place at the concrete level.

I illustrated above that the Court's abstract considerations are intended to serve as a guideline for the balancing of the facts and circumstances of a particular case. In both the case of De Haes and Gijsels v. Belgium and the case of Schöpfer v. Switzerland, the Court considered at an abstract level that the courts as 'the guarantors of justice; whose role is fundamental in a State based on the rule of law – must enjoy public confidence'. Because of the particular circumstances of the cases, however, the outcome in each case could be, and in fact was, different. In the Schöpfer case eventually the functioning of the courts prevailed, whereas in the De Haes and Gijsels case, the interest in freedom of expression prevailed.

Such a difference in outcome is impossible in the approach in the Derbyshire case. Once it concerns a public authority that sues for libel, freedom of expression will always prevail.

Balancing of interests as a method of substantial review can be found under statute law as well as common law and equity. It cannot be said that the courts are more active in protecting freedom of expression in this manner under common law than under statute law. Moreover, balancing of interests is not widespread in English law. However, it has been applied on more than one occasion and in relation to most concepts of law. The English courts are getting increasingly familiar with the concept, and apply it to a large extent in a similar manner to that of the Court.

4.2 Impact of the Human Rights Act 1998

4.2.1 Manner of Protection

S.2, 3 and 6 are the most important sections of the Human Rights Act with regard to the common ground between balancing of interests by the English courts and the European Court of Human Rights. S.2 imposes a duty on the courts to take account of the Strasbourg case law. S.3 requires the courts to 'read and give effect to' primary and secondary legislation 'in a way which is compatible with the Convention rights'.[37] In those cases in which the courts do not conclude that the legislation is incompatible, responsibility to offer sufficient protection to individual rights lies with the courts. S.6 moreover, includes courts in the term 'public authority'.[38] Although the courts have already considered freedom of expression in horizontal situations, s.6 of the Act implies that the courts should also provide protection of the Convention rights between citizens with regard to both statutory and common law.

---

37   S.3 ss.1 HRA 1998.
38   S.6 ss.3(a) HRA 1998.

The compatibility with Convention rights seems to include compatibility with the case law that has determined the meaning of the incorporated rights. S.2 requires the courts to 'take account' of this case law. The manner in which this degree of protection is to be achieved is not specified and as I have remarked before, the Court itself does not require the national authorities to adopt the methods of review it applies. The aim of the Human Rights Act is to provide protection to a degree similar to that of the Court, however, and this will require the English courts to apply balancing of interests consistently as a method of review in those instances in which the protection of freedom of expression does not already meet the requirement of s.3.

The Human Rights Act does prescribe how the courts should take account of the Convention rights, namely when they 'read' or 'give effect to' domestic legislation. Unlike the European Court of Human Rights, they do not only determine consistency with the Convention of the result of application of law, but they also interpret and apply the legislation leading to the decisions. It seems unlikely that the courts have a possibility to give a compatible effect to restrictive law, contrary to the wording of it. That this was not intended by the legislature is evidenced by the availability of the declaration of incompatibility, for use by the judiciary.

The terms 'reading' and 'giving effect' seem instead to refer to the possibilities the courts have to act on the duty formulated in s.2. They will consider the Convention rights in the course of normal duty, i.e. the interpretation and application of the (restricting) legislation. The possibilities to take account of Article 10 of the ECHR should consequently be found in the law itself. The basis for such a possibility can be found in those terms in the legislation that leave room for interpretation, or for different application per individual case. These are 'open norms' and 'vague terms'. 'Open norms' are those norms of which the meaning is clear, but which may cover a range of different situations. These norms should be 'given effect' in such a way that they are compatible with Convention rights. 'Vague terms' are terms whose meaning is not clear, so the courts determine the meaning. These terms should be 'read' so as to be compatible with Convention rights. Both the interpretation of 'vague terms' and the application of 'open norms' can be done by way of balancing of interests.

Under common law, a greater influence of the ECHR was already developing;[39] in particular, with regard to statutory legislation, a change will be achieved. Previously, the ECHR could play a role in those instances in which the wording of the legislation was ambiguous: they should interpret such provisions as if Parliament intended them to be in conformity with the Convention rights. However, in those

---

[39] The courts determine whether common law is uncertain on particular aspects, and if the ECHR can be a help in determining its scope, see also Sir Anthony Hooper, the Impact of the Human Rights Act on Judicial decision-making, 1998, p. 676.

cases in which the wording of the legislation was clear, the ECHR could not be referred to. The obligation provided for in s.3 makes it possible for the courts to consider the ECHR and its case law with regard to all legislation. Moreover, legislation that restricts freedom of expression offers sufficient possibilities to come to a balancing of interests.

S.4 of the Obscene Publications Act, for instance, provides for a public good defence. If the public good of a publication outweighs the damage done by the obscene nature of the publication, the publisher or author cannot be convicted under this Act. Similarly, s.5 of the Public Order Act 1986 provides for a defence for people who plead that their behaviour is 'reasonable'. This term could also be applied by way of a balancing of interests: if the interest in the expression outweighs the damage to the public order, no offence under these sections of the Public Order Act has been committed. As for the Official Secrets Act, the term 'damaging' can be approached in such a manner. The terms 'substantial' and 'seriously' used in s.2 and 'public interest' use in s.5 of the Contempt of Court Act could be approached in this manner as well, as can s.10 of that Act. In fact, in the case of Camelot Group v. Centaur Ltd, the term 'necessary' in that section was already used to carry out a balancing of interests. In the case of Derbyshire County v. Times Newspaper, both the Court of Appeal and the House of Lords opted for a balancing of interests when interpreting defamation law.

4.2.2 Moment of Protection

In the Derbyshire case, the courts balanced the interests at an abstract level and concluded that public authorities could never sue for libel. In fact, this moment of protection is favoured by the English courts and a balancing of interests at the level of the individual case is thought to result in legal uncertainty. As I already observed in this chapter, this approach implies a lack of possibilities to adjust the application of the law to the circumstances of the case.

In opposition to the favoured approach of the English courts, the European Court of Human Rights tends to refrain from judging on the compatibility of legislation with the Convention. Consequently, it will look at the circumstances of the particular case that lead to the decision and determine whether it constituted a violation. This difference in moment of protection may lead to discrepancies in the protection of freedom of expression. Although the moment of protection is not referred to in the Act, s.2 could be used as a basis to opt for consideration of the interests in freedom of expression at the level of the individual case. The fact that the courts are authorised to take account of the ECHR makes such a concrete balancing of interests possible. And, vice versa, this possibility will force the courts to consider all relevant aspects of freedom of expression of the particular case at issue. Legal uncertainty will have to make way for the possibility to differentiate between cases.[40] This will require the courts to define the terminology of the legislation in a manner that makes it possible to balance the facts and circumstances of the particular case, similar to the approach that was taken to the term 'necessary in the interest of justice' of s.10 of the Contempt of Court Act in the Morgan Grampian and Camelot judgments. That the courts recognise this requirement became apparent in the judgment of the House of Lords in Reynolds v. Times Newspapers Ltd and others.[41] In this case the court was asked to accept qualified privilege for publications regarding politicians. This was refused and the House of Lords unanimously referred to the Human Rights Act in the motivations to this judgment. Lord Nicholls of Birkenhead held: 'Freedom of expression will shortly be buttressed by statutory requirements. Under s.12 of the Human Rights Act 1998, expected to come into force in October 2000, the court is required, in relevant cases, to have particular regard to the importance of the right to freedom of expression. The common law is to be developed and applied in a manner consistent with article 10 of the ECHR, and the court must take into account relevant decisions of the European Court of Human Rights (sections 6 and 2). To be justified, any curtailment of freedom of expression must be convincingly established by a compelling countervailing consideration, and the means employed must be proportionate to the end sought to be achieved'. He subsequently went on to consider whether the defence of proof of truth lived up to these requirements and whether the case law of the Court showed evidence of requirements that all publications regarding public figures always be protected. No mention was made of the fact that the Human Rights Act was not yet law. Lord Hope of Craighead's considerations were similar: 'If the category cannot be described precisely, it will be at risk of enlargement or erosion case by case and thus losing touch with the underlying justification for the creation of the category. Where imprecision is unavoidable, the better course would seem to be to take each case on its own facts and circumstances. If the category is of a kind where the communication is made to a particular person or group of persons, and not to the public generally, it may be thought that the advantages of precision outweigh those which come with flexibility'. The individual approach required to determine whether an expression is allowed qualified privilege is called the 'circumstantial test'. In applying this test, Lord Nickolls explicitly referred to recent case law of the Court regarding the requirements formulated in cases such as this one, and came to the conclusion that it could not be said that speech regarding political figures would always outweigh the interest in protection of reputation, and that therefore the circumstances of the case should be taken into account.

---

40 This is also suggested by Markesinis, Privacy, Freedom of Expression, and the horizontal effect of the Human Rights Bill: Lessons from Germany, 1999, p. 74.
41 Reynolds v. Times Newspapers [1999] 4 All ER 609.

CHAPTER IX
CONSIDERATION AND APPRECIATION OF FACTS AND CIRCUMSTANCES

1 INTRODUCTION

In the previous chapters I identified a common ground between the notions of freedom of expression in English law and the ECHR and a common ground between the methods of protection, with some emphasis on the moment of protection, applied in these systems of protection. This leaves one final aspect of the protection of freedom of expression to be examined. Two cases that were decided under both systems of protection illustrate that consideration and appreciation of the facts and circumstances of a particular case is an aspect that also determines the level of protection of freedom of expression. The term 'consideration' refers to the facts and circumstances taken into consideration in a judgment. The term 'appreciation' refers to the importance that is subsequently attached to the facts and circumstances considered.

The two cases referred to are A-G v. Guardian Newspapers which became Observer and Guardian Newspapers v. the United Kingdom before the European Court of Human Rights, and X Ltd v. Morgan Grampian, or Goodwin v. the United Kingdom before the European Court of Human Rights. In the first case, A-G v. Guardian Newspapers, the House of Lords applied a balancing of interests when it decided to continue the relevant interlocutory injunction after publication of the Spycatcher book in the United States. However, this decision was held by the Court to constitute a violation of Article 10 ECHR. The grounds for the Court's decision cannot be found in the method of review applied: a balancing of interests took place in both instances. The Court decided that there had been a breach of Article 10 because the interlocutory injunction constituted too serious a restriction on freedom of expression. This was considered to be the case because the book could be freely imported into the United Kingdom after publication of it was allowed in the United States. The fact that the information was available freely was the main reason for the Court to decide that there had been a violation of Article 10. This aspect of the case was not considered in the majority of speeches in the House of Lords, when it was decided that the interlocutory injunction should be continued. The majority of the judges held that the Attorney General should have a chance to have the case 'judged on the merits on full evidence',[1] that newspapers should not profit from the unlawful

---

1   A-G v. Guardian Newspapers [1987] 3 All ER 316, per Lord Brandon at 351.

conduct of the former secret servant that wrote the book and neither should they regard publication of the information abroad as a possibility to evade an injunction.[2] In this particular case, it was the difference in the aspects that were considered in the balancing of interests that caused the difference in the protection of freedom of expression.

In the case of X Ltd v. Morgan Grampian, a second example, both the Court and the House of Lords considered that the public interest in the protection of sources should be balanced against the interest of the company in keeping the information confidential. Although, in both instances similar facts and circumstances were considered, still the Court concluded that there had been a breach of Article 10 of the Convention. This was caused by the importance attributed to the public interest in keeping the identity of the source secret. The House of Lords had given less weight than the Court to the chilling effect which a court order, entailing an obligation to reveal the identity of a source, would have on the free discussion of matters of public interest. The House of Lords considered the restrictive effect on freedom of expression, but held that the interest in keeping the information secret should prevail, whereas the Court considered the interest in the aim pursued, but held the chilling effect to be restrictive of freedom of expression to such an extent that freedom of expression should prevail.

It is clear that both the English courts and the European Court of Human Rights consider and appreciate the facts and circumstances of a case when coming to their judgments. Also with regard to this aspect of the protection of freedom of expression the supervisory jurisdiction of the Court influences the consideration and appreciation of facts and circumstances. Moreover, the facts and circumstances of a case influence the scope of the review of the Court. To determine a common ground between the consideration and appreciation of facts and circumstances, I therefore first elaborate on the function this aspect of protection of freedom of expression has in the case law of the Court. Then I examine which facts and circumstances are regularly considered by the Court and the weight subsequently given to them. In the third paragraph I discuss the consideration and appreciation of the facts and circumstances by the English courts. And finally in the fourth paragraph I determine a common ground between the approaches of the Court and the English courts.

2   CONSIDERATION AND APPRECIATION OF FACTS AND CIRCUMSTANCES BY THE COURT

The consideration and appreciation of facts and circumstance has two functions in the decisions of the Court. First, they influence the margin of appreciation the Court

---

2   A-G v. Guardian Newspapers [1987] 3 All ER 316, per Lord Templeman at 357.

applies in a particular case. In the chapter on the margin of appreciation as a method of protection I observed that the margin of appreciation doctrine was not (completely) formulated by the Court itself. A number of academic writers derived the doctrine from the decisions of the Court. A certain consistency in the appreciation of the facts and circumstances led them to conclude that, beside the factors of influence explicitly formulated by the Court, other facts and circumstances could be distinguished that influenced the margin of appreciation.[3]

Second, the facts and circumstances that are considered and the weight attributed to them are also are a part of reviewing the proportionality of a measure or the balance between the interests involved. The considerations regarding the margin of appreciation and those regarding the balancing of the facts and circumstances concern appreciation of facts and circumstances.[4] It is the second function which is the topic of this chapter. However, the two functions of the consideration and appreciation of facts and circumstances are difficult to keep apart. A natural consequence of the manner in which the margin of appreciation doctrine has developed, is that the two functions coincide. It therefore is necessary to elaborate on the relation between the two functions before I discuss the consideration and appreciation of the facts and circumstances by the Court in its function of determining the outcome of the case (section 2.1). After that I elaborate on the facts and circumstances that are regularly considered by the Court, and on the appreciation of which some general remarks can be made (section 2.2).

2.1 Consideration and Appreciation of Facts and Circumstances to Determine the Margin of Appreciation and to Conduct a Substantive Method of Review

I clarify the relation between the determination of the margin of appreciation and the review of the substance of the case by giving two examples which illustrate the difference. The first case I discuss is Bladet Tromsø and Stensaas v. Norway.[5] The Bladet Tromsø case dealt with the publication of information on the committing of cruelties to animals during seal hunts, by the crew of a particular vessel. This incident was reported by a journalist, but in his capacity as a seal hunting inspector. The government subsequently suspended publication of the report. The Bladet Tromsø, which obtained the report from the journalist, did publish the information. Although the report only referred to the crew of the vessel in general, the publication was held

---

3   See e.g. Schokkenbroek, Toetsing aan de Vrijheidsrechten van het Europees Verdrag tot Bescherming van de Rechten van de Mens, 1996, p. 226.

4   See e.g. Schokkenbroek, Toetsing aan de Vrijheidsrechten van het Europees Verdrag tot Bescherming van de Rechten van de Mens, 1996, p. 226.

5   Bladet Tromsø and Stensaas v. Norway, 20 May 1999.

by the domestic courts to be defamatory with regard to the hunters. The newspaper and the journalist subsequently took the case to Strasbourg.

The Court held that the national authorities were left a certain margin of appreciation, which went hand in hand with a European supervision, and that the press has a duty to impart information and ideas on all matters of public interest. Consequently it was held that 'in cases such as the present one the national margin of appreciation is circumscribed by the interest of democratic society in enabling the press to exercise its vital role of "public watchdog" in imparting information of serious public concern'.[6] The Court went on to hold that 'also expressions that offend, shock or disturb are protected', and that although 'the media must not overstep the bound imposed in the interests of the protection of the reputation of private individuals, it is incumbent on them to impart information and ideas concerning matters of public interest'. Furthermore, it stated that the public had a right to receive this information, and therefore the public interest aspect of the case should be regarded.[7] It also considered the public interest aspect of the publication and reviewed whether the bounds of publication were overstepped: the newspaper had balanced reporting on the issue of seal hunting and 'the thrust of the impugned articles was not primarily to accuse certain individuals of committing offence against the seal hunting regulations or cruelty to animals'. It went on to consider that although the fact that the article contained factual statements on private individuals, the newspapers' extent of the duty to verify the information was fulfilled because the 'allegations of reprehensible conduct' were not 'particularly serious' and did not identify any specific hunter, whereas the reliability of the report was sufficient for the Court to hold that it acted in good faith, because the author of the report was a hunting inspector and the Ministry had stated that 'it was possible that illegal hunting had occurred'.[8] The Court consequently concluded that the interest in protection of reputation was insufficient 'to outweigh the interest of the public to have an informed public debate over a matter of local and national as well as international interest'.[9]

First of all, the explicit considerations with regard to the margin of appreciation are influenced by the facts and circumstances of the case. The Court, in fact, indicated this by holding that 'in cases such as these' account should be taken of the public interest aspect of the case and the role of the press. An additional indication of the influence of the facts and circumstances of the case on the margin of appreciation can be observed when one compares the considerations in the Bladet Tromsø case with those in the case of Janowski v. Poland. In the latter case, in which a police officer was offended by a journalist, the role of the press was not explicitly

---

6   Bladet Tromsø and Stensaas v. Norway, 20 May 1999, par. 58-60.

7   Bladet Tromsø and Stensaas v. Norway, 20 May 1999, par. 62.

8   Bladet Tromsø and Stensaas v. Norway, 20 May 1999, par. 62.

9   Bladet Tromsø and Stensaas v. Norway, 20 May 1999, par. 62.

considered with regard to the margin of appreciation. Although the Court did not expressly elaborate on this, the fact that the Court held that the plaintiff did not act in his capacity as a journalist, together with the fact that it was a police officer that was offended, seemed to have caused the application of a narrow margin of appreciation.

In the Bladet Tromsø case, there is an additional element that potentially widens the margin of appreciation, namely the fact that the defamatory speech concerns private individuals. The view of the Court that the newspaper had balanced reporting on the issue concerned, had verified the information, had not identified any specific hunter and could have believed the report to be reliable, together with the public interest in the topic, not only negated the possible widening effect on the margin of appreciation, but also led to the conclusion that there had been a breach of Article 10. In other words, these considerations determined both the scope of the margin of appreciation and the outcome of the case. To compare this case to the considerations in the Janowski case once more: the view that the speech in this case offended a police officer, who should be able to perform his duty in order to maintain public order led to the application of a narrow margin of appreciation and also led the Court to conclude that here there had not been a violation of Article 10.

The motivation of the reasons why certain elements of a case are decisive with regard to the margin of appreciation, coincides with the appreciation of facts and circumstances with regard to the outcome of the case. This is not illogical, since the Court will try to persuade the public to agree with its findings: in the Bladet Tromsø case, the public interest aspect was emphasised when the Court held the topic of the article at issue to be of great value to a 'national and international' discussion on the topic; any public interest in criticising the behaviour of police officers on duty is ignored in the Janowski case. The considerations of the Court in each case will be amplified by the facts and circumstances of the particular case, but at a general level the four factors that regularly turn up in the considerations of the Court with regard to the margin of appreciation, can be said to be regularly considered in relation to the appreciation of the facts and circumstances regarding the conducting of substantive review as well. There is, however, one aspect that is regularly considered by the Court that does not influence the scope of the margin of appreciation. This concerns the issue of whether a statement is a statement of fact or a value-judgment. This is regularly considered by the Court in defamation cases. Beside the factors that also determine the scope of the margin of appreciation, the Court's considerations regarding the status of defamatory speech will also be elaborated on, in order to determine the importance awarded to recurrent elements of consideration.

2.2 The Facts and Circumstances Considered and Appreciated by the Court

Although deviations will always occur, looking at the Court's case law as a whole, some recurring aspects of consideration and appreciation of facts and circumstances of particular cases can be distinguished. At the outset of its decisions, the Court usually considers the importance of freedom of expression to a democratic society.[10] This emphasises the favoured position of this fundamental right under the case law of the Court. What this position exactly is, is determined by the importance attached to the facts and circumstances of the particular case. Four aspects regularly appear in the considerations of the Court. These are: the nature of the speech, the existence of a common ground, the aim served with the restriction of freedom of expression and finally the seriousness of the interference.

As observed the Court does not consistently review each of these elements. Their consideration and appreciation will depend on the case at hand, but still some general remarks can be made on the approach to these aspects.

Starting with the nature of the speech, it can be said that the Court attributes relatively great importance to speech that is held to be of public importance. Speech relating to a politician will automatically be considered as such.[11] However, also speech relating to judges or even concerning private individuals may be considered to be of public interest. In such cases, however, the topic of the speech will have to be of great public interest and most likely it will have to be part of a public discussion.[12] Moreover, if the speech concerns private individuals or judges, the Court usually formulates a requirement with regard to the manner of expression and the way in which freedom of expression was used. If, for example, the restriction concerns a publication by a journalist, this as such establishes public interest in the speech because of the function of the press in a democratic society. If this speech concerns a private individual, however, such as in the Bladet Tromsø case, a balance with regard to the topic of discussion will be required.[13] Commercial speech and artistic expression on the other hand seem to be held to be of less importance.[14] Not only does such a circumstance narrow the margin of appreciation, also on occasion the Courts' observations with regard to speech of such a nature have been less

---

10 See e.g. Müller v. Switzerland, (1988) A.133, par. 33; Otto Preminger v. Austria, (1995) A.295, par. 49.

11 See e.g. Lingens v. Austria, (1986) A.103.

12 See De Haes and Gijssels v. Belgium, 24 February 1997, Reports 1997-I and Bladet Tromsø and Stensaas v. Norway, 20 May 1999.

13 See also De Haes and Gijssels v. Belgium, 24 February 1997, Reports 1997-I: The restriction of the publication of an offensive article regarding a judge was held to constitute a breach of Article 10, partly because the extensive research done by the journalists in question was held to be able to support the journalists' findings.

14 E.g.: Markt Intern Verlag v. Germany, (1989) A.165, Casado Coca v. Spain (1994) A.285-A.

'objective'.[15] It is therefore of great importance how the Court qualifies the speech concerned.[16]

The common ground regularly referred to by the Court can be found both in treaties to which a majority of the States party to the Convention are a signatory and in the national legal traditions of these States.[17] With regard to commercial speech, for instance, the Court attributes less importance to speech when it concerns competition law, because this is a fluctuating area of law in the domestic law of the Contracting States.[18] A monopoly position of the State with regard to broadcasting, however, was not accepted because most of the (small) States party to the Convention do not organise broadcasting in this manner.[19] Also, the protection of the authority of the judiciary by way of preventing all publication on cases pending before the courts was not held necessary, because the majority of the party States accept that the judiciary cannot 'operate in a vacuum'.[20] In other words an existing common tradition will be attributed considerable weight.

With regard to the aims pursued, the Court does not seem to attribute great importance to speech if the restriction pursues the protection of morals, of national security and of public order as well as to the protection of rights of third parties when this concerns private individuals or judges.[21] When speech defames politicians the protection of their reputation is of less significance.[22] With regard to aims that are given a lot of weight, the Court will require proportional use of the right to freedom of expression, and will also consider the seriousness of the behaviour that violated the national legislation.[23]

Finally, the seriousness of the restriction is regularly referred to by the Court. In some cases the seriousness of the interference contributed to the Court's motivation

---

15 Otto Preminger v. Austria, (1995) A.295, Wingrove v. United Kingdom, 25 November 1996, Reports 1996-V.

16 See also Hertel v. Switzerland, 25 August 1998, Reports 1998-VI.

17 Schokkenbroek, Toetsing aan de Vrijheidsrechten van het Europees Verdrag tot Bescherming van de Rechten van de Mens, 1996, p. 225.

18 E.g. Casado Coca v. Spain (1994) A.285-A.

19 Schokkenbroek, Toetsing aan de Vrijheidsrechten van het Europees Verdrag tot Bescherming van de Rechten van de Mens, 1996, p. 225-228.

20 Sunday Times v. United Kingdom, (1979) A.30.

21 See also Sunday Times v. United Kingdom, (1979) A.30, par. 59 and see Chorherr v. Austria (1993) A.266-B, Observer and Guardian v. United Kingdom, (1991) A.216. Note here, to confirm the conclusion of the following section, that the Court does not necessarily think such speech not to be important, but the aim pursued leads to the application of a wide margin of appreciation and therefore the importance of the speech is less relevant.

22 Barfod v. Denmark (1989) A.149, De Haes and Gijssels, 24 February 1997, Reports 1997-I.

23 See De Haes and Gijssels v. Belgium, 24 February 1997, Reports 1997-I.

of why Art. 10 ECHR had not been violated.[24] On the other hand, a State broadcasting monopoly was held to be too serious a restriction on freedom of expression,[25] and a complete ban on information was also not favourably received.[26] The Court has also emphasised that prior restraint constitutes a serious restriction of freedom of expression and calls for the most careful scrutiny.[27] Prior restraint does not automatically lead to the conclusion that there has been a breach of Article 10.

Beside these elements, derived from the factors that determine the scope of the margin of appreciation, there is one separate element that is relevant to the consideration and appreciation of facts and circumstances. That element is the consideration and appreciation of facts and value-judgements.

2.3 Statements of Fact and Value-Judgements

The Court considers the distinction between facts and value-judgements in libel cases. This distinction is of relevance to those cases in which the applicant was convicted for libel by the national courts because he was not able to prove the truth of his statements, as well as to those cases in which factual statements were held to be defamatory by the national courts.[28] In Lingens v. Austria, the Court explained why it distinguishes between statements of fact and value-judgements: 'In the Court's view, a careful distinction needs to be made between facts and value-judgements. The existence of facts can be demonstrated, whereas the truth of value-judgements is not susceptible to proof.' On the fact that journalists will be convicted if they cannot prove the truth of their statements, the Court consequently held: 'As regards value-judgements this requirement is impossible of fulfilment and it infringes freedom of opinion itself, which is a fundamental part of the right secured by Art. 10 of the Convention'. When the speech concerns factual statements there is a duty to verify the information by independent research. The extent of this duty depends 'in particular on the nature and degree of the defamation at hand and the extent to which the newspaper could reasonably regard' the source of the information 'as reliable

---

24 Casado Coca v. Spain, (1994) A. 285-A, par. 52; Jacubowski v. Germany, (1994) A. 291-A, par. 25.
25 Informationsverein Lentia v. Austria, (1993) A.276.
26 E.g. Sunday Times v. The United Kingdom, (1979) A.30; Open Door and Dublin Well Woman v. Ireland, (1992) A.246.
27 Observer and Guardian v. The United Kingdom, (1991) A.216.
28 Cases such as these will lead the Court to determine whether the information was verified sufficiently to be able to be held to be factual in nature.

with respect to the allegations in question'.[29] In other words, depending on the nature of the speech, this requirement of proportional use of freedom of expression will be more stringent.[30] If proof of truth of a value-judgement is required, the Court will hold that requirement to constitute a breach of Article 10 ECHR.

Statements of fact have also regularly been restricted in the cases that came before the Court. Some of them concern allegedly defamatory speech. In the Thorgeir Thorgeirson case, a journalist was convicted for publishing an article in which he held that a police officer had been guilty of violent behaviour. This police officer had in fact been convicted in court for such behaviour. The national authorities therefore could not sustain that there was insufficient proof for the statements made by the journalist. Although the article concerned was put in strong terms, it concerned a matter of serious public concern and it was held therefore that the expression should be protected. The information was carefully collected and therefore no further proof of its truth could be required. In the case of Fressoz and Roire v. France, the Court explicitly confirmed that journalists have to publish information on an 'accurate factual basis' and in doing so have to act in good faith, but it also held that the journalist could not be required to prove the truth of his statements. In the Bladet Tromsø case, the source of the information, a report, had been written by a journalist, but in 'an official capacity as an inspector appointed by the Ministry of Fisheries' and although the Ministry had postponed publication of the report it had also held that 'it was possible that illegal hunting had occurred'.[31] In this case the requirement of a 'reasonable' basis for factual allegations was held to have been satisfied.

In most cases before the Court dealing with factual statements, the truth of these statements was not denied, instead it was held by the national authorities that the person or newspaper that published the information had a duty not to disseminate it. These cases concern the protection of government information[32] or information on cases pending before the courts[33] and usually serve to protect national security and public order or serve to maintain the authority and impartiality of the judiciary. However, the factual nature of the statements is not explicitly considered in such cases. Instead the importance of the aim pursued determines the consideration and appreciation of facts and circumstances.

---

29 Bladet Tromsø and Stensaas v. Norway, 20 May 1999, par. 66. The extent of the duty to verify the information in this case is influenced by the fact that the defamatory statements concern private individuals.

30 See also De Haes and Gijssels v. Belgium, 24 February 1997, Reports 1997-I; Bladet Tromsø and Stensaas v. Norway, 20 May 1999.

31 Bladet Tromsø and Stensaas v. Norway, 20 May 1999, par. 68-71.

32 Observer and Guardian v. United Kingdom, (1991) A.216.

33 Sunday Times v. United Kingdom, (1979) A.30.

3 CONSIDERATION AND APPRECIATION OF FACTS AND CIRCUMSTANCES UNDER ENGLISH LAW

In this section I do not elaborate on the mere consideration of freedom of expression as such by the English courts. The extent to which freedom of expression as an interest is taken into consideration by the courts and the manner in which it is done, I discussed in the chapter on balancing of interests. The subject of this section is the elements of a case taken into account by the English courts in deciding which interest should prevail: that represented in the national legislation restricting freedom of expression or the right to freedom of expression, and the importance subsequently attached to these elements. This approach assumes that freedom of expression was considered. Taking the consideration and appreciation of facts and circumstances as point of departure, I examine the consideration and appreciation of the nature of speech, a common ground, the aim pursued, the seriousness of the restriction and the distinction between fact and value-judgements. The element of a common ground in English law refers to the influence of the ECHR on the considerations of the courts.

In the early case of Knuller v. the DPP, which dealt with the protection of 'public decency', Lord Simon referred to the aspect of 'tolerance' that is inherent in a democratic society to come to a restrictive interpretation of the offence of outraging public decency.[34] The majority of the House of Lords, however, only referred to the protection of the public confronted with the indecent speech. Lord Simon's reference to 'tolerance' as an aspect of a democratic society should have led to a restrictive interpretation of the offence of outraging public decency. With regard to the common law offences concerned with the protection of morals as well as the offences under the Obscene Publications Act, freedom of expression has rarely been referred to explicitly. Instead, the main area of concern has been the aim of penalising the criminalised behaviour. The Obscene Publications Act, however, provides for a public good defence, consequently allowing protection to speech that is held to be of value to the general public.[35] If speech is considered to be of general value to the public, it will not be considered obscene under this Act.

With regard to the offence of blasphemy, Lord Edmund Davies referred to the value of freedom of expression to a free society, implying that this consideration should influence the decision on whether a publication constituted the offence. Lord Edmund Davies did require the criticism to be expressed in 'decent and temperate language'. This apparently requires the speech not to be intended to outrage or shock the feelings of Christians. If this requirement is met, the right to criticism should prevail. Because of the absence of a 'pressing social need' the offence of blasphemy was not extended to other religions beside Christianity, in the Choudhurry case.

---

34 Knuller v. DPP [1973] AC 435, per Lord Simon of Glaisdale at 495.
35 R. v. Calder and Boyars [1969] 1 QB 151, per Lord Salmon at 171.

According to these considerations tolerance as a value in a democratic society prevails. Finally, if the expression is of artistic, historical or religious value to society, the likelihood of a film which is in principle blasphemous receiving a certificate increases, as the considerations in the Wingrove decision show. This approach is comparable to the public good defence provided for in the Obscene Publications Act 1959.

With regard to the aim of protection of reputation by means of a libel action, political speech is explicitly protected, as the Derbyshire case and the subsequent judgment in Goldsmith v. Bhoyrul illustrate. It was held in both cases that an open debate on issues of public interest should not be restricted, at least not in the interest of protecting the reputation of public authorities or political parties. In the Derbyshire case, this interest in public debate was held to be of such importance that the interest in protection of reputation of a public authority could never override it. Also in Goldsmith v. Bhoyrul the open discussion on issues of public interest overrode the interest in the protection of reputation of a political party. Fair comment on issues of public interest and publications of factual statements of which proof of truth was possible, was protected by the law. Where the protection of reputation is concerned, the defence of justification, or proof of truth, usually protects the publication from being libellous and similarly, the defence of fair comment provides protection for expression of opinions. In relation to these defences it should be noted that prior restraint is thought to be such a serious breach of freedom of expression that the mere claim of presenting these defences will lead to rejection of the request for a injunction.[36]

With regard to the protection of confidential information such a general rule is not applied. On the contrary; where governmental information is concerned, although the government must show a public interest in keeping the information secret in order to obtain an injunction, apparently any interest can serve to meet that requirement. There is no requirement as to the seriousness of the public interest in confidentiality. However, confidentiality law draws, at least is supposed to draw, the line at information that is already in the public domain. A-G v. Guardian Newspapers illustrates that also the denial of profit from the breach of confidence of a third person, as well as the chance to have the case judged on the merits, might be reasons to accept prior restraint at the interim stage of a case. These were novel considerations in a confidentiality case, but indicate that even if the information is freely available to the public, this does not automatically mean that the 'balance of convenience' will tip to the side of freedom of expression. The aim of protecting national security seems to be of overriding interest under almost all circumstances.

---

36 See the speech of Lord Denning in Fraser v. Evans [1969] 1 QB 349 at 360 already referred to, in which he held that courts will not 'prejudice the issue' by allowing an injunction on publications which may be true or constitute 'fair comment on a matter of public interest'.

Where government information is not concerned, the public interest that may imply a necessity to publish confidential information may concern, for example, public health or the risk of wrongful prosecution. But the mere existence of such an interest does not suffice for the public good defence to be accepted. The public interest must be of sufficient importance to override the interest in confidentiality. The fact that information is already available to the public does override the confidentiality. Although not explicitly stated in the case of Woodward v. Hutchins, even free communication of information of public interest as such seemed able to amount to such a public interest, although here the fact that the plaintiff himself sought public attention on other occasions was an element of consideration in this case.[37] The Official Secrets Act is concerned with the protection of a broad range of government information regarded as meriting secrecy. This Act, however, does not provide for a general public interest exception.

The interest in due administration of justice is protected in the Contempt of Court Act 1981. In this Act discussion of matters of general interest, to which mention of a case is incidental to the discussion, is excluded from the offence. The mere fact that the trial itself is not mentioned does not make the discussion incidental and the discussion of the facts of a case can lead to a serious risk of prejudice. The time between the publication and the trial may be of influence, as may be the nature of the publication. S.10 of the Contempt of Court Act provides for a possibility to keep the identity of sources of journalists secret. This section was adopted to assure an effective press. If, however, the reasons for demanding revelation of the identity of a source lie in the interest of the protection of national security or in prevention of crime and disorder, the provision will not be applied. If knowledge of the identity of the source is necessary in the interest of justice, there will be a more extensive elaboration in the court to decide whether freedom of expression or due administration of justice should prevail. Financial interests of all possible parties will be considered, as the Morgan Grampian case illustrated, as well as the interest in limiting harm suffered by breach of confidence, and preventing repetition of disclosure of confidential information. From the Camelot Group judgment, it became apparent that the chilling effect on other sources who might otherwise come forward may be considered, as well as the interest in further dissemination of confidential information and the benefit of publication of the information for the public, such as where the information would have been published soon afterwards anyway.

Finally, the interest in protection of public order is considered to be of great importance. This is not only illustrated by the reluctance of the courts to take freedom of expression into consideration when they apply provisions of the Public Order Act 1986, but also by the acceptance of a development of this law that significantly

---

37   Hubbard v. Vosper [1972] 1 All ER 1023, at 1024.

increases the restriction of freedom of expression by this Act. This occurred in relation to s.14 of this Act, which governed the offence of trespassory assembly. A peaceful protest which was not obstructing the road could be banned in order to 'curb protests on public roads', according to the Court of Appeal.[38] Such a demonstration was held not to amount to 'reasonable' use of the highway. The public interest, for instance, in receiving critical information, was not considered. The House of Lords was of a different opinion, but was not prepared to hold that peaceful and non-obstructive assemblies in general cannot constitute unreasonable use of the highway.

Under English law the distinction between statements of fact and value-judgements is relevant with regard to libel law. As observed, English libel law provides for a defence of fair comment on a matter of public interest and for a defence of justification. In relation to these defences the distinction between fact and value-judgement can be of great importance to freedom of expression. Defamation law also provides for qualified privilege. If qualified privilege is accepted, proof of truth of a statement is no longer required, even if it is factual in nature. The only requirement that remains when qualified privilege has been accepted is that the publication should not have been done with intent of malice.[39]

When the expression does not touch upon the protection of reputation, but on protection of administration of justice (Contempt of Court Act 1981) or of national security (Official Secrets Act 1989), the fact that the information is true seems an additional incentive to prevent it from becoming public.

Although the different position of value-judgements, as opposed to statements of fact, is recognised and the law appreciates that fair comment on matters of public interest should be protected, the impact of this difference lies mainly in the prevention of prior restraint. With regard to the decisions on the merits, the effect of this defence is limited, because the facts on which the value-judgements are based should be repeated when making the comment, which limits the concept of discussion significantly. This requirement was formulated in the case of Telnikoff v. Matusevitch.

What becomes apparent is that under English law the elements of consideration vary with regard to the aim regarding which freedom of expression is restricted. A public good defence is available under the Obscene Publications Act and under the law of breach of confidence but not under Blasphemy law, the Official Secrets Act or the common law offences regarding the protection of public decency. The public interest in speech can be considered with regard to libel law and Contempt of Court law under s.10, but not to such a general extent under the Obscene Publications Act, in which the protected speech is specified to expressions of historical, artistic or literary value. The Official Secrets Act does not provide for a possibility to take

---

38   DPP v. Jones [1997] 2 All ER 119.
39   See also Reynolds v. Times Newspapers Limited and Others [1999] 4 All ER 609.

freedom of expression of any nature into consideration. Similarly, prior restraint is considered in relation to libel law when the defendant claims justification or fair comment, whereas in relation to confidentiality law and public order law, prior restraint is not considered in relation to the application of the duty or offence. Similarly the importance attributed to certain elements of consideration varies. With regard to the application of the Obscene Publications Act, expression which has artistic, historical or literary value turns out not to constitute an offence under the Act. Under the law of breach of confidence, significant the public interest is required in order for the confidential information to be allowed to be disseminated. Speech that is regarded to be political in nature will not constitute defamatory speech if it concerns public authorities or political parties. The public interest in speech that cannot be considered political is unclear with regard to libel law, but with regard to the Contempt of Court Act it is clear that speech of public interest, be it political or otherwise, has to be of sufficient importance to outweigh the interest in knowing the identity of a source under s.10, when the aim concerns the protection of due administration of justice. The Morgan Grampian judgment as well as the case of Bhoyrul v. Goldsmith show that the interest in due administration of justice is considerable. Not only is prior restraint considered with regard to libel law, but when a defendant claims justification or fair comment, the courts will not grant an injunction to prevent publication. As observed, under confidentiality law the prevention of prior restraint is not a concern. However, prior restraint is automatically prevented when the information is in the public domain, because under such circumstances an action for breach of confidence no longer serves a purpose. This is assuming of course that the law is applied as such: in the A-G v. Guardian Newspapers, the public domain doctrine was not considered and consequently the prior restraint continued even after the information was freely available to the public.

From the degree of ease with which the English courts allow arguments regarding freedom of expression to influence the scope of areas of law that restrict this freedom, the importance generally attributed to the aims pursued by the restrictive legislation can be deduced. The protection of reputation has been given relatively little weight, whereas the interest in the protection of confidential information, due administration of justice and public order law is held to be of great importance. With regard to the offence of blasphemy it can be said that when it concerns the protection of the sensibilities of Christians it is held to be of great importance, but with regard to other religions the offence is held not to exist, because there is no (pressing social) need to protect those interests.

4 COMMON GROUND BETWEEN CONSIDERATION AND APPRECIATION OF FACTS AND CIRCUMSTANCES

4.1 Before the Human Rights Act 1998

In commenting on a common ground concerning the consideration and appreciation of facts and circumstances I successively discuss the consideration and appreciation of the nature of speech, a common ground in the European Court of Human Rights' sense, the aim pursued, the seriousness of the restriction and the distinction between fact- and value-judgements. Beside these four elements I comment on the approach to one additional element: that is, the reference made in the case law of the two systems of protection to the proportional use of freedom of expression.

Starting with the nature of the speech, it can be said that under both systems of law this aspect of a case can be a subject of consideration. In most cases, the Court qualifies expressions as being of a political nature, of a commercial nature or as being artistic in nature, or in a more general manner it will refer to the speech as being of public interest, which amongst other things will be the case when it is the press that is being restricted. The English courts have also considered the nature of the speech in a number of cases. They referred to the nature of the speech in terms of 'the public interest of publication'[40] or of 'matters of public importance'.[41] But they have also referred to the nature of the speech in specific, rather than general, terms. The English courts have referred to the 'commercial nature' of speech,[42] they have taken notice of the fact that information came from the press,[43] that speech was of a political nature,[44] and also the artistic value of speech has been taken into account.[45]

With regard to the nature of the speech, as observed, the Court will attribute additional weight to speech that is considered to be in the public interest, or more specificly political in nature. Under English law, such an approach can also be found. In the Derbyshire case, the importance attributed to political speech is comparable to the importance the Court will allow such speech. Commercial speech on the other hand, and this is also similar to the approach of the Court, as can be concluded from the Schering Chemicals case will be attributed less importance. It should be

---

40 See Hubbard v. Vosper [1972] 1 All ER 1023; Lion Laboratories Ltd v. Evans [1984] 2 All ER 417; Woodward and Hutchins [1977], A-G v. Times Newspapers Ltd [1973] 3 All ER 503; X Ltd v. Morgan Grampian Ltd [1991] 1 AC 1 and Camelot Group v. Centaur Ltd [1998] 1 All ER 251.
41 Telnikoff v. Matusevitch [1992] 2 AC 343, per Lord Ackner.
42 Schering Chemicals v. Feldman Ltd [1981] 2 WLR 848.
43 A-G v. Guardian Newspapers Ltd (No.2) [1988] 3 All ER 545.
44 Derbyshire County Council v. Times Newspapers [1993] 2 WLR 449; Goldsmith v. Bhoyrul [1997] 4 All ER 268, and Reynolds v. Times Newspapers [1999] 4 All ER 609.
45 Under s.4 of the Obscene Publications Act 1959.

remarked, however, that the qualification of the speech can be of great importance both under English law and in the case law of the Court. In the Schering Chemicals case it was held that the information about a company constituted commercial speech, which contributed to the conclusion that there had been a breach of confidence. Although the Court also has approached cases in this manner,[46] there are also examples of judgments regarding information on companies which demonstrate that such speech can also be qualified as being in the public interest.[47]

Unlike the case law of the Court, where the Obscene Publications Act is concerned, speech of artistic or literary value is awarded significant weight. The Müller judgment shows that the Court attributes less importance to such speech. The artistic value of speech with regard to the offence of Blasphemy, however, is considered to be of less importance; in that regard the approach of English law is similar to the case law of the Court.[48] The common ground also plays a role in both systems of law. The Court will refer to the common ground, or the lack of it, that exists among the States party to the Convention regarding the restrictive legislation. Beside the national legislation the common ground may also be conventions or treaties to which a number of States party to the Convention are a party. Under English law, the ECHR and its case law have been referred to as a source of common ground that exists between English law and the ECHR.[49]

The influence of the Convention on English law has increased tremendously over the passed two decades.[50] The Convention has been referred to, in order to establish that English law contains a principle of freedom of expression and that it offers the same protection as Article 10 ECHR.[51] It has influenced decisions on the size of damages awarded in that the amount of the damages should be moderate to the extent that they could be considered 'necessary in a democratic society'.[52] It influenced the scope of defamation law, because 'similar protection' meant protection of political speech, and it influenced the manner of application of s.10 of the Contempt of Court Act 1981 in that the courts apply a balancing of interests to determine whether disclosure of the identity of sources is necessary in the interest of justice.[53] The

---

46 Markt Intern Verlag GmbH v. Germany, (1989) A.165.

47 E.g. Barthold v. Germany, (1985) A.90; Goodwin v. United Kingdom, 22 February 1996, Reports 1996-II.

48 Wingrove v. United Kingdom, 25 November 1996, Reports 1996-V.

49 Especially where the protection of fundamental rights were concerned, other Common Wealth jurisdictions offered limited material for comparison. International treaties, in particular the ECHR, therefore gradually gained influence on the English courts, the process of which was described by Hunt in 'Using Human Rights Law in English Courts', 1998.

50 See Hunt, Using Human Rights Law in English Courts, 1998.

51 Derbyshire County Council v. Times Newspapers [1993] 2 WLR 449.

52 Rantzen v. Mirror Group Newspapers [1993] 3 WLR 954; John v. MGM Ltd [1996] 2 All ER 35.

53 Camelot Group v. Centaur Ltd [1998] 1 All ER 251.

constitutional traditions of other party States and the treaties to which these states are a party influence English law only to the extent that this common ground in turn influenced the decisions of the Court. Treaties to which the United Kingdom is a party are rarely referred to, most likely because they are not adopted into English law and they do not provide for an individual complaints procedure.

However, although the importance attributed to speech of public interest, especially political speech, is comparable to that in the case law of the Court, with regard to libel law, as under the case law of the Court, the aim pursued significantly influences the weight given to speech that is considered to be of public interest. Any political value of the speech in the case of A-G v. Guardian Newspapers is easily overridden by the interest in protection of national security. The value of a free press to a democratic society was initially automatically overridden by the interests in due administration of justice, in the protection of national security and in maintaining public order. The Court, too, tends to attribute less importance to speech that is restricted to protect national security and public order, but with regard to the protection of due administration of justice, the Court tends to attach greater significance to the speech concerned than the English courts. The importance to a democratic society of a free functioning of the press seemed to be the reason for adopting s.10 of the Contempt of Court Act.

With regard to the aim of a restriction, it should be noted that English national legislation which restricts freedom of expression will always pursue an aim. However, because the English courts are not constitutional courts, the aim of the restriction is itself the starting point of litigation, and especially in earlier case law the aim was not really elaborated on. But it could be said that the aim is in fact considered in all cases simply because the restricting legislation exists to achieve an aim. The aims considered by the Court are restricted to those enumerated in the second paragraph of Article 10 ECHR. However, all restricting legislation seems to serve one of the purposes listed there in some way or another.

The Morgan Grampian judgment did suggest that it was possible for the interest in freedom of expression to be of more weight than the interest in due administration of justice, but the English courts still attach greater weight to the latter interest than the Court. The fact that with regard to obscenity the English courts offer greater protection to freedom of expression is not a problem, but the fact that the Court offers greater protection to freedom of expression where due administration of justice is concerned is a problem in the sense that this is consequently an area of law in which violations of the Convention are likely to be caused. As observed, when the aim pursued concerns the protection of reputation, speech of public interest is deemed to be of considerable importance. This is not only the case with regard to who can sue for libel, but also in relation to the granting of an injunction when fair comment or justification is pleaded. The Court does not award great importance to the protection of reputation when the speech concerns politicians or other public figures, but with regard to private individuals it will offer more weight to the interest in a good reputation. Also where judges are concerned this is of great importance. Under English law, however, this will most likely be covered by Contempt of Court law.

The seriousness of the restriction is regularly considered by the Court. This usually implies a reference to the possibilities left to the defendant to disseminate his thoughts and ideas. In relation to this, prior restraint has been referred to. It should be noted that English law offers several possibilities of prior restraint. Both with regard to libellous speech and speech concerned with confidential information, an appellant can ask the courts to grant an interim injunction that may allow for prior restraint of the disclosure of the information concerned. Also Contempt of Court law allows for prior restraint on the reporting of cases when there is a 'substantial risk of prejudice to the administration of justice'.[54] Furthermore s.13 of the Public Order Act 1986 allows the chief officer of police to 'prohibit public processions, or a class of public processions, entirely, when the chief officer of police reasonably believes that the powers to impose conditions on a public procession under s.12 will be insufficient to prevent serious public disorder resulting from public procession held in a district or part of a district, because of the particular circumstances existing in that district or part'.[55] And finally the system of film-censorship brings with it prior restraint. When the mentioned legislation is subject of litigation, the prior restraint aspect is not an issue of consideration except with regard to the granting of injunctions in cases concerning confidential information and defamatory speech.

With regard to the seriousness of the restriction it can be said that prior restraint is considered a serious matter under the case law of the Court, but it is not rejected outright. It is also not an element that is considered to be of great importance as such.[56] Under English law, with regard to libel law, prior restraint is automatically prevented when the defence states it will plead fair comment or justification, because speech will not be restricted 'where no wrongful act' was done. With regard to confidential information, prior restraint is a given, since damage done by publication is irreparable and will therefore always outweigh the interest in immediate publication. Finally, also the Contempt of Court Act allows for prior restraint when there is a 'significant risk of prejudice to the administration of justice'. The fact that the prejudice should be significant seems to imply that the risk must be of some importance: not any risk will satisfy that requirement. However, as remarked previously, the other circumstances of the case will determine whether the importance attributed to prior restraint is comparable to the weight attached to it by the Court.

---

54   Contempt of Court Act 1981, s. 4 (2). See also Feldman, Civil Liberties and Human Rights in England and Wales, 1993, p. 765-781.

55   Feldman, Civil Liberties and Human Rights in England and Wales, 1993, p. 823.

56   A-G v. Guardian Newspapers Ltd (No.2) [1988] 3 All ER 545.

Finally, the distinction between facts and value-judgements can be found in the case law of both the Court and the English courts. With regard to the appreciation of facts and value-judgements, it can be said that under libel law the initial protection of value-judgements is comparable. Fair comment will not be restricted under English law, and although fair comment with regard to libel law is not attributed that much weight under the case law of the Court, prove of truth cannot be required with regard to value-judgements. The nature of the speech will determine the extent of the protection of such speech. A judge, for instance, is held not to be in a position to defend himself, and therefore restrictions on opinions about such a person will not be tolerated that easily.[57]

Beside the factors that I discussed so far, there is one other consideration that frequently appears in the case law of the English courts, that is the requirement of proportional use of freedom of expression. In some judgments that are considered of significance with regard to the protection of freedom of expression, it is striking that the manner in which freedom of expression was used was an aspect of consideration. In the case of A-G v. Guardian Newspapers, the view that the papers should not profit from another man's wrongdoings seemed decisive to the outcome of the case; similarly in X Ltd v. Morgan Grampian the way of obtaining the information was an important aspect of consideration. Under the case law of the Court, also the manner in which freedom of expression was used is a recurrent matter of consideration. This consideration is not as such an element that will determine the outcome of a case, but it is attributed to the findings of the Court. Usually such considerations determine that the information concerned was collected carefully, which will then, together with the public interest in the speech, justify the conclusion that there was a violation of Article 10.[58] The weight awarded to the proportional use of freedom of expression in cases such A-G v. Guardian Newspapers and X Ltd v. Morgan Grampian, which more or less required people to give up expressing themselves freely when the basis of the information to be disseminated could be contrary to legislative provisions is, however, unfamiliar to the Court.

All recurrent elements of consideration can be found under both systems of protection. There is a problem, however. As observed, the Court and the English courts do not consistently apply these elements to each case. Moreover, the nature of the inconsistency differs. The inconsistency of the elements considered by the Court seems to be caused by the fact that the Court's considerations do not only reflect the process of thought at the basis of the case, but also attempt to gain support for the outcome of the case. Whereas under English law, the inconsistent application of the elements considered is not only the result of the attempt to convince the public that

---

57 Barfod v. Denmark, (1989) A.149.
58 Bladet Tromsø v. Norway, 20 May 1999, De Haes and Gijssels v. Belgium, 24 February 1997, Reports 1997-I.

the court came to the right conclusion, but also of the fact that the aspects that can be considered are to a large extent determined by the kind of law that is the topic of the litigation at hand. As observed, not all concepts of law provide for a public good defence. And when English law does provide for some explicit protection, it is usually not of a general nature. The Contempt of Court Act in s.10 offers the press the possibility to keep sources secret, but this protection is overridden when knowledge of the identity of the source is necessary in the interest of the protection of national security, the protection of public order or in the interest of due administration of justice. S.4 of the Obscene Publications Act does not offer protection to speech of public interest generally, but only to expressions of artistic, historical or literary value.

The lack of consideration of certain facts and circumstances by the English courts could be the cause for a conviction by the Court. In the Sunday Times case, the nature of the speech and the seriousness of the restriction was not considered by the House of Lords and the appreciation of these elements subsequently led the Court to convict the UK for a breach of Article 10. A more recent example is the case of A-G v. Guardian Newspapers, in which the original aim of protection of confidential information was not considered by the House of Lords, which meant that it did not lift the injunction on the publication of Spycatcher even after it was possible to import the book freely into the UK. The lack of interest in realising the aim of the injunction once the information was freely available caused the conviction of the UK for a breach of the Convention. In this case it is obvious that the conviction could have been avoided by way of applying the public domain doctrine provided for under the law of breach of confidence. The common law of contempt of court, however, did not provide for a possibility to take the nature of the speech or the seriousness of the restriction of freedom of expression into account. Interestingly enough, the Contempt of Court Act 1981 does not offer any explicit possibility to do so either.

However, as observed in the introduction to this chapter, even if the English Court and the Court consider similar elements of a case, this does not automatically mean that the outcome of the case is the same. This has to do with the importance attributed to the various aspects of the case that are considered. Common ground with regard to the consideration and appreciation of facts and circumstances exists to the extent that all elements of consideration can be found under both systems of protection and that the appreciation of those facts and circumstances is similar to a certain degree as well. However, in the case of the Court all aspects of consideration could play a role in any case regarding freedom of expression, if such a consideration is relevant to the outcome of the case. Under English law, this is not always possible due to limitations imposed by legislation. Under influence of the decisions of the Court, the English courts have found the national legislation to be more lenient in that regard than is evident at first sight. Similarly with regard to the appreciation of facts and circumstances there exist some differences in the importance attached to freedom of expression and to the interests in restricting speech. But also here, it shows that such approaches may change, as the Derbyshire case shows.

Before drawing a conclusion on the existence and the extent of common ground with regard to the protection of freedom of expression, as far as its concept, the methods of protection and the consideration and appreciation of facts and circumstances are concerned, I first discuss the impact the Human Rights Act 1998 may have on a common ground regarding the protection of freedom of expression. That the Act will have an impact seems obvious since it aims to incorporate the ECHR into English law.

4.2 Impact of the Human Rights Act 1998 on a Common Ground

The last issue of consideration in this chapter is the extent to which the Human Rights Act influences the consideration and appreciation of facts and circumstances.

In those cases in which balancing of interests already occurs at the individual level, the English courts are already in a position to consider any aspect of a case they like, as the Morgan Grampian case and the Camelot case showed. The most important effect of the Human Rights Act lies in the fact that the courts now have the possibility to consider freedom of expression and its protection under the ECHR explicitly. This will not only make it possible for the courts, but will also encourage them to study closely the relevant judgments of the Court. The facts and circumstances the Court tends to consider and the weight subsequently given to them are the most obvious aspects of the Court's judgments and are consequently the easiest to take account of, as the courts under s.2 are obliged to do. Especially with regard to the Contempt of Court Act and possibly regarding s.4A and 5 of the Public Order Act[59] this will imply a change in emphasis. It is with regard to these two acts that the protection of freedom of expression is most likely not to be up to the minimum standard set by the Court. I have emphasised earlier that the concept of margin of appreciation as room left to the initial decision-making authorities has no place in cases in which the courts themselves are the initial interpreters of legislation instead of a public authority. However, the influence of the margin of appreciation applied by the Court, in relation to the margin of appreciation applied by the English courts, is relevant. It influences the consideration and appreciation not so much as a

---

59 See also Criminal Justice and Public Order Act 1994 which was the topic of litigation in DPP v. Jones (1997) 147 New Law Journal 162. This Act provides for a prohibition order on the holding of any trespassory assemblies involving more than twenty people. In this case such an order was given to an assembly that was held within a four mile radius of Stonehenge. The provision was held by the High Court to extend to any demonstration in the area on the public highway, regardless of how peaceful or non-obstructive such a protest happened to be. Mr Justice Collins made clear that in his view this ban was not only lawful in Britain but was also in compliance with Article 11 of the ECHR. See also Ewing and Gearty, Rocky Foundations for Labour's New Rights, 1997, p. 150.

doctrine, but in the way it affects the resultant degree of protection after its application by the Court. In other words it influences the degree of protection the Court requires the States party to the Convention to give to freedom of expression. Although the English courts are free to provide greater protection than required, because the Court tends to allow a wide margin of appreciation with regard to, for instance, the protection of Public Order and national security, s.4 of the Public Order Act 1986 and the Official Secrets Act are less likely to be inconsistent with the Convention. Consequently, in relation to these restricting provisions the approach of the English courts will not have to change significantly. In relation to Contempt of Court and the restriction of political speech under s.4A and 5 of the Public Order Act 1986 on the other hand, a narrow margin of appreciation might well be applied by the Court. In such cases not only the application of a balancing of interests at the level of the individual case, but also the consideration and appreciation of facts and circumstances similar to the approach of the Court, would help avoid future convictions of the United Kingdom in Strasbourg. However, the extensive possibilities to restrict freedom of expression under domestic law such as the Official Secrets Act might even bring cases under legislation that has a lesser risk of resulting in a conviction into the danger zone. The Spycatcher-decision shows that it may be wise not to change the approach to cases restricting freedom of expression selectively, that is in those instances in which the Court generally applies a narrow margin of appreciation. In the Spycatcher case the protection of national security was at stake, and consequently a wider margin of appreciation was applied by the Court. However, even in this case, the Court concluded that there was a violation of freedom of expression when the injunction was not lifted once the book could be freely imported from the United States. Cases in which speech on governmental information concerning national security is restricted might also require a change in the consideration and appreciation of facts and circumstances. In those areas of law where a change will be necessary, the Human Rights Act provides a basis for such a change in approach by the courts.

CHAPTER X
SUMMARY AND CONCLUSIONS

1 INTRODUCTION

The primary aim of this study was to identify a common ground between the protection of fundamental rights in English law and under the ECHR, on which the required protection of the rights of the Convention as incorporated into English law by the Human Rights Act 1998 can be based. In order to do so, I examined the requirements set out by the Human Rights Act and searched for a common ground between the protection of freedom of expression in English law and under the ECHR. The term common ground concerned all the aspects that together establish the protection of freedom of expression. Consequently I defined common ground as follows: common ground refers to the approach of a system of protection to the notion of a right, the role of the judiciary and legislature in providing protection for a right (location of responsibility), the substantive methods of protection applied by the courts and the consideration and appreciation of facts and circumstances.

In chapter II I described the requirements of the Human Rights Act 1998 with regard to the protection of the rights incorporated by the Act. In this chapter I concluded that the wording of the Act regarding the level of protection is indeterminate as to the degree of protection provided for the incorporated rights. The courts are supposed to 'take account' of the Strasbourg case law regarding the rights concerned, and they are required to do so as far as possible when 'reading' and 'giving effect' to legislation. Under s.6 they are moreover obliged not to act in a way which is incompatible with a Convention right, the application of common law, equity and judicial review are all included in the obligation to act in accordance with the Convention rights. Although 'taking account of' Strasbourg case law in fact gives little indication of the degree of protection the courts are required to provide, one of the main objectives of the Act is to provide protection to a degree that makes it unnecessary for UK citizens to bring their case before the European Court of Human Rights to see their rights sufficiently protected. This suggests that the degree of protection provided under English law should be at least the same as that provided by the Court. In carrying out their task of reading and giving effect to legislation, the English courts should therefore provide protection to that level as far as it is possible to do so. If it is not possible for the courts to provide 'sufficient' protection, the obligation to provide this degree of protection rests on the legislature.

In chapter III I drew a general picture of the current position of freedom of expression in English law. I examined seven areas of law as to the formulation of the law concerned and their application by the courts. These areas were: criminal libel and related offences, civil libel, breach of confidence, official secrecy, contempt of court, public order offences and finally judicial review. These areas of law involve statutory law, common law and equity. In the preliminary conclusions to this chapter I observed that although freedom of expression in English law is not protected as such as a fundamental right, English law on a number of occasions, by exceptions and defences, provides for some protection of freedom of expression. Moreover, the courts increasingly refer to freedom of expression in interpreting and applying legislation and reviewing acts of decision-making authorities. This development coincides with the increasing occurrence of Article 10 ECHR in the reasoning of the courts, even though the Convention was not yet a part of English domestic law. I observed also that the English courts' active attitude towards the protection of freedom of expression, was initiated with regard to common law rather than statute law. Finally I commented that the laws and case law discussed in chapter III would be examined in great detail on the notion of freedom of expression that could be derived from them, on the methods of protection applied in English law and the case law of the courts and on the consideration and appreciation of facts and circumstances that could be derived from this.

In chapter IV I identified the methods of review that are applied by the Court to provide protection to freedom of expression. I concluded that three methods of protection could be distinguished: application of a margin of appreciation, review of the proportionality of a measure and balancing of interests. The application of a margin of appreciation concerns the scope of the review by the Court and is related to the division of the responsibility between the States Party to the Convention and the Court for the protection of the rights guaranteed under the Convention. The margin of appreciation is variable and influenced by the facts and circumstances of a particular case. The other two methods of protection are substantive in nature, meaning that they concern the criteria a restriction has to meet in order for it to be considered 'necessary in a democratic society'. I distinguished three forms of review of proportionality: review of the suitability of a measure, review of whether a less restrictive alternative was available and balancing of means and ends. I observed that the third method of protection, balancing of interests, should be distinguished from the review of proportionality. Balancing of interests concerns an evaluation of the importance of the countervailing interests involved in the case, whereas the review of proportionality concerns considerations regarding the means and ends of a restriction. The means and ends of a restriction are indissolubly connected, the opposing interests exist separate from each other.

In chapter V to IX I examined the existence and scope of a common ground. I recapitulate the conclusions of those chapters in the following section.

2 COMMON GROUND

The second part of this study contained the search for a common ground. In chapter V I examined a common ground between the approach to the notion of freedom of expression in English law and under the ECHR. In chapter VI I examined a common ground between their application of a margin of appreciation. In chapter VII and VIII I examined successively a common ground for the review of proportionality and the application of balancing of interests in English law and by the European Court of Human Rights. Finally in chapter IX I searched for a common ground concerning the consideration and appreciation of facts and circumstances.

2.1 Notion of Freedom of Expression

I concluded in chapter V that the notion of freedom of expression is similar in both systems of protection. The scope of this freedom is not restricted by a limited perception of the nature of the expression governed by it. Furthermore, under both systems of protection a horizontal effect of freedom of expression is accepted, and also prior restraint is in principal allowed as a restriction to freedom of expression. The English courts explicitly refer to freedom of expression and refer to it as a principle or even a right.

2.2 Margin of Appreciation

The search for a common ground between the application of a margin of appreciation in the two orders concentrated on a common ground between application by the Court and by the English courts in relation to their task of judicial review. The application of a margin of appreciation by the Court is also of relevance with regard to the appellate jurisdiction of the English courts. The search for a common ground in that regard, however, takes place with regard to balancing of interests and consideration and appreciation of facts and circumstances, since the application of a margin of appreciation by the Court results in requirements as to the degree of protection provided in the areas of law governed by the English courts' appellate jurisdiction. The margin of appreciation applied by the Court can vary from reviewing whether the necessity of a restriction was 'absolutely certain' to whether a state party to the Convention was 'entitled to think' that the restriction was necessary. The widest scope of the margin of appreciation is where the Court reviewed whether it was not unreasonable for the State to think that the measure was necessary. Van Dijk and Van Hoof defined these varieties of the margin of appreciation as the 'narrow approach', the 'reasonable' test and the 'not unreasonable' test. The margin of appreciation applied by the Court does not imply an obligation on the national authorities to apply the same scope of review. The margin of appreciation influences the degree of protection the national authorities are required to provide. With regard to national administrative law this implies that only when the application of the margin of appreciation leads to specific requirements of protection, the national courts are in fact also required to apply such a scope of review.

The application of the 'not unreasonable' test is common to both systems of protection. The Wednesbury reasonable test amounts to the application of a similar scope of review. The suggested scope of review in the Brind case and the review applied by Steyn LJ. in the Leech case, amount to the application of a reasonable-test. So although not applied frequently, the occurrence of this scope of review in the case law of the English courts, extends the common ground to the 'reasonable-test'. The narrow approach of the European Court of Human Rights cannot be found in English case law, however.

I distinguished four factors that influence the scope of the margin of appreciation applied by the Court. These were: the nature of the expression concerned, the common ground that can be found for the protection of a right in the systems of protection of the States party to the Convention, the legitimate aim invoked and, finally, the seriousness of the interference. These factors overlap and influence each other. They do not make the scope of the margin of appreciation predictable, but they do provide a certain measure of probability. Some general conclusions can be drawn with regard to the influence of these factors. These are that political speech, especially when coming from the press, will attract the application of a narrow margin of appreciation, whereas the determination of the necessity of the restriction of commercial speech and artistic speech will largely be left to the national authorities of the states. If the aim invoked is the protection of national security or the prevention of disorder or crime, the Court is inclined to apply a wide margin of appreciation, despite the nature of the expression. Protection of the authority of the judiciary, on the other hand, is governed by the principle that the courts cannot operate in a vacuum and, depending on the topic of the speech, may sometimes attract a narrow margin of appreciation. Similarly, the protection of rights of others, depending on the subject of the speech, may also bring the Court to apply a narrow margin of appreciation. With regard to the seriousness of the restriction, the margin applied will depend on the other factors which influence the margin of appreciation, except when it amounts to an (almost) complete ban of dissemination of the information concerned. A ban will lead the Court to apply a narrow margin of appreciation. The cases in which the English courts apply a narrower margin of appreciation than the traditional Wednesbury test, are those where a fundamental right is restricted. Moreover, the circumstances of the cases in which such a decreased margin of appreciation was applied recall the factors that lead the European Court of Human Rights to apply a narrow margin of appreciation: the public interest in the speech and the aim of the restriction were both referred to when the English courts applied a narrower margin of appreciation than the traditional Wednesbury review.

Similar circumstances lead to the application of a narrower margin of appreciation, but the scope of the review of the Court in those circumstances is narrower than the scope of the review of English courts.

2.3 Review of Proportionality

After chapter VI, I turned to the substantive methods of protection, starting off with an analysis of a common ground with regard to the review of proportionality in chapter VII. The European Court of Human Rights understands the review of proportionality to be a consideration on the relationship between means and ends of a restriction, but also understands it to be a balancing of interests. With regard to the review of means and ends, the Court applies two sorts of review. These are the review of whether a less restrictive alternative was available and a balancing of means and ends. In English law, reference to a requirement of proportionality is rare, but in fact a number of cases can be found, as I pointed out, in which the existence of a less restrictive alternative was reason to quash a decision of the authorities. A balancing of means and ends can also be found in the case law of the courts. The former occurred with regard to the penalty imposed in criminal law cases, but also in judicial review cases. The latter form of proportionality review occurs in libel law cases in which an interim injunction is requested, and can also be found in judicial review cases. In one judicial review case, a balancing of interests was suggested in order to review the proportionality of a restriction, when Staughton LJ. suggested that review of proportionality amounted to a balancing of the risk to life against the threat to national security. Where review of proportionality is applied, however, it usually concerns a review of means and ends. A common ground exists between the types of proportionality review that can be found in English case law and the judgments of the Court, including balancing of interest. However, as with the application of a narrower margin of appreciation than the usual Wednesbury review, a common ground between the two types of review of proportionality ends at the frequency with which the courts apply this type of substantive review. The English courts do not review proportionality, that is including considerations regarding the interest in the restricted right, as consistently as the Court in judicial review cases.

2.4 Balancing of Interests

A common ground between the application of a balancing of interests in English law and under the ECHR was examined in chapter VIII. Balancing of interests occurs in the case law of the Court both as a method of protection applied to support findings regarding the proportionality of a measure, and also as an independent method of protection. Balancing of interests by the Court always entails considerations regarding the two opposing interests involved in a case, and always involves considerations on

289

the level of the concrete case. I refer to balancing of interests entailing considerations of both interests involved as a 'full balancing of interests'. Considerations regarding the interest in freedom of expression in English law do not occur in relation to all areas of law I discussed in chapter III. Where application of the Public Order Act 1986 is concerned, the courts are reluctant to consider any interest in freedom of expression. They will apply the wording of the law, without specifically taking consideration of the restricted freedom. With regard to the scope of the offence in regard to obscene publications no balancing of interests occurred either, although with regard to this offence a defence of public good is available which limits the restrictive effect on freedom of expression. On occasion, the jury has even been invited to apply a full balancing of interests in order to determine whether a publication could be considered obscene in the sense of the law. The restrictive law as such gives evidence of a balancing of interests by the legislature on a number of occasions. The Obscene Publications Act is an example, since it provides for a public good defence. Also libel law, which provides for qualified privilege, a defence of fair comment and justification, and breach of confidence, which provides for a public domain doctrine and a public interest exception, demonstrate that freedom of expression is taken account of in statutory law, in common law and equity. Also the Contempt of Court Act provides for some protection of freedom of expression, since it determines that discussion of matters of public interest in which reference to a case is incidental to the discussion, cannot constitute a contempt of court. Moreover, this Act lays down that journalists cannot be obliged to reveal their sources, unless it is necessary in the interest of justice, or national security or for the prevention of disorder or crime.

This evidence that a balancing of interests exists in the law itself does not necessarily imply that English courts carry out a balancing of interests. However, evidence can be found of full balancing of interests. Initially this method of protection was used to diminish the effects of defences that were available to protect freedom of expression. The Schering Chemicals case is a good example. In this case, the public domain doctrine should have made it impossible for the Schering company to obtain an injunction preventing publication of confidential information. A balancing of interests was applied in which the fact that the drug which was held to cause deformities in unborn children, was already withdrawn from the market and the fact that the information was obtained in breach of confidence led the court to allow the injunction. A similar approach was taken in the more recent case of A-G v. Guardian Newspapers. With regard to s.10 of the Contempt of Court Act in the Morgan Grampian case, a balancing of interests took place after the court had first extended the interest in protection of the administration of justice beyond proceedings that are active before a court of law.

However, the English courts increasingly take account of the interest in freedom of expression in order actually to provide protection to this right. The English courts apply the law that represents the aim with regard to which freedom of expression is restricted; in addition they tend to consider the scope of legislation on an abstract level. These two facts lead to the situation that they apply an implied balancing of interests, meaning that they only explicitly consider the interest in freedom of expression. Balancing of interests at an abstract level will necessarily lead to lack of subtlety in the protection of freedom of expression, in the sense that if a particular characteristic is fulfilled, the speech will either be protected or not, regardless of the particular circumstances of the case. The Derbyshire case illustrated this. The result of the application of an abstract, implied, balancing of interests was that any defamatory statements on public authorities were excluded from the possibility of a libel suit. Also with regard to the scope of the offence of blasphemy this occurred. Speech that concerns religions other than the Christian religion can never be blasphemous in nature. The application of the defence of fair comment leads to absolute protection of freedom of expression as well, at least in terms of interim measures. Whenever the defendant claims fair comment, an injunction will be refused. It is worth noting that the application of the public domain doctrine, which would be expected to be applied in this manner in relation to a request for an injunction, can in fact still lead to a balancing of interests as the Brind case and the Schering Chemicals case illustrated.

In the meantime, a number of other decisions have occurred in which a full balancing of interests was applied. This full balancing of interests is then automatically combined with considerations at a concrete level, i.e. involving evaluation of the facts and circumstances particular to the case. This was in relation to Contempt of Court law and, under influence of the expected requirements of the Human Rights Act, with regard to the defence of qualified privilege in libel law.

The existence of a common ground between balancing of interests as method of protection does not necessarily imply that the resultant degree of protection is the same. This depends on the consideration and appreciation of facts and circumstances.

2.5 Consideration and Appreciation of Facts and Circumstances

An examination of a common ground between the two systems, with regard to consideration and appreciation was done in chapter IX. The consideration and appreciation of facts and circumstances is affected by the factors that influence the scope of the margin of appreciation. The restriction of freedom of expression in order to protect national security or public order will usually lead to the application of a wide margin of appreciation, implying that the interest in national security and public order is held to be of great importance. With regard to those facts and circumstances that lead the Court to apply a narrow margin of appreciation, the level of protection the Court gives to freedom of expression is not implied in the scope of the margin of appreciation but is more directly evident. Where speech of public interest is concerned and, particularly when it is of a political nature and disseminated by the press, the interest in freedom of expression will be considered extensively and is held to be of great importance, regardless of whether the aim invoked concerns the protection of rights of others, or protection of the authority of the judiciary.

In addition to the aspects that influence the scope of the margin of appreciation, consideration as to the difference between facts and value-judgements in cases concerning the protection of reputation are facts and circumstances which occur time and time again, as does the proportional use of freedom of expression. These aspects are not considered in every case, but are usually considered whenever they support the decision of the Court.

These facts and circumstances considered by the Court are all familiar to the English courts. And, like the Court, the English courts are not consistent in considering each aspect every time in cases in which freedom of expression is considered. The consistency depends partly on the importance attributed to the facts and circumstances, since courts tend to emphasise those aspects that support their decision, especially when the outcome of the case is clear (to them).

A common ground with regard to the appreciation of facts and circumstances exists with regard to the importance attributed to political speech where libel law is concerned.

The importance attributed by the English courts to speech of public interest when they apply libel law is comparable to the weight given to such speech by the Court. A common ground also exists with regard to the importance given to freedom of expression when the aim pursued concerns national security or the protection of public order or crime. Under such circumstances the English courts attach little weight to freedom of expression and the Court applies a wide margin of appreciation. Also the importance attributed by the Court and the English courts to obscene speech and blasphemous speech is similar to the extent that with such speech, the Court will be inclined to apply a wide margin of appreciation. The seriousness of a restriction may also lead the English courts to hold a restriction disproportionate to the aim pursued. This is, for instance, the case when fair comment is pleaded in libel cases. In such cases common ground is restricted to the scope of protection the Court would provide in a particular case.[1]

Concerning damages awarded in libel cases, the seriousness of the restriction is taken into consideration to the extent that the courts can adjust the amount of damages to an amount that can be considered necessary in a democratic society. In such cases, the seriousness of the restriction is influenced by considerations regarding freedom of expression. The seriousness of the restriction is also considered when the courts determine whether an injunction should be allowed, but in fact this aspect

---

[1] See par. 3.2.3.2. of chapter VIII on balancing of interests at a concrete level, which decreases the possibilities of differentiation according to the circumstances of the particular case.

cannot overrule the interest in keeping information confidential. Depending on the nature of the information protected and the aim served with keeping it confidential, the Court may come to a different evaluation of the case. Prior restraint is accepted as a necessary restriction under both systems of protection. However, when prior restraint results in an absolute ban on the dissemination of information, depending on the nature of the information concerned, the speech may be held to be of greater importance that the aim pursued. Also when protection of national security is involved. The importance the English courts attach to the protection of national security seems to be even greater than the importance the Court attaches to it.

A common ground finds it limit at the appreciation of speech of public interest, especially when disseminated by the press, when the aim pursued is protection of the authority of the judiciary. Also it should be remarked with regard to libel law that the application of a full balancing of interests at a concrete level, where a defence of qualified privilege is concerned, in my view led to lack of protection for speech of public interest. Finally, a common ground with regard to the circumstance that speech is in the public domain seems to be lacking.

2.6 Concluding Remarks

From the previous sections of this concluding chapter it has become apparent that an extensive common ground exists on which the protection of the incorporated rights can be based. A final remark with regard to the conclusions as to the search for a common ground is required however. It should be noted that apart from the narrow approach of the Court to the margin of appreciation, all methods of protection applied by the Court as well as the facts and circumstances considered and the importance attributed to them can be found under English law. This implies that the approach of the Court to the protection of freedom of expression is available to English law. However, I wish to note that the application of these aspects of the protection of freedom of expression is inconsistent.

With these considerations I come to a discussion of the implications of the Human Rights Act 1998. I elaborate on the changes that are required under English law to meet the requirements of the Human Right Act.

3 CHANGES REQUIRED AFTER THE HUMAN RIGHTS ACT 1998 BECOMES LAW

The changes required of the English system of protection to meet the requirements of the Human Rights Act 1998, depend on the extent of incorporation of the system of protection of the ECHR. A limited number of rights are incorporated. Beside the rights themselves, the case law of the Court is also incorporated, to the extent that the courts have a duty to 'take account' of it. The Act provides that the courts give protection to the rights when they read and give effect to legislation, as far as it is possible to do so. This provision as such does not indicate the required degree of protection. But it can be argued that the resultant degree of protection should at least meet the degree of protection required by the Court. In this study I elaborated on a common ground between the ECHR and English systems with regard to the aspects of the protection of freedom of expression that together establish the resultant degree of protection. I concluded that the approach to the notion of freedom of expression is similar in the two systems of protection. Moreover, the methods of protection applied by the Court are all familiar to the English system of protection, and even the consideration and appreciation of facts and circumstances shows a significant common ground. The scope of common ground provides a good foundation on which to base the application of the Human Rights Act. However, as the conclusions from the previous section show, some changes are required to realise fully the aim of providing protection to the degree the Court does. In this section, I indicate the changes required and the manner in which the Human Rights Act provides for possibilities to realise these changes.

3.1 Margin of Appreciation

It has been suggested that the margin of appreciation doctrine is not something that can be applied in the protection of rights in a national context, and that consequently in that context it is possible to provide much more protection to the incorporated rights than the Court does, since the margin of appreciation no longer plays a role once the Convention is incorporated.[2] The fact that s.2 speaks of 'taking account of' the case law of the Court was to support that approach. This expectation could be realised under the Act. However, in my opinion, when one thinks of the level of protection given to freedom of expression by the English courts so far, this seems an unlikely development. Instead, the margin of appreciation does remain of influence to the national system of protection. The margin of appreciation applied by the Court influences the degree of protection required of the States party to the Convention. As the margin of appreciation gets narrower, the domestic courts will increasingly be obliged to follow the Court's approach to such cases to achieve a similar level of protection.

In relation to judicial review cases, the resultant degree of protection can be achieved by the courts only if they adjust the scope of the review. In private law and penal law cases, the required degree of protection that is partly the result of the application of a margin of appreciation can be achieved by the national system of protection by a balancing of interests, and by adjustments in the consideration and appreciation of facts and circumstances. The English courts, in my opinion, will be

---

2   Singh, Hunt and Demetriou, Is there a role for the 'Margin of Appreciation' in National Law after the Human Rights Act?, 1999, p. 17.

most likely to offer just enough protection to freedom of expression to meet the requirements of the Court, and these requirements are influenced by the margin of appreciation left to the States party to the Convention. Nevertheless, it is always possible to offer more protection than required by the Court; it is not necessary for the English courts to change their stance with regard to defamation of democratically elected public bodies and political parties, even though in such cases the extent of the protection goes further than is required by the Court. A limit to more extensive protection is set only by the requirement of protection of other incorporated Convention rights, such as privacy.

As I observed, the English courts leave the decision-making authorities a degree of discretion in exercising their powers. But although the review of Wednesbury unreasonableness is more stringent in cases concerning fundamental rights, the closeness of the review of cases in which fundamental rights are restricted is never as rigorous as the scrutiny of the Court under circumstances which, according to the Court, justify such closeness of review.[3] Although the English courts apply closer scrutiny to cases in which fundamental rights are restricted, the scrutiny goes no further than the 'reasonable-test' applied by the Court. The 'narrow approach' of the Court has not been applied so far. The question now is whether the Human Rights Act provides for a possibility for the English courts to apply such a narrow approach. The relevant provisions with regard to the relationship between the judiciary and the executive are s.2 and s.6 of the Act. S.6 contains the obligation for public authorities to act in conformity with Convention rights. Primary responsibility to live up to this obligation lies with the public authorities. Looking at the Brind case, for instance, in which a broad discretionary power was granted, the public authority has a duty under the Human Rights Act to interpret that power in accordance with the Convention. The extent to which the courts can review the public authorities' view of what is consistent is not regulated in the Act.[4] S.7 of the Act merely provides that a person who claims his rights have been violated by a public authority may 'bring proceedings against the authority under' the Human Rights Act or may 'rely on the Convention right or rights concerned in any legal proceeding'. A combination of factors, however, could support the stance that the Human Rights Act provides a basis for closer scrutiny. First, s.2 of the Human Rights Act determines that, in a situation in which the appellant claims a breach of a right a court must take into account the case law of the Court and Commission. Moreover, one of the aims of incorporating the ECHR was to reduce the number of convictions of the UK by the Court. The courts could understand s.6 together with s.2 to mean that they have a duty to ensure

---

3   Singh, Hunt and Demetriou, Is there a Role for the 'Margin of Appreciation' in National Law after the Human Rights Act?, 1999, p. 16.
4   See also Lord Lester of Herne Hill, The Art of the Possible – Interpreting Statutes under the Human Rights Act, 1998, p. 668.

295

a degree of protection of the Convention rights in judicial review cases similar to that offered by the Court. This would imply that they would have to narrow substantially the margin of appreciation allowed to the public authorities substantially. Closer scrutiny would at least be required in those cases in which the facts and circumstances would lead the Court to apply a 'reasonable-test' or a narrow margin of appreciation.

Although s.6 of the Act suggests that the initial responsibility for the protection of Convention rights is with the decision-making authority, s.2 provides a possibility for the courts to apply close scrutiny in order to attain a sufficient degree of protection. Whether or not the Act will be applied in this manner depends on the willingness of the courts to take such a big step away from their current position with respect to the executive.[5] The case of R. v. DPP, ex p. Kebeline suggests that there does exist such a willingness to come to an extensive change in attitude.[6] This case dealt with the Prevention of Terrorism Act according to which the defendant is asked to prove that he did not intend a terrorist act when he has behaved in a way which leads to the assumption that he did so intend. In this case, s.6 of the Human Rights Act 1998 was used to state that public authorities putting that obligation on a person act contrary to Article 6 of the Convention and that this constitutes 'abuse of power'. The House of Lords did not condone this approach, for a number of procedural reasons and because the Human Rights Act was not in force yet.[7] However, the approach of the Court of Appeal does show that the courts may regard the Act as containing a general duty to protect the Convention rights, leading to a significant change in the relation between the executive and the judiciary.

3.2 Influence of the Human Rights Act on the Review of Proportionality

The substantive method of protection ostensibly applied by the English courts is the Wednesbury unreasonableness test. We have seen that this test may vary in content and that in fact occasionally this test amounts to a review of the proportionality of a measure in cases in which human rights are restricted. The application of this method of protection is controversial. The objections regarding the review of proportionality mainly concern the scope of the review by the courts. We have seen above that to provide protection to the degree the Court does, this scope should be narrowed when the circumstances of the case call for it. Review of the proportionality of a restriction, however, does not necessarily imply close review. Proportionality can and has been reviewed by the English courts and in this section I discuss the extent to which the

---

5   See also Feldman, Proportionality and the Human Rights Act 1998, 1999, p. 122.
6   R. v. DPP, ex p. Kebeline [1999] 3 W.L.R. 175, CA; 28 October 1999, HL.
7   Note the remarkable difference with the Reynolds case in which the Human Rights Act had been reason to come to a balancing of interests at a concrete level.

Human Rights Act 1998 forces the courts to review the proportionality of acts consistently, that is in all cases in which freedom of expression is restricted. Feldman convincingly held that if the English courts were to refrain from using proportionality as a method of review, this 'would lead to too wide a rift between the interpretation of Convention rights in the UK and their interpretation under the ECHR, and would undermine the main purpose of the Bill'.[8]

As for the scope of the review, the criteria of review are not specified in the Human Rights Act either. However, if the Act is intended to offer protection similar to that offered by the Court, the restriction on fundamental rights such as freedom of expression will have to be necessary in a democratic society. The Court determines this necessity by reviewing the proportionality of a measure or even by balancing the interests involved. The Human Rights Act requires protection to the degree provided by the Court and s.2 can serve as a ground for providing such protection. This section could be used to narrow the margin of appreciation, just as it can be used to justify the application of review of proportionality in cases in which fundamental rights are restricted, even though the Act does not say explicitly that the methods of protection of the Court should be adopted by the English courts. The review of proportionality already occurs in English law and therefore I expect the regular review of proportionality to be less of a step away from the traditional approach to judicial review than the narrowing of the margin of appreciation.

3.3 Influence of the Human Rights Act on Balancing of Interests

The Act imposes a duty on the courts to take account of the Strasbourg case law under s.2. This and sections 3 and 6 are the most important provisions of the Act with regard to balancing of interests. S.3 requires the courts to 'read and give effect to' primary and secondary legislation 'in a way which is compatible with the Convention rights'.[9] In those cases in which the courts do not conclude that there is incompatibility of the legislation, responsibility to offer sufficient protection to individual rights lies with the courts. S.6, moreover, includes courts in the term 'public authority'.[10] Although the courts already considered freedom of expression in horizontal situations, s.6 of the Act explains that the courts should also provide protection of the Convention rights between citizens with regard to both statutory and common law.

First of all it should be remarked that the degree to which the courts can take account of the provisions of the ECHR and its case law has increased compared to the situation previous to the Human Rights Act becoming law. Although under

---

8   See also Feldman, Proportionality and the Human Rights Act 1998, 1999, p. 121.
9   S.3 ss.1 HRA 1998.
10 S.6 ss.3(a) HRA 1998.

common law a greater influence of the ECHR was developing already,[11] there will be a change especially with regard to statutory legislation. Previously the ECHR could play a role in those instances in which the wording of the legislation was ambiguous: the courts were supposed to interpret such legislation as if Parliament intended it to be in conformity with the Convention rights. However, in those cases in which the wording of the legislation is clear, the ECHR could not be referred to. The obligation provided for in s.3 makes it possible for the courts to consider the ECHR and its case law with regard to all legislation. The Act regulates when the courts are supposed to live up to this duty, namely when they 'read' or 'give effect to' the domestic legislation. Because the duty to take account of the Convention rights should be found in the legislation itself, this in my opinion leaves the courts two possibilities to come to a balancing of interests.

The foundation for balancing of interests can first of all be found in a law itself, when it provides for exceptions and defences that accord protection for freedom of expression. These should then be applied in the same way as Lord Simon suggested applying the public good defence of the Obscene Publications Act in DPP v. Whyte. If the legislation includes a public good defence, such as s.4 of the Obscene Publications Act, the possibility of a balancing of interests is obvious. Similarly s.4A and 5 of the Public Order Act 1986 provide a defence for people who plead their behaviour to be 'reasonable'. And the defence of qualified privilege could serve that purpose under defamation law. As the example of DPP v. Whyte shows, the application of section s.4 already led to the suggestion to apply a balancing of interests. However, the Contempt of Court Act and the Official Secrets Act, for instance, lack such a provision. With regard to such legislation the vagueness of the terms used to formulate the offence at issue can be used to come to a balancing of interests. In the Contempt of Court Act such terms can be found in s.2 and s.5 of the Act. S.5 exempts discussion of matters of public interest if 'risk of impediment or prejudice' to particular legal proceedings is merely 'incidental' to the discussion. The terms 'public interest', 'risk' and 'incidental' should leave sufficient room to come to a balancing of interests in which all aspects relevant to the protection of freedom of expression are considered. However, even outside the scope of s.5 there are possibilities to take account of freedom of expression. S.2 of the Contempt of Court Act requires 'substantial risk' of 'seriously' impeding or prejudicing legal proceedings. Regarding the Official Secrets Act the term 'damaging' can be regarded as vague. The usual approach would be to define such terms. The resultant scope of the restriction would at the same time implicitly would determine the scope of freedom of expression. The terms in inverted commas, however, are suitable to take account of the interests in freedom of expression explicitly. The change required in

---

11   See also Sir Anthony Hooper, the Impact of the Human Rights Act on Judicial decision-making, 1998, p. 676.

the approach of the courts is that they explicitly consider the interests in freedom of expression and the opposing interest in the administration of justice to determine the meaning of the wording of the legislation. The fact that the Courts are authorised to take account of the ECHR makes such an explicit balancing of interests possible. And vice versa, this possibility will force the courts to consider all relevant aspects of freedom of expression.

The balancing of interests can be done at two different moments. First, when the legislation is actually considered abstractly, that is when the facts and circumstances of the particular case at issue are not considered yet, such as was done in the Derbyshire case regarding defamation law. And second, when the legislation is applied to the case.

As I mentioned in the chapter on balancing of interests, the first moment of consideration may lead to discrepancies in the protection of freedom of expression. Although the moment of protection is not referred to in the Act, again s.2 could be used as a basis to opt for consideration of the interests involved at the level of the individual case. As I observed, the Court usually tends to apply substantive methods of protection at the level of the individual case, whereas the English courts when they balance interests, are inclined to do this at an abstract level, apparently to avoid uncertainty of law.[12] However, in order to reach the goals of the Human Rights Act, it would be legitimate for the English courts to assume a similar approach to that of the Court and make it possible to balance interests at the level of the individual case. This would require the courts to define the terminology of the legislation in a manner that makes it possible to balance the facts and circumstances of the particular case at a concrete level. This approach would be similar to the approach that was taken to the term 'necessary in the interest of justice' of s.10 of the Contempt of Court Act in the Morgan Grampian case and the Camelot judgment. In these cases, although the Human Rights Act at that time was not even an issue of consideration in Parliament, the courts referred to Article 10 ECHR at the level of the individual case and balanced the particular interests in revealing the source of confidential information and in freedom of expression. This would also be possible under defamation law, by means of the defence of qualified privilege. Instead of determining in general that public authorities cannot sue for libel, qualified privilege could be used to come to a balancing of interests at the individual level, consequently leaving room for a more differentiated approach to a case. The English courts seem to be aware of the necessity of a change towards balancing of interests at a concrete level, as the approach to the case of Reynolds v. Times Newspapers demonstrated.

A last remark concerns s.12 of the Human Rights Act. Although the press is not a 'public authority', as a result of the horizontal effect of the Convention rights, the

---

12   This is also suggested by Markesinis, Privacy, Freedom of Expression, and the horizontal effect of the Human Rights Bill: Lessons from Germany, 1999, p. 74.

Act will establish a new restriction of freedom of expression under English law, namely the right to privacy as adopted in Article 8 of the Convention. In order to make sure that the interest in freedom of expression is not disregarded by the courts in those cases in which the two conflict, s.12 was adopted. This section instructs the courts not to grant an interim injunction in cases in which the applicant 'is likely to establish that publication should not be allowed', and that the courts 'must have particular regard' to the interest in freedom of expression when the information concerns 'journalistic, literary or artistic material'. This section causes a change to the protection of freedom of expression with regard to defamation law. It can no longer be sufficient to argue justification or proof of truth to avoid an interim injunction. Instead the interest in the publication of the information must outweigh the interest in privacy. S.12 could to a certain extent also be of relevance to cases under the Contempt of Court Act and breach of confidence cases, when these cases involve a private person. I doubt, however, that s.12 requires the court to strike a different balance from that under sections 2 and 3 of the Act.

3.4 Influence of the Human Rights Act on Consideration and Appreciation of Facts and Circumstances

In those cases in which balancing of interests already occurs at the individual level, the Human Rights Act has no influence on the consideration of facts and circumstance, since the courts are already in a position to consider any aspect of a case they like. The most important effect of the Human Rights Act lies in the fact that the courts now have the possibility to consider freedom of expression and its protection under the ECHR explicitly. This will not only enable, but also encourage the courts closely to study the relevant judgements of the Court. The facts and circumstances the Court tends to consider and the weight subsequently given to them are the most obvious aspects of the Court's judgments, and are consequently the easiest to take account of, as the courts under s.2 are obliged to do.

The facts and circumstances that led the European Court of Human Rights to apply a wide margin of appreciation do not imply that freedom of expression under those circumstances should be awarded little weight by the English courts, nor that the opposing interests should be awarded much weight. It merely means that the national authorities have relatively more room to decide on the importance they attach to either interest. Therefore with regard to the protection of blasphemous speech or commercial speech, or with regard to speech that touches upon the protection of public order or national security, English law is left a great deal of leeway as to the degree of protection it provides for freedom of expression. This will imply a change in emphasis, especially with regard to the Contempt of Court Act, and possibly regarding s.4A and 5 of the Public Order Act. It is with regard to these two acts that the protection of freedom of expression is most likely not to be up to the standard set by the Court. I have emphasised earlier that the notion of margin of appreciation has no place in cases in which the courts themselves are the initial interpreters of legislation. However, the influence of the margin of appreciation applied by the Court, in relation to the margin of appreciation applied by the English courts, is still of relevance. It influences the consideration and appreciation of the English courts not so much as a doctrine, but in the way it effects the resultant degree of protection after its application by the Court. In other words it influences the degree of protection the Court requires the States party to the Convention to give to freedom of expression. The Court tends to allow a wide margin of appreciation with regard to, for instance, the protection of Public Order and national security; for that reason s.4 of the Public Order Act 1986 and the Official Secrets Act are less likely to be inconsistent with the Convention. Consequently, in relation to these restricting provisions, the approach of the English courts will not have to change as significantly. In relation to Contempt of Court and the restriction of political speech under s.4A and 5 of the Public Order Act 1986 on the other hand, a narrow margin of appreciation might well be applied by the Court. In such cases, it would help avoid future convictions of the UK in Strasbourg if balancing of interests were applied at the level of the individual case, and also if there was a similar consideration and appreciation of facts and circumstances to the approach taken in Strasbourg. However, the extensive possibilities to restrict freedom of expression under certain domestic law, such as the Official Secrets Act, might even bring cases under legislation that has less risk of resulting in a conviction into the danger zone. The Spycatcher decision shows that it may be wise not to change the approach to cases restricting freedom of expression selectively. Cases in which speech on governmental information concerning national security is restricted might also require a change in the consideration and appreciation of facts and circumstances. In those areas of law where a change will be necessary, the Human Rights Act provides a basis for such a change in approach.

3.5 Conclusions

In general I conclude that the Human Rights Act, with all that it implies, is not so much a radical step away from the traditional approach to the protection of fundamental rights, but more a step in a development towards a rights-based protection of rights and freedoms. With regard to public law, the development towards a narrower margin of appreciation is underway already. The Human Rights Act may serve as an encouragement for the courts to continue this development and apply an even narrower margin of appreciation. Whether they will dare to apply a narrow enough margin of appreciation to offer similar protection to the Convention rights as the Court, remains to be seen, especially in those cases in which the Court comes to its closest review.[13] In those instances in which the Court applied a narrow margin of appreciation, close scrutiny by the English courts will be required to provide a similar degree of protection.

The review of the proportionality of a measure or balancing of interests, will be unavoidable if the English courts want to achieve the aim of the Human Rights Act. However, under public law, both a narrowing of the margin of appreciation left to the decision-making authorities, and also a balancing between means and ends of a restriction are already taking place. In order to realise the objectives of the Act, the impact of the application of a proportionality-test will have to be supplemented with a narrower margin of appreciation.

The Human Rights Act makes it necessary for the courts to apply a balancing of interests in private and penal law cases, and this balancing of interests should be at a concrete level.

The possibility for such a balancing of interests, by means of s.2, can be found in the 'vague' terms of certain legislation; and in those cases in which such a balancing of interests already takes place and takes place at the right moment, the Act offers the possibility to consider similar circumstances and to give them similar weight. Also with regard to this last aspect, the development of a more extensive common ground had already set in.[14]

The incorporation of the ECHR in the manner done by the Human Rights Act could well achieve 'a change in attitude towards civil rights'. Only in those instances in which the wording of restrictive legislation leaves no room for interpretation and constitutes a breach of the Convention, will the English courts not be able to offer protection. In such cases it is up to the legislature to protect the rights concerned.

4 BROADER FRAME OF RELEVANCE OF THIS STUDY

The remarks in this section serve to indicate that the problem I dealt with in this study has a broader frame of relevance than the central problem addressed in this book. This book has been concerned with a common ground between the protection of freedom of expression in English law and the ECHR. This study was aimed at determining the extent to which the aims of the Human Rights Act were realised already and at the same time the study determined the changes in approach to the protection of freedom of expression that were required of the English system of protection to realise the aims of the Act.

---

13 Hunt in Using Human Rights Law in English Courts, 1998, p. 184, remarked that this whole development does not 'constitute dramatic new departures for the common law'. In reviewing discretionary powers the courts were accustomed to attaching greater weight to some interests that were thought to be of great value 'such as the right to property and other economic interests'.
14 See Hunt, Using Human Rights Law in English Courts, 1998.

The integration of different systems of protection in general, and that of the ECHR and English law in particular, is relevant also to the protection of fundamental rights within the European Union. The protection of human rights within the European Union is topic of a current discussion. Emphasis in this discussion lies on the insufficient protection of fundamental rights in the European Union.[15] Now that integration within the Union has developed to the extent that it has, it is held that the Union can no longer leave the protection of human rights to ad hoc development of such protection by the European Court of Justice.[16]

With regard to an integrated protection of fundamental rights within the EU there are several problems that could be singled out for a more extensive examination. Questions regarding the scope of the protection of fundamental rights by the European Court of Justice and whether the people residing within the European Union should be protected from breaches of their fundamental rights by the Members States completely. Also questions arise regarding the improvement of the effectiveness of protection of fundamental rights within the Union. A problem with regard to integrated protection of fundamental rights within the EU is also the existence of different systems of protection, among which that of the ECHR and the English system of protection.

I do not intend to start an extensive discussion on the consequences of the conclusions of this research to the integration of human rights within the European Union at this moment. The only comment I want to make is that the development of the protection of fundamental rights in English law is also of significance to the protection of fundamental rights within the European Union.

---

15 Alston and Weiler, An 'Ever Closer Union' in Need of a Human Rights Policy: The European Union and Human Rights, 1999, p. 14-15; the writers observe that in the EU there is lack of protection against for instance racist and xenophobic behaviour, unequal treatment, various types of discrimination, against shortcomings in the enjoyment of economic, social and cultural rights of disadvantaged and vulnerable groups, unsatisfactory treatment of refugees and asylum-seekers and degrading treatment of detainees.

16 See for a more extensive argumentation of why the European Union needs a harmonized human rights policy: Alston and Weiler, An 'ever closer Union' in need of a human rights policy: the European Union and Human Rights, 1999.

SAMENVATTING

VRIJHEID VAN MENINGSUITING IN ENGELAND EN ONDER HET EVRM: OP ZOEK NAAR GEMEENSCHAPPELIJKE GRONDSLAGEN. EEN BASIS VOOR DE TOEPASSING VAN DE HUMAN RIGHTS ACT 1998 IN HET ENGELSE RECHT

De centrale vraag van dit onderzoek is: welke gemeenschappelijke grondslagen bestaan tussen de bescherming van vrijheid van meningsuiting in het Engelse recht en onder het EVRM. Het boek bestaat uit twee delen. Het eerste deel bestaat uit 4 hoofdstukken en het tweede deel bestaat uit 6 hoofdstukken.

De aanleiding voor dit onderzoek is de Human Rights Act 1998, die op 2 oktober 2000 kracht van wet zal krijgen. De Human Rights Act maakt een deel van de rechten zoals opgenomen in het EVRM en haar protocollen, onderdeel van het Engelse recht. De Act markeert een omslagpunt in het Engelse recht betreffende de bescherming van fundamentele rechten: van een voornamelijk op algemene vrijheid gebaseerde bescherming is er vanaf 2 oktober een vooral op gedefinieerde rechten gebaseerde bescherming. De vraag die zich vervolgens opdringt is wat de Human Rights Act nu precies verlangt van het Engelse beschermingssysteem. Met andere woorden, in hoeverre wordt het EVRM feitelijk door deze wet geïncorporeerd en in welke mate vereist dat een verandering in de reeds bestaande bescherming van fundamentele rechten in het Engelse recht. Het bepalen van gemeenschappelijke grondslagen in de bescherming van fundamentele rechten geeft aan in hoeverre de bescherming die door de Act wordt verlangd reeds aanwezig is en bepaalt tevens waarop eventueel vereiste verdergaande bescherming van de opgenomen rechten kan worden gebaseerd.

In dit onderzoek heb ik mij beperkt tot studie naar de gemeenschappelijke grondslagen tussen de bescherming van het recht op vrijheid van meningsuiting, een recht met betrekking waartoe er in zowel het Engelse als het Europese beschermingssysteem een uitgebreide jurisprudentie bestaat. Hierdoor leent het zich goed voor een onderzoek als het onderhavige. Wat betreft het Engelse beschermingssysteem richt het onderzoek zich bovendien op de rol van de wetgever en de rechter bij de bescherming van vrijheid van meningsuiting.

Tenslotte wordt in het inleidende hoofdstuk de centrale vraag opgesplitst in een aantal deelvragen, die tevens verraden wat er onder de term 'gemeenschappelijke grondslagen' wordt verstaan. De bescherming van rechten is opgedeeld in drie aspecten. Het eerste is wat er onder het concept 'vrijheid van meningsuiting' wordt verstaan. Het tweede aspect is de wijze waarop er in een beschermingssysteem bescherming wordt geboden aan een recht. Het derde aspect tenslotte is de waardering van feiten en omstandigheden in zaken waarin een recht wordt beperkt. Met betrekking tot elk van deze aspecten wordt naar gemeenschappelijke grondslagen gezocht.

In de hoofdstukken II tot en met IV wordt vervolgens de informatie verschaft om te komen tot bepaling van gemeenschappelijke grondslagen tussen de Engelse en de EVRM-bescherming van vrijheid van meningsuiting.

In hoofdstuk II wordt aangegeven in hoeverre het EVRM door de Human Rights Act wordt geïncorporeerd in het Engelse recht. Belangrijk daarbij is onder andere dat niet alleen de tekst van de opgenomen rechten wordt geïncorporeerd, maar dat ook rekening moet worden gehouden met de uitleg die door het Europese Hof voor de Rechten van de Mens aan die rechten is gegeven. Daarnaast hebben 'public authorities' onder de Act een zelfstandige verantwoordelijkheid om niet in strijd met de geïncorporeerde rechten te handelen. Bovendien biedt de Human Rights Act de rechterlijke macht vergaande mogelijkheden om de bescherming van de Conventie-rechten, zoals er aan wordt gerefereerd in de Act, te realiseren: zij moet wetgeving zoveel mogelijk in overeenstemming met de rechten interpreteren. Als via interpretatie niet te voorkomen is dat er strijd met de rechten is, kan een aantal met name genoemde hogere rechtscolleges een zogenaamde 'declaration of incompatibility' maken, waarna de verantwoordelijkheid voor het respecteren van de rechten bij de wetgever ligt. Burgers kunnen bovendien een actie bij de rechter aanhangig maken tegen 'public authorities' die niet in overeenstemming met de Conventie-rechten hebben gehandeld. De benaderde rechterlijke instantie kan ook dan de bescherming van de opgenomen rechten realiseren, tenminste voor zover de betreffende 'public authority' niet door wetgeving gedwongen was te handelen zoals het gedaan heeft. Interessant is bovendien dat rechters zelf door de Act als 'public authority' worden aangemerkt. Dit opent allerlei perspectieven voor horizontale werking van de opgenomen rechten, ook omdat deze bepaling de werking van de Act uitbreidt naar 'common law'. Tenslotte wordt in dit hoofdstuk opgemerkt dat voor de verwezenlijking van de mogelijkheden die de Human Rights Act biedt voor de bescherming van de Conventie-rechten, de doelstelling van de wetgever van belang is. De doelstelling is namelijk om een tijd- en kostenbesparing te creëren voor mensen die hun rechten beschermd willen zien en om burgers de mogelijkheid te geven deze bescherming, als dat nodig is, af te dwingen bij de nationale rechter.

In hoofdstuk III wordt vervolgens een indicatie gegeven van de bestaande bescherming van vrijheid van meningsuiting in het Engelse recht. Dit wordt gedaan middels de bespreking van een zevental rechtsfiguren die van invloed zijn op de ruimte die aan vrijheid van meningsuiting wordt gelaten. Het gaat hierbij om rechtsfiguren uit wetgeving, 'common law' en 'equity', waarbij dan steeds de regelgeving zelf en de daarop gebaseerde jurisprudentie wordt bekeken op de benadering van vrijheid van meningsuiting.

In hoofdstuk IV, het laatste hoofdstuk van deel I van het boek, worden de methoden van bescherming die door het Hof worden toegepast aangegeven. Er worden drie methoden van bescherming onderscheiden: ten eerste de toepassing van de 'margin of appreciation', welke gebruikt wordt om aan te geven in hoeverre het Hof de nationale autoriteiten de verantwoordelijkheid laat om de betreffende rechten te beschermen. Daarnaast worden twee methoden van bescherming onderscheiden die niet zoals bij de 'margin of appreciation' intensiteit van de toetsing betreffen, maar die de methoden van toetsing van het Hof zijn die de eisen behelzen waaraan de inhoudelijke beperking van het recht door de nationale autoriteiten moet voldoen. Dit is in de eerste plaats de eis dat de beperking proportioneel moet zijn. Proportionaliteit zoals gebruikt door het Hof kan bepaald worden door de geschiktheid van de beperkende maatregel, door de mate waarin voor de minst beperkende maatregel geopteerd is en door de mate waarin het middel (de beperkende maatregel) in evenwicht is met het doel van de beperking.

De tweede inhoudelijke methode van bescherming van het Hof betreft het toetsen of het belang bij de beperking van het recht en het belang van de persoon bij het vrij kunnen uitoefenen van zijn recht van vrijheid van meningsuiting in evenwicht zijn.

De 'margin of appreciation' wordt vanzelfsprekend in elke uitspraak toegepast door het Hof. De inhoudelijke methoden van bescherming worden niet steeds elk door het Hof gebruikt om te bepalen of een beperking op een recht gerechtvaardigd is. Deze methoden worden door elkaar gebruikt. Alleen het evenwicht tussen doel en middel en het evenwicht tussen de betrokken belangen kunnen afzonderlijk leiden tot een conclusie betreffende de gerechtvaardigdheid van een beperking.

Na het vaststellen van het algemene kader waarin de centrale vraag van dit onderzoek speelt, wordt vervolgens in de hoofdstukken V tot en met X een antwoord geformuleerd op de deelvragen. Steeds wordt bekeken hoe de situatie was voor het kracht van wet krijgen van de Human Rights Act 1998, en daarna wat de invloed van de Human Rights Act verwacht wordt te zijn op gemeenschappelijke grondslagen tussen de bescherming van vrijheid van meningsuiting in de beide beschermingssystemen.

In hoofdstuk V worden gemeenschappelijke grondslagen tussen de benadering van de notie van vrijheid van meningsuiting gezocht. Die gemeenschappelijke grondslagen zijn aanzienlijk. Zowel in het Engelse recht als onder het EVRM worden uitingen niet op hun aard uitgesloten van de mogelijkheid van beroep op vrijheid van meningsuiting. Het gaat daarbij dan wel steeds om uitingen middels gesproken woord, geschrift of beeld. Er ligt een grens bij gewelddadige handelingen. Bovendien maakt het beroep of de hoedanigheid van degene die de uiting doet geen verschil voor de mogelijkheid van beroep op vrijheid van meningsuiting. Onder beide systemen is daarenboven sprake van een, hoewel niet uitdrukkelijke, horizontale werking van het recht van vrijheid van meningsuiting. Tenslotte wordt onder beide systemen voorafgaande beperking van de uiting gezien als een onder omstandigheden noodzakelijke beperking.

Na in hoofdstuk V te hebben vastgesteld dat beide systemen het bij benadering over hetzelfde hebben als gerefereerd wordt aan vrijheid van meningsuiting, wordt in hoofdstuk VI een begin gemaakt met het zoeken naar gemeenschappelijke grondsla-gen tussen de methoden van bescherming. Hoofdstuk VI zoekt hiernaar met betrekking tot de door het Hof toegepaste methode van 'margin of appreciation'. In de inleiding van dit hoofdstuk wordt aangegeven tot op welke hoogte de toepassing van deze methode vergelijkbaar is met de bescherming die in een nationaal rechtssysteem als het Engelse aan een recht wordt geboden: het toepassen van de 'margin of appreciation' door het Hof is van invloed op het niveau van bescherming gegeven door het Hof. In het geval van strafrecht of privaatrecht, wordt het bereiken van het niveau van bescherming in een nationaal systeem van bescherming gerealiseerd middels inhoudelijke methoden van bescherming. Echter in het administratieve recht, waar de nationale rechter de beslissingsinstantie onder omstandigheden (ook) ruimte laat om de situatie zelf te beoordelen, wordt door die nationale rechter ook een bepaalde beslissingsruimte gelaten. Waar de intensiteit van de toetsing van de Engelse rechter beduidend minder is dan die van het Hof, wordt het moeilijk voor de Engelse rechter om tot een vergelijkbaar niveau van bescherming te komen. Hoewel het concept van de 'margin of appreciation' in beide systemen dus verschillend is, is dit het niveau waarop het zinvol is om naar gemeenschappelijke grondslagen te zoeken.

De 'margin of appreciation' zoals gebruikt door het Hof is variabel, en haar reikwijdte hangt af van de omstandigheden van de zaak. Ook de 'margin of appreciation' die door de Engelse rechter wordt gelaten aan de beslissende organen is inmiddels variabel. Deels wordt de omvang van de 'margin of appreciation' beïnvloed door dezelfde omstandigheden van een zaak. Vooral waar de uiting van publiek belang is, zal de 'margin of appreciation' klein zijn. Echter, de kleinste 'margin of appreciation' gelaten door de Engelse rechter is minder klein dan die toegepast door het Hof. In die omstandigheden waar het Hof de 'margin of appreciation' bijna reduceert tot nul, zullen Engelse rechters in administratieve zaken betreffende de uitoefening van discretionaire bevoegdheden grote moeite hebben om een vergelijkbaar niveau van bescherming te bieden. In dit hoofdstuk wordt echter opgemerkt dat de Human Rights Act goede mogelijkheden biedt aan de Engelse rechter om de ruimte gelaten aan de beslissingsorganen verder te beperken. Volgens deze wet moet wetgeving zoveel mogelijk in overeenstemming met het EVRM en haar rechtspraak worden uitgelegd, 'public authorities' hebben de plicht voor zover wetgeving dat mogelijk maakt, in overeenstemming met het EVRM te handelen. Waar het discretionaire bevoegdheden betreft is die ruimte er altijd, deze plicht kan bovendien afgedwongen worden bij de rechter, die zelf ook de plicht heeft zoveel mogelijk in overeenstemming met het EVRM te handelen. Geen expliciete opdracht om de ruime 'margin of appreciation' te laten varen, maar gezien een van de doelen van de wet, namelijk besparing van tijd en kosten van burgers, die nu niet meer naar Straatsburg hoeven, lijkt een aanpassing van de 'margin of appreciation' wel voor de hand te liggen.

In hoofdstuk VII wordt gezocht naar gemeenschappelijke grondslagen tussen de toepassing van de proportionaliteitstoets. In beide systemen bestaat die toets voornamelijk uit het afwegen van doel en middel en het nagaan of er een minder vergaand alternatief voorhanden was. Het toetsen van de geschiktheid van de maatregel vindt een enkele keer plaats, maar dergelijke overwegingen zorgen nooit zelfstandig voor vernietigen van een besluit of het concluderen tot strijd met artikel 10.

In hoofdstuk VIII wordt gekeken naar gemeenschappelijke grondslagen betreffende de methode van het afwegen van de betrokken belangen. In beide systemen van rechtsbescherming wordt deze methode door rechters toegepast. In de loop van de tijd is de invloed van het EVRM op het Engelse recht toegenomen, waardoor vrijheid van meningsuiting en de daaraan verbonden belangen steeds uitdrukkelijker een plaats kregen in de Engelse jurisprudentie. Een belangrijk onderscheid tussen het toepassen van deze methode in de beide systemen is echter het moment van bescherming. Het Europese Hof voor de Rechten van de Mens past deze methode altijd toe op de concrete omstandigheden van het geval. Tot voor kort paste de Engelse rechter om redenen van rechtszekerheid deze methode echter toe op abstract niveau, waardoor nuancering van bescherming naar de omstandigheden van het geval onmogelijk was. Inmiddels lijkt de Engelse rechter zich bewust van dit verschil en van de invloed die dit heeft op de mogelijkheden om bescherming te bieden aan vrijheid van meningsuiting op een niveau als geboden door het Hof. Er vindt reeds een verschuiving plaats richting een concrete toetsing door de Engelse rechter. Gezien de doelstelling van de Human Rights Act om op nationaal niveau voldoende bescherming te bieden aan de rechten van de Conventie, ligt het doorzetten van deze ontwikkeling voor de hand.

In hoofdstuk IX tenslotte, wordt ingegaan op de gemeenschappelijke grondslagen tussen de waardering van feiten en omstandigheden door de rechter in beide systemen van rechtsbescherming. In de uitspraken van het Hof is een bepaalde lijn aan te geven in de waardering van feiten en omstandigheden die voor het grootste deel samenvalt met de omstandigheden die de omvang van de 'margin of appreciation' bepalen. Als de meningsuiting van publiek belang is, bijvoorbeeld in geval van politieke uitingen, neemt het belang van de uiting toe, dit in tegenstelling tot commerciële uitingen die niet van groot belang geacht worden te zijn. Doelen als de bescherming van nationale veiligheid en het voorkomen van criminaliteit worden van relatief groot belang geacht. Gemeenschappelijke tradities in het beschermen van meningsuiting doen het belang van de uiting toenemen en zeer ernstige inbreuken op vrijheid van meningsuiting beïnvloeden het belang dat aan het doel wordt toegekend.

Met betrekking tot bepaalde rechtsfiguren deelt de Engelse rechter de globale waardering van feiten en omstandigheden van het Hof. Echter, deze waardering is niet consistent: hij varieert per rechtsfiguur. Niet elk rechtsfiguur waarbij verschillend belang wordt toegekend aan de feiten en omstandigheden van het geval vertegenwoordigt bovendien een van de omstandigheden waarbij het Hof normaliter een ruime 'margin of appreciation' zal laten of waar het Hof in het algemeen groot belang hecht aan het nagestreefde doel. In dergelijke gevallen, wanneer het belang door het Hof toegekend aan de feiten en omstandigheden groter is dan dat toegekend door de Engels rechter (en wetgever), is er een risico dat het Hof een inbreuk op het recht als ongerechtvaardigd zal bestempelen. De verschillen in waardering die leiden tot een verschillend niveau van bescherming zijn gemakkelijk aan te passen en de Human Rights Act biedt daarvoor de ruimte. De doelstelling van de Act om op nationaal niveau voldoende bescherming te bieden aan de rechten van de Conventie moedigt een dergelijke aanpassing bovendien aan.

In hoofdstuk X worden de bevindingen van de voorgaande hoofdstukken kort samengevat en wordt geconcludeerd dat de gemeenschappelijke grondslagen tussen het EVRM en het Engelse beschermingssysteem aanmerkelijk zijn. De benadering van de notie van vrijheid van meningsuiting, en tot op grote hoogte de toegepaste methoden van bescherming en de waardering van feiten en omstandigheden, hebben beide systemen gemeen. Vooral de omvang van de 'margin of appreciation' levert een belangrijk struikelblok voor het verwezenlijken van de doelstelling van de Human Rights Act om op nationaal niveau bescherming aan de Conventie-rechten te bieden. Hoewel in Engeland reeds een verschuiving naar een meer intensieve toetsing plaatsvindt, schiet deze nog tekort ten opzichte van de meest intensieve toetsing door het Hof. De Human Rights Act biedt goede mogelijkheden om dit op te lossen. Zowel het moment van toetsing als de waardering van feiten en omstandigheden ontwikkelen zich nu reeds in de richting van de benadering van het Hof. De Human Rights Act laat voldoende ruimte voor een dergelijke ontwikkeling, en de verplichting om rekening te houden met de uitleg zoals door het Hof aan de rechten van de Conventie wordt gegeven, moedigt die ontwikkelingen aan.

SELECTED BIBLIOGRAPHY

Allan, T.R.S., *Law, Liberty, and Justice, The Legal foundations of British Constitutionalism.* - Oxford: Clarendon Press, 1993.

Amnesty International, *Annual Report 1998.* - London: Amnesty International, 1998.

Bailey, S.H. and M.J. Gunn (eds.), *Smith and Bailey on the Modern English Legal System.* - London: Sweet & Maxwell, 1991.

Bailey, S.H., D.J. Harris and B.L. Jones, *Civil Liberties cases and materials.* - 4th ed. - London, Dublin, Edinburgh: Butterworths, 1995.

Barendt, E., Libel and Freedom of Speech in English Law. In: [1993] *Public Law* 449, p. 449-464.

Barendt, E., *Freedom of Speech.* - Oxford: Clarendon Press, 1996.

Besselink, L.F.M., Fundamentele Rechten in het Gemeenschapsrecht. In: L.F.M. Besselink and H.R.B.M. Kummeling (eds.), *Grenzen aan grenzenloosheid, algemene leerstukken van grondrechtenbeschermingin de EU.* - Deventer: Tjeenk Willink, 1998, p. 7-29.

Blake, Nicholas, Judicial Review of Discretion in Human Rights Cases. In: *European Human Rights Law Reports* [1997] 391, p. 391-403.

Bonner, D. and R. Stone, The Public Order Act 1986; steps in the wrong direction?. In: [1987] *Public Law* 208, p. 208-230.

Bosma, H., A Bill of Rights for the United Kingdom. In: Mielle Bulterman, Aart Hendriks and Jacqueline Smith (eds.), *To Baehr in our Minds, Essays from the Heart of the Netherlands.* - Utrecht: SIM Special No. 21, 1998, p. 107-123.

Boyle, Allan, Freedom of Expression as a Public Interest in English Law. In: [1982] *Public Law* 547, p. 574-612.

Boyle, Kevin, Freedom of Expression. In: P. Sieghart (ed.), *Human Rights in the United Kingdom.* - London and New York: Printed Publishers, 1988, p. 85-94.

Boyron, S., Proportionality in English Administrative Law: A Faulty Translation?. In: *Oxford Journal of Legal Studies* Vol. 12 (1992) 237, p. 237-264.

Bradley, A.W., The courts in conflict with Parliament. In: [1999] *Public Law* 384, p. 384-390.

Brems, E., The Margin of Appreciation Doctrine in the Case-Law of the European Court of Human Rights. In: *Zeitschrift fur ausländisches öffentliches Recht und Völkerrecht* (1996) 240, p. 240-314.

Brown, D. and T. Ellis, Criminalizing Disrespect. In: [1995] *Criminal Law Review* 98, p. 98-100.

Brusse, P., E-G-voorzitterschap Verenigd Koninkrijk: Brits instinct en conservatieve eensgezindheid. In: *Internationale Spectator* nr. 9, september 1992, p. 17-22.

Card, R., *Public Order: the new law.* - London: Butterworths, 1987.

Card, Cross and Jones, *Criminal Law.* - 13th ed. (R. Card ed.) - London, Dublin, Edinburgh: Butterworths, 1995.

Clapham, A., *Human Rights in the Private Sphere*. - Oxford: Clarendon Press, 1993.

Council of Europe, *Collected Edition of the 'Travaux Préparatoires' of the European Convention on Human Rights*, Vol. I; Den Haag, 1975.

Cross, C. and S. Bailey, *Cross on local government law*. - London: Sweet & Maxwell, 1986.

Deans, M., *Scots Public Law*. - Edinburgh: T&T Clark, 1995.

De Búrca, G., The Principle of Proportionality and its Application in EC Law. In: (1993) 13 *Yearbook of European Law* 105, p. 105-150.

De Búrca, G., Proportionality and Wednesbury Unreasonableness: The influence of European Legal Concepts on UK law. In: *European Public Law* 1997, Vol. 3, p. 561-586.

Dijk, P. van, and G.H.J. van Hoof, *Theory and Practice of the European Convention on Human Rights in Theory and Practice*. - 3rd. ed. - The Hague, London, Boston: SIM Kluwer Law International, 1998.

Eissen, M.A., The Principle of Proportionality in the Case-Law of the European Court of Human Rights. In: T.St.J. MacDonald, F. Matcher and H. Petzhold (eds.), *The European System for the protection of Human Rights*. - Dordrecht, Boston, London: Martinus Nijhoff Publishers, 1993.

Emiliou, N., *The principle of proportionality in European Law*. - London, The Hague Boston: Kluwer Law International, 1996.

Ewing, K.D. and C.A. Gearty, *Freedom under Thatcher - Civil Liberties in Modern Britain*. - Oxford: Clarendon Press, 1990.

Ewing, K.D. and C.A. Gearty, Rocky Foundations for Labour's New Rights. In: [1997] 2 *European Human Rights Law Reports* 146, p. 146-151.

Ewing, K.D., The Human Rights Act and Parliamentary Democracy. In: *The Modern Law Review* [1999] 1, p. 79-99.

Fawcett, J.E.S., *The Application of the European Convention on Human Rights*. - Oxford: Clarendon Press, 1987.

Feldman, D., *Civil Liberties and Human Rights in England and Wales*. - Oxford: Clarendon Press, 1993.

Feldman, David, Remedies for Violations of Convention Rights under the Human Rights Act. In: *European Human Rights Law Reports* [1998] 691, p. 691-711.

Feldman, D., Proportionality and the Human Rights Act 1998. In: Evelyn Ellis (ed.), *The Principle of Proportionality in the Laws of Europe*. - Oxford: Hart Publishing, 1999, p. 117-144.

Frankel, M., *The Official Secrets Bill*. - Internet: http://www.cfoi.org.uk/osareform.html.

Gardner, J.P., The Protection of Freedom of speech in Constitutional and Civil Law. In: J.P. Gardner (ed.), United Kingdom Law in the 1990's, United Kingdom Comparative Law series Vol. 10, *United Kingdom National Committee of Comparative Law* 1990, p. 375-384.

Gardner, John, Freedom of Expression. In: C. McCrudden and G. Chambers (eds.), *Individual Rights and the Law in Britain*. - Oxford: Clarendon Press, 1994, p. 209-238.

Gearty, C., Freedom of Assembly and Public Order. In: C. McCrudden and G. Chambers (eds.), *Individual Rights and the Law in Britain*. - Oxford: Clarendon Press, 1994, p. 39-67.

Gurry, F., *Breach of Confidence*. Oxford: Clarendon Press, 1984.

Heringa, A.W., The 'Consensus Principle', The role of the 'common law' in the ECHR Case-

Law. In: 3 *The Maastricht Law Journal* (1996), p. 108-145.

Himsworth, C.M.G., Legitimately expecting proportionality?. In: [1995] *Public Law* 46, p. 46-52.

Hoffmann, Lord, A Sense of Proportion. In: C. Forsyth and I. Hare (eds.), *The Golden Metwand and the Crooked Cord, essays in honour of Sir William Wade.* - Oxford: Clarendon, 1998, p. 149-161.

Hoffmann, Lord, Human Rights and the House of Lords. In: *The Modern Law Review* [1999] 159, p. 159-166.

Hooper, Sir Anthony, The Impact of the Human Rights Act on Judicial Decision-making. In: [1998] *European Human Rights Law Reports* 676, p. 676-686.

Hope of Craighead, Lord, Devolution and Human Rights. In: [1998] *European Human Rights Law Reports* 367, p. 367-379.

Human Rights Watch, *Human Rights Watch World Report 1998 - Events of 1997.* - New York: Human Rights Watch, December 1998.

Hunt, M., *Using Human Rights Law in English Courts.* - Oxford: Hart Publishing, 1998.

Hunt, M., The 'Horizontal Effect' of the Human Rights Act. In: [1998] *Public Law* 423, p. 423-443.

Irvine of Lairg, Lord, Judges and Decision-Makers: The Theory and Practice of Wednesbury Review. In: [1996] *Public Law* 59, p. 59-78.

Irvine of Lairg, Lord, The Development of Human Rights in Britain under an Incorporated Convention on Human Rights. In: [1998] *Public Law* 221, p. 221-236.

Jones, B.L. and K. Thompson, *Garner's Administrative Law.* - 8th ed. - London, Edinburgh, Dublin: Butterworths, 1996.

Jones, T.H., The Devaluation of Human Rights Under the European Convention. In: [1995] *Public Law* 430, p. 430-449.

Jowell, J. and A. Lester, Beyond Wednesbury; substantive principles of administrative law. In: [1987] *Public Law* 368, p. 368-382.

Jowell, J. and A. Lester, Proportionality; Neither Novel Nor Dangerous. In: J. Jowell and D. Oliver (eds.), *New Directions in Judicial Review.* - London: Stevens, 1988, p. 51-69.

Jowell, J., Is Proportionality an Alien Concept?. In: *European Public Law* 1996, Vol. 2, p. 406-411.

Jowell, J., Of Vires and Vacuums: Constitutional Context of Judicial Review. In: [1999] *Public Law* 448, p. 448-460.

Kistenkas, F.H., *Vrije Straatcommunicatie, de rol van de locale overheid bij de regulering van vrije meningsuiting in rechtsvergelijkend perspectief.* - Deventer and Arnhem: Kluwer and Gouda Quint, 1989.

Krüger, Hans Christian, The Practicalities of a Bill of Rights. In: *European Human Rights Law Reports* [1997] 353, p. 353-359.

Lange, de R., *Publiekrechtelijke Rechtsvinding.* - Zwolle: Tjeenk Willink, 1991.

Lavender, N., The Problem of the Margin of Appreciation. In: (1997) *European Human Rights Law Reports* 380, p. 380-390.

Laws, J., The Ghost in the Machine: Principle in Public Law. In: [1989] *Public Law* 27, p. 27-31.

Laws, J., Is the High Court the Guardian of Fundamental Constitutional Rights? In: [1993] *Public Law* 64, p. 59-79.

Laws, J., The Limitations of Human Rights. In: [1998] *Public Law* 254, p. 254-265.

Laws, J., Wednesbury. In: C. Forsyth and I. Hare (eds.), *The Golden Metwand and the Crooked Cord, essays in honour of Sir William Wade.* - Oxford: Clarendon, 1998, p. 185-201.

Leigh, L.H., United Kingdom. In: M. Delmas-Marty (ed.), *The European Convention for the protection of Human Rights; International Protection versus National Restrictions.* - Dordrecht, Boston, London: Martinus Nijhoff Publishers, 1992, p. 259-278.

Lester of Herne Hill, Lord, European Human Rights and the British Constitution. In: J. Jowell and D. Oliver (eds.), *The Changing Constitution.* - 3rd ed. - Oxford: Clarendon Press, 1994 p. 33-53.

Lester of Herne Hill, Lord, First Steps Towards A Constitutional Bill of Rights. In: *European Human Rights Law Reports* [1997] 124, p. 124-131.

Lester of Herne Hill, Lord, The Art of the Possible - Interpreting Statutes under the Human Rights Act. In: [1998] *European Human Rights Law Reports* 665, p. 665-675.

Le Sueur, A., Taking the soft option? The duty to give reasons in the draft Freedom of Information Bill. In: [1999] *Public Law* 419, p. 419-427.

Loveland, I., *Constitutional Law, A critical introduction.* - London, Dublin, Edinburgh: Butterworths, 1996.

Lyell, N., Whither Strasbourg? Why Britain Should Think Long and Hard Before Incorporating the ECHR. In: [1997] *European Human Rights Law Reports* 132, p. 132-140.

MacDonalds, Ronald St. John, The Margin of Appreciation in the Jurisprudence of the European Court of Human Rights. In: *International Law at the time of its Codification, Essays in honour of judge Roberto Ago.* - Milano: Giuffre 1987, p. 187-208.

Mahony, P., Judicial activism and judicial self-restraint in the European Court of Human Rights: two sides of the same coin. In: 11 *Human Rights Law Journal* (1990), p. 57-88.

Mahony, P., Universality versus Subsidiarity in the Strasbourg Case Law on Free Speech: Explaining Some Recent Judgments. In: [1997] *European Human Rights Law Reports* 364, p. 364-379.

Markesinis, B.S. and S.F. Deakin, *Tort Law.* - 3rd. ed. - Oxford: Clarendon Press, 1994.

Markesinis, B., Privacy, Freedom of Expression and the horizontal effect of the Human Rights Bill: Lessons from Germany. In: (1999) 115 *Law Quarterly Review* 47, p. 47-88.

Marshall, G., Two Kinds of Compatibility: more about section 3 of the Human Rights Act 1998. In: [1999] *Public Law* 377, p. 377-399.

Martens, S.K., Incorporating the European Convention: The Role of the Judiciary. In: [1998] *European Human Rights Law Reports* 5, p. 5-14.

Merills, J.G., *The Development of International Law by the European Court of Human Rights.* - Manchester: Manchester University Press, 1988.

Miller, C.J., *Contempt of Court.* - 2nd ed. - Oxford: Clarendon Press, 1990.

Morisson, C.C., Margin of Appreciation in European Human Rights Law. In: *Droits de l'homme-human rights*, Vol. 6, 1973, p. 263-286.

Nourse, L.J., The English Law of Defamation - is trial by jury still the best? In: *NILR* 1990 nr. 2, p. 182-192.

O'Boyle, M., D.J. Harris and C. Warbrick, *Law of the European Convention on Human Rights.* - London, Dublin, Edinburgh: Butterworths, 1995.

O'Donnel, T.A., The Margin of Appreciation Doctrine: Standards in the Jurisprudence of the

European Court of Human Rights. In: *Human Rights Quarterly* Vol. 4, 1982, p. 474-496.

Palmer, S., Tightening Secrecy Law; The Official Secrets Act 1989. In: [1990] *Public Law* 243, p. 243-256.

Penner, R., The Canadian Experience with the Charter of Rights; Are there lessons for the United Kingdom? In: [1996] *Public Law* 104, p. 104-125.

Prakke, L. en C.A.J.M. Kortman, *Het bestuursrecht van de landen der Europese Gemeenschappen.* - Deventer: Kluwer, 1986.

Robertson, G. and A. Nicol, *Media Law.* - 3rd ed. - London: Penguin, 1992.

Scarman, Lord, *English Law - The new dimension,* 1974.

Schokkenbroek, Jeroen, Judicial review by the European Court of Human Rights; constitutionalism at a European level. In: R. Bakker, A.W. Heringa, F. Stroink (eds.), *Judicial Control, Comparative essays on judicial review.*- Antwerpen: MAKLU Uitgevers, 1990.

Schokkenbroek, J.G.C., *Toetsing aan de vrijheidsrechten van het Europees Verdrag tot Bescherming van de rechten van de Mens.* - Zwolle: Tjeenk Willink, 1996.

Singh, R., Privacy and the Media after the Human Rights Act. In: [1998] 6 *European Human Rights Law Reports* 712, p. 712-729.

Singh, R., M. Hunt and M. Demetriou, Is there a Role for the 'Margin of Appreciation' in National Law after the Human Rights Act? In: [1999] 1 *European Human Rights Law Reports* 15, p. 15-22.

Smith, J.C. and B. Hogan, *Criminal Law.* - 7th ed. - London, Dublin, Edinburgh: Butterworths, 1992.

Smith, de S.A., H. Woolf and J.L. Jowell, *Judicial Review of Administrative Action.* - 5th ed. - London: Sweet and Maxwell, 1995.

Steyn Lord, Incorporation and Devolution - A Few Reflections on the Changing Scene. In: *European Human Rights Law Reports* [1998] 153, p. 153-156.

Straw, Jack and Paul Boateng, Bringing Rights Home: Labour's Plans to Incorporate the European Convention on Human Rights into U.K. Law. In: *European Human Rights Law Reports* [1997] 71, p. 71-80.

Wade, E.C.S. and Bradley A.W.; A.W. Bradley and K.D. Ewing (eds.), *Constitutional and Administrative Law*; - London and New York: Longman, 1993.

Wade, Sir William, Human Rights and the Judiciary. In: [1998] *European Human Rights Law Reports* 520, p. 520-533.

Wadham, J., Bringing Rights Half-way Home [1997] *European Human Rights Law Reports* 141, p. 141-145.

Walker, D.M., *The Oxford Companion to Law.* - Oxford: Clarendon Press, 1980.

Walker, Neil, Setting English Judges to Rights. In: *Oxford Journal of Legal Studies* [1999] 19 (1) 133, p. 133-151.

Wiarda, G.J., Extensieve en restrictieve verdragstoepassingen door het Europese Hof voor de rechten van de mens; een middenkoers? In: H. Franken, A. Heijder, C.F. Rüter and E.M. Enschedé, *Ad Personam, Opstellen aangeboden aan Prof. Mr. Ch.J. Enschedé ter gelegenheid van zijn zeventigste verjaardag.*- Zwolle: Tjeenk Willink, 1981, p. 371-385.

Williams, G., *Learning the Law.* - 9th ed. - London: Stevens and Sons, 1973.

Woolf of Barnes Lord, Droit Public - English Style. In: [1995] *Public Law* 57, p. 57-71.

Woolf, H., The tension between the Executive and the Judiciary. In: (1998) 114 *Law Quarterly Review*, October, p. 578-593.

TABLE OF CASES

European Court of Human Rights

INDEX

CURRICULUM VITAE

Heleen Bosma (1971) studied law at the University of Groningen. She graduated in constitutional and administrative law, and company law and social security law in 1995. Her Master's thesis concerned family-life of homosexuals in Dutch law and under the ECHR. She has been employed as a Ph.D. candidate at the Institute of Constitutional and Administrative Law of Utrecht University since 1996.

SCHOOL OF HUMAN RIGHTS RESEARCH SERIES

The School of Human Rights Research is a joint effort by human rights researchers in the Netherlands. Its central research theme is the nature and meaning of international standards in the field of human rights, their application and promotion in the national legal order, their interplay with national standards, and the international supervision of such application. The School of Human Rights Research Series only includes English titles that contribute to a better understanding of the different aspects of human rights.

Editorial Board of the Series: Prof. dr C. Flinterman (Utrecht University), Prof. dr W.J.M. van Genugten (Tilburg University), dr M.T. Kamminga (Erasmus University Rotterdam), dr H. Werdmölder (Utrecht University) and dr R.E. de Winter (Maastricht University).

Published titles within the Series:

1   Brigit C.A. Toebes, *The Right to Health as a Human Right in International Law*
    ISBN 90-5095-057-4

2   Ineke Boerefijn, *The Reporting Procedure under the Covenant on Civil and Political Rights. Practice and Procedures of the Human Rights Committee*
    ISBN 90-5095-074-4

3   Kitty Arambulo, *Strengthening the Supervision of the International Covenant on Economic, Social and Cultural Rights. Theoretical and Procedural Aspects*
    ISBN 90-5095-058-2

4   Marlies Glasius, *Foreign Policy on Human Rights. Its Influence on Indonesia under Soeharto*
    ISBN 90-5095-089-2

5   Cornelis D. de Jong, *The Freedom of Thought, Conscience and Religion or Belief in the United Nations (1946-1992)*
    ISBN 90-5095-137-6

6   Heleen Bosma, *Freedom of Expression in England and under the ECHR: in Search of a Common Ground. A Foundation for the Application of the Human Rights Act 1998 in English Law*
    ISBN 90-5095-136-8